Chile

Arica Desert to Tierra del Fuego

ROYAL CRUISING CLUB
PILOTAGE FOUNDATION

Revised by
ANDREW O'GRADY

from original material by Ian and Maggy Staples,
Tony and Coryn Gooch

Imray Laurie Norie & Wilson

Published by
Imray Laurie Norie & Wilson Ltd
Wych House The Broadway St Ives Cambridgeshire
PE27 5BT England
☎ +44 (0)1480 462114 *Fax* +44 (0) 1480 496109
email ilnw@imray.com
www.imray.com
2004

First edition 1998
Second edition 2004

© Text: RCC Pilotage Foundation 2004
© Plans: RCC Pilotage Foundation 2004
© Photographs: as credited

ISBN 0 85288 721 3

British Library Cataloguing in Publication Data.
A catalogue record for this title is available from the
British Library.

The last input of technical information was November
2003.

Printed in Great Britain by Butler and Tanner Ltd.

CORRECTIONAL SUPPLEMENTS

This pilot book will be amended at intervals by the issue
of correctional supplements. These are published on the
internet at our web site www.imray.com and may be
downloaded free of charge. Printed copies are also
available on request from the publishers at the above
address.

CAUTION

Whilst every care has been taken to ensure that the
information contained in this book is accurate, the
RCC Pilotage Foundation, the authors and the
publishers hereby formally disclaim any and all
liability for any personal injury, loss and/or damage
howsoever caused, whether by reason of any error,
inaccuracy, omission or ambiguity in relation to the
contents and/or information contained within this
book. The book contains selected information and
thus is not definitive. It does not contain all known
information on the subject in hand and should not
be relied on alone for navigational use: it should
only be used in conjunction with official
hydrographic data. This is particularly relevant to
the plans, which should not be used for navigation.

The RCC Pilotage Foundation, the authors and
publishers believe that the information which they
have included is a useful aid to prudent navigation,
but the safety of a vessel depends ultimately on the
judgment of the navigator, who should assess all
information, published or unpublished.

PLANS

The plans in this guide are not to be used for
navigation – they are designed to support the text
and should always be used together with
navigational charts. Even so, every effort has been
made to position harbour and anchorage plans
adjacent to the relevant text.

It should be borne in mind that the characteristics
of lights may be changed during the life of the book,
and that in any case notification of such changes is
unlikely to be reported immediately.

All bearings are given from seaward and refer to
true north. Scales may be taken from the scales of
latitude. Symbols are based on those used by the
British Admiralty – users are referred to *Symbols and
Abbreviations* (NP 5011).

Contents

The RCC Pilotage Foundation

In 1976 an American member of the Royal Cruising Club, Dr Fred Ellis, indicated that he wished to make a gift to the Club in memory of his father, the late Robert E Ellis, of his friends Peter Pye and John Ives and as a mark of esteem for Roger Pinckney. An independent charity known as the RCC Pilotage Foundation was formed and Dr Ellis added his house to his already generous gift of money to form the Foundation's permanent endowment. The Foundation's charitable objective is 'to advance the education of the public in the science and practice of navigation', which is at present achieved through the writing and updating of pilot books covering many diffent parts of the world.

The Foundation is extremely grateful and privileged to have been given the copyrights to books written by a number of distinguished authors and yachtsmen including the late Adlard Coles, Robin Brandon and Malcolm Robson. In return the Foundation has willingly accepted the task of keeping the original books up to date and many yachtsmen and women have helped (and are helping) the Foundation fulfill this commitment. In addition to the titles donated to the Foundation, several new books have been created and developed under the auspices of the Foundation. The Foundation works in close collaboration with three publishers – Imray Laurie Norie and Wilson, Adlard Coles Nautical and On Board Publications – and in addition publishes in its own name short run guides and pilot books for areas where limited demand does not justify large print runs. Several of the Foundation's books have been translated into French, German and Italian.

The Foundation runs its own website at www.rccpf.org.uk which not only lists all the publications but also contains free downloadable pilotage information.

The overall management of the Foundation is entrusted to trustees appointed by the Royal Cruising Club, with day-to-day operations being controlled by the Director. All these appointments are unpaid. In line with its charitable status, the Foundation distributes no profits; any surpluses are used to finance new books and developments and to subsidise those covering areas of low demand.

Imray
The Baltic Sea
North Brittany and the
  Channel Islands
The Channel Islands
Faroe, Iceland and Greenland
Isles of Scilly
North Biscay
South Biscay
Atlantic Spain and Portugal
Atlantic Islands
Islas Baleares
Corsica & North Sardinia
Mediterranean Spain –
  Costas del Sol & Blanca
Mediterranean Spain –
  Costas del Azahar, Dorada & Brava
North Africa

Adlard Coles Nautical
Atlantic Crossing Guide
Pacific Crossing Guide

On Board Publications
South Atlantic Circuit
Havens and Anchorages for the
  S American Coast

The RCC Pilotage Foundation
Supplement to Falkland Island
Shores
Cruising Guide to West Africa

Foreword

The first edition of this guide, published in 1998, was six years in preparation. It was not anticipated that a second edition would be required for many years. However, Chile has become an increasingly popular cruising destination and sales of the guide exceeded expectations. At the same time the guide stimulated many people to provide further information and corrections and it was realised that a new edition would be required.

When Andy O'Grady sent in some corrections he had not expected to be asked to edit a second editon. The RCC Pilotage Foundation is very grateful to Andy for agreeing to take on this task. His painstaking work in updating and expanding this guide is greatly appreciated, as is Ulla Norlander's excellent work on the plans.

In addition to their work on Chile, Andy and Ulla have also provided pilotage information for South Georgia which can be downloaded free of charge from the Pilotage Foundation website at www.rccpf.org.uk

Comments, corrections and updates are always welcome and can be sent either to Imray, or to the Pilotage Foundation by email to rccpf@clara.co.uk

Francis Walker
Director
RCC Pilotage Foundation
October 2003

Preface

The cruising grounds of Chile, in particular to the S of Puerto Montt, are vast. This is one of the last easily accessible places on the planet where yachts can explore little known waters and find previously unreported anchorages. No one person could expect to produce a guide covering such a vast area. This book is a collaborative effort involving many people over many years. Appendix F lists the names of known contributors; in reality there are many more. Modern sailors can visit waterways and anchorages that are virtually unchanged since the days of Magellan, Sarmiento and Drake. The charts bear witness to the phenomenal work done by the crew of HMS *Beagle* and commemorate, amongst many others, such giants as Pringle Stokes, Robert Fitzroy and Charles Darwin. Echoes of expeditions from Spain, Chile, Britain, Italy, France and Germany amongst others are to be found in place names across the area. Who would not be thrilled to find themselves sharing an anchorage with the spirit of the *Goleta Ancud, Golden Hind, Spray* or *Mischief?*

Some people deserve especial mention due to the amount of effort that they contributed directly towards this volume. They are: Oz Robinson, the first editor; Tony and Coryn Gooch who provided detailed information on the whole region; and the couple who made the greatest contribution of all: Ian and Maggy Staples, who in the 1997/98 season covered as many anchorages as possible between Valdivia and Puerto Williams on *Teokita*. Maggy Staples drew or redrew every one of the sketch charts in the original edition. The result of their work was an easy-to-follow, substantially accurate volume that has proved its worth to hundreds of visiting yachts.

The work of Imray in the preparation should not be underestimated nor should the contribution of Francis Walker, Director of the RCC Pilotage Foundation, and Ros Hogbin, Assistant Director (Editorial) for the Foundation. I would like to thank my wife, Ulla Norlander, who has provided all the new sketch plans as well as making the necessary corrections and additions to the originals.

It is not the aim of the guide to cover every possible anchorage; this would result in an excessively long book and spoil the joys of exploration and discovery that enliven cruising in Patagonia. The intention has been to provide the cruising yacht with accurate information so that whatever area she finds herself in there will be a safe haven within reach. Therefore some marvellous spots are omitted where they are close to those already included. Some contributors also assisted Capitán Alberto Mantellero in the preparation of his book *Una Aventura Navegando Los Canales Del Sur Chile;* thus there is a degree of overlap. The present editor has deliberately avoided using suggested anchorages already included in that book where this guide has acceptable alternative recommendations in the vicinity.

No guide can guarantee complete safety in every location. So much depends upon the particular conditions of the visit. Confirmation that particular places have proved suitable in adverse conditions is very important. Several anchorages that were found dangerous have been dropped from the present edition as a result of information received. The guide should be considered as an evolving collection of knowledge and yachtsmen are urged to contribute and to ensure that they are carrying the latest set of corrections available from www.imray.com. Corrections and contributions are requested and greatly appreciated.

Andrew O'Grady
October 2003

Preface to the first edition

In 1992 the Pilotage Foundation of the Royal Cruising Club (the RCC) realised the increasing interest of yachtsmen in cruising in Chile and began to collect information on the area. Early contributors were members of the RCC and the Ocean Cruising Club of Great Britain, with whom the Pilotage Foundation shares information. They included Hugh Clay, Willy Ker, David Lewis, Laurence Ormerod, Knick and Lynn Pyle, Harry Ross-Skinner, Hal Roth, Bill Tilman, Chris West and his father, Mr West Sr. Some of these contributors also assisted Capitán Alberto Mantellero in the preparation of his book, *Una Aventura Navegando Los Canales Del Sur Chile*, which is the prototype of books of this nature on the area. Later a significant addition to our stock of knowledge was the contribution of John and Fay Garey and whilst most of their work has been absorbed into the body of the text, their note on flora and fauna remains in an appendix as it stood. The next major step resulted from a chance meeting with Tony and Coryn Gooch who without comment absorbed the fact of the Foundation's interest in the area, sailed away in *Taonui* for their second cruise from Arica to Cape Horn and later returned a detailed report with plans and including the note on the tandem anchoring system; theirs was a major contribution. During the season of 1997, two other boats, *Ardevora* (Tim and Sophie Trafford) and *Plainsong* (Francis Hawkings) cruised through the Magallanes and reported on anchorages. But the greatest contribution came from *Teokita* (Ian and Maggy Staples), which in the 1997/98 season set out to cover as many anchorages as possible between Valdivia and Puerto Williams. *Teokita's* crew checked and corrected information which had already been collected and provided information on anchorages not previously recorded. More importantly, plans most helpfully provided by *Taonui* were amplified then re-drawn by Maggy Staples who went on to draw all the other plans which appear in this volume, a very significant work.

Teokita had met *Toupa* (Yves Beauvillen and Marie Goaourit) in Tahiti and *Morgane* (Yves and Florance Monier) in Valdivia. They both produced many anchorage plans. During her travels, *Teokita* met and was helped by others who visited anchorages to verify and draw them. These were notably *Gordian* (Miles Horden), *Parmelia* (Roger Wallace), *Noomi* (Greger and Eva Dahlberg), *Ardevora* (Tim and Sophie Trafford), *Felice* (Hans-Petter Lien), as well as members of the Valdivia Yacht Club, especially *Oscar Prochelle* (Yate Clipper). *Northanger* (Greg Landrein and Keri Pahuk), *Najat* (Keith and Liz Post) and *Pelagic* (Skip Novak and Hamish Laird) also provided useful information. All these contributions greatly helped and are much valued as is the contribution of Katherine Thornhill who read the very first draft. In addition Pedro Llera of Diseño Malla in Valdivia was most helpful in digitising and transmitting the charts by email to Imray.

This work is therefore a compilation of reports, believed reliable, from numerous sources and if the Editor has failed to single one out, he can only apologise. He points out again, however, that by far the greatest contributions came from *Taonui* and *Teokita* and in particular that the work of Maggy Staples, based on inputs of varying standards of draughtsmanship and often checked in difficult conditions, is a vital contribution. To save time , her drawings were sent to Imrays from Chile via the internet which contributed to the difference from the usual Imray style of plans.

It is a matter of regret that the Pilotage Foundation came to learn of the excellent work being done by *Saudade III* (Mariolina and Giorgio Ardizzi) in this field too late for it to be fitted into our production schedule. As it is, this guide only mentions some of the hundreds of anchorages that there are in the south. It would take another year or two to collect information about them and to include them all in one volume dealing with the whole of Chile is not practicable; one has to draw a line somewhere. It is to be hoped that the *Saudade* information too will be made available to the yachting fraternity in due course, possibly by means of a supplement to this book.

As ever, much painstaking and detailed work has been done by Imray staff, particularly Julia Knight, Alan Shepherd and Christine Coveney (who spent hours on the internet). Their contribution towards putting the work together was essential.

This compilation is not, of course, a Pilot but a Guide. The intention of the Pilotage Foundation is to bring it up to date from time to time. In that context, contributions and comments from cruising yachts will be greatly appreciated.

Oz Robinson
Editor
June 1998

Introduction

Chile – an overview

Organisation and government

The Republic of Chile is headed by an elected President and Congress (seated in Valparaíso though the Administration remains in Santiago). The country is organised into a metropolitan district and twelve other regions each with its own elected government and raising its own taxes; each region is subdivided into provinces.

Chile is a progressive and orderly democratic state. However, the armed forces play a significant part in the life of the country. Most visitors come with strongly held notions of the rights and wrongs of the period of Military Dictatorship. Chileans, once they know that you have an open mind, are happy, even eager, to discuss the issues. Be prepared to meet many people who believe strongly that what happened was for the best as well as those who suffered or saw their dreams of social justice demolished.

The country

Most of the population of 14 million is of mixed ancestry. Only about 15% live outside towns and some five and a half million live in the metropolitan district of Santiago. Spanish is the common language but there are enclaves where Indian languages are spoken and in some communities, such as those between Valdivia and Puerto Montt, German speakers are fairly common. Though English is taught to every schoolchild it is rare to find someone who speaks it, particularly away from population centres. The experience of cruising will be enhanced by some knowledge of Spanish; take a good Spanish dictionary. Spanish speakers will find that Chileans speak a distinctive dialect, especially people from Chiloé. Delightful *chilenismos*, words and expressions peculiar to Chile, are common.

There is religious freedom. Traditionally most Chileans are Roman Catholics. In recent years evangelical churches have started to predominate. Episcopalian and Lutheran congregations are found in areas where foreigners have played a significant role in economic life.

Mining and agriculture are the main economic activities. Chile is the world leader in production of copper. Fishmeal and farmed salmon are major exports and Chile is one of the world's largest exporters of fruits. Forest and cellulose products are also major income earners. There is comparatively little mechanical industry; Chile's light industry is competent though limited in scope and geared to the internal market. However, ships are understood. Besides the navy, known in Spanish as *la armada*, there is a considerable inshore fishing fleet and some commercial vessels. In the central area of Chile there are a growing number of yachts and cruising in the *canales* (channels) of the S is increasingly popular. Valdivia and Puerto Montt are developing expertise in light shipbuilding as a result of the demands of the salmon and tourist industries. Some very nice luxury yachts have been built in Valdivia.

Arts and academic life are strong. Music, painting, poetry and prose thrive – Chile numbers two Nobel Prize winners for poetry. Pre-Columbian cultural influences are evident in arts and crafts, especially in the music of the Andes and in textiles. In many areas, notably Chiloé, the large island at the northern end of the Patagonian *canales*, time honoured rural traditions survive that are a rich blend of the indigenous and Spanish cultures. Primary education is free and obligatory, the literacy rate is high and numerous universities top the education ladder, though university education is beyond the financial means of many.

The people

Though their language is Spanish, Chileans have diverse origins. Traces of pre-Columbian peoples are still evident in the appearance of many Chileans. In areas such as between the Río Bio-Bio and Valdivia there are many relatively pure blooded Mapuche. A relatively small number of Spaniards arrived in the time of the conquistadores; these men rapidly fathered children with indigenous women. Even after the arrival of Spanish women, mixing of the races went on apace. Despite the apparently closed nature of the Spanish Empire, people were arriving from other nations even before Chilean independence. Perhaps the most notable of these was Don Ambrosio O'Higgins, born in Ballinvary, Co Sligo, Ireland, who rose to become governor of Chile and then Viceroy of Peru, of which Chile was a dependency. His son, Bernado Riquelme O'Higgins is celebrated as the father of Chilean independence. The British naval commander Lord Cochrane, the model for Jack Aubrey in the acclaimed sea stories of Patrick O'Brien, is a national hero. He engineered Chile's naval victory in the war of independence. Later came many settlers from the British Isles drawn by military and business opportunities in the new republic. Towards the end

Arica
Iquique
Mejillones
C H I L E
Caldera
Coquimbo
Valparaíso
ARGENTINA
Concepción
Valdivia
P Montt
Chiloé
Aysén
Golfo San Jorge
Cabo Ráper
Golfo de Penas
Puerto Edén
Bahía Grande
Puerto Natales
Strait of Magellan
Punta Arenas
Ushuaia
P Williams
Cape Horn
Borders are approximate

20°S
30°S
40°S
50°S
75°W
65°W

N

1
2
3
4
5
6
7
8
9
10

40°S

N

P Montt

G de Ancud

Chiloé

Península Valdés

Golfo Corcovado

2

4

3

Archipiélago de los Chonos

Aysén

Golfo San Jorge

Cabo Rapér

CHILE

Cabo Banco

Golfo de Penas

ARGENTINA

Cabo Tres Puntas

5

Puerto Edén

50°S

Bahía Grande

6

Puerto Natales

7

CHILE

Strait of Magellan

I Riesco

Punta Arenas

Isla Grande de Tierra del Fuego

ARGENTINA

8

Ushuaia

P Williams

I de los Estados

I Hoste

I Navarino

Borders are approximate

Cape Horn

75°W

65°W

9

10

Natural History
(by John and Fay Garey)

PLANTS

Stretching from the Tropics to Antarctica, from the driest deserts to the wettest rain forest, Chile is home to an astonishing range of plants. About half of the 5,000 or so flowering species are exclusive or endemic to the country, and there are entire families of plants that are found nowhere else but in Chile. Arriving in Chile, one's first impression is of stepping into a foreign landscape, where the trees, flowers and even the weeds are different. In the central zone, with its Mediterranean-type climate, are trees with unheard-of names (*Peumus boldus, Maytenus boaria, Lithraea cuastica*), characterised by hard, small, often aromatic leaves designed to withstand the arid conditions. The Chilean palm (*Jubaea chilensis*) grows here, although its numbers have been much reduced by felling for the extraction of 'palm honey', together with bromeliads or pineapple-relatives (*Puya* species), with weird metallic blue or greenish-yellow flowers.

In the N desert of Atacama are vast tracts of land which are totally devoid of vegetation. However, nearer the coast and in the high Altiplano bordering Bolivia, there is sufficient moisture for many types of cactus, shrub and herbaceous plant to exist. These include the giant candelabra cactus, which grows 5mm a year, flowers once a year for 24 hours, and lives to hundreds of years old; and the equally long-lived, slow-growing *llaretales* or cushion plants, at altitudes over 3500m.

Two of Chile's most distinctive conifers grow in the coastal range and Andes in the S, their populations now shrunk to isolated pockets. The monkey-puzzle tree *Araucaria araucana*, with its umbrella-like canopy, reaches heights of 150 ft and more. The alerce (*Fitzroya cupressoides*) has become almost extinct because its wood is so highly prized. It can live to around 5,000 years of age.

The richest area is undoubtedly that S of the Río Bio-Bio and Concepción, which includes the temperate rain forest of Valdivia and the island of Chiloé. It is a great thrill to see fuchsia, escallonia, berberis, buddleia and other familiar garden shrubs actually growing in the wild. Indeed, Chile has contributed many ornamental plants to our gardens, such as alstroemeria, calceolaria, nasturtium, hippeastrum and schizanthus, and it has also supplied the ancestors of two common foods, the potato and the strawberry.

Recommended reading

Flora Silvestre de Chile, Palmengarten Sonderheft 19 (1992), translated from German into Spanish
Flora Silvestre de Chile, Zona Araucana (2nd edition, 1991)
Flora Silvestre de Chile, Zona Central (1978)
Cactáceas en la Flora Silvestre de Chile (1989)
all by A Hoffmann (Ediciones Fundación Claudio Gay)
Arboles Nativos de Chile Claudio Donoso Zegers (Marisa Cuneo Ediciones, 1991), with English and Spanish text.

BIRDS

One of the great excitements of crossing the Equator and arriving in the S Hemisphere is the first sighting of an albatross, the largest of all seabirds. The commonest species are the wandering, the royal and the black-browed albatross, all unmistakable with their huge wingspans and soaring flight. They are often accompanied by pintado petrels, which habitually follow ships and are instantly recognisable from the black and white chequered upper parts. Another ship-follower is the white-chinned petrel, a large, entirely dark brown bird, except for a white chin and pale yellow bill. Attractive but very difficult to distinguish are several gadfly petrels that nest in the Juan Fernandez islands and roam the ocean; these small or medium-sized birds are grey and white, with an open 'M' marking across the wings and back. The pink-footed shearwater, a big, rather clumsy-looking bird, also breeds in the archipelago.

As one approaches the mainland, it is a delight to see pelicans – in this case the huge Peruvian or Chilean pelican, the avian equivalent of a giraffe in that it seems to have been designed by a committee, but a master of the air and sea. The silly, open-mouthed, cross-eyed expression of the Peruvian booby similarly belies its expertise; like the pelican, it is found from Arica to Chiloé. More surprising is to encounter penguins, diving and swimming in the clear water and sometimes giving a curious mooing sound exactly like that of a cow. Although their more spectacular kin live in the far S and Antarctica, the Humboldt and closely related Magellanic penguin are much in evidence along the coasts of Chile and Peru. Among the numerous species of tern that inhabit or visit Chile and its off-lying islands, perhaps the most striking is the Inca tern; this is endemic to the Humboldt Current and its dark grey plumage is enlivened by bright red legs and beak. The colourful red-legged shag shares the inshore waters with the imperial or blue-eyed shag, the rock shag, the guanay cormorant and the olivaceous cormorant, the latter often occurring in rivers and lakes as well. Several types of grebe can be observed in freshwater areas. These include the pie-billed grebe, which has a stubby banded beak and lacks the usual crest on the head; and the great grebe – or *haula* as it is known, possibly because of its poignant meowing cry – with a long pointed beak and slim, reddish brown neck. Some of the more interesting gulls are the grey gull, of central Chile, which runs across the sand pretending to be a sandpiper; and the kelp gull, the only large, black-backed, white-tailed gull in the S oceans. A regular summer visitor is the black skimmer, unique in having the lower mandible longer than the upper; at dawn and dusk, flocks of these birds fly low over the water, scooping up food with their extraordinary scissor-like beaks. At the water's edge, snipes, oystercatchers (both the familiar American species and the black oystercatcher), herons and hawks are always busy.

The bird life of Chile is as varied as the country itself and comprises an estimated 439 breeding and migrant species, about 5% of the total world population. One of the most notable natives is the Juan Fernández hummingbird, which makes its presence felt on Robinson Crusoe Island with noisy shrilling from the eucalyptus trees; the male is orange-red, the female bright green and smaller, and for many years they were thought to be different species. The famous condor, depicted in the national coat of arms, is increasingly scarce, but vultures are widespread and it is a strange experience to have one perch on top of the mast. The Andean flamingo, largest of the three endemic species, dwells in the salt lakes and coastal areas of the N desert. In such barren surroundings, it seems unbelievable to come across this exotic bird, with its pinky-white plumage and long neck, standing motionless by the water on one stilt-like leg, or, when it takes flight, displaying vivid flame-coloured wings edged with black. Equally memorable is the black-necked swan, of coastal lagoons, particularly in Valdivia and Chiloé, which has a pure white body, jet-black neck and crimson beak. In Patagonia, on a still day in a secluded anchorage, a loud hammering, exactly like the noise of a building site may disturb the tranquillity. There are two spectacular woodpeckers that may be responsible for the racket: the *Carpinterito* or little carpenter or the *Carpintero negro*, a giant that can reach nearly half a metre in height. Both species have a dramatic red crest.

Recommended reading

Seabirds of the World, A Photographic Guide Peter Harrison (Christopher Helm, 1987)
Guía de Campo de las Aves de Chile Baulio Aray M & Guillermo Millie H (Edvisitorial Universitaria, 1991), with English index

Note Professor Julius Schlatter, of the Universidad Austral de Chile, Valdivia, is a leading ornithologist in the country, who would be pleased to hear of unusual sightings or to help with identification.

MAMMALS

Sea lions (*Lobos marinos*) are common all along the coast of Chile. Hefty creatures up to 6 feet long, they seem to be equally at home draped over a surf-swept rock, or basking in the calm water of a sheltered harbour, or even swimming far inland up a river. Their curiosity tends to get the better of them when a yacht is at anchor and they will surface just a few yards away, with a loud exhalation of breath; they will also follow a dinghy, diving around playfully and without fear.

The Juan Fernández fur seal is unique to that archipelago and the only mammal native there. When Alexander Selkirk was marooned on Robinson Crusoe Island in 1704, these animals were so numerous that he hunted them for sport. By the beginning of this century, they were on the verge of extinction, but the population has now recovered to about 8,000.

Of dolphins, the sturdy bottlenose and the smaller, more slender spinner dolphin, with a pronounced upright fin, are probably the most likely to be encountered in the open ocean and sometimes even quite close to land. They are always a delight to watch performing leaps and somersaults apparently for their own benefit, or rushing towards the boat to ride in the bow wave. Much more restricted in distribution are the Chilean or black dolphin, small and black with white underparts, and the similar black porpoise, both inhabiting cold inshore waters S of Valdivia and both considered rare. In these lower latitudes, the piebald dolphin and the blackchin dolphin are reportedly fairly frequent, together with the southern right whale dolphin in deeper waters; all of them variously patterned in black and white. One of the most widespread whales in the world is the orca or great killer whale, generally seen in coastal areas and estuaries. It is immediately recognisable from the tall dorsal fin, forward pointing in the male, and the distinctive white markings on the black body.

Sightings of other species of whale are a matter of chance, although yachtsmen venturing as far as Antarctica may be rewarded by the appearance of an enormous blue whale, feeding on krill.

Recommended reading
Whales of the World, A Complete Guide to the World's Living Whales, Dolphins and Porpoises Lyall Watson (Hutchinson, 1985)

of the nineteenth century, following a treaty with the Mapuche people who inhabit much of the rich agricultural land to the north of Patagonian Chile, German colonists arrived in the south. Their influence remains very strong. Chilean names also come from all parts of the world and in the far south there are many people of Yugoslav desent. The people of Chile are vivacious and hard working. Despite the wide social hierarchy, racial prejudice is virtually unknown. Yachtsmen will meet people from all levels of society and be greeted with unaffected warmth and hospitality.

The fishermen warrant particular mention. These hard-working men possess little other than great warmth of heart, good manners and unbounded generosity, all of which they lavish upon yacht crews in an unforgettable manner.

Geography

CONTINENTAL CHILE

Most of Continental Chile is contained between the Andes and the Pacific, between 17°30'S and 55°50'S, from the tropics to beyond the roaring forties. In terms of nautical miles, though some 2300M long it is on average only about 97M wide except in the far S where the country reaches the Atlantic. The dominant feature is the Cordillera de los Andes, the chain of mountains and volcanoes that runs the length of the country, the crest of which forms the boundary with Argentina. The Andes are highest (7000m and more) in the middle and N of the range. At a short distance offshore, depths of 7000m have been recorded. Tectonic movements that created the still growing Andes produce stresses in the earth's crust. These occasionally result in earthquakes and tsunamis (tidal waves), sometimes catastrophic, for example at Valdivia in 1960 when the level of the ground sank 1m and two ships in the river were sunk. A vivid reminder can be seen in Castro where the present quayside is built upon the tortured concrete remains of the one destroyed by the 1960 earthquake.

In the N, the rainless Atacama Desert covers the land from Arica on the Peruvian border to Copiapó, some 550M south. It has high daytime temperatures and cold nights. Mining – copper, nitrates, sulphates and salt – is the chief industry. To its S is a zone of semi-desert, still arid but with slight winter rainfall and irrigated agriculture. This area then merges with the fertile central valley, the Chilean heartland, between Illapel and Concepción. The valley is protected from the ocean by the Cordillera de la Costa and is the main farming region of the country. Fruit, vegetables and cereals are grown, cattle raised and viticulture is practised in a Mediterranean climate. Temperatures average 28°C in summer and 10°C in winter, when most of the annual 350mm of rain falls. Santiago is situated in this valley.

Between Concepción and Puerto Montt rainfall increases markedly, reaching some 2500mm annually in the southern part. There is an important agricultural and timber industry. Summers are sufficiently warm and sunny (peaking over 30°C) to attract many tourists to the Lake District, south of Temuco, a beautiful landscape of lakes, rivers, forests and snow-capped volcanoes. One of the world's three temperate rain forests, Bosque Valdiviano, flourishes near Valdivia. It is an incredibly rich and complex assembly of trees and plants, many of them unique to the region.

South of Puerto Montt, the Cordillera de la Costa subsides into Isla Chiloé and the central valley is drowned behind Chiloé and the Archipiélago de Chonos to form one of the world's finest cruising grounds. Annual rainfall decreases here to about 2000mm. At all times of year there may be rain and high winds for days. These periods are offset by long spells of fine weather that can occur in winter or summer. Chiloé is a popular place for summer holidays. It has similarly lush, but subtly different, vegetation to that of Valdivia. Much of the forest has been cleared for agriculture which, with tourism and salmon farming, is the main economic occupation. On the mainland, opposite the Chonos, the countryside is less accessible by road, though the Carretera Austral winds more than 500M S to Villa O'Higgins. The road has not yet displaced the ferry services of the area. The Chonos themselves are a fascinating wilderness area. Economic necessity means that their sheltered waters will see a great development in salmon farming over the next few years.

Beyond Cabo Ráper (47°S) the spine of S America, here renamed Cordillera Patagónica, runs to the shoreline and disintegrates into a myriad of islands, *canales* (channels) and fjords, with spectacular glaciers and mountains. The N and S Patagonian icefields in this area are the third largest in the world, after those of Antarctica and Greenland. The southerly regions are frequently cold, rainy and windswept but spectacular, especially during the occasionally prolonged periods when the sun shines. In Magallanes, the most southerly region, the scant population is dependent on sheep farming, fishing and, more recently, on oil and gas extraction and tourism. Despite the new industries most areas that will be seen by visiting yachts remain little changed from the thrilling descriptions to be found in Estephan Lucas Bridge's book *Uttermost part of the Earth*. The only major change is that the hardy people who inhabited the area for thousands of years are no more.

Moving west to east, at any latitude N of Puerto Natales, both terrain and climate are dominated by the Andes. In the far S, on the E side of the Cordillera Patagónica, there are dry, low-lying grasslands (*pampas*) swept by the westerlies. This is one of the world's great sheep farming regions but is in decline due to depressed markets.

THE ISLANDS

Isla de Pascua (Easter Island) is the remnant of extinct volcanoes. A fertile island, it has a rugged coastline and variable weather which, along with its isolation, is challenging for visiting yachts. Perhaps partly because of the difficulties, the island retains a unique romanticism and mystery, and it can be rewarding to visit if one is lucky with conditions.

The island is famous for its unique statues, carved by early Polynesian inhabitants. Thor Heyerdahl's theory of settlement from the South American mainland is no longer accepted. Ample evidence points to pre-European contact between the island and other parts of Polynesia. The Pacific-wide presence of the sweet potato (*kumara* in New Zealand) originating from Chiloé or Bolivia and the earth oven (*hangi* in New Zealand and *curanto* in Isla Pascua and Chiloé) point to incredible Polynesian voyages of discovery, colonisation and trade.

The islands of Archipiélago de Juan Fernández are attractive and well worth visiting. They are warm and humid, with a variety of flora, some of which is unique. Facilities are limited and there is no absolutely secure shelter. There has been offshore seismic activity but nothing on-shore and nothing serious within the last 150 years.

Communications

TELEPHONES

There are several telephone companies in Chile, which has one of the world's most competitive communications markets. Pre-paid mobile phones are inexpensive and readily available with good coverage around population centres. Telephone and fax calls may be made and telephone cards (*fichas*) bought from call offices (*Centros de Llamada*) that are open early to late. Phone boxes accept either *fichas* or coin, not both; *fichas* may also be bought at cafés, newsagents etc. which may also allow the use of their phone. Not all phone boxes handle international calls.

When making an international call away from a call office, the selected company's access code is first entered, then 00, then the country code. The efficacy of the companies varies with the destination of the call; inquire locally which company is best for the circumstance of the call and for its access code. The international code for calls to Chile is 56. Within Chile 0 precedes national area codes.

MAIL

Each town and many small villages have a post office signed as *Correo*. Usual hours are 0830-1230 and 1430-1700 Monday to Friday and 0900-1230 on Saturday. Either buy stamps or have mail franked at the *Franqueo* counter and then post it at the office. Street post boxes (*buzon*) are rare. Airmail to and from Europe or N America takes about 5 days, sea mail ten weeks with luck.

Yacht clubs and marinas will hold mail. It is usually only necessary to name the club and the port if the full address is not known.

Poste restante facilities are available but mail is held for 30 days only (ask for the *lista de correos*). The envelope will be filed alphabetically under the first letter in the address. The address must start with the surname; do not put an initial or a title first. If staying awhile in Chile, it may be worth renting a post office box (*casilla*).

INTERNET

Chile is moving ahead very rapidly in this area and internet facilities are found in the smallest towns, though not, as of 2001, in isolated island communities. Larger centres have several different places for connection. Look for a *Centro de Llamados* with internet facilities or for a cybercafé.

TRANSPORT

For more detail about public transport see *Guía Turistel*, full title: '*Turistel – Guía Turística de todo Chile*'. It is said to be available from newsstands, bus and rail stations. The English version, ISBN 956-7206-03-1, is hard to find within Chile and should be acquired before arrival. An up-to-date copy of the Lonely Planet or Travel Companion volumes, both titled *Chile and Easter Island* are invaluable.

Air

Many companies serve Chile from the E and N and prices vary enormously, especially to the USA and Latin American destinations. From the W, Chile is served only by Air New Zealand from Auckland and LanChile (Lineas Aereas Nacionales de Chile) from Papeete and Isla de Pascua (heavily booked in January and February).

Within Chile, LanChile, Ladeco and smaller carriers maintain separate and extensive nets serving places and ports from Arica in the N to Puerto Williams in the S. Centres such as Puerto Williams are served by small airlines with light aircraft. There is a small airport tax.

Rail

Except for the line from Arica to La Paz, passenger services do not run N of Valparaíso. Southwards the line runs as far as Temuco. It is very rough and extremely slow. A *Guía Turística* is available at major stations.

Santiago has an efficient French-built metro.

Buses

Medium and long distance bus services are very good. The best provide meals, refreshments and sleeper-seats (but do not sit at the back near the toilets). *Salón-cama* has 25 fully reclining seats, three to each row, *semi-cama* 34 fully reclining seats, four to each row and *salón-ejecutivo* 44 normal seats. Tickets are obtained from the bus terminal, which is often particular to one or two companies with several terminals in large towns. Book ahead in the high season. Arica – Santiago 28 hours; Santiago – Puerto Montt, 12 hours. Bone-shaking minibuses work local routes, with few formal stopping places and very low fares.

Car hire

There are many car hire firms, expensive and often short of cars at peak holiday times. Prices quoted generally do not include IVA (Chilean value-added tax) or insurance – be careful about the latter for if it is inadequate, a foreign driver involved in an accident may find himself staying in Chile longer than planned. The Automóvil Club de Chile runs an agency with discounts for affiliated members.

Taxis

Taxis have meters (50% extra after 2100hrs and on Sundays) but they will often negotiate fares for out of town and long journeys. Tips are not expected unless for some extra service such as baggage handling. All cities have *collectivos*, which have fixed fares little more expensive than bus fares. Like buses, they work between collecting points.

Other issues

HEALTH

If coming from Panama, Colombia or Bolivia, yellow fever inoculations may be required. Otherwise there are no requirements, but typhoid and hepatitis A vaccinations should be considered.

All towns have medical and dental centres. Attention is quick and efficient. Credit cards are often accepted. Most prescription drugs are available over the counter at pharmacies.

Rabies is not common but is present in Chile. If bitten by dogs or wild animals medical advice should be sought. There is a big problem with wandering dogs and cruising yachtsmen have frequently reported attacks.

Hanta virus (a flu-like illness that frequently progresses to respiratory failure and death) may pose a significant threat to hikers in Patagonia where it is spread by aerosolised mouse dropping particles in shelters or mouse infested accommodation. (Mice are frequent visitors on board in the S *canales*.)

In the S, ultra-violet radiation is strong compared to that in low latitudes. Pay particular attention to the prevention of sunburn.

SECURITY

Chile is one of the safest countries of Latin America. Thefts from yachts are rare and generally owners have not found it necessary to remove deck-stowed working gear whilst in port. It is a matter of judgement whether to lock up if leaving the boat for a few hours. Any club with reasonable facilities tends to be security conscious, often with a 24-hour guard, and many owners employ a *marinero* to keep a boat shipshape; the system discourages pilfering. Ashore, centres attract the usual petty criminals – pickpockets at bus terminals and so forth. The port areas of Valparaíso and Puerto Montt have a reputation for petty theft.

To avoid loss of papers when going ashore, it is advisable to carry photocopies of ships papers and passports. The later have proved acceptable to the *armada* or as ID for credit card use. The only time the original document is required is when renewing a visa in the passport. A yacht that had their papers stolen on a bus found the *carabineros* (police) and *armada* were helpful.

Security on the border with Argentina remains a sensitive matter and yachts visiting the Tierra del Fuego area must take particular care to obey the regulations.

MONEY

The unit is the Peso, indicated by the dollar sign $. Notes are $10,000, $5,000, $2,000, $1,000 and coins $100, $50, $10 & $5. Large denomination notes are difficult to change. In 2002 one US dollar was worth about 600 Pesos.

Credit cards are widely used. Identification by passport (photocopy the ID page) is usually required. Cash against electronic banking or credit cards is almost universally available from automatic tellers (*cajeros automaticos*). These are often located in the foyers of banks and can be accessed out-of-hours by swiping the card at the doorway. Generally only isolated spots will present problems. S of Chiloé carry a good supply of small denomination pesos on board.

It is useful to have a supply of low denomination US dollar notes to trade for pesos where banking facilities are limited. In Puerto Williams the Banco de Chile will advance cash against credit cards.

Travellers cheques denominated in US dollars can be cashed for pesos at large hotels and some supermarkets, also at travel agencies and *casas de cambio* (which may give a better rate than other change agencies). However places that do not have facilities for cash withdrawals may also have difficulties with travellers cheques.

In certain circumstances, for instance staying in a hotel with a published tariff, it is possible to avoid the 18% IVA if paying by credit card or in US dollars by cash or cheque.

TIME
Standard time is UTC −4 hours. Summer time, UTC −3 hours, operates between early October and early March.

PUBLIC HOLIDAYS
1 January New Year's Day
March/April Easter
1 May Labour Day
21 May Navy Day
25 May Corpus Christi
29 June St Peter and St Paul
15 August Assumption
18 September Independence Day
19 September Army Day
12 October Columbus Day
1 November All Saints
8 December Immaculate Conception
25 December Christmas
In addition, there are numerous local religious, folk and cultural festivals. January to March is the main holiday season.

Cruising in Chile
Cruise planning
Most vessels arrive in Valdivia, Puerto Montt or Puerto Williams in November and December. Many find themselves making the entire passage through the *canales*, N or S, in the summer. This may be unavoidable for those with time constraints. Vessels with more time have found that prolonged summer cruises in the area between Puerto Montt and Laguna San Raphael or in the Beagle Channel are delightful. They have also reported making enjoyable passages through the *canales* in winter. The key to a memorable passage between the Beagle Channel and Golfo de Penas (against the prevailing winds) seems to be to have plenty of time to wait for the fair weather which invariably comes. The passage could be achieved in a month but it would most likely be a miserable slog with a high proportion of headwinds.

A yacht can be laid-up satisfactorily at Algarrobo, Valdivia, Puerto Montt and Puerto Williams. Yachts have been left elsewhere, such as Castro, but at some risk.

THE NORTH
This 1400 nautical mile section of the nation stretches from the border with Peru (18°S) to the Canal Chacao (42°S) which leads to Puerto Montt. It spans first a hot, dry, desert, then from about Quintero southwards, a Mediterranean climate, which in turn merges into a temperate, very wet, zone. The coast has long stretches of inhospitable cliff and unapproachable beaches. It is punctuated by commercial harbours, some of which can handle yachts, and numerous anchorages of varying quality. S of Quintero yachting facilities improve. Valdivia (40°S) has good facilities and sheltered sailing in the river. Approximate distances between harbours, often considerable, are given in the text.

The area offers warm sailing and many interesting places to visit; too many yachts skip it completely in their desire to reach the *canales* of the S.

CHILOÉ, CHONOS AND PENÍNSULA TAITAO
Once into the archipelago of Chiloé and *canales* of Patagonia the yacht enters a magnificent cruising ground. Though the climate can be harsh, this contrasts with some of the most secure and tranquil anchorages to be found anywhere. This guide and other works provide much information on Patagonian waters yet the crew sailing there can feel as though they are amongst the first to do so. Indeed, information available covers only a tiny proportion of the available waterways and anchorages; the scope for exploration is almost unlimited.

The area lies between Puerto Montt, 41°30'S, and the S end of Estero Elefàntes, 47°S, some 300M to the S as the crow flies. The last 60M of the S fjord of this region, Elefantes, is a cul-de-sac. In the N are miles of delightful cruising: through and around Chiloé, its off-lying islands and the more rugged, mountainous islands and *canales* of the Archipiélago de los Chonos. It has few urban centres and the whole region, with many colourful working boats, ox carts and fascinating wooden churches, deserves some months for exploration. On the coast at the S end, Península Taitao leads round to Golfo de Penas, where the first (or last when coming from the S) of more consistently difficult weather may be expected.

THE SOUTH

Golfo de Penas to Cabo de Hornos is roughly a thousand miles in a straight line. Civil administration is divided between the *Regións* of Aysén and Magallanes. The two regions are even more sparsely populated than Chonos. Puerto Edén (49°S 74°W) is the only settlement of any size on the main *canales*. In the far S Punta Arenas is a major city but a poor yacht anchorage and Puerto Williams is a small naval and fishing settlement. Puerto Natales, a major tourist town and source of supplies, is 60M off the main route. The route passes through many famous *canales*, including Magellan and Beagle. Rugged, wet, often extremely windy with *ráfagas* (williwaws) churning the water into flying spume and *rachas* (another term for williwaws) spinning yachts on their anchors (if they hold), the *canales* are awe-inspiring but quite delightful and incredibly scenic whatever the conditions. There are numerous anchorages where, with care, a yacht can be perfectly secure.

The routes described do not stray far from the main *canales* used by commercial shipping which the *armada* favours. Indeed, in the far S it is difficult to obtain permission to move away from them. N of Magellan Strait it should be possible to obtain a *zarpe* to cruise away from the main routes.

THE ISLANDS

Of the three Pacific territories, Islas Desventuradas (the Miserable Group of San Félix and San Ambrosio) are hardly worth visiting. Isla de Pascua (Easter Island) and the Archipiélago de Juan Fernández (which includes San Juan Bautista or Robinson Crusoe Island) can be fitted into a passage northwards from Valdivia or visited en route for Chile.

Getting there

There are essentially four routes by which yachts arrive in Chile:
1. Via the South Atlantic
2. From the N Pacific or Central America
   a. Offshore around the S Pacific High or
   b. Inshore along the coasts of Ecuador, Peru and Chile
3. Across the S Pacific.

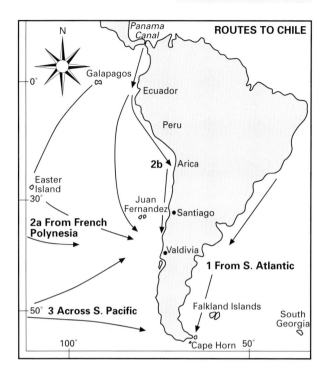

1. **VIA THE SOUTH ATLANTIC**

The Brazilian coast is renowned as a pleasant and interesting cruising area. S of Brazil there are fewer sheltered anchorages. The Río de Plata area offers all facilities a yacht could wish for. The Argentine coast is shallow with strong N/S tidal flows. The river mouths are shallow and treacherous.

There are two schools of thought about the best strategy for sailing south. The first is to stay close to the coast along the 50-metre depth line. Here it is said that the wind and waves are lighter. The other is to stay well offshore (150–200 miles) to avoid the bad seas and strong winds that blow off the coast.

Of seven yachts passing to or from Tierra del Fuego along the Argentinian coast S of Mar del Plata during November and December 2001, all stopped in at least one place. The following anchorages have been used by yachts to provide shelter from some wind directions, to exchange crew, do repairs etc:
Puerto Madryn (42°45'S 63°15'W)
Fondeadero Cracker (42°57'S 64°29'W) said to be easy to enter
Bahía Janssen (44°02'S 65°13'W)
Puerto Santa Elena (44°32'S 65°22'W)
Caleta Carolina or **Sara** (44°54'S 65°36'W)
Caleta Horno (45°03'S 65°42'W) said to be easy to enter
Isla Tova (45°06'S 65°58'W) said to be easy to enter
Comodoro Rivadavia (45°51'S 67°27'W) said to be easy to enter
Puerto Deseado (47°46'S 65°54'W) In Puerto Deseado yachts can tie up to a barge with gives good protection from all winds. Fuel and water can be arranged with jerrycans. There is a good

entry in the *South America Pilot Vol. II.*

Puerto Hoppner, Isla de los Estados
(54°47'S 64°24'W) see 10·29. This is a very
good anchorage and is highly recommended as
a place to recuperate before heading for the
Beagle Channel.

Some of these places can be dangerous to
enter or to stay in with bad weather. A pilot
book and a tide table are required. The Pilotage
Foundation Guide, *South Atlantic Havens &
Anchorages* covers some of this area.

2a. THE PACIFIC OFFSHORE ROUTE

This is the traditional sailing ship route from the
Pacific coast of North America to S Chile or the
Horn. The theory is to sail close-hauled on a S
course between 90° and 120°W until westerlies
are encountered around 35° to 40°S, and then
run into Valdivia (39°50'S) or Puerto Montt
(41°30'S). Much depends upon the time
available for the passage. If coming through
Panama in January or February, some yachts
visit the Galápagos, about 900M. They then go
on to Tahiti and the Australs before turning
towards Valdivia or the Horn; going this way,
the distance from the Galápagos to Valdivia is
about 8800M. A middle route lies via Gambier,
about 7000M and an even shorter route passes
by Isla de Pascua, about 4000M.

A more direct route is to sail S from Panama
to Salinas, Ecuador, about 670 miles, and then
make an off-shore loop of about 3100M to
Valdivia or crawl down the coast. At first, the
winds in the Gulf of Panama are light and
variable and thunderstorms are common. It is
advisable to stay well off the coast of Colombia,
closing the coast around the border with
Ecuador. If going offshore, most of the
remainder is close hauled, beating across the SE
trades with a reach or run in to the coast at the
end. For a boat that is happy beating in rough
conditions, this route may be preferable as it
takes less time than the other routes.
Unfortunately the high is unstable. In the centre
of the high the winds will be very light.

2b. THE PACIFIC INSHORE ROUTE

The inshore route is almost all against the
prevailing S wind and the Humboldt Current. A
not untypical passage following the coast from
Salinas, Ecuador to Valdivia logged a total of
3360M, 1460M under motor and 1,900 under
sail.

The Humboldt Current flows up the coasts of
Peru and Chile at a rate of 0·5 to 1·5kts. The
prevailing wind is from the S and follows the
coast. During the day it is reinforced by the
thermal effect of air flowing over the cold waters
of the Humboldt Current and onto the warm
land. The strength of the thermal wind increases
during the summer months. It is often easier to
travel at night when the wind is lighter and
frequently has an offshore slant.

Dealing with the officials in Peru is time
consuming, frustrating and expensive.
Fortunately there are anchorages where there
are no settlements and hence no officials. The
Peruvian coast is 1150M long with few
sheltered anchorages, necessitating several
overnight legs. In Chile, the anchorages and
towns become more frequent. The straight-line
distance from Arica to Valparaíso is 870M but
under sail as much as 1150M may be logged
and the average distance between anchorages
rises to about 60M. Although the prevailing
winds are decidedly from the S, there are
occasional N winds lasting 12–24 hours with
calms during the night. There are fewer
anchorages along the 600M from Valparaíso to
Valdivia, though there is a greater likelihood of
W or SW winds making for easier sailing on a
close reach.

This route takes more time than the offshore
route but has a number of attractions. The
coastal towns in N Chile are worth visiting. So
few yachts travel this coast that the welcome is
generous. The anchorages in the Atacama
Desert are a unique experience. With the
availability of anchorages, the inshore route is a
great deal easier than the rough offshore
passage, particularly for smaller yachts.

Local advice, concerning the prevailing
southerlies, is that November and December
are the months of strongest winds. Two yachts
travelling S in these months experienced no
night-time decrease in winds S of Caldera.
Wind strength varied between 15 to 25 knots
with, occasionally, 30–35 knots (off Caldera,
Puerto Huasco and Valdivia).

3. ACROSS THE S PACIFIC

Several yachts each year make the crossing
direct from Australia or New Zealand. The
weather along the 5000M route from New
Zealand is dominated by the depressions which
track across the Southern Ocean between 50°
and 60°S producing a strong W flow up to
about 35°S. Gales are most common in winter
and their number lessens in November.
Tropical cyclones, which generally keep to the
W end of the S Pacific, are most likely between
January and March and can affect conditions in
higher latitudes. With an eye to cruising
Patagonia in the spring, the best choice appears
to be to cross in November or December
between 40° and 45°S but the decision will be
affected by conditions at the time of the start. In
January some vessels have experienced
frustrating E winds along this route as far S as
50 degrees. Places to aim at are Puerto Williams
after rounding Cape Horn, Puerto Montt via
Canal Chacao or Valdivia. To enter the
Patagonian *canales* elsewhere is more difficult:
the landfall is highly complex and there are no
ports of entry.

The sea

The Peru or Humboldt Current comes inshore near Cabo Ráper and drifts N along the coast in a band some 50 to 150 miles wide at about half a knot. It often slants towards the coast, which can be dangerous, as it cools the surrounding air and causes fog. Off Cabo Ráper the current may drift any way, even E, but the tendency is either N or S. Along the S coast the W wind drift moves SE and increases up to 1 knot towards Cabo de Hornos. Between summer and winter, sea temperatures vary from 20°–15°C in the N and 9°–5°C in the S. Once or twice a decade, the system is upset by El Niño, a mass of warm Pacific surface water. This, when it reaches the coast around Ecuador, pushes S, blocking the lower rungs of the food ladder and causing wide disruption to dependant life as well as upsetting the climate in places as far apart as Australia and Brazil, California and Tierra del Fuego. Hearsay suggests that El Niño years are more settled in the far south.

Tides are noticeable along the N Coast but tidal ranges are generally less than 1m. Between Puerto Montt and Cabo Ráper, tidal ranges can be as much as 10m and there are strong to very strong (8kt) tidal streams in some of the *canales*. The tide tables *(Tabla de Mareas)* of the Chilean Hydrographic Office (SHOA, or *Servicio Hidrográfico y Oceanográfico de la Armada de Chile)* are very useful; see Hydrographic Information below. The SHOA publication is numbered N3009. Many people have found that computer based tidal predictions are accurate.

Swell is almost always present on the coast. Storms in the S produce swell in the N days after it was generated.

Tsunamis (tidal waves, *maremotos* in Spanish), caused by submarine earthquakes, are of little consequence to a vessel at sea in deep water because the swell, though high, is exceedingly long. Their effect on shore can be serious. New Zealand and the USA run a tsunami warning system. Warnings are issued from Oahu (Hawaii) and promulgated from Arica, Antofagasta, Coquimbo, Valparaíso, Talcahuano and Puerto Montt.

Weather systems

The S Pacific High sits within the area bordered roughly by the Galapagos to the N, Easter Island to the W, and the continent of S America to the E. It moves N in winter and S in summer. The N part of the Chilean coast is on the fringe of the SE trades; to the S is a wide area of moderate southerlies gradually becoming stronger westerlies. Inshore, the westerlies may be diverted by the Andes, generally to the N. Winds from an E quadrant are rare or short lived on the coast although they may blow 200 or 300M offshore.

The S Pacific High is generally powerful enough to keep the frontal systems of the roaring forties to the S of Valparaíso. Some systems slip through, especially in winter. In winter, the extreme cold of the mountains and Argentine pampas can result in the temporary development of a stable high over Patagonia. This can push depressions to the N or S. It is not unknown for the Golfo de Penas to be calm and sunny whilst a gale rages in Valdivia.

RAIN AND TEMPERATURE

In the N, on the borders with Peru and Bolivia, rainfall is zero, the land is hot (more than 30°C in summer), stony and deserted. In the S the hot desert region gives way to a mediterranean climate with winter rainfall which increases as latitude increases until at Valparaíso it is some 360mm a year. Then quite sharply there is a change to a temperate climate with warm summers, cool winters and much more rain. At Valdivia (40°S) the annual rainfall is 2460mm, varying from less than 100mm per month in summer to around 400mm in midwinter. The inland waters of the cruising grounds from Puerto Montt to Cabo de Hornos (Cape Horn) are given some shelter from the heaviest rainfall by the seaward ranges but rain and snowfall is little short of 2000mm a year. S of Cabo Ráper, rain falls on more than half the days of the month though there is slightly less in winter than in summer. Temperatures in the far S seldom rise above 20°C in summer (14°C is a common midday temperature) and not far above freezing in winter. Sea temperatures in summer range between 10° and 12°C. In the S fog is rare but squalls and low cloud can reduce visibility to very low levels.

WEATHER FOR THE SAILOR

Sailing down the long N coast the predominant winds are from the S. These winds are weak in the N and there are frequent calms. By Valparaíso (33°S) the southerlies are often strong and there are also strong sea breezes blowing onshore. At San Antonio, for example, S of Valparaíso, vessels are

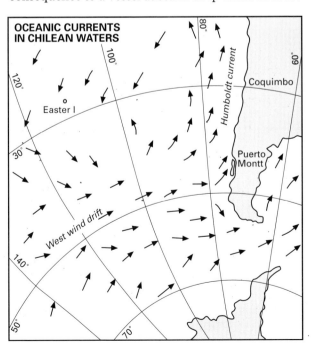

OCEANIC CURRENTS IN CHILEAN WATERS

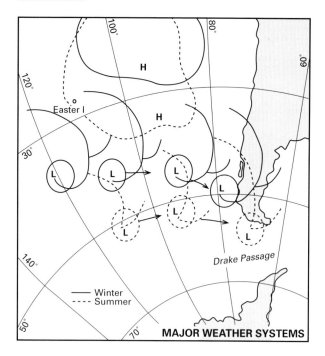

MAJOR WEATHER SYSTEMS

— Winter
---- Summer

advised to enter at night or at daybreak when the SW winds, which raise a heavy swell, are at their lowest. Along this stretch there is scant protection from the occasional N gales. Caldera (27°S) is usually reckoned to be the N limit of N winds.

Around Valdivia westerlies begin to make themselves known but, as indicated, they tend to be deflected either N or S by the Andes. Near Puerto Montt southerlies predominate in summer, northerlies in winter. Further S, northerly winds become predominant at all times of year. Active fronts regularly cross this region. It should be kept in mind that there may be a strong but usually short-lived southwesterly change following the passage of a front. Fronts can pass quickly and go through overnight. Many anchorages have adequate security in NW winds but are less good in SW. The better anchorages are sheltered from N through to SW. The best are those where wind direction is not seriously modified by mountains.

Below the Archipiélago de Chonos the incidence of bad weather increases. The winds are stronger and more from the W and N. The weather is strongly influenced by the mountains. They can turn an expected fair wind into a headwind, generally from the N. Of great importance in S Chile are the violent squalls resulting from eddies set up in high level winds by the mountains. These squalls can come from any direction and are known to exceed 100 knots on occasion; locally they are called *rachas*. *Rachas* can uproot poorly moored boats with ease and not infrequently also uproot the trees to which the boats were moored.

Between Golfo de Penas and the Estrecho de Magallanes the South Pacific high continues to have an influence. As a low passes to the S, it creates a 'crush zone' between it and the high, packing the isobars closely together and causing a band of very strong NW winds. As the low moves away to the SE,

the high pushes back down creating softer and warmer weather. However the wind usually stays in the N. Most of the *canales* in this area slant from SE toward the NW. This funnels winds with any W in them down the *canales* from the NW. Similarly, the E winds that occasionally blow during the winter are funnelled up the *canales* from the S. So, even when it's blowing SW offshore, the wind is bent to NW in the *canales*. This makes a trip north up the *canales* during the summer an almost continuous slog directly to weather, usually into about 25kts apparent wind. A vessel requires either a powerful engine and fuel capacity to motor-sail the entire way or good sails and the time and patience to tack. Use can be made of calm periods that occasionally occur between weather systems. The trip can be made in a month, but two months is needed for a pleasant trip and 3 or 4 months for a relaxing one. A trip S is generally much more pleasant. Some yachts prefer to sail S on favourable wet and windy days and spend the intervening spells of good weather exploring on shore.

The notes above apply to Estrecho de Magallanes with the difference that the orientation of the strait dictates that winds here are generally from the W and exceptionally strong.

Daytime warming of the land strongly affects winds in the *canales* from Golfo de Penas to Canal Beagle. The normal westerly winds drop by 10–20kts during the night (often going absolutely calm) and build during the day, peaking about 3pm. This effect is particularly pronounced in the E/W oriented Canal Beagle and Estrecho de Magallanes, and it is usually much easier to go west in these two *canales* during the night or very early in the morning.

Most winters a temporary high establishes itself over Argentine Patagonia. This situation can give calm settled weather with cloudless skies over the *canales*. The air is extremely cold and anchorages without steadily flowing water can freeze, usually at night but sometimes for days on end. In the valleys leading into the Andes katabatic E winds can blow strongly whilst it is calm in the *canales* between. Those who have experienced these conditions, in yachts with good heating and winter clothes, highly recommend winter cruising in this area. These fine periods can last for one month or more.

Between Estrecho de Magallanes and Canal Beagle it is much rainier, with a day or two of steady heavy rain, frequently mixed with hail or snow squalls, when a low tracks overhead. Also the winds are strong as they come in directly from the ocean, undeflected by land or hills. The hilltops here are mostly bare stone covered by snow and the few small trees cowering from the wind in gullies and coves are gnarled and twisted. Narrow *canales*, such as Seno Garibaldi, can funnel winds down their entire length so that moderate wind conditions elsewhere blow at gale force within the Seno.

The deep southern ocean lows (975mb is not exceptional) are the dominant feature in the Beagle area. These come through about every 3–5 days.

The centres track across the southern Drake Passage and the Antarctic Península during the summer (roughly mid-December to mid-March). As a low approaches, the barometer drops, and the wind blows hard from the NW for 24 hours with heavy rain and sometimes snow. After the low passes overhead, the barometer starts to rise, and it blows harder from the SW for around 12 hours (a steady 40kts with gusts to 50 is pretty common) with bright sun and occasional rain or snow squalls. Finally, it goes calm and sunny for a day or two until the next low approaches. The barometer provides a reliable indicator of wind direction and is frequently of more assistance than the weather reports.

During the spring and autumn the lows occasionally track above the Beagle, producing easterly winds which can make some of the recommended anchorages very uncomfortable. In the winter a high often establishes itself over southern Argentina, pushing the lows either far south or far north, providing very cold, but calm, or easterly, weather with cloudless skies in the *canales*.

Weather forecasts

Times are UT unless stated otherwise.

NAVTEX

Navtex transmissions in Chile are in English and Spanish; in Argentina, English only. The area code for Chile is XV and Argentina, VI. Station identities are as follows:

Station	English	Spanish
Antofagasta	A	H
Valparaíso	B	I
Talcahuano	C	J
Puerto Montt	D	K
Magallanes	E	L
Isla de Pascua	F	G
Ushuaia	A	

See the list of Radio Signals for times of transmission.

VHF

Ports and major lighthouses broadcast weather information twice a day on a working channel (usually 14) following an announcement on channel 16. Detailed information may be found in the list of radio signals. In practice times and contents of forecasts vary. Unless one is in port or in the far S, it is rare to be within range of a VHF station. VHF weather forecasts are in Spanish. Published forecast times are mainly between 0205 and 0215 and 1405 and 1415 with local exceptions. All stations keep a listening watch on channel 16 and will gladly repeat the latest forecast on request.

HF

HF forecasts vary considerably in time of broadcast. Refer to the list and obtain up to the minute advice from other yachts. Most stations broadcast on 2738kHz following a call on 2182kHz.
Forecasts are generally given on 4146kHz morning and evening at some time after the reception of position reports. Times seem to be variable and are not given in the radio list.

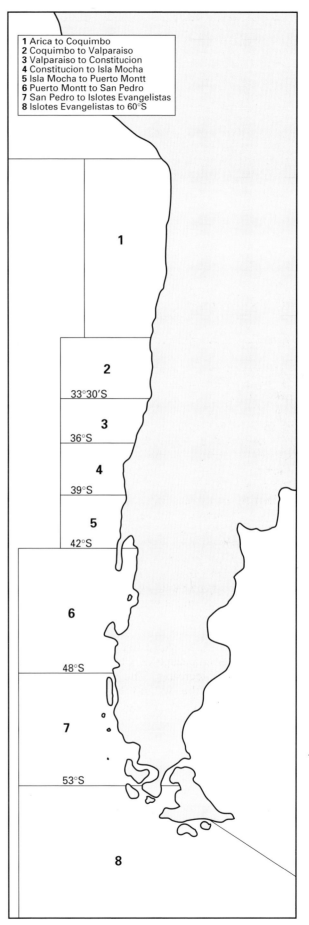

1 Arica to Coquimbo
2 Coquimbo to Valparaiso
3 Valparaiso to Constitucion
4 Constitucion to Isla Mocha
5 Isla Mocha to Puerto Montt
6 Puerto Montt to San Pedro
7 San Pedro to Islotes Evangelistas
8 Islotes Evangelistas to 60°S

CHILE FORECAST AREAS

WEATHERFAX BROADCASTS

Frequency 4228·2, 8675·2 & 17144·6kHz

Note at the time of compilation, some of the weather charts actually broadcast were not listed in the current list of radio signals. 1115 and 2315 UT seem to be the reliable times.

Time	Content
1115	Surface Analysis 0600UT plus satellite image
1915	Sea State Analysis plus satellite image
2200	Surface Analysis plus Antarctic ice chart
2315	forecast for 1200UT the following day plus satellite image

Another useful weatherfax, particularly for an offshore passage or when crossing the Drake Passage, is transmitted by New Zealand (ZKLF) at 1030 on 13550·5kHz.

Except when there is a large stationary high sitting over the area, the specific interpretation of the weatherfax and forecast information is difficult. This becomes increasingly true the further S one travels, particularly in the area of Magallanes and S. At best this information protects the yachtsman from extreme weather. The low systems move and change so quickly that daily predictions and reality rarely coincide. In a day it is possible to have sunny weather, light and gale force winds, squalls and even snow. The weatherfax picture in the morning is already history by the time it is received and the pattern of the lows can have changed markedly a few hours later. The use of a barograph enables the observer to update the information provided by the fax and so gain a better understanding of the prevailing conditions.

Local terminology: *ráfaga* and *racha* both mean williwaw, or sudden and violent short-lived squall, usually without precipitation. *Chubasco* is a term used by the *armada* and in this context means squalls, though in inland forecasts it generally indicates showers.

OTHER INFORMATION

Inmarsat C provides regular weather information, similar in nature to that broadcast by the *armada*, but in English.

Vessels that can receive email can access very good weather data in a compressed computer file 'grib format' from www.saildocs.com

Formalities

THE *ARMADA*

The Chilean Navy, referred to as the *armada*, based at Valparaíso, has absolute authority over every movement of all shipping throughout Chile.

BEFORE ARRIVAL

Make photocopies of passports, of a crew list with passport details and of the ships papers. The end product is more impressive if stamped with the ship's rubber stamp. You will in due course also be asked for details of fuel and water tanks, how many days' supply of food is aboard, the range of the ship (in miles or in days) and of life saving equipment. Some people have been asked for evidence of insurance, skippers and radio officers qualifications and radio licence. One case has been reported in which a *zarpe* was refused because insurance cover was lacking, but most skippers seem to have been able to obtain a *zarpe* even when insurance cover has been lacking. Details (factory numbers) of the engine, all transceivers and specialist radio equipment (weather and other fax) and possibly of autopilots may be requested. It is useful to have them listed and copied. It is also useful to copy papers issued to you by the Chilean authorities. This is easily achieved in the towns.

Photocopies of passports are acceptable as ID for everything except entering and leaving the country.

ENTRY

There are three authorities that must be attended upon: the *armada* (navy), the *aduana* (customs) and the *policía internacional* (international police) a division of *policía investigaciones* ('plainclothes' police). The *armada* will usually come to the yacht to check in. The *aduana* and *policía investigaciones* may come to the yacht but may have to be visited at their offices. Generally speaking, yachts may enter Chile at any major port – Isla de Pascua, Arica, Iquique, Antofagasta, Talcahuano, Valparaíso, Valdivia, Puerto Montt, Punta Arenas or Puerto Williams. The *aduana* office for Valdivia is at Osorno, two hours away by bus.

Chacabuco is technically a port of entry but a yacht using it as such may run into trouble since she will have been in Chilean waters for some time.

IMMIGRATION

Requirements change but in 2002 the situation was as follows:

Citizens of the EU, the USA, Canada, New Zealand and Australia do not need visas. It would be wise to check before departure, especially for those who are not citizens of the above nations. All require valid passports. All visitors receive a 90-day entry permit on arrival. This is to be kept securely with the passport. In most cases the entry permit may be renewed once before expiry (don't take no for an answer) and failure to do so before expiry will mean getting involved in a lot of paperwork and perhaps a fine. Sailing is no excuse so far as immigration is concerned. In addition to entry ports, the entry permit can be renewed in Puerto Aysén and Puerto Natales. An alternative is to bus to Argentina and then re-enter Chile to collect another 90-day permit (some people have had problems re-entering on the same day, though it is generally permissible). Sailing to Ushuaia will achieve the same thing but visitors needing a visa should bear in mind the requirement for a multiple entry visa if shuttling between Argentina and Chile in the far S or elsewhere.

Application can be made, via the local government offices, for a 1-year temporary residence permit. The cost of this depends upon charges levied by your home country to Chilean citizens. Thus British citizens have to pay about US$350 whilst for Swedes there is no charge. Those staying for some time would be well advised to make enquiries soon after arrival. For longer stays, the temporary permit can be renewed once; thereafter residence can be applied for.

CUSTOMS

On first arrival a *Declaración de Admision Temporal* must be made to the *aduana* and a certificate for the yacht obtained. Details of the ship and her equipment – safety, communications, propulsion etc. – may be recorded. The certificate is free and is usually issued for a four-month period, renewable for further four-month periods up to a total of two years. Allow time for this: renewals may have to be processed through the customs office at the original port of entry but other customs offices are generally happy to assist with this. Renewals during the second year may require more time and special attention from the regional inspector. Generally a different reason from the first year needs to be given in the application (such as the necessity to wait for the appropriate season to continue the voyage). The officials are universally helpful and considerate. After two years the yacht is liable for import duty and IVA (*impuesto de valor agregado* – value added tax) on its current estimated value. (It may be possible to import a vessel via one of the duty free areas – *Zona Franca* in Punta Arenas or Iquique.) Renewing a certificate can take a week to ten days; start the process in good time.

PAPERWORK

The procedures may be tedious at first but the form must be observed. Once a cruise is launched, matters become more relaxed. All reports mention the unfailing patience, courtesy and helpfulness of the *armada* in assisting yachts to keep to the rules.

On departing from any Chilean port, a vessel requires a *zarpe* or permit, even if going to another Chilean port. This is a document issued by the *armada* giving information on the ship, her stores and crew. The route, destination and ETA are included. In addition, when clearing out of the country, you will need to contact immigration and customs (through the *armada*).

The principal *armada* stations, such as Castro, Puertos Melinka, Aguirre and Chacabuco are manned by navy personnel and are known as *Capitanías de Mar*. Small villages and settlements often have a post, an *Alcalde de Mar,* run by an agent of the navy, usually the police *(carabineros).* Depending upon the personnel, the level of interest in yachts shown by *Alcaldes de Mar* may vary; they have been know to decline to accept a QTH (radio shorthand for present position) and not to respond to the VHF.

OBTAINING A *ZARPE* (PERMIT)

Some ability in Spanish is a real asset in negotiating the document and the effort of speaking in Spanish is appreciated.

It is best to make written application, though this is not always required.

The information required is:

1. Boat information.
2. Crew list and passport information.
3. Water, fuel, cruising range and period of self-sufficiency.
4. Any changes to equipment since entry.
5. Route to be followed, identifying each main *canal* or pass if appropriate.

  The first *zarpe* has to be referred to Valparaíso, which may take a few days. It pays to cast your programme as far forward as possible, even though it is not possible to be precise about dates. For instance, it is possible to get a *zarpe* for a passage from Arica to Valparaíso or Valdivia to Ushuaia. Subsequently, unless it has to be referred to Valparaíso again, the *zarpe* is prepared locally for your signature and that of the Port Captain and generally takes no more than half an hour to obtain.

6. Port of destination and ETA.

On reaching port, intermediate or final, the *armada*, if present, will examine the *zarpe;* details of passports and the yacht will be required. It is useful to have them ready on a handout.

On a lengthy cruise, it is usually a good plan to make the application as wide as possible without going into detail – make it long on *canales* and short on ports. A successful application involving a crew change at Puerto Chacabuco and stop at Puerto Natales was as follows on the next page:

Place and date
Señor (Gobernador Marítimo de Puerto Montt)
Date
Presente
Estimado Señor
Mediante la presente, solicito a Vd. la autorización de
    navegación en aguas interiores para mi yate:
(Name of yacht)
(Date of Departure)
(Crew List)
Ruta Puerto Montt – Seno Reloncaví – Golfo Ancud –
    Golfo Corcovado – Islas Chonos- Laguna San Rafael
    – Seno Aysén – Puerto Chacabuco
(Estimated date of arrival)
(Estimated date of departure)
(Different crew list)
Ruta Puerto Chacabuco – Islas Chonos- Golf de Penas –
    Canal Messier – Puerto Natales- Estrecho de
    Magallanes – Canal Cockburn – Canal Brecknock –
    Canal Beagle – Puerto Williams
(Estimated date of arrival)
Motivo: Fines Turisticos
(Signed)
Capitán

This allowed scope to pick and choose anchorages
en route. Depending upon the official you deal with
the route may be copied directly from your
application or more specific details may be added. N
of Valdivia where yachts are less common the
officials tend to be stricter and require more detail.
In Puerto Williams it is usual to be told which routes
and anchorages are permitted without any room for
argument. This is particularly frustrating, as they are
not necessarily those that appear to be most
appropriate for a yacht. When heading N from
Puerto Williams the *zarpe* is usually less specific
than one for that port's immediate area of control.
Don't be too worried by a *zarpe* that appears unduly
restrictive. In practice it is accepted that yachts have
different needs from commercial vessels and that
anchorages or *canales* not mentioned on the *zarpe*
can be used if weather or seamanship dictate.

REPORTING YOUR POSITION

HF radio is not compulsory. One of the instructions
given on each *zarpe* is that all vessels should call the
armada at 0800 and 2000 each day to report its
position (QTH) on HF, known as its PIM – *Posición
e Intención de Movimiento*. Trying to get through to
the *armada* at those times can be very difficult. If
you have, or admit to having, SSB then twice-daily
reporting is likely to prove quite a chore!

If they do not have HF, yachts are nevertheless
expected to report their PIM on VHF which they
are obliged to carry. They should also report to
lighthouses as they are passed and to ships, whose
Pilots will relay the report to the *armada*. They may
be called by *armada* stations ashore at any time and
asked for their PIM.

At 0800 and 2000, the *armada* station
(particularly the local posts in the far south) may call
vessels known to be in the area, and you may be one
in a queue. The shore radio calls the yachts name
por QTH (pronounced *ku tay achay*) followed by
cambio (over). The response is to give the yacht's

name and call sign. When recognised, the shore
station gives the go ahead which is normally the
word *adelante*. The response which should all be in
Spanish is '*Navigando de* (from) . . . *a* (to) . . .
Latitud . . . *Longitud* . . ., *Romeo Victor* (give true
course) . . . *grados*, *Andar* (give speed) . . . *knudos*,
Echo Tango Alpha' (give your ETA in local time
plus day if appropriate). If you are at anchor, the
response is '*Fondeado en* (place) . . ., *Latitud* . . .,
Longitud . . ., *Sin novedad*' (if you have nothing to
report). You may wish to give your ETD and ETA
and place of your next planned stop. At the end,
when the shore station has acknowledge your
message, it will either call the next ship or say
'*proximo*' if it wants the next ship to call in.

It may be handy to have the Spanish numerals
written out. The other words, which tend to vanish
from the memory in moments of stress are *grados*,
minutos, *norte*, *sur*, *este*, *oeste*, *knudos*, *horas*.

RESTRICTIONS IN THE SOUTH

Strictly speaking, travel in the region is restricted to
the *canales* used by commercial traffic. However, in
the waterways N of Magellan Straits it seems to be
recognised that yachts will deviate from the
commercial route to explore glaciers. S of Magellan
the *armada* is more sensitive, partially because of its
responsibility to aid vessels in distress and therefore
the need to know who is where and partially because
of the sensitive relations between Chile and
Argentina in this region. In the Beagle Channel the
armada is particular that the intended anchorages
are listed on the *zarpe* and there are certain
prohibited anchorages which the *armada* will not
allow on a *zarpe*. It is understood that in bad
weather or an emergency a yacht may use any
anchorage along their authorised route. Yachts have
been expelled from Chile for using prohibited
anchorages without good cause.

That said, there are certain *canales*, such as Canal
Bárbara and Canal Acwalisnan, which are not on
the commercial route but are regularly used by
fishermen and quite frequently by yachts. It may be
possible to use such *canales* if the *zarpe* is
indeterminate about the matter but that is a matter
for judgement on the spot. Descriptions are
included in case they come in handy.

REPORTING IN THE S

The matter of reporting becomes more serious once
the far S is reached. A good station to report your
PIM to is Felix Radio, 4146·0kHz USB, between
0700–0800 and 1900–2000hrs; if you have not got
HF, use VHF at those times whether or not you
think you will be heard – some station may pass your
message on. Some yachts have found a log of their
PIM calls helpful when queried by the *armada* for
failing to report (see introduction to Chapter 10).

In summary: be patient. The *armada* is good
humoured, helpful, very well behaved and has a job
to do.

Radio communications

RADIO

VHF is mandatory. It is worth asking the *armada* for their publications on maritime telecommunications services but their information is not always up to date, even in respect of their own schedules. Most stations appear to use United States VHF channels rather than International channels. This is not a problem on most commonly used channels like 16 and 14 but some, like channel 22 (a weather channel in the States and occasionally used in Chile for calling non-official shore stations), are different. Some VHF units are capable of switching between the two standards; some will be blocked from transmission on the weather channels.

SSB radio is not mandatory for cruising in Chile.

RADIO STATIONS

Most coast radio stations have both HF and VHF, a few smaller marine posts, *Alcaldes del Mar*, not operated by the *armada*, do not monitor HF frequencies nor are they particularly reliable in answering calls on VHF.

DISTRESS

At the time of writing Chile is implementing Digital Selective Calling (DSC – *Llamada Selectiva Digital*, in Spanish) for distress signals for VHF (Ch 70) and HF (2187·5; 4207·5; 6312; 8414·5; 12577 and 16804·5kHz). VHF channel 16 and HF channel 2182kHz continue to be monitored for distress calls.

CALLING FREQUENCIES
VHF

All ports, *armada* vessels and manned lighthouses keep a listening watch on channel 16.

HF

Major ports and lighthouses monitor 2182kHz. In addition many monitor 4146kHz, this frequency is used at 0800 and 2000 local time for ships reporting QTH. At those times the frequency is busy but contact is almost guaranteed, whereas perseverance may be required at other times.

RADIO SERVICES

All stations will accept official traffic including position reports and will give meteorological information and advice on local conditions (such as whether the port is open for traffic or large vessels are transiting a channel).

Stations in some major ports offer free emergency medical advice (users are encouraged to use the medical section of the international code of signals). A few stations offer public radiotelephone services. Valparaíso – Playa Ancha radio/CBV offers all services. Major stations will be able to offer varying levels of English.

Users are referred either to SHOA 3008 *Radioayudas a la navigacion en la costa de Chile* or the ALRS.

INMARSAT

Users of Inmarsat C will be able to obtain weather and safety bulletins.

CRUISING NET

The SSB Patagonia Cruising Net meets daily on 8164kHz at 0900 local time. Be prepared for a frequency change shortly after this time if conditions dictate. Juan Carlos Szydlowski (see Añihué, Chapter 3·2) is a lynch pin of the net and has been active in collecting information for this guide and with lobbying in Santiago for the interests of cruising yachts.

EMAIL BY HF RADIO

JC Szydlowski has organised a Seamail service. Cruisers with a HF modem may use this at no cost. Unfortunately Sailmail coverage in this area is currently variable and requires exceptional propagation conditions.

Amateur operators using Winlink have had good success with the following stations (PMBOs – pactor mailbox operators): ZS5S, K4CJX, K6IXA, and WBOTAX. 20 metres was consistently useable, K4CJX was often good on 17m. ZS5S uses a beam antenna and has special times but will turn towards the area on request.

Hydrographic information

CHARTS
(See appendix D)

General

Chilean charts are of very high quality and represent an impressive body of hydrographic effort. Other authorities' charts are derived from Chilean information. Therefore it is strongly recommended that Chilean charts are used wherever possible.

Chilean, British and US navies swap information and that obtained by one can be expected to appear in another's publication. The Chilean authority is the *Servicio Hidrográfico y Oceanográfico de la Armada* (SHOA). SHOA charts are about the same price as those of the UK Hydrographic Office. They are obtainable from their office in Valparaíso, at chart agencies (*agencias de cartas*) in major ports (including Puerto Montt and Punta Arenas), through UK chart agencies (but that takes months) and the Armchair Sailor Bookshop, Newport, Rhode Island which often has the *Atlas Hidrográfico* (see below) in stock.

SHOA produces its own Pilots but the UK Hydrographic Office Pilots to S America, NP 6 & 7, are comprehensive.

A very useful website is www.shoa.cl from where the complete catalogue of Chilean charts, which includes notes on renumbering, electronic charts and corrections for varying datums in use with Satellite Navigation, is available free. It would be wise to have a copy on board.

Official Chilean chart numbers at May 2003 differ from many of those in the 2001 *Atlas Hidrográfico*. This guide uses the latest numbering available. Appendix H gives conversions between present numbers and those in the 2001 Atlas.

The large-scale Chilean charts are a necessary adjunct to this guide if going S of Puerto Montt. SHOA's *Atlas Hidrográfico de Chile* contains all the Chilean charts and is priced at US$120; it represents remarkable value for money. The charts are reduced, beautifully printed and clear but a really good magnifying glass, preferably with an interior light, is necessary. The atlas as a whole is difficult to handle in a seaway but individual sheets can be abstracted for chart work. New editions of the Atlas are published regularly. As new charts are constantly being added, particularly around the Chonos Archipelago and in the far S, it is important to have the latest edition (presently December 2001) and the catalogue should be consulted for the most recent charts. The charts in the Atlas are not intended for navigation and are therefore NOT corrected later than their date of publication (the chart's publication date, not that of the atlas). This means that lights are frequently not shown or have different characteristics from the Light List and that additions and changes, such as the placing of overhead cables are omitted.

Warning

The *armada* has been producing many new charts in recent years particularly in the far S. Older charts have many inaccuracies, especially in longitude. Discrepancies of up to 2 miles have been observed between GPS and charts. It would be wise not to try to compare between new and old charts and to use new charts in conjunction with GPS wherever possible. SHOA 3000, the chart catalogue, has a series of corrections to apply to correct different datums to WGS84, useful as these are it seems that in many cases the errors are in the original plotting of positions rather than in the datum used.

Unofficial information

When cruising S of Puerto Montt, the *Navigator Guide – Una Aventura Navegando los Canales del Sur Chile* (Yachtsman's navigator guide to the Chilean channels) by Alberto Mantellero is very helpful and has provided many suggestions which have been followed up by contributors to this volume. It is believed that a further guide with particular emphasis on the S area is due to be published in the near future, but no details are available to the Pilotage Foundation at this stage.

LIGHTS

A branch of the *armada*, the Dirección General del Territorio Marítimo, DIRECTEMAR, supervises lights and the standards are high. A light list (N3007 *Lista de Faros y Señales de Niebla*) is issued annually. The UK equivalent is the Admiralty *List of Lights Volume G* NP80. One or the other should be aboard. Many major lights are still manned. In the S the long distances and stormy conditions can result in delays to repairs and occasionally lights or marks are absent. Note that positions given for lights are charted positions and may not agree with the GPS. The Chilean list specifies the number of the chart to which the position refers.

TIDES

A certain amount of tidal information is given in the text based on the UK Admiralty *Tide Tables Vol. 3* NP203. The information is, however, patchy and the tide tables (N3009 *Tabla de Mareas*) produced by SHOA should be obtained. Note that the times used in this publication are Chilean Standard Time and need to be corrected for summer time in the appropriate season. The free PC tide programme WXtide32, covers the whole world and proved to be accurate to within 10 minutes between Canal Chacao and Cape Horn. However the tidal stations are mainly in the outer areas and not in the mainland inlets. Other computer based tidal programs have been found accurate.

BUOYAGE

Buoyage direction conforms to the IALA region B (red right returning).

The direction of buoyage for lateral marks is as follows:

From S to N along the coast with the exception of the Straits of Magellan where it is N to S.

From W to E in transverse *canales* with the exception of the Straits of Magellan and Canal Cockburn where it is E to W.

Running into ports whatever the geographical direction.

In the Canal Beagle between longitudes 68°36'·64W and 66°25'W the colours of lights and structures does not indicate the direction of Buoyage and does not comply with IALA.

All other buoyage complies with IALA.

Warning – salmoneras (salmon farms)

At present these are only found in the area between Puerto Montt and Melinka, Seno Aysén and in the environs of Puerto Natales. A vast expansion of the industry is currently in progress, by 2003 they can be expected all the way down to the Golfo de Penas and not long after to the Magellan Straits. *Salmoneras* adversely affect anchorages aesthetically and by the large amount of thoughtless disposal of non-biodegradable waste that pollutes adjacent waters. In 2001 one yacht was nearly lost after fouling both propeller and rudder during a gale on drifting nets from abandoned installations. Active salmon installations do not present a serious navigation hazard but the practice of cutting loose old salmon pens and allowing them to drift into adjacent beaches and coves appears quite widespread. Beware of trailing ropes and nets. It is sad that such an important aspect of Chile's national economy, with obvious benefits in terms of employment and development of the local infrastructure, is also associated with so much avoidable pollution.

RDF BEACONS

Although superceded by new techniques, RDF beacons are listed in Appendix A. If working, they remain as back up to other systems. An estimated range in nautical miles is given for marine radio beacons and the power of the transmitter is given for aero beacons. RDF is of exceedingly limited usefulness S of Puerto Montt. If a vessel is dependant upon RDF then a recent list of radio signals should be carried.

Ship's stores and equipment

PROVISIONS

In N and central Chile very good foodstuffs are commonly available. S of Chiloé, there are good supplies in Aysén, Puerto Natales and Punta Arenas. Ushuaia has excellent shopping, though fresh food may have been refrigerated and not keep well, this problem is less common in Chile. Puertos Edén, Aguirre and Melinka have very limited supplies. Most necessities are available in Puerto Williams though selection and quality are poor. There are excellent wines, many unknown outside Chile, good local spirits (notably *Pisco*), and some genuine but little known Scotch whiskies that are very good value.

SHELLFISH

Shellfish, particularly mussels and clams, are plentiful. In the S *marea roja*, the red tide, a bloom of algae discolouring the water, is frequently a problem. The algae produce neurotoxins that are concentrated by bivalves feeding upon them. Eating affected bivalves is to risk paralytic shellfish poisoning which is often fatal; there is no antitoxin. As the toxin persists in the shellfish long after the algae has dispersed it is unsafe to take shellfish unless laboratory testing has cleared the area. The coastline is too large to permit this to be thoroughly undertaken. Currently (2002) the collecting and consumption of shellfish S of 44°S is prohibited and the *zarpe* is always endorsed to this effect. In practice only a few areas are contaminated at any one time. Commercial collection is allowed but each batch of shellfish harvested is tested prior to a certificate being issued permitting sale for consumption. Therefore, in places like Puerto Natales, the presence of local mussels in the shops is NOT an indication that they are safe to gather.

GAS

Propane Gas is widely used and almost universally available. Many boats have encountered problems with filling due to the different fittings used in Chile. Bigger centres seem to have the required connectors but smaller towns such as Castro or Aysén do not. Several people have recommended buying local cylinders and installing the appropriate connector. The cost is not great and the cylinder can then be exchanged for a full one with ease. Other people make up a connector tube and drain the Chilean cylinder into their own using gravity.

FUEL (*COMBUSTIBLE*)

Diesel *(petroleo)* is of a very pure and clean burning type (kerosene Primus stoves run well on it). Quality is usually good at the pump. Smaller ports may have stored fuel in rusty drums so filtering is recommended. Petrol/gasoline *(gasolina)* is universally available. Paraffin/kerosene *(parafina or kerosina)* is cheap and also of a very high, clean burning, quality. It seems to be available in all towns except Puerto Williams. Lubricating oils *(lubricantes)* are good and easily obtained. Methylated sprit is best bought from a pharmacy *(farmacia)* where it is known as *alcohol blanco*. *Alcohol de quemia* (burning alcohol) is widely available in hardware stores and marginally cheaper, but gives off foul fumes.

SPARE PARTS

Spares for equipment other than basic motor necessities are hard to come by. Chilean engineers are used to making do and will be very helpful. Take spares for all mechanical and electrical gear. See the comments below on importation of spares.

Consider taking cigarettes to trade with fishermen. Their lives are short and tough and our concerns about the health implications seem laughable to them when a cigarette provides a touch of comfort and luxury in a hard existence. Wine boxes are also welcome. Basic supplies such as cooking oil, tea, maté or aspirin are appreciated. Newspapers and magazines, too, will be pounced upon.

SPECIAL REQUIREMENTS

Apart from heavy weather, cold weather and ocean going gear, the importance of really strong ground tackle cannot be overemphasised when cruising S of Puerto Montt. Plenty of long mooring lines are essential. Radar is of great assistance, much more useful than GPS. Heating and insulation is vital for comfort except for summer visits north of Laguna San Raphael.

LEAVING THE SHIP UNATTENDED

At some ports, a visiting yacht left unattended whilst the owner or captain is out of the country can be put in bond with the *aduana*. Inquire locally wherever you are as views of officials can vary.

IMPORTING EQUIPMENT FROM ABROAD

Duty-free importation of equipment for the vessel is definitely allowed. However, many people have had trouble. The problem seems to be that the local agents of the courier companies (none of the major ones seem to have an office of their own in Chile) appear to add the duty themselves (possibly acting as agents for the customs and collecting a commission). The agency then refuses to release the goods without payment. No particular company appears to be secure in this respect. If possible, contacting the local agent beforehand and ensuring that they will not charge duty is a good idea. It is essential that the package is marked *Rancho de Nave* and it seems to help if it is sent to a well-known marine business such as Alwoplast in Valdivia or Oxxean in Puerto Montt. It costs a lot to send goods by courier and it is not unusual for the delivery to take the same time as mail. In case of problems, contacting the parent company in the country of origin and refusing to pay seems to work but may take weeks. In such cases the local customs office appears to be sympathetic to your case but lacks the power to do anything about it.

One boat found that arranging for packages to be repacked and sent by regular postal airmail in a plain wrapper, labelled 'radio spares' or such, worked better than the courier at a fraction of the cost. Chileans tend to have a poor opinion of the postal service, yet reports of problems are less common than with the courier companies.

Search and rescue

The Search and rescue organisation (*Sistema Chileno de Búsqueda y Salvamento*) is run by the *armada* and commanded by a Vice Admiral. Besides inshore waters and Chilean Antarctica, it covers the Pacific S of 18°12'S and between 120°00'W and 67°16'W; S of 58°21'S the E boundary is 53°00'W. Failure to comply with *zarpe* requirements may initiate a search, especially in the far S. The national system of reporting is known as CHILREP.

In the S rescue boats are stationed at Puerto Montt, Castro, Chacabuco, Puerto Natales, Punta Arenas and Punta Williams.

The *armada* maintains 2 dedicated search and rescue helicopters (daytime only), one at Puerto Montt and the other at Punta Arenas. These are painted grey with a red stripe, carry VHF and may call a vessel on Ch 16.

Additional notes on cruising in S Chile

A factor to reckon with if cruising for an extended period in the far S is that the day rapidly shortens after mid-summer. Around 53°S, in January there are 16 or more hours of daylight. By mid-April it is down to 11 hours and by mid-June, 7 hours. To make the point another way, the distance that can be covered in daylight is about halved between summer and winter.

ANCHORING

Anchoring techniques are as varied as the yachts and crews that practice them. The following is intended only as a guide to aid crews in preparing themselves for conditions in S Chile.

The strong winds and *rachas* found in the *canales*, particularly the S portion, require the most secure anchoring techniques. The weather can change very quickly and what was a calm anchorage at 1700 can turn into a scene of wind-whipped white water and rain by 0200. There are many tales of boats being blown out of what had been a calm, sheltered cove. Even in settled weather it is prudent to anchor in a manner that assumes gales in the middle of the night. In many locations this means using shorelines as well as one or more anchors. The rationale for this is to pull the vessel into a more sheltered spot, usually below the trees, where she will miss the most violent winds. If such a spot is not available then swinging to an anchor is preferable as long as the holding is good and the tackle very heavy.

For getting through kelp in an emergency, a Fisherman's anchor has a lot to commend it. Take one as a reserve. It goes without saying that all gear should be very strong and heavy.

Tandem anchoring

Many consider that this is safer and more secure than lying to two separate anchors. With a little practice, tandem anchors are easy to deploy and recover. Two bow rollers, port and starboard bow cleats and a good chain and rope windlass are required. The 'first-down' anchor lies in the port side roller. Its shaft is connected by 6–10m of chain, running around the outside of the pulpit and back to the crown of the main anchor lying in the starboard roller. A retrieval line, 3m longer than the chain, leads from the shackle on the shaft of the 'first-down' anchor to the shackle on the shaft of the main anchor. For a 'Rolls-Royce' set-up, the retrieval line should be floating polypropylene with snap shackles spliced into both ends but it works fine with regular line.

Prior to anchoring, the 'first-down' anchor is held in place on its roller by the retrieval line cleated to the port bow cleat. The main anchor is held in place by the chain from the windlass. With the boat slowly in reverse, let go the 'first-down' anchor by hand using the retrieval line. Then release the windlass and pay out the main anchor. Set it hard with the

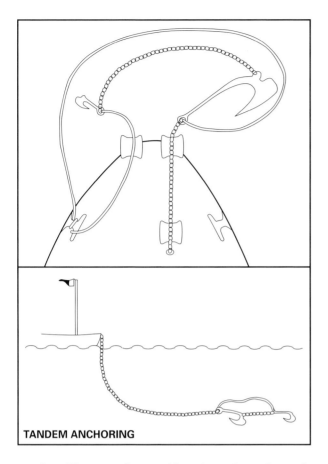

TANDEM ANCHORING

engine. Place a nylon snubber (5–7m) on the main anchor chain. Take the chain off the windlass and loosely secure it to the starboard cleat. Make sure that the snubber is protected from chafe over the roller.

To retrieve the anchors, haul up the main anchor on the windlass until the shaft reaches the roller. Lock the windlass. Reach around from the port side of the pulpit and bring the retrieval line over the port bow roller. By hand, haul up the 'first-down' anchor. Initially, the only weight is that of the anchor. When the anchor is almost on board the weight will be that of the anchor and half of the chain. Pull the 'first-down' anchor over the roller and secure with the retrieval line to the port cleat. Bring the main anchor all the way home. Disconnect the chain from the crown of the main anchor and store the 'first-down' anchor. If the 'first-down' anchor is particularly hard to raise, take the chain of the main anchor off the windlass to the starboard bow cleat and use the rope gypsy of the windlass to haul up the retrieval line.

LINES ASHORE

Although tandem anchoring is very secure, the strength of the *rachas* and their variable direction dictates that two or three lines ashore are often required. Generally speaking the objective is to anchor as close to the shore as possible and preferably in a notch where the boat can be secured by lines from all four corners or from the two stern quarters and the bow. In some anchorages, e.g.

Morris and Sofia, it is better to anchor out in the open because there is no notch or because the obvious notch is close to the head of the anchorage and subject to more *rachas* than prevail in the open area to one side.

In some locations the bottom shelves too steeply to swing to an anchor but with stern lines ashore the anchor can be laid so that it is pulling uphill and will hold very well.

The best gear is two to four 100m lines. Lines can be tied around trees or lengths of chain may be used to loop around rocks or trees and brought back to be shackled to eye splices on the ends of the lines. Three-strand polypropylene is preferred. Unlike nylon, it floats, tends to stay above the kelp, tows easily from a dinghy and does not have a life of its own. It is also relatively inexpensive and can be purchased easily in hardware stores (*fereterías*) ashore. If there is space, rope reels on deck are a great asset.

Anchoring and taking lines ashore often has to be carried out quickly before the boat is blown out of position. There is a fair tide range so it is important to tie the lines ashore at points above high tide. One method is to tie the eye spliced end of the line around your own waist, the dinghy painter around a leg and then row as fast as possible to a pre-selected tree or rock. Leap ashore, leaving the dinghy to fend for itself, secure the chain and line as quickly as possible and rush back to the boat for the next line. Every boat seems to develop its own variation on this theme. Watch out for rotten trees as they are covered with moss and it is hard to tell good from bad.

In very fierce offshore winds it is not uncommon for vessels to have dragged away from the anchorage before lines have been set up. It may be preferable to get the lines ashore prior to dropping the anchor. This way it is easier for the boat to maintain her position.

KELP

Kelp is both a blessing and a curse. It grows only on rocks and as such is a useful marker of danger and areas to be avoided both on passage and when anchoring (though the rock to which it is attached may be much deeper than the draught of the boat). It makes for poor holding. A machete is useful for cutting away bundles that come up on the anchor. Rowing through kelp is either difficult or impossible. Outboards tend to clog up if run slowly.

DEPTHS

The combination of relatively warm, saline, oceanic water flowing into the deep canals and near freezing, fresh, glacial melt water results in discrete layers of water of different densities. This phenomonen may cause misleading echos to be returned on depth sounders. It is not unusual to experience a reading of 6m where the actual depth is many hundreds of meters. Be particularly alert near the confluence of tidal and river or glacier water.

SHIP'S STORES

Puerto Edén has only the most basic supplies. Puerto Natales has good shoreside facilities (and easy access to Punta Arenas) but is well off the main routes. Ushuaia, in Argentina, is a better place to stock up than Puerto Williams. Punta Arenas has excellent stores and facilities but is not a good anchorage (consider using Bahía Mansa 8·26). If coming from the Atlantic and aiming at the Beagle Channel, it is worthwhile calling at Ushuaia and then backtracking to Puerto Williams to enter Chile. If coming from the W, make sure that you clear out of Chile before entering Argentina. Those who are obliged to have a visa for Chile will heed a possible need for a multiple entry visa if calling at Ushuaia.

FUEL

One characteristic of cruising in the S is that in general a very high proportion of the distance is made good under engine. After leaving Chiloé, the next fuel is about 1000 miles away unless a hefty premium is paid at Puerto Edén or a detour made to Chacabuco or Puerto Natales. It is worth carrying as much fuel as possible in cans as the cost of the cans is quickly recovered if set against the cost of fuel in remote places.

Empresa Abastecimiento Zonas Aisladas (EMAZA) can supply fuel at Puerto Edén and Tortel. However prior notice may be necessary (contacting the local *armada* station via HF or telephone may be one way to do this). Fuel bought at such sites may be up to 50% more expensive than that bought in population centres.

At Puerto Natales, Punta Arenas and Puerto Williams (considerably more expensive than in Ushuaia in 2002) there are the usual commercial sources. Ushuaia is well supplied with filling stations and has a YPF fuel dock to the E of the main wharf.

Most fishermen in the S have a supply vessel that calls at regular intervals (usually 7–10 days) to bring them food and fuel and to buy the catch. These vessels have been known to supply yachtsmen. In case of need, ask the local fishermen who will generally be delighted to assist.

HEATING

After a cold, windy and wet day a heater provides a great deal of comfort and few boats cruise the area without one. Whilst there may be no problems with a ducted warm air heater, such as a Webasto, with other types the back-pressure in the chimney created by *rachas* may well put out the flame and with a drip-feed diesel type, such as a Dickinson or Reflex, fill the cabin with diesel fumes. One solution is to fit a domestic rotary chimney to the existing chimney pipe. The other is to raise the height of the flue to around 2 metres above deck level. All Chilean towns in the S have workshops (*hojalatareias*) that sell or make up flues and tops. The result may not be pleasing aesthetically but it works.

ICE

Winter cruising is highly recommended, the scenery is spectacular and the weather frequently settled and sunny. During periods of cold still weather many of the more sheltered anchorages will freeze over. At first the idea of using your beloved vessel to break ice is frightening, however the thin ice is easily broken and causes only minor scratching. (It is a bad idea to renew antifouling before heading S: much of it will be scratched off and the level of fouling is so low that even old antifouling will quickly become clean.) An anchor hanging ahead can help to break the ice. Look for spots where a quick flowing stream enters the bay as it is less likely to freeze. Beware of shallow inlets well inland such as Seno Eberhardt where the ice may become too thick to break. Once the settled spell is over the ice disperses rapidly and the more sheltered anchorages are once again available.

Using this guide

The Pilotage Section of this guide works from N to S. The area of the Chonos archipelago is too large for one chapter though the logical coverage is N to S, therefore Chapters 3 and 4 share the same overall map to assist in planning when traversing E-W or vice versa. Chapter 5 onwards first follows the main channel from Canal Messier down to the Magellan Straits and past Cape Froward to Dungeness. Subsequent sections follow the main channel from Cabo Froward to Puerto Williams and beyond. Working southward, departures from the main channel are marked as 'diversion' and the end of the diversion is marked as 'continuation'. Additional notes on routes likely to be followed are headed 'passage'. In the far S geography dictates that there has to be some doubling back and a few Argentinian anchorages are included. The chapter on Isla de Pascua and Islas Juan Fernandez comes at the end. Antarctica is not covered.

The guide is an assemblage of information about ports and anchorages from visiting yachtsmen whose work has been made available to the Pilotage Foundation of the Royal Cruising Club and to the Ocean Cruising Club. Further detailed information is available in official publications. Reference has been made to publications of the *armada* and of the British Hydrographic Office in Taunton. The coastal notes of the first section were largely gleaned from published geographical descriptions.

Important notes on the anchorage information and sketches

Numbering of anchorages

Users of the first edition will note that anchorages have been renumbered in order to incorporate changes. Therefore it is not possible to cross-reference between editions using these numbers.

Numbering of Chilean charts

Since publication of the first edition SHOA has instituted completely new numbering of charts in Chilean waters. This edition uses the new numbering. If old charts are carried it will be necessary to refer to the SHOA catalogue or the latest *atlas hidrográfico*. See note above and Appendix H.

Correctional supplements

This pilot book will be amended at intervals by the issue of correctional supplements prepared by the RCC Pilotage Foundation. Supplements are available free at www.imray.com.

Positions

All positions must be treated with caution. Charted position has been given unless otherwise stated and reported GPS positions have not been included where they are in agreement with the chart. For GPS readings the datum in use is WGS84, but note that where the datum used to report the position is unknown there is an exclamation mark (!) as a warning. (Contributors providing corrections should indicate whether their positions are Chart or GPS and the datum used for GPS should be WGS84.)

The different co-ordinate systems used in Chile provide a maximum difference in position of approximately 200m. Many of the positions reported were taken pre-2000 in the days of selective availability so may have even greater errors. The total possible error of doubtful GPS positions may be in the order of 500m. There are many instances where charts disagree with GPS and with each other. Actual differences between the chart and GPS may be more than a mile. **Positions given in the text and on plans are intended purely as an aid to locating the place in question. They should always be treated with caution.**

Lighthouses

The Pilotage Foundation recommends that all vessels navigating this coast at night should carry an up-to-date light list. In the area covered by Chapter 1 night passages off-shore are usually required, though few people would think of entering port at night without very up-to-date information and charts. Therefore Chapter 1 only has a selection of the major coastal lights in Appendix G. Useful leading marks and other significant lights are included with the anchorage notes wherever relevant throughout the book. Light information is provided from the Dec 2001 Chilean list (SHOA 3007) and

needs to be treated with caution. Positions of lights are the charted positions, usually the largest scale chart available; the Chilean list of lights specifies the chart used.

Plans

The plans in this guide are not to be used for navigation. Plans have been prepared from yachtsman's sketches and are not based upon hydrographic surveys. They are designed to support the text and should always be used with navigational charts (though in many cases they are more accurate than the charts!). Where no detailed chart exists, even though a plan is available, a vessel should still navigate as though in uncharted water.

All bearings are from seaward and refer to true N. Depths are in metres. Symbols are based on those used by the British Admiralty – users are referred to *Symbols and Abbreviations* (NP 5011). Where marine farms have been shown, the positions should be treated with caution, as changes in position are very common.

Anchoring positions

Many corrections submitted have incorporated comments on the positioning of anchors and lines. Anchoring techniques are as varied as the yachts and crews that practice them. Please regard positions of anchors and shorelines described in this book or depicted in the sketches as a guide only. Everything depends upon the conditions on the day.

Comments about the suitability of an anchorage need to be assessed with regard to other nearby possibilities. If an anchorage was uncomfortable in a storm but there was no reasonable alternative and the vessel was safe then the anchorage was considered suitable for inclusion. If an alternative is found to be far superior in particular conditions, this is valuable information for which the editor would be grateful. Obviously much depends upon the circumstances of the visit.

Names

Many of the names used in this guide have been coined by yachtsmen and have no official status whatsoever. Hopefully some of the more historical ones will become recognised, as appears to be the tradition in Chile (Mischief Narrows and Tilman Island are excellent examples). The present editor has bestowed many names on anchorages: usually they have been called after vessels or people who provided information. Any users who are aware of a local name or official name for such anchorages are urged to report these for inclusion in future editions.

1. Arica to Canal Chacao

General

This coast has hundreds of miles of inhospitable beach and cliff with only a few widely-spaced places to land or shelter. There is a N-going current and S winds predominate, these are often light to non-existent in the N and strong in the S. In the N there is rainless desert and in the middle a mediterranean climate with winter rains. In the S the climate is temperate with greatly increased rainfall and more frequent N winds in the winter.

Tides

The following are listed:
a. Mean Spring Range
b. Mean Neap Range
c. The time difference with the standard port, Valparaíso. Variation in the differences between HW and LW is usually zero and never more than 12 minutes.

Lights

Navigation at night off this shore should only be conducted with an up-to-date light list. In case of emergency for passage making vessels forced inshore a selection of lights that may be of use to a vessel making a passage (correct to the *Chilean Light List* of December 2001) is included in Appendix G.

1·1 Arica

18°28'S 70°19'W
Distances
Callao–570–Arica–70–Pisagua
Charts BA *3070;* US *22221;* Chile *1000, 1100, 1111*
Tides
a. 0·9m
b. 0·5m
c. –0103hrs
Port communications
Port Ch 16 ☎ 23 22 84.
Club de Déportes Náuticos Ch 68 ☎ 22 43 96

General

Arica, pop. about 170,000, rainless and warm (average 24°C in summer, 19°C in winter), sits under the Morro de Arica, a granite headland, scene of a 19th-century battle with Peru. It is a resort for Bolivians, with surfing, bathing, restaurants, hotels etc. About half Bolivia's foreign trade passes through Arica and it is the terminal for the oil pipeline to Bolivia. The port has a fishing fleet, the town has fishmeal plants and a car assembly plant; it also has a reputation as a transit centre for narcotics. If this is the first port of call in Chile, on arrival visit the *policía* for immigration, the *aduana* for clearance

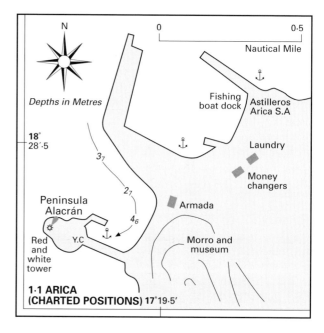

1·1 ARICA
(CHARTED POSITIONS) 17°19·5'

and the *armada* for a *zarpe*; the Club de Déportes Náutico will help.

Approach

A traffic separation scheme operates in the approach; see charts. The yacht harbour is behind Península Alacrán.

The hills, Morro Arica (150m) and Morro Gorda (216m) are conspicuous, the red granite of Morro Arica showing white in the sun. The prevailing wind is SW, strongest in the afternoon, dropping at night, and a land breeze sets in from early morning to about 0900. There may be a 1–2kt set in the roadstead running in either direction parallel to the shore. Swell is common. The entrance to the yacht club anchorage is narrow with shallows to N and S. Call the club on Ch 16 and they will send out a launch to lead you in.

Arrival

Arriving in Arica from the N, boats should call the *armada* on Ch 16 VHF, from at least 10 miles out. The *armada* and other authorities (*aduana* and *armada* offices are on the E side of the commercial harbour) will give instructions for clearance. Most yachts less than 40ft can then proceed to the yacht club just to the S of the town.

Anchorage

Yacht Club moorings are on the NE side of Península Alacrán (Isla Alacrán is joined to the mainland by a causeway) and protected by a

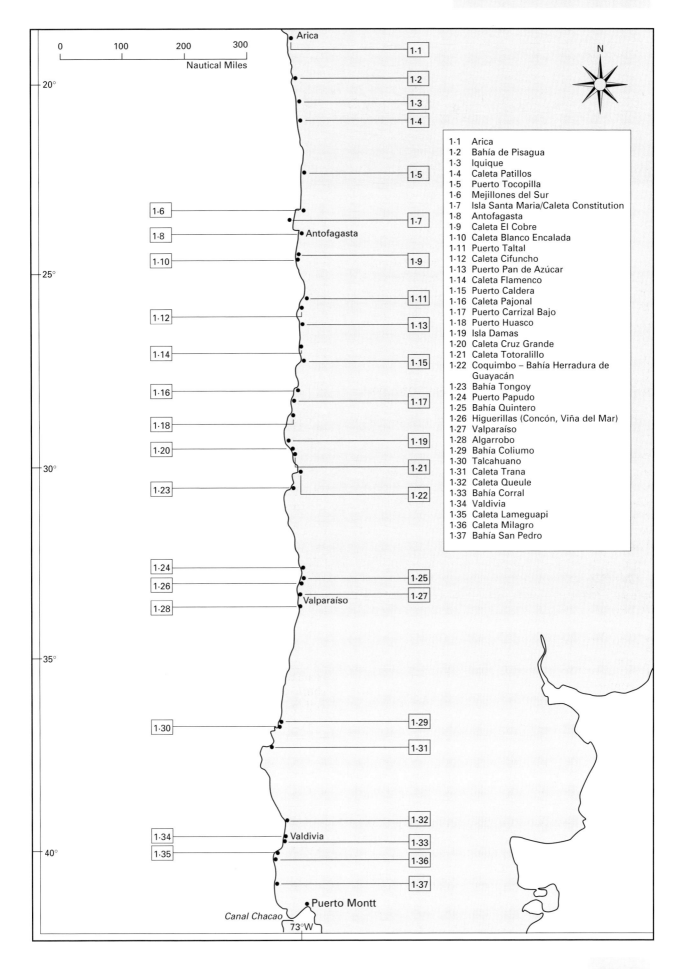

1·1   Arica
1·2   Bahía de Pisagua
1·3   Iquique
1·4   Caleta Patillos
1·5   Puerto Tocopilla
1·6   Mejillones del Sur
1·7   Isla Santa Maria/Caleta Constitution
1·8   Antofagasta
1·9   Caleta El Cobre
1·10   Caleta Blanco Encalada
1·11   Puerto Taltal
1·12   Caleta Cifuncho
1·13   Puerto Pan de Azúcar
1·14   Caleta Flamenco
1·15   Puerto Caldera
1·16   Caleta Pajonal
1·17   Puerto Carrizal Bajo
1·18   Puerto Huasco
1·19   Isla Damas
1·20   Caleta Cruz Grande
1·21   Caleta Totoralillo
1·22   Coquimbo – Bahía Herradura de
        Guayacán
1·23   Bahía Tongoy
1·24   Puerto Papudo
1·25   Bahía Quintero
1·26   Higuerillas (Concón, Viña del Mar)
1·27   Valparaíso
1·28   Algarrobo
1·29   Bahía Coliumo
1·30   Talcahuano
1·31   Caleta Trana
1·32   Caleta Queule
1·33   Bahía Corral
1·34   Valdivia
1·35   Caleta Lameguapi
1·36   Caleta Milagro
1·37   Bahía San Pedro

breakwater. The yacht club anchorage is within the breakwater, which gives good protection from the prevailing S winds. The anchorage is subject to surge, which lasts several days when major storms in the S send large swells up the coast of Chile. This occurs most frequently in the winter months. Club mooring buoys are no longer available to visiting yachts. Anchor fore and aft in rock. The club launch will place you and help. The anchorage requires caution because of the harbour surge and rocky bottom. The anchoring charge in 2000 was US$10·00/day which included a free launch service ashore.

Facilities

Astilleros Arica SA (travel-lift and hard standing) a major boat construction and repair yard for large fishing boats in Arica, have been very helpful to visiting yachts. Contact details: Maximo Lira 1099, Casilla 202 Arica ☎ 251784 or 225043 Fax 251412.

Andino Ship Supply Co. owner Leonardo D. Moreno, speaks English and is very helpful to visitors. He has a connection to West Marine USA. Andino is located at No. 050 Manuel Rodriguez. ☎/Fax 058-257308, VHF Ch 15, email andinoship@arica.cl.

Fuel from garages in town.

Water from the Club's pontoon (depth 2m); pick up the buoy and secure stern-to.

Fincard; Banco Osorno (VISA); many Casas de Cambio on the corner of 21 Mayo and Colon.

Market at Mercado Central (Sotomayor, between Colón and Baquedano, mornings only) and Terminal Agropecuario (buses marked 'Agro'); supermarket at San Martin and 18 de Septiembre.

Laundries: Lavandería Moderna, 18 de Septiembre 457; Americana, Lynch 260 ☎ 231 808.

Club de Déportes Náuticos, ☎ 253 847 excellent facilities – restaurant, showers, swimming area.

British Consulate: Baquedano 351 ☎ 231 960 Casilla 653. Also Consulates of Brazil, Bolivia, Denmark, Italy, Norway, Peru & Spain.

Tourism

Day tour: Parque Nacional Lauca and Lago Chungará (4600m, cold).

Half day: Valle de Azapa.

Local Catedral San Marco and old Custom House, now Casa de Cultura (Mon-Sat 1000–1300, 1700–2000), both designed by Gustave Eiffel (of the tower); footpath up Morro de Arica, 10 minutes walk from Colón, good views.

The pre-Colombian Museo Arqueologico San Miguel de Azapa is worth visiting. The 12km bus route from Arica passes enormous petroglifos (stone drawings).

Communications

Air, rail and bus connections to Chile & Bolivia, air, rail and bus connections to Peru, air connections to Ecuador

Car hire: Hertz, Budget, American, GP, Viva.

Telephone: ENTEL, CTC and VTR, 21 de Mayo 345, 0900–2200. Area Code 58.

Passage

Between Arica and Caleta Chica (19°20'S 70°17'W) the cliffs are broken only by two *quebradas* (ravines), Vitor and Camarones. S of Caleta Chica there are cliffs and beaches. The few bights are either deep and steep-to or rock strewn.

1·2 Bahía de Pisagua

19°35'S 70°13'W

Distances
Arica–70–Pisagua–38–Iquique

Charts BA *3030*; US *22205*; Chile *1000, 1100, 1141*

Lights

To the SW

1978 **Punta Pichalo** 19°35'·9S 70°14'·2W
Fl.12s55m13M White GRP tower, red band 4m

General

Pisagua is the first available shelter S of Arica. It is a reasonable anchorage provided the swell is light. Under the military regime, the town became a notorious prison camp in the 1970s. It was rebuilt in the early 1990s. The clock tower (designed by Eiffel) on a prominent mound is a good landmark. It shows a blue and white light. There is an *armada* station. Offshore, there may be rafts of petrels, many shearwaters and albatross.

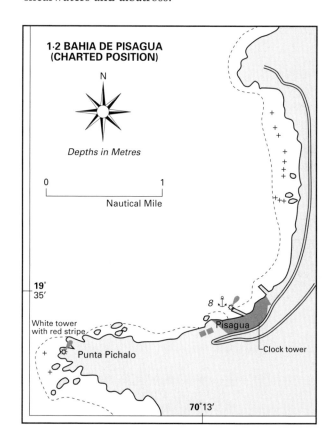

1·3 Iquique

20°12'S 70°09'W

Distances
Pisagua–38–Iquique–35–Caleta Patillos

Charts BA *3070, 3076;* US *22233;* Chile *1000, 1100, 1200, 1211*

Tides
a. 0·9m
b. 0·5m
c. –0100hrs

Port communications
Port Ch 16, Pilots Ch 08, ☎ 42 28 48/42 34 98.

General

A naval base, oil, commercial and fishing port, Iquique is also the capital of Región 1, Tarapacá, with a population of 140,000. There is an artificial harbour and behind it, an anchorage sheltered from the S and SW. The city has kept much of its late 19th-century character but with improved facilities for visitors – hotels, restaurants and so forth. It is located on a small coastal plain with beaches; either side the coastline is one of cliffs, up to 800m, interspersed with beaches.

Zona Franca in the suburb Zofri is a duty free zone said to be useful for photographic and electronic goods; there is a limit of US$650 on purchases made by tourists.

This harbour and yacht club is the only one on the N Coast where it is comfortable to over-winter.

Approach

N of Iquique, inshore currents are variable and are occasionally strong (4kt).

The port is entered between Punta Piedras, 3M to the N (with rocks and breakers 400m off-shore) and Península Serrano which has a light tower, white with red bands, 22m high with three 18m radio masts and a wooden tower, 25m, nearby. There is a traffic separation scheme off the immediate entrance.

Anchorage

The fishing boats anchor in about 7m in the centre of the bay S and E of Roca Patilliguaje

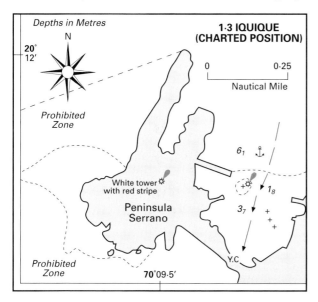

```
Depths in Metres            1·3 IQUIQUE
N                           (CHARTED POSITION)
20°
12'                  0                    0·25
                                    Nautical Mile
Prohibited
  Zone

                        6₁  ⚓

         White tower ✿          ⚓  1₈
         with red stripe

          Peninsula          3₇  +
          Serrano                  +
                                   +
                              Y.C
Prohibited
  Zone       70°09·5'
```

(Fl.G(2+1)14s, iron and concrete G with R stripe). After rounding the breakwater pass Roca Patilliguaje to starboard. Leading marks on shore lead to the yacht club marina. The channel has a minimum depth of 1·7m at low water. The club monitors Ch 80 and is very helpful. In 2000 the rate in the marina was three free days and then US$5·00/day.

Formalities

Inform the *armada* by VHF of the vessels arrival and visit their office.

Facilities

Trawler shipyard, engine and other repairs.
800-ton slipway, mobile cranes.
Yachts of up to 14 tons have been lifted out by crane onto a hard standing area at the club. Crane rates are US$80·00/hr.
Water and electricity on the wharves.
Fuel by truck with long hose at rates slightly below that in service stations.
Fincard at Serrano 372 and Zona Franca. Casas de Cambio.
Municipal market Barros Arana Block near Latorre.
Supermarkets etc.
Laundry: Bulnes 170, Obispo Labbé 1446.
Club de Yates, Recinto Portuario, restaurant.

Tourism

Excursions: Rock paintings at the Reserva Nacional Pampa del Tamarugal, 95km. The abandoned nitrate workings at Humberstone. The three-day Altiplano tour offered by most tour companies takes in a very impressive variety of scenery and wildlife. Try Avitour at 997 Baquedano, ☎ (56) 473775. Owner Marco Muhlenbrock, who speaks English, leads many of these tours himself and is very good.
Also recommended is Sergio Cortez at Bolivar and Ramirez. Sergio has a shop that does stainless and aluminium welding, machine work and fabrication. His Altiplano tours are a 'hobby' and he can tailor the tour to suit tastes – including land sailing – and numbers.
Local There is a very interesting wooden tower in the main square of Iquique that was built in 1877 and designed by Eiffel. The Naval Museum contains an excellent display of the famous naval battle of 1879 between Chile and Peru that led to the expansion of Chile's border to the N.

Communications

Diego Aracena airport at Chucumata 40km S, internal services to Arica, Antofagasta, Santiago.
Car hire: Automóvil Club de Chile, Budget, Hertz, Rent's Procar.
Buses to Bolivia and Argentina.
Telephone: Area code 57.

Passage

Along the coast between Iquique and Antofagasta there are foul grounds and breakers with cliffs and offshore rocks interspersed with beaches and *caletas*. The chief ports are Tocopilla (22°05'S 70°12'W) and Mejillones del Sur (23°05'S 70°28'W). Tocopilla is a major port in terms of tonnage

handled. It has a population of 25,000, a thermal
power station supplying electricity to most of N
Chile and a mineral port where 80,000-ton bulk
carriers are advised to take lines out to 'help damp
the Pacific swell'; it has a fishing fleet, some hotels
and restaurants and a reputation for game fishing.
At Mejillones del Sur, away from its explosives and
nitrates facilities, an area near the fishing harbour is
being developed for holidaymakers.

1·4 Caleta Patillos

20°44'·5S 70°11'W
Distances
Iquique–35–Patillos–75–Tocopilla
Charts BA *3070;* US *22234;* Chile *1000, 1200, 1231, 1232*

General

Patillos is a good day's run 35 miles S of Iquique.
There is reasonable shelter to the N of the pier in
12m. The bottom is rocky but the holding is good.
Swell comes into the bay and a stern anchor may be
useful to cut down rolling. The long pier is used to
load salt. There are no officials. The Pan-American
Highway is close to the coast at the head of the bay.

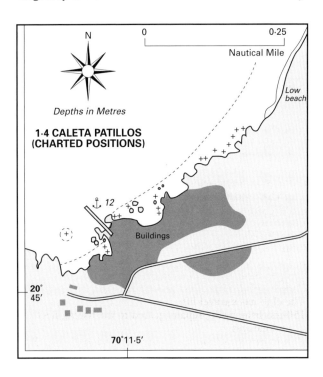

1·5 Puerto Tocopilla

22°05'·4S 70°12'·5W
Distances
Patillos–75–Tocopilla–60–Mejillones del Sur
Charts BA *3077;* US *22221;* Chile *1000, 1200, 1300, 1311*

Lights

1956 **Punta Algodonales (Islote Blanco)** 22°05'·5S
70°13'·0W Fl.12s24m16M White round GRP tower,
red band 8m 048°-vis-041°

General

Tocopilla provides good shelter at the end of a long

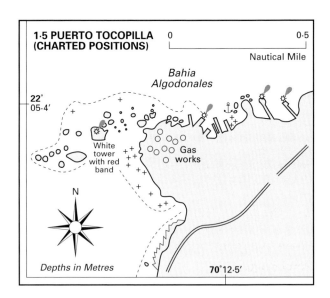

75 mile beat S from Patillos. It is a dirty industrial
port with many piers and cranes and is the seaport
for Chuquicamata, the world's largest open pit
copper mine, 75 miles to the E. Anchorage is
possible in front of the main group of piers.

1·6 Mejillones del Sur

23°05'S 70°28'W
Distances
Tocopilla–60–Mejillones del Sur–40–Antofagasta
Charts BA *3076;* US *22251;* Chile *1300, 1330, 2000*

Lights

1952 **Punta Angamos** 23°01'·4S 70°30'·9W
Fl.10s109m14M White GRP tower, red band 8m
036°-vis-267°
1953 **Puerto Mejillones del Sur** 23°05'·7S 70°27'·1W
Fl.G.3s20m6M On harbourmaster's office balcony
038°-vis-326°

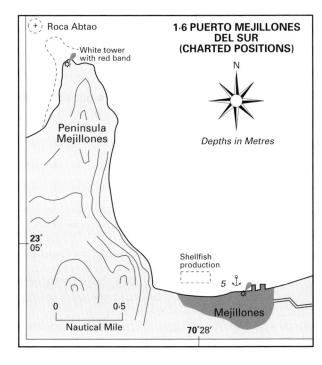

General

The town of Mejillones is located on the S side of a wide bay that provides excellent shelter from the prevailing S and SW winds. The anchorage is close to the beach in 5m of water, in front of the *armada* building. Alternative anchorage can be found in front of a sand beach approximately ¾ mile WNW of the village in 10m.

The town itself is quite small with limited supplies. Fresh water can be obtained from the *armada* station.

1·7 Isla Santa Maria/Caleta Constitution

23°26'S 70°37'W

Charts BA *3071, 3077;* US *22225;* Chile *1300 1322, 2000*

Anchorage

Enter the bay to the N of Isla Santa Maria and anchor on E side of the island in front of sand beach in 3–5m. Well protected anchorage – exactly on the Tropic of Capricorn – and good shellfish diving.

1·8 Antofagasta

23°38'S 70°24'W

Distances
Mejillones del Sur–40–Antofagasta–215–Caldera

Charts BA *3071, 3077;* US *22222;* Chile *2000, 2111*

Tides
a. 0·9m
b. 0·6m
c. −0050hrs

Port communications
Port Ch 16, 9, 14 ☎ 26 33 63 or 26 82 75
Club de Yates Ch 16 ☎ 26 85 83

General

Antofagasta, capital of the Región of Antofagasta, is a somewhat rough town but it is a major commercial centre with a population of 185,000 and has two universities, good stores, restaurants etc. The port is important for Bolivian imports and exports, handling minerals (particularly copper, trainloads are shunted into the port daily along the road outside the yacht club) and fishing.

Approach

A large white anchor is inscribed on a hill about 1½ miles E of the Molo de Abrigo which, from the N, may be seen after rounding Punta Tetas. The shore of the Rada de Antofagasta has rocks up to 400m off it. Head for the small harbour just to the north of the main commercial port.

Entry

Enter between two rock breakwaters (new, not on charts) marked by red and green lights on 3m high steel towers on a heading of about 130°. Yacht club marina is immediately to starboard. Tie between mooring buoys and wharf. For yachts more than 35ft LOA it is recommended that a bow anchor be laid out as the mooring buoys are too close to the wharf. On shore, behind the marina, is a 17-storey blue and cream building. Considerable harbour surge. In 2000, the first three days were free, daily

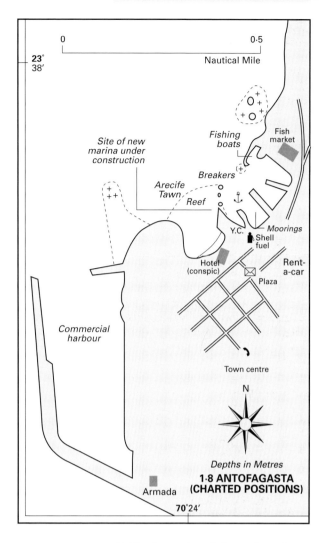

rates were unavailable from the club at that time. The Club keeps watch on VHF Ch 16 and will send out a launch to help with anchoring.

Formalities

The *armada* office is opposite the entrance of the commercial harbour, two miles S of the Club.

Facilities

The club has a travel-lift.
150-ton fishing slip; repairs geared to the fishing fleet and garages.
Fuel in cans from the Shell station next door to the Club de Yates.
Water by 400m hose laid by the Club; potable but with a curious aftertaste of sulphur and chlorine.
Banks and Cambios including Fincard, Av. Prat 431.
Provisions: Municipal market at the corner of Uribe & Matta; 'Las Brisas' supermarket near to Yacht Club.
Laundry: Lavandería Pronor on the outskirts will collect and deliver – see the local yellow pages; Laverap, 14 Febrero 1802.
Club de Yates restaurant, showers etc.
Consulates: Argentina, Belgium, Bolivia and France.

Tourism

Numerous organised out of town excursions to the Atacama desert and its towns, mines, geysers, salt pans and resident flamingos. Nearer, bus or hired car excursions to Mejillones, Caleta Coloso or Taltal. In town, the centre is Plaza Colón, which has many important public buildings

Communications

Air: American, Iberia, Lloyd, Aéreo Bolíviano, and Lufthansa to N America, Europe and Bolivia. Alta, LanChile, Ladeco & National to Arica, Iquique, Santiago.

Buses: National and to Argentina; organisation of internal services is complex – bus companies have separate booking offices and terminals.

Car hire: Avis, Rent-a-Car, Budget, and Hertz. Try near the Shell station by the Club de Yates.

Telephone: Area code 55. CTC Matta 2625, ENTEL Condel 2142.

Passage

The coast between Antofagasta and Caldera is rocky and steep, often with foul ground off it. There are several possible fair weather anchorages for small boats and a small port, Taltal, which has a straightforward approach.

1·9 Caleta El Cobre

24°13'·8S 70°31'·5W

Distances
Antofagasta–35–El Cobre–8–Blanco Encalada

Charts BA *3071;* US *22225;* Chile *2000, 2123*

General

Although only 35 miles S of Antofagasta, the passage could be a beat of more than 50 miles and

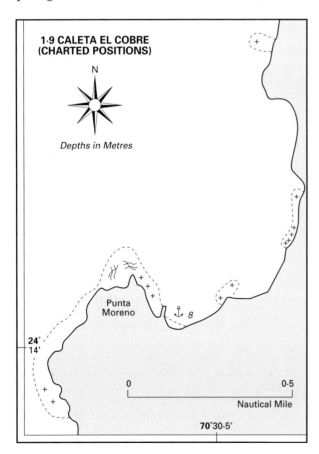

1·9 CALETA EL COBRE (CHARTED POSITIONS)

therefore El Cobre may be convenient for a night stop. The holding is good on a sand bottom in 7·5m but the swell can make around the point and the air can be very dusty from the mine just to the S.

1·10 Caleta Blanco Encalada

24°22'·1S 70°32'·5W

Distances
El Cobre–8–Encalada–62–Taltal

Charts BA *3077;* US *2225;* Chile *2000, 2121*

General

Blanco Encalada is one of the better anchorages on this part of the coast. The point and the rocks to the NW stop the swell but a stern anchor may still be useful to cut down rolling. Anchor just N of the mooring buoys in 8m, sand. There are a large number of low stone walls built on the hill to the W with no apparent purpose.

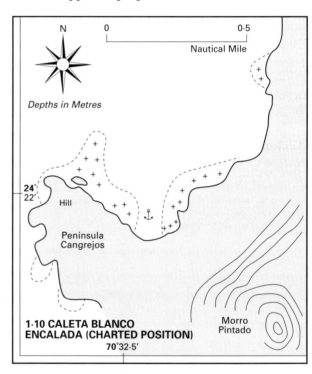

1·10 CALETA BLANCO ENCALADA (CHARTED POSITION)

1·11 Puerto Taltal

25°24'S 70°29'W

Distances
Encalada–62–Taltal–25–Cifuncho

Charts BA *3078;* US *22225;* Chile *2000, 2214*

General

The anchorage is underneath the hill in the SW corner of the bay amongst the fishing boats. The small town of Taltal is very friendly. Fresh vegetables were readily available. A large statue of the Virgin Mary looks down from the hill in the centre of the town and the view from the top is well worth the climb.

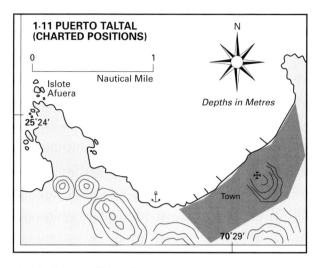

1·12 Caleta Cifuncho

25°38'·2S 70°38'·6W

Distances
Taltal–25–Cifuncho–33–Pan de Azúcar
Charts BA *3071, 3072;* US *22225;* Chile *2000, 2212*

General

Cifuncho provides a sheltered anchorage and some excellent hiking in the dry rocky hills to the E and on the point above the anchorage. Small trawlers use it. Campers use the beach.

Anchorage

Anchor to the E of the fishing boats in about 10m sand. There is a wharf for landing a dinghy.

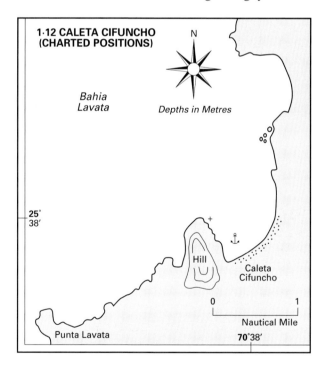

1·13 Puerto Pan de Azúcar

26°09'S 70°39'·7W

Distances
Cifuncho–33–Pan de Azúcar–56–Caldera
Charts BA *3072;* Chile *2000, 2213*

General

Pan de Azúcar gives immediate access to the National Park of the same name, which is known for its cacti. It is approached by a narrow channel, with shoals either side, behind Isla Pan de Azúcar. Although *NP7* describes Caleta Sur as being more protected, local fishermen consider it dangerous and prefer Caleta Norte, about ½M NE of Punta Rodriguez, with 12m and sand.

1·14 Caleta Flamenco

26°35'·3S 70°43'W

Distances
Cifuncho–60–Caleta Flamenco–32–Caldera
Charts BA *3071, 3072;* US *22225;* Chile *2000, 2213*

Anchorage

Anchor just to the E of moored fishing launches and in front of rocks in about 8 to 10m. Land on sandy beach between rocks marked by fishing dinghies drawn up on shore.

Facilities

Two small grocery stores and some restaurants in the village.

1·15 Puerto Caldera

27°03'·8S 70°49'·5W

Distances
Pan del Azúcar–56–Caldera–63–Carrizal Bajo
Charts BA *3078;* US *22250, 22252;* Chile *3000, 3111*
Tides
a. 1·0m
b. 0·6m
c. –0035hrs
Port communications
Port Ch 16 ☎ 31 55 51

General

A rather spartan anchorage, Caldera is an ore-shipping port with a population of 12,000 and a few shops and restaurants. However it is popular as a holiday resort and accommodation is heavily booked in season. Caldera is the most northerly place where N winds can be encountered and is exposed to the rare blows from that direction. It has excellent shelter from the prevailing S winds.

Immediately to the S are two other bays, Puerto Calderilla and Bahía Inglésa, both of which would provide good shelter in the event of strong S winds.

Approach

From the N, leave Punta Francisco (no mark) one mile to port and head S and then SE to the anchorage. From the S, round Punta Caldera at a distance of about one mile, and then head approximately SE to the anchorage. Green buoy Ra Chango (27°02'S 70°50'W Fl.G.5s), not shown in atlas, should be left to port. A substantial pier, formerly used for ore shipments, with two concrete dolphins on either side of the pierhead, should be left to starboard. On the SE side of the pier is a small commercial shipyard and next to that the yacht club.

1·15 PUERTO CALDERA
(CHARTED POSITIONS)

N

Depths in Metres

Punta Francisco

Punta Caldera

27°
03·8'

0   1

Nautical Mile

Puerto Caldera

70°49·5'

Anchorage

The yacht club has free mooring buoys for visitors along with some private moorings, these are situated off the dinghy dock. Anchorage may be taken among the fishing boats nearby, in about 6m, rock.

Formalities

The *armada* offices are about half a mile round the bay.

Facilities

Maestranzas Navals SA a commercial yard just to the W of the club has a large lift and can handle yachts. Contact owner Luis Herrera at ☎ (052) 315200.

There are two other slips for small craft, limited workshops.

Fuel: COPEC station, Edwards & Montt.

Provisions: Supermarket Carvallo, between Montt & Ossa Cerda.

Club de Yates bar, cold showers, WC.

Tourism

Santuario de la Naturaleza, about 15km N past the deserted Playas Ramada and Rodillo, has unusual spherical granite boulders. There is an interesting 50-mile bus trip through the nearby wine-growing country to Copiapó where there is an excellent mineral museum and many old Colonial buildings. The green of the river valley makes a welcome change from the arid Atacama desert.

Communications

Buses, local and national (e.g. 4 services a day to Santiago).

Telephone: Area Code 52.

Passage

The coast between Caldera and Coquimbo is the usual mix of rock and sandy beaches, often fringed by off-lying rocks and islets. There are several anchorages.

1·16 Caleta Pajonal

27°44'·1S 71°02'·8W

Distances
Caldera–40–Caleta Pajonal–24–Carrizal Bajo

Charts Chile *3000, 3121*

Anchorage

Well protected anchorage. Fishermen advise that in rough conditions the swell can build up in the shallow (6m) water to the E of the mooring buoys and to anchor to the W of the buoys in 11m.

1·17 Puerto Carrizal Bajo

28°04'·6S 71°09'·5W

Distances
Caldera–63–Carrizal Bajo–22–Huasco

Charts BA *3072;* US *22250;* Chile *3000, 3122*

General

This shallow river mouth harbour provides a quiet anchorage in S and SW winds. There is a small village with a couple of small grocery stores and a restaurant.

Approach

The light I Carrizal, Fl.3·9s15m W GRP tower with R stripe, is not shown in the atlas.

Anchorage

Anchor either N (7m) or S (4m) of fishermens' buoys. The bottom is mud with good holding in 3m.

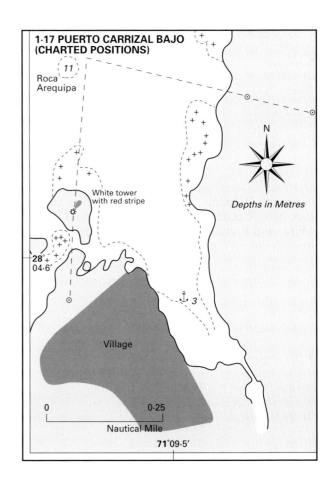

1·17 PUERTO CARRIZAL BAJO
(CHARTED POSITIONS)

Roca Arequipa

11

White tower with red stripe

N

Depths in Metres

28°
04·6'

Village

3

0   0·25

Nautical Mile

71°09·5'

1·18 Puerto Huasco

28°27'·5S 71°14'·5W

Distances
Carrizal Bajo–22–Huasco–75–Totoralillo
Charts BA *3079;* US *22250*; Chile *3000, 3211*

General

Anchor in front of the town in 4–5m. A large number of fishing boats are on buoys and there is a launch service to the dock. Unfortunately the anchorage is exposed to the swell making around the point. A stern anchor helps. A copper processing plant produces a considerable amount of airborne dust. This is a very dirty anchorage.

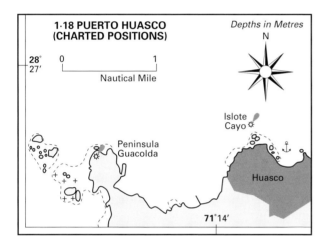

1·19 Isla Damas

29°13'·5S 71°31'·7W

Distances
Carrizal–74–Isla Damas–18–Cruz Grande
Charts Chile *3000, 3212*

General

One of three small uninhabited islands in Bahía Choros. A reef with a conspicuous rock extends about 400m S from the S end. A National Reserve of enchanting beauty. Paths have been marked and laid with seashells. It is a nesting site for Humboldt penguins. Dolphins, sealions and sea birds may be seen here. Cactus and desert flowers bloom behind white sand beaches. Gorgeous anchorage protected from the prevailing S quadrant winds.

Anchorage

Anchor in Caleta Lynch on the E side of the island. Good holding, sand, in 8–10m, sheltered NW–SW–SE. Give a wide berth to the reef that forms the S limit of this cove.

1·20 Caleta Cruz Grande

29°26'·8S 71°19'·8W

Distances
Damas–18–Caleta Cruz Grande–32–Guayacan
Charts Chile *3000, 3213*

General

An abandoned iron ore shipping port with a large dock for ore vessels blasted out of solid rock and now used by many fishing boats.

Basic provisions in the pleasant village, some restaurants and bars. Two *armada* ratings live in the ex-port manager's house beautifully sited on a promontory above the bay. They are not part of the *zarpe* system and offered use of their showers. They do monitor Ch 16 and will take a QTH.

Anchorage

The two silver fuel storage tanks mentioned in the *Admiralty Pilot* NP7 have been painted in camouflage by the *armada* and are just slightly more difficult to see. Either moor using the large *armada* buoy or anchor nearby in about 10m. Best to land the dinghy in the ore dock and walk into town.

1·21 Caleta Totoralillo

29°28'·2S 71°20'W

Distances
Huasco–75–Totoralillo–30–Guayacán
Charts BA *3080*; US *22250*; Chile *3000, 3121*

General

Totoralillo is at the S end of the Atacama desert and the beginning of grasslands and scrubby trees. The anchorage itself is very sheltered in 6m in front of a steep, black stone beach. There are a number of old ruins on shore together with remains of garden plots, protected by well made stone walls and irrigated by laid stone canals. For those who like hiking, the stony hills to the E are very enjoyable.

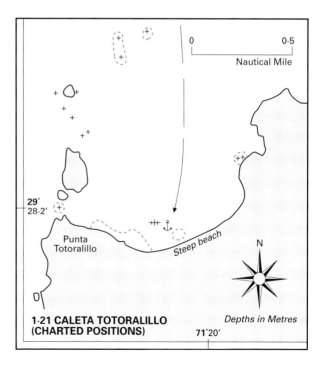

1·22 Coquimbo – Bahía Herradura de Guayacán

29°59'S 71°21'·5W

Distances
Totoralillo–30–Guayacán–23–Tongoy

Charts BA *3073, 3080;* US *22250, 22282;* Chile *3000, 4000, 4200, 4111*

Tides
a. 1·1m
b. 0·7m
c. –0017hrs

Port communications
Port (Coquimbo) Ch 16 ☎ (51) 31 11 04
Club de Yates ☎ (51) 32 12 80

Lights

1896·7 **Islotes Mewes** 29°57'·8S 71°21'·8W
  Fl(3)G.9s9m3M Green GRP tower 3m 309°-vis-175°
1896·6 **Punta Herradura** 29°58'·0S 71°22'·2W
  Fl.5s20m10M White GRP tower, red band 3m
  101°-vis-103°, 111°-vis-298°
1897 29°58'·9S 71°22'·0W **Ldg Lts 140°**
  Front F.R.18m3M White board, red diagonal stripes,
  5m high by 3m wide
1897·1 bearing 140·5°, 304m behind 1897
  Rear F.G.33m3M White board, red diagonal stripes,
  9m high by 3m wide
Note there are 4 other sets of leading lights within the
  bay, all with F.G rear and F.R front; if using lights
  check that the bearing is correct.

General

The town of Coquimbo is built on a península looking N over Bahía de Coquimbo and S over Herradura de Guayacán (*herradura* = horseshoe). It

has a population of 115,000 and has facilities to match (and regattas in September and February). Coquimbo is now the less important port but is the port authority. Guayacán handles much of the copper and iron ore exported from the region. La Serena (population 120,000), 12km N, is the capital of Región IV, Coquimbo.

Approach

From the N, there are groups of clearly charted but unmarked rocks lying 1M NW of Punta Tortuga which itself is 2M N of Guayacán. Passage is possible between the groups. From the S, Punta Lengua de Vaca has to be passed which is well known for abnormally strong local winds. The bay is invisible until one is off the entrance (note that Punta Herradura light cannot be seen from the S).

Entry

On 140° towards leading marks between Islotes Mewes and Punta Herradura. Ignore other leading marks (particularly two sets on 112°, which will be crossed in succession). Continue on 140° until the end of the long pier projecting into the bay bears 090°, then turn to 193° towards the yacht club. This avoids the fish farms on the W side of the bay (these are reported to be extending to the N and E).

Anchorage

In 4–5m, off the yacht club pier, sand. Yachts have over wintered here but be prepared to move to the NE corner of the anchorage in strong winter northerlies. In 2000 the yacht club gave two weeks free in the anchorage, and then 15000 pesos/month. The club has hot showers, a restaurant and monitors VHF Ch 68.

Formalities

The office of the *armada* is in the middle of Coquimbo

Facilities

Private dockyard in Coquimbo, engine repairs possible.
Fuel by can from a garage in Herradura. Fishing craft fuel at the Muelle Mecanizado.
Banks in Coquimbo and La Serena.
Small supermarket, fruit, vegetable and liquor shops in Herradura. Otherwise Coquimbo or La Serena.
Laundry: Lavachic self-service, Aldunate 852 Coquimbo.
Water in containers from the yacht club.
Yacht club has a bar, restaurant, and phone. Use of the swimming pool requires an introduction from a member and an entry fee.

Tourism

To the N are La Serena and the Elqui Valley, famous for its production of *Pisco*, a grape spirit and the national alcoholic spirit of Chile. La Serena is a most interesting city with many old Colonial buildings and churches. There is a long boulevard in the centre of town, which contains some magnificent sculptures. It is a university town, and is well known for its pottery. In the centre of town there is a good vegetable, fish and artisan market.
To the S is the Parque Nacional Fray Jorge, with forests dependent upon mist or fog for water (if planning a visit, it is important to check opening times).

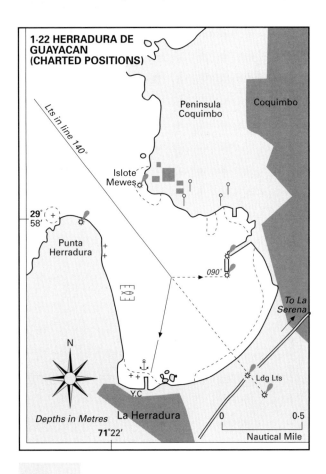

1·22 HERRADURA DE GUAYACAN (CHARTED POSITIONS)

Communications

*Herradura Collectivo*s and taxis to Coquimbo and La
    Serena.
Coquimbo national buses.
La Serena national buses (48 a day to Santiago); airport
    (La Florida) with national flights.
Car hire in La Serena.
☎ Area code 51. Telephone at the yacht club de Yates.
    CTC, ENTEL in Coquimbo, La Serena.

1·23 Bahía Tongoy

30°17'S 71°37'W
Distances
Guayacán–23–Tongoy–135–Papudo
Charts BA *3080;* US *22275;* Chile *3000, 4000, 4200, 4113*

General

Tongoy provides excellent shelter from the
prevailing S winds. The best anchorage is deep into
the SW corner of the wide bay in front of the village.
The holding is good on a sandy bottom in 6m.
There is also a good anchorage under the point in
Bahía Guanaquero, ten miles to the NE of Tongoy.

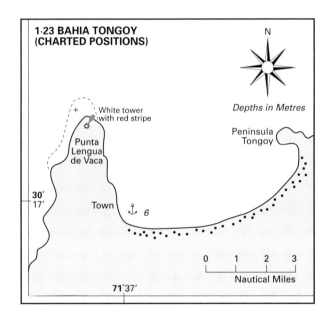

1·24 Puerto Papudo

32°31'S 71°26'·5W
Distances
Tongoy–135–Papudo–14–Quintero
Charts BA *3073*; US *22293, 22261;* Chile *4000, 4313*

General

In the S corner of the bay is a small fishing village
and many old summer homes with lovely gardens.
Anchor off the beach where the colourfully painted
fishing boats are drawn up each day. Limited
supplies are available in the town in the off-season
when the small yacht club is deserted.

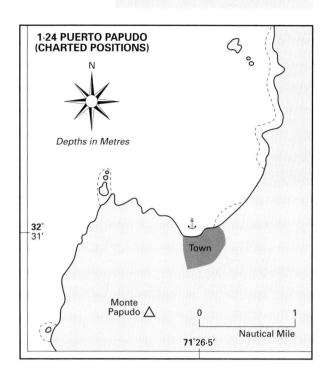

1·25 Bahía Quintero

32°46'·5S 71°31'·3W
Distances
Papudo–14–Quintero–10–Higuerillas
Charts BA *3073;* US *22293, 22263;* Chile *4000, 5000, 4320,
4321*

General

Bahía Quintero is a large open bay surrounded by
low-lying land, and is somewhat exposed to the
occasional N storm. Gas, oil, chemicals and coal are
handled commercially. There is an active yacht club
inside the península. The yacht club will check
visiting yachts in with the *armada*.

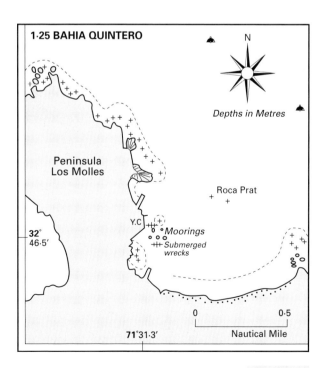

Approach
There is a traffic separation scheme in the approach.

Anchorage
The yacht club has a string of rather closely packed mooring buoys which visitors are welcome to use. Many fishing boats are also moored in this area.

Facilities
The club can haul boats up to about 30ft in length, and there is a storage area on land for the winter storage of members' boats.

The town is an area of summer homes and there are few shops.

1·26 Higuerillas (Concón, Viña del Mar)
32°55'·8S 71°32'·4W

Distances
Quintero–10–Higuerillas–26–Algarrobo

Charts BA *3073*; US *22259, 22293*; Chile *4000, 5000, 4320, 4322*

Tides
a. 1·1m
b. 0·7m
c. 0000hrs

Port communications
Club de Yates de Higuerillas Ch 68 ☎ 90 38 39 *Fax* 81 17 69

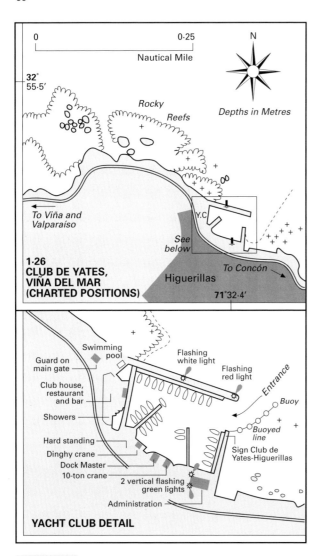

General
Valparaíso, the port for Santiago, does not cater for yachts and the nearest club, Club de Yates Recreo, though welcoming, is on an open roadstead. For visitors, the Club de Yates Viña del Mar (or de Higuerillas) is the nearest haven to the N and Algarrobo the nearest to the S. Higuerillas is a village between Concón and Viña del Mar, itself just to the N of Valparaíso. All the facilities of Viña del Mar (an international resort crammed with hotels and restaurants), Valparaíso and Santiago can be reached easily from Higuerillas.

The area has fog for about two days a month in summer, more frequently in winter. Strong southerlies blow in summer in clear weather with a high barometer; the afternoon sea breeze can also be strong.

The yacht harbour provides considerable protection in bad weather but it is not totally secure, particularly in winter. 2m tides have been experienced and storms can create a surge within the harbour rising and falling 1m within a minute – particular attention must be paid to warps and chafe if a yacht is to be left. Yachts wintering under the N wall have been covered in shingle. Most yachts haul out for the off-season. Visitors have been accommodated. If leaving a boat even for a few days, negotiate with the club manager for the services of a marinero to care-take; the marinero must be given a detailed brief.

Approach
There is a traffic separation scheme off Valparaíso. Strong winds can produce strong currents inshore, sometimes with an onshore set, especially in summer.

From the N pass either side of Rocas Concón, 3M N of Punta Concón and covered by the red sector of its light; when past, head for Punta Concón. From the S, round Punta Concón about ½M off. The yacht club is just over ½M E of Punta Concón.

Anchorage
In the summer season, there is limited space available along the dock. A very friendly club. Call the club on VHF Ch 68 and they will come out to provide directions to the appropriate mooring buoy outside the club basin (in summer it is crowded and it may be necessary to anchor). The completion of a new breakwater in 2001 may allow room for visitors in a new basin with increased protection. No charge for mooring or hot showers for yachts in transit.

Formalities
On arrival the club manager may examine the ship's papers and report by radio to the *armada*. It will nevertheless be necessary to call on the *armada* at the *Gobernación Militar* with papers and passports. If this is the first port of call, the *aduana* and *Imigración must* be visited. All are in Valparaíso port or town; obtain the addresses from the Club. It will take more than a day to sort everything out.

Facilities

10-ton crane, sail repairs, stainless steel welding at the Club. Large DIY store in Viña.

Chandlers in the port area of Valparaíso but quality (even of cordage) doubtful. Better quality at Alfredo Kauer, Frederico Reich 143, Santiago, by the Viña del Mar bus terminal. He also machines brass.

Electronics: agents of European and N American manufacturers are to be found in Valparaíso. Diagnostic skills good but repair skills hampered by, amongst other factors, lack of spares.

Fuel from garage on road to Viña.

Propane bottles can be filled at the large filling station in Concón and in Uruguay St, off the main square in Valparaíso. The yacht club also knows of a place in Viña.

Water on pontoons.

Banks: nearest Fincard is in Viña.

Provisions: simple shops & fish stalls in Higuerillas; supermarket in Reñaca; sophisticated shops of all types in Viña.

Laundry can be arranged by the Club. Alternatively there are facilities in Reñaca and Viña.

Club de Yates de Higuerillas: very well found. Swimming pool, security guard at gate and night watchman.

British Consul: Errázuriz 730, (Casilla 82-V), Valparaíso ☎ 25 61 17 Fax 25 53 65. Also Argentinian, Belgian, Danish, Dutch, German, Japanese, Peruvian, Spanish and Swedish consulates.

Tourism

There is a highly developed international resort at Viña. The charming old city of Valparaíso with its scenic walks, staircases and funicular railways is well worth a visit. Santiago, the capital, is just a 1½ hour bus ride away. Chile's main international airport is on the route to Santiago.

Communications

No 9 bus from Concón to Viña via Reñaca every half-hour in winter along the coast road, more frequently in summer but the coast road is then crowded with holiday traffic.

No 10 bus from the top of the hill behind the village, in winter more frequent than the No 9, takes the main road which is also served by *collectivos*.

At Viña buses and trains to Valparaíso, buses to Santiago. Airport at Santiago.

Telephone: Area code 32.

1·27 Valparaíso

33°02'S 71°37'W

Charts BA *1314*; US *22293, 22259*; Chile *4000, 5000, 4320, 5111*

General

Valparaíso is a major shipping port and a large old town. In the port is the headquarters of the *armada* and on the opposite side of the square is the headquarters of the Chilean Customs. Very few yachts anchor at Valparaíso itself, it is much easier to stop at Higuerillas and travel here by bus. The Valparaíso Yacht Club (Club de Yates Recreo) is located in the bay to the E of the port, but the anchorage is very exposed.

Facilities

Chilean charts and publications are available from:
Servicio Hidrográfico y Oceanográfico de la Armada, (SHOA) Melgarejo 59, Local 5 Valparaíso ☎/*Fax* (38) 25 77 31

Passage

The Valparaíso traffic separation scheme runs roughly 350° or 170° NE of Punta Curaumilla and a crossing at right angles (or thereabouts) should present little problem. To the S, the coast is one of headlands and beaches.

1·28 Algarrobo

33°21'·5S 71°41'W

Distances
Higuerillas–26–Algarrobo–220–Coliumo

Charts BA *3073, 3074*; US *22293, 22295*; Chile *5000, 5100, 5113*

Tides
a.　1·1m
b.　0·7m
c.　0000hrs

Port communications
Ch 16 ☎ 48 11 80.

General

The Confradía Náutica del Pacífico (not to be confused with the Club de Yates) has developed a marina with floating pontoon berths, which offers protection in any wind. The marina accommodates over 50 yachts and has an extensive hard standing served by a travel-lift. It is very expensive but it is the safest place in the area to leave a yacht.

During the season, it would be wise to check availability of berths before arriving. Out of season, there is plenty of room.

Algarrobo is a pleasant, pine-clad area, convenient for weekenders from Santiago. It has long been a

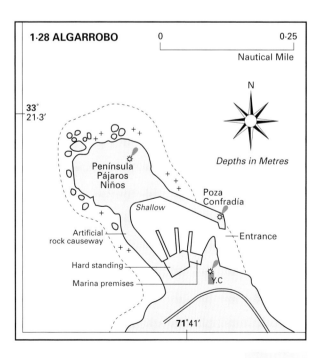

popular centre for yachting regattas. It is only a few miles from Isla Negra, where Pablo Neruda, the famous Nobel Prize-winning poet, constructed his intriguing seaside home, now a museum. However, there are no shops and no buses and it is almost essential to have a car or use taxis to get around.

Approach

The approach is easy in most conditions, although a wide berth should be given to Los Farallones, an unlit but charted group of mainly above-water rocks, lying about a mile NW of the harbour. Light 1866 Península Pájaros Niños Fl.R.10s4m R GRP tower has a sector light Fl.5s 150°-163° that marks Los Farallones.

Facilities

Travel-lift.
Hard standing.
Engine repairs.
Showers and a restaurant.

Passage

Puerto San Antonio is a major port with a reputation for heavy swell between September and March. The rest of the coast is as inhospitable as ever, with inshore currents accelerated by strong winds and often with an on-shore set. Bajo Rappel (33°51'S 71°52'·5W) has a particularly bad reputation; keep out. The coast between 35°S and 36°30'S is said to be incorrectly charted; keep out.

1·29 Bahía Coliumo

36°32'S 72°57'W

Distances
Algarrobo–220–Coliumo–15–Talcahuano
Charts BA *3074*; US *22290*; Chile *5000, 6000, 5300 6110*

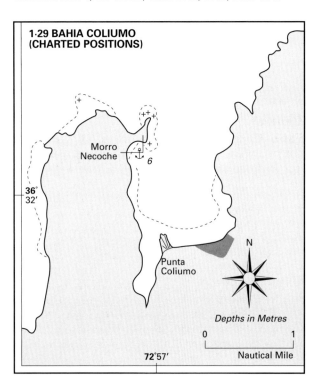

General

This is a quiet, picturesque anchorage just inside the headland on the W shore in 6m, in front of the small village.

1·30 Talcahuano

36°42'S 73°06'W
Distances
Coliumo–15–Talcahuano–50–Trana
Charts BA *3074*; US *22290, 22311*; Chile *5000, 6000, 6110, 6111*
Tides
a. 1·1m
b. 0·7m
c. +0025hrs
Port communications
VHF Ch 16 ☎ (41) 54 52 49

General

Talcahuano is a timber and fishing port and a Chilean Naval base. It is on a peninsula on the W side of Bahía de Concepción. The harbour is a little dirty from airborne dust. Shore facilities are fairly basic (better facilities in Concepción, half an hour by bus) but there is accommodation and there are restaurants. Mainly, however, it offers safe shelter in winds from every direction.

The municipal nautical centre, Cendyr, which oversees the moorings, has a helpful staff who will allow the use of their telephone.

Approach

Isla Quiriquina may be passed either side. Cargo vessels are advised to use the E channel, Boca

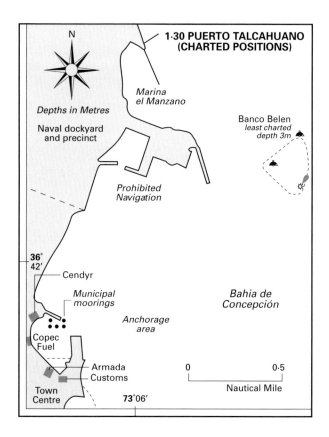

Grande, where there is a traffic separation scheme. The W channel, Boca Chica, has irregular streams, which are strong at springs.

Anchorage

Pass 1814 Banco Belén (3–5m) and anchor in the basin in mud. Land at fishermen's wharf or yacht club. Alternatively, the new marina El Manzano, is very welcoming and helpful. All facilities, club house with bar, workshop, email service.
☎/*Fax* 041 745743
email marina.elmanzano@entelchile.net

Formalities

Check in on Ch 16 and the *armada* will come and inspect the ship's papers. To check out, a visit to their office is necessary.

Facilities

Repairs; try at the Navy yard (but they are not used to yachts).
Fuel at a station across the street from fishermen's wharf and club or from Copec shown on sketch.
Covered market, basic shops and a supermarket.
Club de Yates – restaurant, toilets but no washing facilities.

Communications

Bus to Concepción every half-hour; eight daily to Santiago, Puerto Montt.
Airfield at Concepción.
Telephone: Area code 41. CTC Avenida Colón.

Passage

A traffic separation scheme operates at the entrance to Bahía San Vincente, off Punta Guálpen. Most of the coastline N and S of Isla Mocha (which can be passed either side) is sandy beach, usually with heavy swell. S of Punta Nihué (39°18'S 73°14'W) there are rocky headlands interspersed with beaches.

1·31 Caleta Trana

37°09'·5S 73°34'·5W
Distances
Talcahuano–50–Trana–175–Valdivia
Charts BA *3074, 3075;* US *22290, 22312;* Chile *5000, 5300, 6000, 6120, 6122*

General

Going S, this makes a welcome stop with shelter from the strong S winds. The anchorage is tucked in behind the point of Cabo Rumena. It is a small bay with a sandy beach, no officials and one small farm.

1·32 Caleta Queule

39°22'·9S 73°13'·5W
Charts Chile *6000, 6231*

Anchorage

Anchor in the bay in 5–10m on sand. Small village with basic provisions and a fuel station ½ mile up river (accessible only by dinghy). Good protection from S winds.

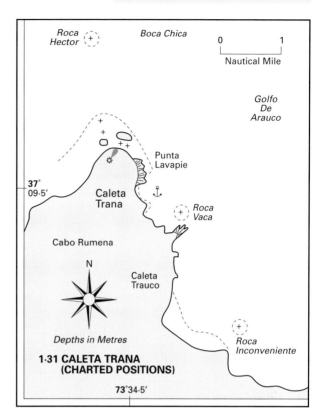

1·33 Bahía Corral and entrance to Río Valdivia

39°53'S 73°24'W
Charts BA *3075, 3081;* US *22335;* Chile *6000, 7000, 6241*

Lights

1726 **Morro Gonzalo** 39°50'·9S 73°28'·0W
  Fl.5s44m10M White square tower, red band 4m, hut. 026°-vis-272°
1728 **Morro Niebla** 39°51'·9S 73°24'·0W
  Fl.10s50m13M White GRP tower, red band 8m 343°-vis-210°
1730 **Roca El Conde** 39°52'·1S 73°25'·2W
  Fl.R.5s6m6M Red framework tower 4m 147·5°-vis-006°
303 (Chile) **Wreck of Haverbeck** 39°52'·7S 73°25'·1W
  Fl.G(2+1)14s 3M Green buoy with horizontal red band

General

Bahía Corral is at the entrance to Río Valdivia. There are two anchorages, which may be useful.

The first, Puerto Corral, is on the W coast of Bahía Corral, opposite the entrance to Río Valdivia. If breaking seas caused by a strong N wind close the river entrance, a boat may wait at Puerto Corral for improved conditions. The best anchorage, close in, will probably be crowded with large fishing boats also taking shelter but a deep-water anchorage can be made S of them.

The second, Isla Mancera, gives shelter from W winds. The island should only be approached from the NW. Anchor just beyond the small ferry pier in about 3–4m of water. Good holding in mud. The tide runs quite strongly. Mancera is a favourite anchorage for the yacht club and is much visited by day-trippers. There is a good restaurant.

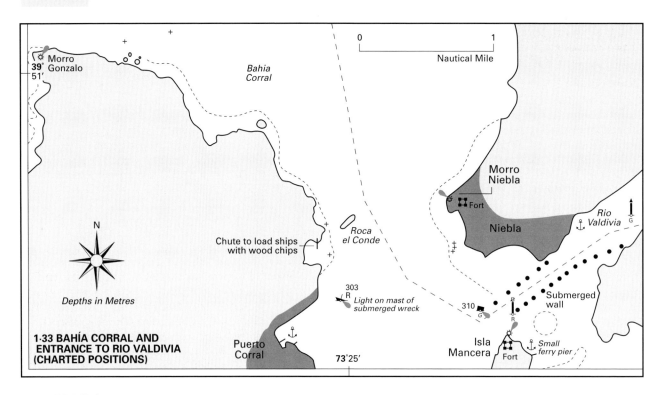

1·33 BAHÍA CORRAL AND ENTRANCE TO RIO VALDIVIA (CHARTED POSITIONS)

1·34 Valdivia

39°48'S 73°15'W

Distances
Trana–175–Valdivia–50–Milagro

Charts BA *3075, 3081*; US *22335*; Chile *6000, 7000, 6251, 6254*

Tides
Puerto Corral
a. 1·0m
b. 0·6m
c. +0100hrs
Valdivia
a. 0·7m
b. 0·3m
c. +0236hrs

Port communications
Corral Ch 16, 13 Irregular
Valdivia Port Ch 16, 88
Club de Yates Ch 68 (24hrs) ☎ (063) 21 30 28
Port captain ☎ (063) 291305

Lights
Entrance to River
1736 **Isla Mancera** 39°53'·1S 73°23'·6W
  Fl(3)R.9s6m3M Red conical GRP pillar 2m 043°-vis-309°
310 (Chile) **Mouth of Río Valdivia** 39°52'·9S
  73°23'·8W Fl.G(3)9s4M Green buoy, then a host of lights and beacons marking the channel

General
Valdivia lies 10M up the Valdivia River with very good facilities for both yachts and general shopping; it is probably the best port in Chile to lay up. Club de Yates Valdivia, with very friendly members and staff, lies about half a mile from the centre of town. Club De Yates Valdivia have an outstation at La Estancilla (39°50'S 73°19'W), well before the city is reached, on the north side of the river beside Alwoplast (see Berthing and Facilities below). The Club is a very good source of information on the *canales* of the south. Valdivia is an attractive, cultured university city with a population of 110,000. It has a strong German influence and German is still widely spoken. It is one of the wetter

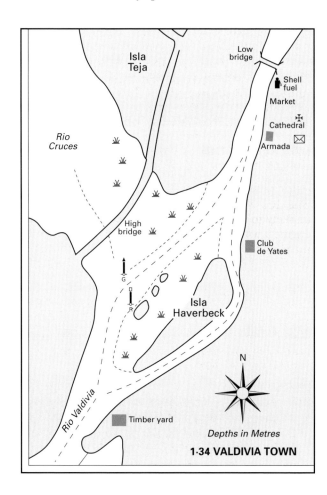

1·34 VALDIVIA TOWN

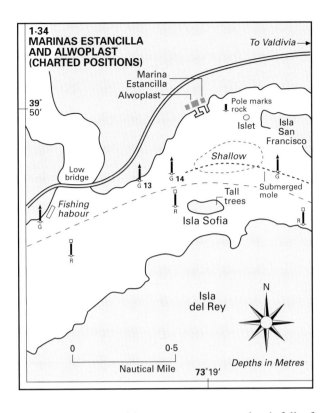

1·34
MARINAS ESTANCILLA AND ALWOPLAST (CHARTED POSITIONS)

To Valdivia →

Marina Estancilla
Alwoplast

Pole marks rock

Islet

Isla San Francisco

39° 50'

Shallow

Low bridge

G 13   G 14

Tall trees

Submerged mole

Fishing habour

Isla Sofia

Isla del Rey

N

0   0·5

Nautical Mile   73°19'

Depths in Metres

places in Chile, with an average annual rainfall of 2·4 metres; most falls in winter though it rains throughout the year. Temperatures rarely fall below zero and in January can reach 31°C. The combination has favoured the nearby growth of one of the world's three temperate rain forests, the Bosque Valdiviano, which has an extremely rich diversity of species, many of them unique to the area. The city was devastated by earthquake in 1960 (9 on the Richter scale) which caused a general subsidence of about a metre. Many riverside farms were flooded and the river is now bordered by marshes. Some remains are still visible along the waterfront and two ships wrecked by the accompanying tsunami lie in the approaches, one visible in the river and the other off Corral.

Approach

The Río Valdivia is tidal. In summer the ebb is unlikely to be critical for most yachts with auxiliary engines; with a favourable wind, the passage can be made under genoa. The channel (3m) is buoyed but there are submerged moles intermittently on both sides of the river from the entrance off Isla Mancera to within two miles of the city. It is advisable to keep in the middle of the fairway. Call the *Capitán del Puerto* on Ch 88 before entering the river. In strong northerly winds breaking seas north of Isla Mancera may close the entrance. In this condition shelter may be had in Puerto Corral.

Berthing

There are three possibilities
1. **Alwoplast** (39°50'·S 73°19'W), ☎ (063 203200 *Fax* 063 204142 *email* alwoplast@telsur.cl This boatyard is owned and run by Alec and

Dagmar Wopper. 4M up the river, Alwoplast will come into view behind the point, which has buoy 14 off it. Pass midway between buoy 13 and buoy 14, where the submerged mole starts again. Alwoplast Ltda is not only a complete shipyard, but also a full service marina. With a 35-ton marine travel-lift with 9m internal clearance, the yard can handle boats up to 65ft in length and 16ft draught. Facilities: Floating docks with water, 220VAC, showers, toilets, laundry, storage, fuel truck, pub, phone, fax and email service. English and German spoken, assistance for import and export, customs clearance and travel needs. Dagmar is a sailmaker.

2. **Marina Estancilla** (39°50'S 73°19'W), alongside Alwoplast.
Moor between the pontoon and the off-lying posts. It may be worth anchoring off the end of the marina pontoon to wait for slack water as the current runs very strongly, particularly on the ebb. The marina has deep water with room for yachts up to 20m. 24-hour guard, toilets, showers and water. Charges are low and the marina is very welcoming, well-sheltered and secure. In 2002 charges were less than US$4 per day. It is one of the few places a yacht may be left in comfort over the winter. Public transport to and from Valdivia is frequent and economical.

3. **Club de Yates Valdivia** ☎/*Fax* 063 213028 is 4–5M further up river on the east bank near the town centre. (2002 charges were US$160 a month.) The railway hoist is able to haul out yachts of up to 24 tons and 16m. It is heavily used by club members so it is worth enquiring about availability. It is usually free at the end of the summer from February to July. Members will advise on workshops, which can carry out a wide range of repairs.

Formalities

Call the *Capitán del Puerto* on Ch 88 on entering the river. He will arrange to visit the yacht. The *aduana*, however are in Osorno, a two-hour bus ride through beautiful countryside. If entering Chile, the task of clearing customs can be combined with a pleasant day's sightseeing. The bus service is very frequent.

Facilities

Chandler: Fibronavales Libertad 15, Gen. Lagos 1049, ☎ 218 742.
General repairs; M&F Naval Service (Casilla 1422, ☎/*Fax* 228 699, English spoken) can cope with stainless steel, aluminium, fibreglass, refrigeration, electrical work, paint work and interior work.
Electronics: Juan Manuel Fabres, Av. Pedro Aguirre Cerda 1330, ☎ 218 189 (authorised Furuno technician). 'STEP', Valentín Lopez, Ismael Valdés 236, ☎ 218 674 (shop).
Good hardware stores (Ferretería Valdivia and Sodimac).
Mecanica Valdivia can solve technical problems.
Fuel: Shell station on quay immediately below the low bridge over Río Calle Calle or Copec on a pier at Niebla just inside entrance to river.
Propane: Engas

Water at the yacht club, possibly at the Shell station.

Fish & vegetable market on the river close to the *armada*.

Well stocked supermarkets, shops etc.

Several laundries in town.

Club de Yates: secure, quiet, showers. 25-ton 16m slip. Water and showers included but electricity metered and charged separately. The yacht club marina at La Estancilla has showers, water and electricity (but not for heating), 24hr guard included in the charges.

Tourism

From Valdivia it is well worth taking the time to visit the Villarica area and the famous Lake District. There are excellent bus services to points all over Chile. For instance it is a 7hr bus ride to Bariloche in Argentina, one of South America's major ski resorts. A trip to Bariloche will trigger a new entry into Chile and start the 90-day visitor permit running again. Closer to hand is the charm of the city, the bird sanctuary Río Cruces which can be visited by boat (not yachts, however) and across the river on Isla Teja the botanical garden, an arboretum and the Museo Austral. Films in English are screened – see the Univ. cinema schedule.

Consulates: German, Italian, Spanish and Dutch.

Communications

Local buses from club to town centre nos. 1, 2 and 3, cost 35 cents US; from La Estancilla, every half hour 50 cents or a *collectivo*, 75 cents.

National airport at Pichoy 32km north. Buses (26 a day to Osorno, the *aduana* station and bus junction for Argentina).

Car hire: Automóvil Club de Chile, Hertz, First Rent-a-Car and others.

(Area code 63.)

Many email cafés.

Post: Club de Yates Valdivia, Casilla 454, Valdivia, X region Chile and

Alex and Dagmar Wopper, Alwoplast Ltda, Casilla 114, Valdivia, will hold mail.

Passage

The distance from Bahía de Corral to the Canal de Chacao is about 120M. The narrows of the Canal are about 10M and it is a further 40M or so on to Puerto Montt.

The prevailing strong SW wind can make this a hard passage, especially as it is against the Humboldt Current. If sailing S in these conditions the passage can take several days. When it is sunny and warm in Valdivia there are almost certainly strong SW winds outside. If it is necessary to depart in these conditions, leave in the late afternoon from Valdivia as the winds generally slacken overnight allowing the yacht to motor-sail in lighter conditions. Several boltholes can then be used en route to shelter from the strong daytime winds. These include Caleta Lameguapi, Caleta Milagro and Bahía San Pedro. It may be better to wait until the winds shift to the N; the passage is then generally easy, taking a day. This shift occurs generally when conditions in Valdivia are wet, chilly and overcast.

Tidal streams in Canal de Chacao are very strong and timing is crucial; there is no slack water and the transit must be made with a fair tide. There are waiting places at both ends of the canal.

1·35 Caleta Lameguapi

40°11'S 73° 43'·5W

Distances

Bahía Corral–26–Caleta Lameguapi–10–Caleta Milagro

Charts BA *1289*; US *22335*; Chile *6000, 7000, 7111*

General

If pushed this *caleta* may serve as a short-term bolthole. There are frequently several large fishing boats taking shelter in this bay. They leave at night and resume fishing a few miles off the coast. However, there is plenty of room to anchor in 12–15m close in. The holding is good but some swell enters the bay in strong SW conditions.

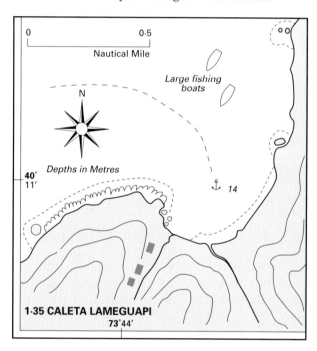

1·36 Caleta Milagro

40°20'S 73°45'W

Distances

Valdivia–50–Milagro–35–San Pedro

Charts BA *1289, 3075*; US *22335*; Chile *7000, 7111*

General

The best anchorage is in 4–5m in the SW corner. The holding is good, but the anchorage is rolly. Caleta Milagro is a more secure anchorage than Caleta Lameguapi.

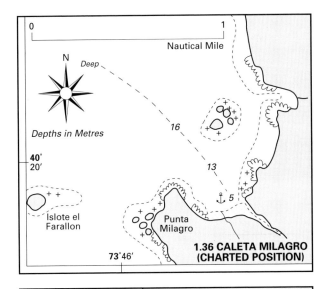

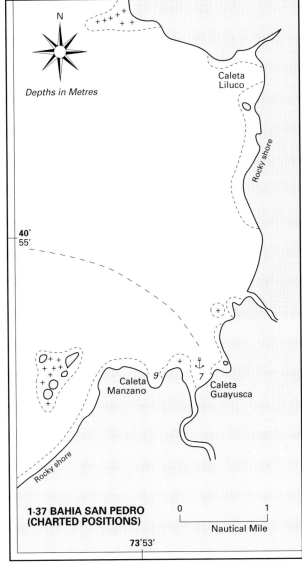

1·37 Bahía San Pedro

40°56'S 73°53'W

Distances
Milagro–35–San Pedro–55–Puerto Inglés
Charts BA *1289*; US *22335*; Chile *7000, 7111*

General

Bahía San Pedro provides the best anchorage between Valdivia and Canal Chacao if strong SW winds are encountered. Caleta Guayusca provides the most secure anchorage. There is a small village here. Caleta Lliuco looks as though it would provide protection in NW winds. However when winds blow strongly from the N or NW they tend to veer to the W as the low passes over. In these conditions the bay becomes a dangerous lee shore. In the 1960s two *armada* vessels were wrecked here with loss of life. If a yacht encounters strong N winds when travelling towards Valdivia it would be better to turn back to either Caleta Godoy or to Puerto Inglés. In these conditions Puerto Inglés should be approached when the current is on the flood through Canal Chacao.

Caleta Godoy (41°39'S 73°45'W – Chile chart *7210*) lies in the N of Bahía Maullin and is protected from the N by Morro Varillasmo. Holding is good at 7–10m in sand.

2. Seno Reloncaví, Golfo de Ancud and Golfo Corcovado

General

The area between Puerto Montt and Golfo Elefantes has been described as one of the best cruising grounds in the world. It is spectacular, with numerous isolated anchorages, fascinating country and few developed harbours; this section deals with the N part of the area. The Guide starts from Canal Chacao, works clockwise around Seno Reloncaví and then southwards down both sides of Golfo Ancud and Golfo Corcovado listing anchorages in order of increasing latitude.

Climate

In the summer the common winds are light S to SW (mean 5–8kts), temperatures are cool to warm (mean max. 18°C, mean min. 10°C) with sun and good visibility. When the winds come from the N, a direction associated with passing lows, they may bring warmer weather and rain or overcast conditions. In winter, N winds are more frequent. Gale force winds are infrequent in summer and in winter they occur on only a few days each month. These generally light wind conditions and the sheltered nature of the waters in Seno Reloncaví and the Golfo de Ancud make the sailing quite relaxing, more in the nature of sailing on a large lake than on the open sea. That said, *rachas* do occur, especially in mountainous areas (they are uncommon amongst the lower lying islands) and good ground tackle is necessary to cope with them as well as a large tidal range and strong streams.

Rainfall in the area is high, averaging about 1900mm a year. The highest falls are in winter, on the W coast and near to the mountains.

Salmon farms

Salmon farms, *salmoneras,* have been widely established. Rounding a headland expecting to find convenient shelter for the night, the pens of a *salmonera* are often encountered. However, in most places there is space between the pens, their anchoring buoys and the shoreline for a small craft to anchor. The staff, *Salmoneristas,* are helpful in making visitors moorings secure – which is in their interest. The pens provide a lee, which gives a little protection from wind and swell. Their detritus promotes the growth of algae on the bottom, which can make it more difficult to dig in an anchor.

Salmon pens have been marked on the sketch plans. However there is continuing investment in

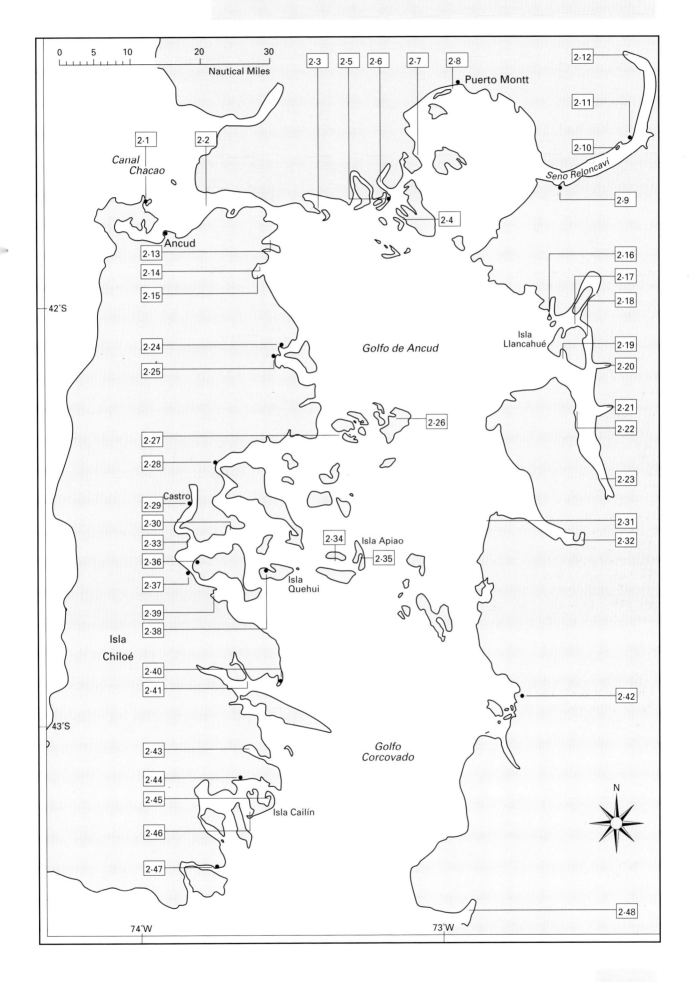

fish pens and their positions and numbers change frequently. A flashing yellow light generally marks salmon farms. Mussel farms are also common and are often found inside the *salmoneras*. They are generally not lit and do not show up well on radar.

Lights and marks

The few lights of passage are not listed here; consult the appropriate chart or light list. Channels are well posted with day-marks and beacons. Experience confirms the wisdom of securing well before dark.

Fuel

Fuel is available alongside at Marina Oxxean in Puerto Montt. It can be obtained by can from *gasolineras* in Puerto Montt, Castro, Quellon and Aguirre and in the larger villages in the area.

Kelp

This is not usually a problem in this area but can grow in strands 75m long (and therefore in deep channels) and in massive beds.

Approach from seaward

Canal Chacao has a straightforward approach; the lighthouse at Punta Corona willingly gives information on tide times and the direction of flow in the channel via VHF. Puerto Inglés is a suitable anchorage in which to shelter and await favourable conditions for traversing the canal.

2·1 Puerto Inglés

41°48'S 73°53'W

Charts BA *1289, 1313;* US *22341, 22342;* Chile *7000, 7210, 7212*

Port communications

You should report your position to Faro Punta Corona on Península Lacui. The Faro (lighthouse) will provide tidal and weather information.

Lights

1676 **Punta Corona** 41°47'·1S 73°53'·3W
Fl.10s66m32M White tower, red bands 9·5m, house. 135°-vis-342°, Racon, RDF beacon, fog signal manned

General

Located S of the light at Punta Corona, this is an excellent anchorage and a good spot in which to wait for the flood tide before entering Canal Chacao. The holding is good, in sand, 6–7m at low water, just outside the entrance to the lagoon (Estero Chaular). It is also possible to anchor just inside the entrance in 3·5m; here the anchorage is windy in northerlies but the water is calm. Alternatively anchor to the NE of the salmon pens with the wreck on the stony beach bearing 332°. If the wind is too strong from the N, an alternative is Estero Dique, round the corner of Punta Arenas, 2·5M W of Ancud.

Ancud is not a recommended anchorage for yachts. The approach is across shallows, which dry, and there is virtually no protection from the W. There is no proper harbour and mooring areas are crowded with small fishing vessels.

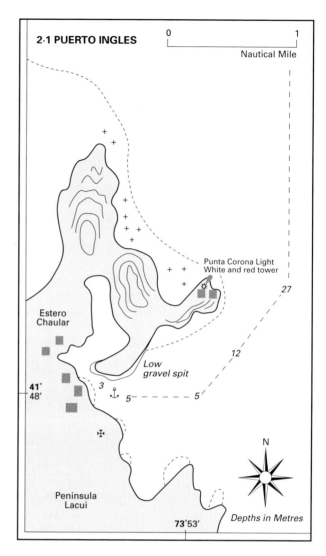

2·1 PUERTO INGLES
0 1 Nautical Mile
Punta Corona Light White and red tower
27
12
Estero Chaular
Low gravel spit
41° 48'
3
5 — — — — 5
N
Peninsula Lacui
73°53'
Depths in Metres

2·2 Canal Chacao

Charts BA *1289, 1313;* US *22341, 22342;* Chile *7000, 7210*

General

Canal Chacao separates Isla Chiloé from the mainland. When approaching, particularly from the W, it is important to establish VHF radio contact with Corona light – call *Faro Corona* on Ch 16. The station is very helpful and will give conditions in the canal plus a local weather forecast. The station also transmits local conditions each day, in Spanish, at 0050, 0650, 1250, 1850 UT on VHF Ch 14.

When approaching from the N keep at least 4M off the W end of Isla Dona Sebastiana as shallow water to the W of the island can create steep and potentially breaking seas. Turn E through the canal when on a line 1 mile S of the island.

A useful short cut, especially when coming from Bahía Maullín is to enter the canal between the E end of Isla Dona Sebastiana and the mainland. Rocks extend out about 1M to the E of the island. Even during calms there are overfalls in this gap although in these conditions they are not dangerous. The passage itself is well marked and wide. It is important to travel to the E on the flood, or to the

W on the ebb. There are strong tidal flows along its 15 mile length, with areas of overfalls in the shallow waters at both ends and also in a line extending to the SW from Península Challahué. In the canal, the W-going stream begins 1 hour before high water and the E-going stream 1 hour before low water. At springs, the stream may be more than 10kts in the centre and there are tide rips. With wind against tide, very steep and high (5–8m) waves may be encountered, some of which break. It is dangerous for a small craft to enter the channel in these conditions.

There is considerable traffic in the canal, including a ferry service, at the E end, that runs from the mainland to Chacao. Anchorages at the E end of the canal are Manao, Hueihue, Linao and, on the N shore, Abtao.

From Canal Chacao to Puerto Montt and Seno Reloncaví

2·3 Puerto Abtao

41°48'S 73°22'W

Charts BA *1289, 1313*; US *22341, 22342*; Chile *7000, 7210, 7300, 7310, 7311*

General

Puerto Abtao is located at the E end of Canal Chacao between Isla Abtao and Península Challahué. Favour the side of Isla Abtao when entering from the S through Canal Abtao to avoid the sandbank off the point. Also beware of the numerous salmon pens along the route. There is a prominent church to the E of the village. Good anchorage can be had S of the village between the

beach and the salmon pens. Depth is 6m at low water and the holding is good in mud and sand.

2·4 Canal Chidguapi

41°50S 73°05'·5W

Charts BA *1289*; US *22341*; Chile *7000, 7300, 7310, 7311*

General

A well-sheltered but deep anchorage on the SW side of the canal between Islas Chidguapi and Puluqui. Anchor in 10–15m (rapidly shoaling bottom) between the W end of the salmon pens and the white beach. Restaurant ashore (booking necessary).

2·5 Calbuco

41°46'S 73°08'W

Charts BA *1313*; US *22341*; Chile *7000, 7300, 7310, 7311*

General

Calbuco is a town perched on top of a hill overlooking the sea and is linked to the mainland by a causeway. It was a settlement founded by the Spanish in 1604, many decades before Puerto Montt. The town has all the usual facilities and it is a good place from which to visit Puerto Montt by bus.

Anchorages

There are three anchorages
1. The most secure if the yacht is to be left for some time is to the W of the causeway. The approach is straightforward through Canal Caicaén but keep to the centre to avoid mussel farms on either side. Very good holding in 10–15m.
2. If a yacht wants to collect fuel or visit the town, the best anchorage is to the N of the town, close E of the causeway in about 10m. This is a good overnight anchorage but show an anchor light as

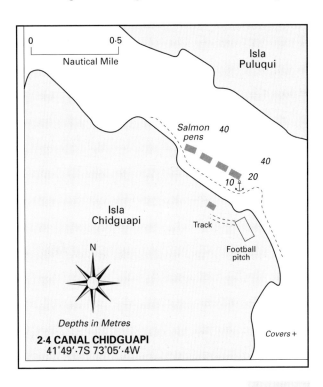

a considerable number of fishing boats move in the area. Put the anchor light in the statutory position, the fore-triangle, not at the top of the mast, or it will not be observed, especially when it is raining and the helmsman is steering from within his cuddy. The dinghy can be landed near the causeway by the Copec station, which has both clean fuel and water.

3. The third is Surgidero La Vega on the S side of the NE corner of the island. Keep to the W shore. Food supplies and fuel (take cans). Open to the S so pick your time and do not stay long.

Formalities
There is an *armada* station in the town.

2·6 Estero Huito
41°45'S 73°10'W
Charts BA *1313*; US *22341*; Chile *7000, 7300, 7310, 7311*

Approach
Watch for rocks off the S shore; favour the N shore. A cable crosses the *estero* with 17m clearance at HW (greater clearance on S side of channel).

Anchorage
Delightful and secure anchorage within the *estero* with good holding in sand and rocks. There are many salmon cages. A useful alternative anchorage is in the bay on the N side of the entrance.

2·7 Isla Huelmo
41°39'·6S 73°04'W
Charts BA *1313*; US *22341*; Chile *7000, 7300, 7310*

General
If it is necessary to wait some time in the area of Puerto Montt, this is a pleasant place to do so, within a few hours sail yet clear of city distractions.

Approach
A rocky spit extends S of the island. Go through the *salmoneras* and mussel rafts towards a small tree-covered hill on the mainland.

Anchorage
There are two anchorages:
1. To the E a sandspit gives good protection from southerlies up to 30 knots. The anchorage is very secure in all other winds. Charts show the inner pool as drying out; this is not so and there is plenty of water. Anchor about 100m offshore in 6m, sand (tidal range about 6m) and far enough in for protection from the S. An anchor light is advisable as local boats use the passage to the N of the island at HW.
2. The second anchorage is off the beach on the W side in 11m, sand. This is exposed between S and SE but is a pleasant anchorage with the more usual W winds.

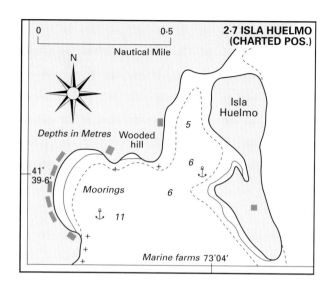

2·8 Puerto Montt
41°29'S 72°57'W
Charts BA *1289, 1313*; US *22341, 22345*; Chile *7000, 7300, 7321*
Tides
a. 5·8m Mean Spring Range
b. 2·3m Mean Neap Range
This is a Standard Port
Port communications
Port Ch 16 ☎25 23 89
Marina del Sur ☎ 25 91 95
Marina Oxxean ☎ 25 55 44

General
Yachts coming in from the Pacific often make Puerto Montt their first port of call. It has good facilities for repairs, maintenance and for restocking the ship.

Puerto Montt is a major tourist centre. Tours to the Lake District start here, as do ferries to Aisén, San Rafael and Puerto Natales.

Approach
Do not try to enter from the NE without local knowledge. There are often very large ships in the main port and cables may stretch right across the channel. The shallows at Angelmó may only be passed at high water. The entrance to Canal Tenglo from the SW is well marked and easy to enter day or night.

Mooring
There are three organised places to moor, prices are reasonable and seem to be open to negotiation, especially in winter.
1. Marina Oxxean was the most economical in 2001 and the staff are exceptionally helpful and friendly. Vessels may dry out here against a concrete wall on firm sand. A pressure hose is available for cleaning. Water and electricity on the marina piers. Fuel by hose at dock.
2. Marina del Sur at the W end of Canal Tenglo can accommodate vessels up to 65ft.
3. Club de Yates, Reloncaví has a small marina and moorings. Prices are reasonable and there is a waterboat service.

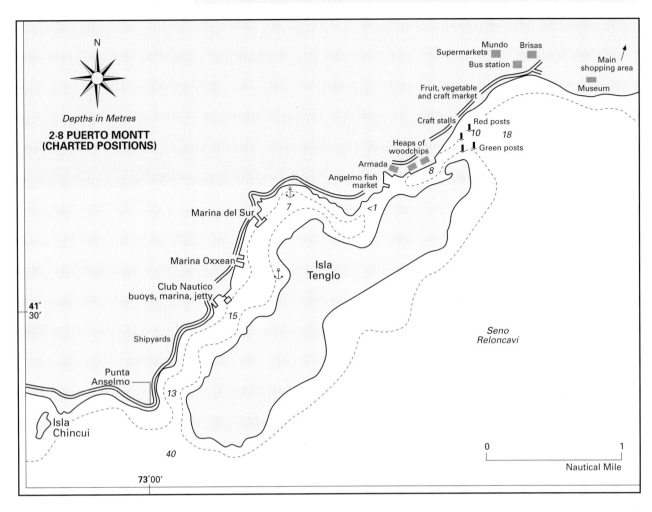

It is also possible to anchor opposite the yacht club and to the NE of Marina del Sur although there is a lot of boat traffic in the canal. Anchoring behind the N end of Isla Tenglo is prohibited. There is no safe anchorage in front of the town itself.

From the marinas there are frequent and inexpensive buses and *collectivos* to Puerto Montt via Angelmó where the *armada* has its office and where there is a major market.

Formalities

Check with the *Capitán del Puerto* on Ch 16. *Aduana* and immigration in town. Staff at the marinas will assist.

Facilities

At marinas
Specialist services such as sail-makers, welders, engine fitters and stores such as propane can be arranged.
Drying-out wall (6m tides at Springs).
Diesel and petrol.
Electricity 220V 50Hz on floats.
Showers and water.
Marina del Sur has a 40-ton platform hoist but no hard standing (the boat is left on the platform during repairs) and a laundry service.

In town
There are excellent supermarkets in the town.
Hardware: Weitzler on Lota and Perez Rosales and many others.

There are many banks that will accept a wide variety of cards as well as numerous moneychangers.
Market at Angelmó, the ferry port and naval base halfway between the marina and the centre of town: vegetables, fish, vacuum-packed smoked salmon, cheese. There are many good and inexpensive restaurants here.
Laundries (including one at Las Brisas).
Alternative energy specialists (batteries, solar and wind power): Wireless Energy Chile, ☎ 292100 or 292101 or *email* wireless@entelchile.net. They are very helpful and knowledgeable.
Consulates: Argentinian, German and Spanish.

Communications

Air: Services to Santiago, W coast ports and to Punta Arenas. Buses to Santiago, Chiloé and many other Chilean destinations and to Argentina. Ferries and cruise ships to Chiloé, Chonos, Aysén, San Rafael and Puerto Natales.
Car hire: Automóvil Club de Chile, Avis, Budget and others.
Telephone: Area code 65, ENTEL Ramírez 948; Telefónica Sur, Chillán 98.
Many email cafés.

Diversion: Seno Reloncaví

2·9 Caleta Martin

41°44'S 72°34'W

Charts BA *1313*; US *22341*; Chile *7000, 7300, 7330*

General

A useful spot if the run up to Ralún is disrupted by weather.

Approach

The anchorage is a fairly small inlet within Caleta Martin on the W side of Punta Chaparano. Enter Caleta Martin until the cove is seen, behind a small promontory with a rock or islet off it, and then approach mid channel. Anchor and run a line to the orange-painted concrete block and another line aft. The local car ferry sometimes moors in the *caleta* and occupies almost all the space.

2·10 Isla Marimeli

41°40'·8S 72°26'W

Charts BA *1313*; US *22341*; Chile *7000, 7300, 7330*

General

The small bay at the NE end of this island is one of the most secure and sheltered anchorages in Seno Reloncaví. Rocks obstruct the N entrance, enter from the E. The anchorage is used for storing salmon pens so the amount of space available will vary. Local boats use the channels between the islands, be careful not to obstruct their passage with mooring lines.

2·11 Bahía Sotomo

41°39' 72°23'W

Charts BA *1313*; US *22341*; Chile *7000, 7300, 7330*

General

Good shelter can be found by anchoring in 15–18m close-to in the SW corner of the bay and taking lines ashore. Thermal springs run directly into the sea on the beach at the head of a small indentation (that appears as an island on the chart) about 300m to the E of the anchorage. They are exposed below half tide.

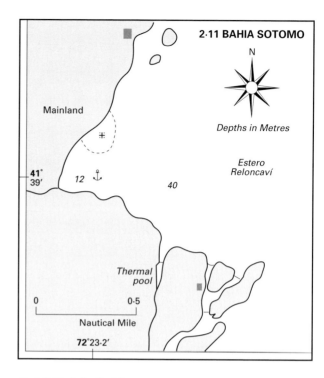

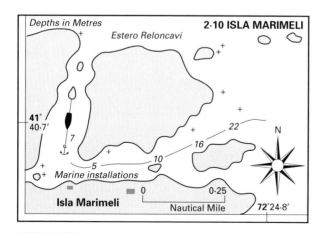

2·12 Bahía Ralún

41°24'S 72°19'W

Charts BA *1313*; US *22341*; Chile *7000, 7300, 7330*

General

Keep to the S shore until Punta Veriles, opposite 1699 Cayo Nahuelhuapi (Fl.R.5s6m5M red GRP tower, 3m), has been passed. About 0·75M WSW approx. there is a pier ashore; anchor in 25m. There is little protection against the N wind and this is recommended only as a temporary anchorage in fine weather. The hotel and restaurant has a good reputation.

Continuation: Canal Chacao southwards – Golfo de Ancud

2·13 Bahía Manao

41°52'S 73°32'W

Charts BA *1313*; US *22341*; Chile *7210, 7000, 7300, 7362*

General

This is a useful anchorage if waiting for a fair tide through Canal Chacao or after coming through the Canal from the W late at night. It is open to the E but there is good holding at the head of the bay in about 10m.

2·14 Bahía Hueihue

41°54'S 73°31'W

Charts BA *1313*; US *22341*; Chile *7210, 7000, 7300, 7362*

General

A small anchorage open to the S with a tidal range of 5–6m. In strong N winds there is little shelter and yachts have reported dragging here. If uncomfortable, consider Linao.

Approach

From the S, Punta Lamecura is clear; from the N, Punta Chilén has foul ground SE and Bajo Cholche lies S of Punta Hueihue. Pass about half way between Punta Concura and Punta Hueihue.

Anchorage

Go up near the head of the bay but check depth against swinging room and tidal range. Access to the lagoon, which has good shelter, may be possible at high water; check the approach by dinghy.

2·15 Bahía Linao

41°58'S 73°32'W

Charts BA *1289, 1313*; US *22341*; Chile *7000, 7300, 7362*

General

Fifteen miles S of the E entrance of Canal Chacao, Bahía Linao offers two sheltered anchorages. Reports vary on their quality in bad weather, the anchorage in the E hook giving best protection in S winds. Unfortunately there is a large oyster farm in the E basin that takes up much of the anchoring space. A bow and stern anchor are necessary to hold the boat in position. The basin is quite shallow, 3–6m at the entrance and 1·8–2·7m N of the oyster farm. The anchorages are at 41°57'S 73°33'·8W and 41°58'S 73°32'W (GPS). Beware submerged rocks E of 1664 Punta Guapilinao (Fl.G.5s52m5M Green GRP tower 3m 012°-vis-343°). The hamlet at Linao, about a mile away, can supply eggs, bread and beer (in bulk, bring bottles).

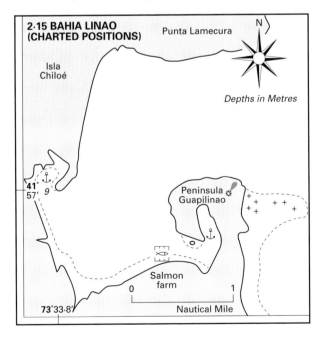

2·16 Isla Malomacun

42°03'·6S 72°37'·75W

Charts BA *1313*; US *22341*; Chile *7000, 7300, 7340*

General

There is a good all-weather anchorage between Malomacun and Isla Toro to the E. Rocky bottom in 10m but good holding has been found. Chart *7340* would suggest that this anchorage should only be approached from the N.

Diversion: Canal Hornopirén and Estero Comau

In settled weather a detour up Canal Hornopirén provides a spectacular passage. There are two bays, open to the SW but otherwise well protected, at the N end of Isla Pelada, one in the NW corner (41°59'·8S 72°28'·7W by GPS) and the other in the NE corner. Access to both is clear. Anchor in 10-15m with shorelines.

Isla Llancahué and Estero Comau offer several anchorages and magnificent mountain scenery as well as excellent thermal baths.

2·17 Isla Llancahué – Caleta Los Baños

42°05'S 72°32'W

Charts BA *1313*; US *22341*; Chile *7000, 7300, 7340*

General

Caleta Los Baños is open to the N but it has running hot water and a hotel. The rock marked at the W entrance of the bay is well offshore and covered at high water (no surf). The river delta, W of the hotel, is shallow. Anchor in 10-15m. A more secure anchorage, although still open to the N, can be found in Caleta Andrade, 1M to the W of Caleta Los Baños. The entrance to this long bay is simple with no dangers. Anchor in 15m silt, good holding. The head of the bay shelves quickly.

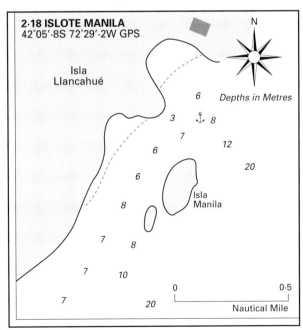

2·18 Islote Manila (Rada Potreros de Cholgo)

42°05'·8S 72°29'·2W (GPS position)

Charts BA *1313*; US *22341*; Chile *7000, 7300, 7430*

General

Local advice is to anchor to the N of Islote Manila ½M NE of Rada Potreros de Cholgo. Apparently strong winds, even from the S, are almost unknown in that spot. Coming from the N the island is easily seen. From the S, look out for two houses, one blue, nearest the point below the high hill. Holding in mud with a few rocky patches. Exceedingly pretty. Vessels have also tied between the island and Llancahué, this is not recommended as the passage is frequently used, day and night, by small launches.

2·19 Isla Llancahué – Estero Bonito

42°08'·0S 72°35'W

Charts BA *1313*; US *22341*; Chile *7000, 7300, 7340*

General

The shape of the bay varies with the charts, *7340* appears to be accurate. However it is an enclosed bay offering a very well protected anchorage, good for all winds. Located on the S side of Isla Llancahué it is a useful stop if going S or W. The narrow entrance is hard to spot but a house on the hill is a landmark. The small bay is full of fishing installations with intense commercial activity all night long. The only available anchorage is open to the S. However the fishing vessels are happy for yachts to tie up with them especially if the weather is bad.

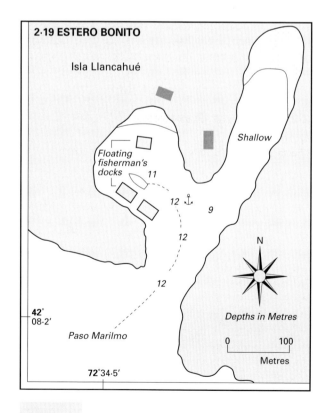

2·20 Estero Quintupeu

42°10'S 72°26'W

Chart BA *1289*; US *22352*; Chile *7000, 7300, 7340*

General

The entrance is very narrow but once inside, it opens out. Leave a *salmonera* to port. The fjord has deep water (the battleship *Dresden* hid here for a short while in 1914) but about 3M up, near the head, depths fall quickly to a narrow sandspit. Estero Quintupeu has been described as spectacular, a dramatic landscape of snow-capped volcanoes and cascades. Beware *rachas*.

Anchorage

There are two places that have been recommended as anchorages. The first anchorage is in the cove on the S shore one mile inside the entrance. There are now several *salmoneras* here but good anchorage can still be found. Watch out for underwater mooring cables between the *salmonera* and the shore. Anchor close to the shore in 15m with lines ashore. The second and better option is to go to the head of the bay and anchor in 6–8m on the edge of the sandspit. This requires care as the bottom shelves very quickly and it is very easy to run aground and be left high and dry on the ebb.

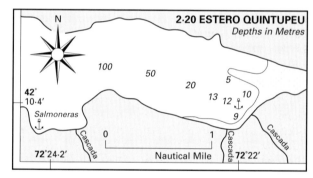

2·21 Estero Cahuelmo

42°15'S 72°24'W

Charts BA *1289*; US *22352*; Chile *7000, 7300, 7340, 7350*

General

In settled weather Estero Cahuelmo makes a spectacular anchorage with the added attraction of thermal pools. The entrance is clear and deep. Proceed towards the head of the *estero*. Well before the end of the fjord it shelves very quickly with

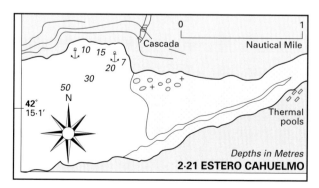

depths decreasing from 80m to a drying sandspit within a few boat lengths. Anchor behind the rocky projection about half a mile to the W of the sandspit. Shelter is marginal in W winds. This *estero* has an evil reputation and should be considered a fair weather only anchorage. Quintupeu is better for an overnight stop.

At low water it is possible to walk across the sandspit to the thermal pools, which are marked by a large wooden sign. At high water use a dinghy to cross the sandspit.

2·22 Península Huequi – Caleta Telele

42°16'S 72°31'W
Charts BA *1289*; US *22352*; Chile *7000, 7300, 7350*

General
With shelter from the NW and some from the N (though the wind may come round the corner of Punta el Cajon), Caleta Telele is on Estero Leptepu, opposite Estero Cahuelmo, and has served well as an overnight anchorage.

2·23 Caleta Porcelana

42°29'S 72°29·5'W
Charts BA *1289*; US *22352*; Chile *7000, 7300, 7350*

General
Caleta Porcelana is a spectacular anchorage in Estero Leptepu, under snow-covered peaks with hot springs nearby.

Anchorage
The anchorage off the beach is not easy as it is deep (20m), steep-to and has a rocky bottom. Anchor facing E as winds blowing down the *estero* produce a swell that bends around the point and turns W. A light tidal current makes a stern line essential. Ask permission to visit the hot springs at the small farmhouse. They are about 800m up a stream, to the north of the house, after crossing a log bridge. There is a charge.

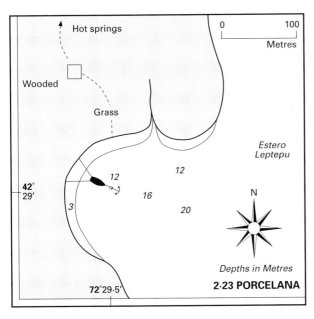

2·23 PORCELANA

The majority of exploration of the canals by yachtsmen has all taken place in the last 10–20 years. However between the two World Wars a small handful of yachtsmen from the Club de Yates, Valdivia, had started to sail among the N islands and fjords. These included Otto Stolzenbach. In the mid-70s, Justo Schuler, President of the yacht club for many years, and other members of the club used the log of Otto Stolzenbach to rediscover beautiful places like Caleta Porcelana.

Continuation

2·24 Estero Tubildad

42°07'S 73°29'W
Charts BA *1313, 1289, 2987*; US *22341*; Chile *7000, 7300, 7362*
Tides
Spring range about 6m

General
A very pretty spot. Not illustrated as it is well drawn on Chile *7362*.

Anchorage
Anchor clear of the mussel rafts in 4–6m, sand, on W side or near the head of the inlet. Good mussels and clams. Puerto Huite, 2 miles to the E along Estero Calcahué has also been used, though it is not so pretty and is filled with *salmoneras*.

2·25 Quemchi

42°08'S 73°29'W
Charts BA *1313, 3749*; US *22341*; Chile *7000, 7300, 7362*

General
The anchorage is off the S shore of the village, mud and sand. It is picturesque, with black-necked swans. The village has old wooden buildings (those with red flags outside are butchers), a supermarket which has accepted dollar travellers cheques, shops, basic restaurants, post and telephone. Bus to Castro and Ancud.

2·26 Islas Buta Chauques

42°17'S 73°08'W
Charts BA *3749*; US *22341, 22352*; Chile *7000, 7300*

General
This group lies to the E of Canal Chauques and consists of two islands, Isla Buta Chauques and Isla Aulin. It is a sparsely populated area of attractive sand spits and rolling hills around a substantial lagoon. The approach is more straightforward than suggested by the chart, and there are a number of excellent anchorages.

Approach
Chile chart *7300* shows two kelp patches (Bajo Del Medio and Boca Pájaros) in the W entrance from Canal Chauques. No kelp was seen in 2000 although the area may be shoal. The approach should be made with caution from the N part of

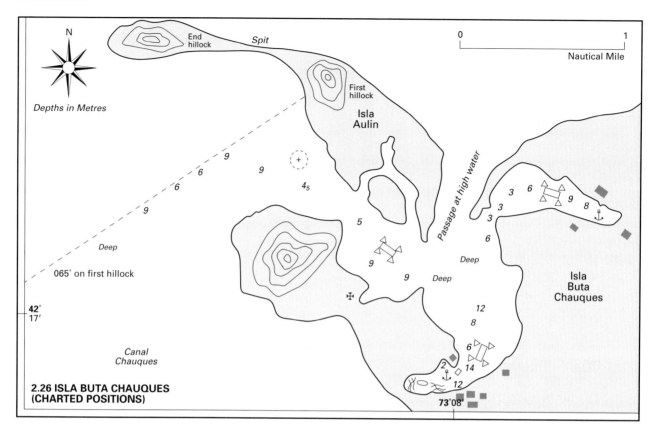

2.26 ISLA BUTA CHAUQUES (CHARTED POSITIONS)

Canal Chauques using the bearings shown in the diagram. The lagoon itself is relatively free of dangers.

Anchorages

The E part of the lagoon divides in two. The N branch is entered through a narrow channel formed by a sand spit. The channel is clear of obstructions and has a minimum depth of 3m. Anchor at the E end of this bay in perfect shelter, 10m mud. Anchorage can be found in the S branch S of the fish farm in about 10m.

2·27 Isla Mechuque

42°19'S 73°15'W

Charts BA *3749*; US *22341, 22352*; Chile *7000, 7300, 7390, 7392*

General

The anchorage in front of Mechuque village is very picturesque and a safe anchorage in settled conditions. The fishing village is particularly attractive as the houses are built on stilts (*palafitos*). There has been considerable investment in salmon farming and there are many salmon pens in this group of islands. Smoked salmon may sometimes be purchased – ask in the village. In the event of strong W winds try the shallow basin to the NE of the town and anchor on the W side due E of a large *palafito*. This position is pretty but space is limited and holding suspect. The anchorage shown to the NE of Isla Añihué is very pretty and secure.

The channel between Isla Mechuque and Isla Añihué to Isla Taucolon is navigable with several well-sheltered anchorages along the way. The passage through the islands is a little difficult to follow when travelling through them. The sketch plan shows the canal with the best route through.

There are several good anchorages around the group, including a spectacular anchorage in the lagoon N of Isla Taucolon. In 2000 this area was crowded with *salmoneras* and, as they are frequently moved, it may be worth investigating. The entrance is straightforward; anchor in 4m just before the final pool. It has good protection except between NE and SE. There are good views of snow-capped mountains on the mainland. A pleasant anchorage can also be found in Puerto Voigue though the anchorage on the E side of the sandspit is full of fish cages.

2·28 Dalcahue

42°23'S 73°40'W

Charts BA *3749*; US *22352*; Chile *7000, 7370, 7371*

General

Dalcahue (the name derives from a traditional three-plank canoe) has a population of 7,000 and many fine old wooden buildings, including one of the oldest wooden churches in Chiloé. It is an interesting place to visit, especially on a Sunday when in addition to the general market, there is a covered craft market with a vast array of woollen knitted and woven goods – sweaters, ponchos and jackets. There are many small shops and bars.

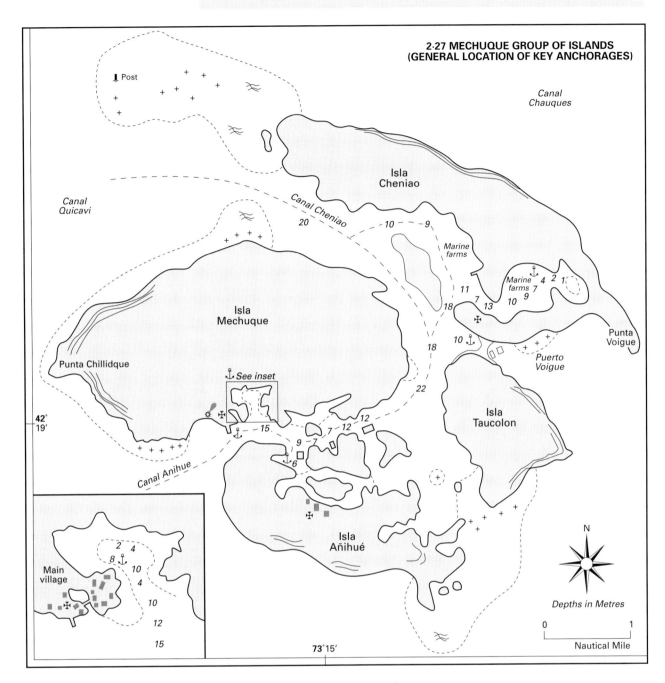

2·27 MECHUQUE GROUP OF ISLANDS
(GENERAL LOCATION OF KEY ANCHORAGES)

Anchorage

Anchor in about 10m near the jetty and the covered market. The current runs very strongly past Dalcahue and the anchorage is crowded with local fishing boats. These boats anchor with a long rope rode so when the tide turns it is easy to become tangled up with them. Anchor as clear from the jumble as possible. There is a more secure anchorage under the power line (43·9m), with a good lee in a strong SW and good holding. Land on the beach or at the ferry ramp. Reasonable shelter can be found on the S shores of the canals near or inshore of the mussel rafts.

2·29 Castro

42°28'S 73°46'W
Charts BA *3749*; US *22352*; Chile *7000, 7370, 7372*

General

Castro is the capital of Chiloé. It has one of the best timber churches on the island, with a fine interior and twin pink and blue towers. The church is a national monument and is in fine condition internally; externally, needful repairs are being carried out. The anchorages at Castro are effectively landlocked. A few foreign yachts over-winter, though it can be choppy in a gale when the wind comes either from S or N.

Shoreside facilities are good in terms of shops, modern supermarkets, hotels, and restaurants. It is a busy place in the high season (January and

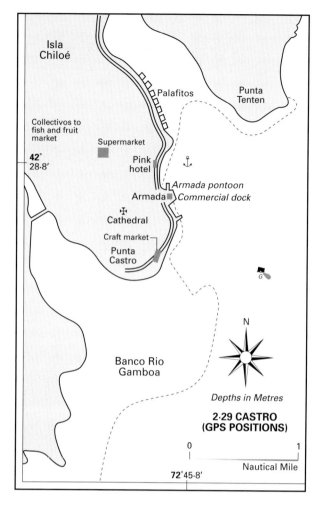

February). There are good general workshops directly opposite the *armada* station with a range of light engineering skills, such as repairing exhausts and welding, but little other support for a yacht.

Approach

Straightforward but the Banco Río Gamboa immediately S of the town is said to be slowly extending SE. It is well marked, with a large green buoy, so poses no problem for a yacht.

Anchorage

The anchorage is to the N of the *armada* station, in 6–14m, well sheltered from the usual passage of fronts. Holding is very good. Vessels that have passed winter here report better weather than Puerto Montt or Valdivia. Strong winds from the E are infrequent and do not seem to be a problem.

Formalities

Check in on Ch 16 and visit the *armada* by using their floating pontoon. The *armada* is very helpful and if asked will allow a visiting yacht to use their pontoon to tie up the dinghy. This gives total security to the dinghy while ashore.

Facilities

The best and most economic place to buy vegetables and fish is at the *Feria*. Catch a *collectivo* from Avenida San Martin, near the Cathedral. The *Feria* operates every

day but is most popular on Saturday morning.
The best supermarket (HiperBecker) is up San Martin, N of the cathedral. There is a wide variety of shops.
There are many hardware shops and small engineering establishments.
Fishing boats dry out alongside the harbour wall (the tidal range is about 5m).
Diesel at service station on harbour wall (jerry cans required; go at high tide with the dinghy and a length of rope) or from stations elsewhere in Castro. Small open trucks, *fletes*, operate like taxis and are useful in this context.
Propane is widely used and easily obtainable however only Chilean type fittings are catered for.
Small shops (including a butcher selling lamb), fresh fish, vegetable markets on foreshore.
Laundry on the road up to Plaza de Armas.
Several hotels will make available their bathrooms for showers.
Water by container at the service station or from the *armada*. The *armada* will also allow a yacht to come up alongside their vessels at the pier to refill by using their long hose. Ask at the office for permission first and warn the captain of the ship that you will go alongside.
Handicrafts on the foreshore.
Credit cards are widely accepted and all banks have ATMs.

Communications

Through buses to Puerto Montt, Santiago (18hrs), Punta Arenas and local buses within Chiloé. Ferries serve the small islands, arriving in Castro in the morning and leaving in the afternoon.
Telephone Area code 65. Phone offices on and near the Plaza de Armas.
Internet café Años Luz on the E side of the Plaza near the top of Blanco.

2·30 Caleta Rilán
42°32'S 73°38'W
Charts BA *3749*; US *22352*; Chile *7000, 7370*

General

The water shoals quickly towards the head of the bay. This is a very quiet anchorage. Anchor near the ramp at the head of the inlet or, with total security but limited space, inside the mussel rafts at the SW end.

2·31 Caleta Poza de Chumildén
42°30'·4S 72°48'·9W
Charts BA *3749*; US *22352*; Chile *7000, 7300, 7392, 7400*

General

A snug anchorage but likely to be uncomfortable in strong northerlies especially at high tide. The inner pool to the SE of Isla la Leona is small and supports a small fishing fleet. Restricted swinging room may necessitate a stern line to the island, to one of the reefs or a stern anchor.

Approach

Approaching from the N, a red and yellow mark painted on the rocks on the E side of the entrance is visible, depending on the light, from 400m. The entrance channel runs SSW between Isla Quemada

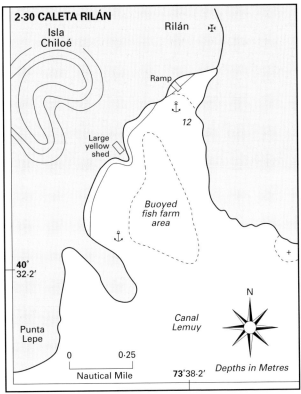

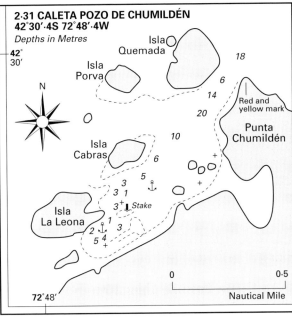

2·32 Estero Reñihué – Estero Pillán

42°34'S 72°31'W

Charts BA *1289*; US *22341, 22352*; Chile *7000, 7400*

General

Estero Pillán is a very beautiful and sheltered anchorage at the head of Estero Reñihué. The anchorage can only be entered at high water. When approaching, take care of rocks which cover at high water and which extend about 100m off the most E end of the two Islas Nieves. To stay in adequate depths (5–6m) keep within about 10m of the N shore. Once inside depths increase quickly. Anchor in about 15–18m on the N side of the lagoon with lines ashore. Vegetables may be purchased from the farm building and there are small trout in the stream. There is some salmon farming.

2·33 Caleta Linlinao

42°34'S 73°45'W

Charts BA *3749*; US *22352*; Chile *7000, 7370*

General

Located 6 miles S of Castro, Linlinao provides good shelter, but is a little open to a N wind whistling down Estero Castro. A light on the S end of Isla Linlinao aids in identification. There are several fish pens to be avoided. The best entrance route is along the S shore. The holding is good in 15m on a mud bottom.

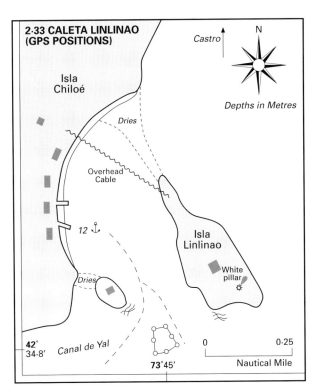

and Punta Chumildén. Keep to the middle of this channel and then pass with care about 30m from the SW end of Isla Cabras. A submerged reef (of rocks) extends N from the rock marked by a stake. Stay on the Isla Cabras and Isla la Leona side of the channel.

Anchorage

The main anchorage is tucked up under Isla la Leona as far as depth permits but beware of the reef in the SE corner of the bay. Reports state that tidal flow is too strong for comfort.

2·34 Caleta Huechun

42°36'S 73°19'W

Charts BA *3749*; US *22352*; Chile *7000, 7390, 7400*

General

This anchorage lies to the E of the long hook of land at the W end of Isla Alao.

Anchorage

Approach from the E, to avoid the shoals off the low spit. Good holding in silt, 6–12m.

To the S, there is a rather beautiful anchorage on the N side of Isla Chaulinec (42°37'S 73°18'W), in 13m close to the shore in front of a small farm and to the W of the village. There is no protection from W or N winds.

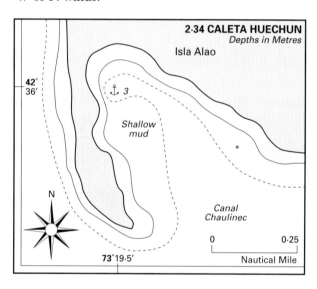

2·35 Isla Apiao – Estero Pellú

42°37'S 73°13'W

Charts BA *3749*; US *22352*; Chile *7000, 7390, 7392, 7400*

General

The anchorage in Estero Pellú on Isla Apiao is one of the most delightful and best protected in the islands off Chiloé. The entrance needs care but is straightforward if approached from the SW at half tide. The spring range is 5·5m. At half tide the two large flat rocks marking the entrance are visible. Leave the W flat-topped rock close to port and then favour the W side of the entrance channel.

Anchorage

There is plenty of room to anchor in 3-6m inside the *estero*; the deeper water is on the W side and it shoals to the N of the second narrows. The best shelter from northerlies is under the bluff of the second narrows. When leaving, the W flat rock becomes visible 1–2 hours after high water and marks the exit.

There are no shops but it is possible to buy potatoes, parsley, and other vegetables in season from Luis, who lives on a smallholding (*parcela*) on the E side of the *estero*.

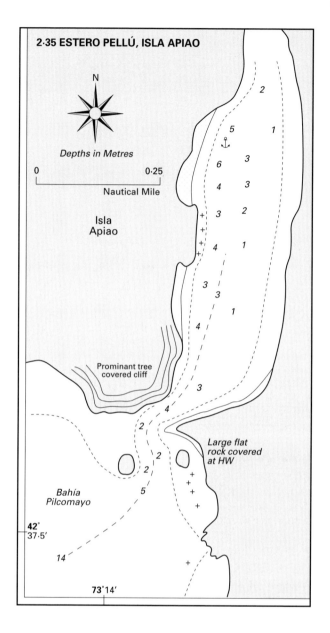

2·36 Estero Ichuac

42°37'S 73°44'W

Charts BA *3749*; US *22352*; Chile *7000, 7370, 7400*

General

On the W side of Isla Lemuy, opposite Chonchi, Ichuac (Chuac on *7370*) is open to the W but sheltered from the SW and has good shelter from the N. Anchor in about 8m at low water, with good holding in mud. This is a very pretty inlet with a small village at the head of the bay.

2·37 Puerto Chonchi

42°37'·6S 73°47'W

Charts BA *3749*; US *22352*; Chile *7000, 7370, 7372, 7400*

General

Chonchi is a very poor anchorage. It is exposed to the N and the E with an uncomfortable swell developing S of the quay. E of the quay the water deepens very quickly. The quay is very busy with

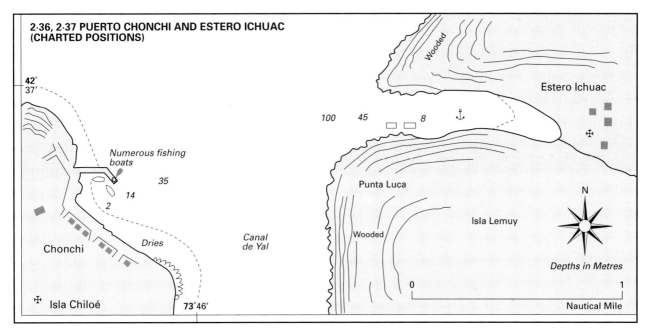

2·36, 2·37 PUERTO CHONCHI AND ESTERO ICHUAC (CHARTED POSITIONS)

fishing boats. Ask permission to go alongside a fishing boat or anchor just S of the pier in about 10m. A stop at Chonchi would be temporary to provision or make a crew change. It is better to cross Canal de Yal to Estero Ichuac.

Canal de Yal

There is an electricity cable across Canal de Yal with 28m clearance. When rounding Punta Yal, in the S part of the canal pass the low-lying Islote Yal on its E side. The canal is safe, clean and deep.

2·38 Isla Quehui – Puerto Pindo

42°37'S 73°30'W

Charts BA *3749*; US *22352*; Chile *7000, 7370, 7400*

General

This is a beautiful anchorage with soft rolling countryside around Estero Pindo. The village of Los Angeles has about 800 inhabitants, several small shops, a pretty wooden church and a pleasant bar. The narrow tracks are perfect for walking with good views of the surrounding area from the top of the island.

Approach

Approaching from the W, head for the church; the light structure (Puerto Pindo Fl.G.5s8·5m4M green GRP tower, 5·5m) is not visible at a distance. The entrance looks wide but the deep water is close to the N shore.

Anchorage

Anchor off the houses just beyond the ramp or further to the NE in 10–12m. The local boats anchor off the ramp using rope with a lot of scope and therefore swing a long way as the tide turns. The anchorage is well protected in all winds but has a modest chop in southeasterlies.

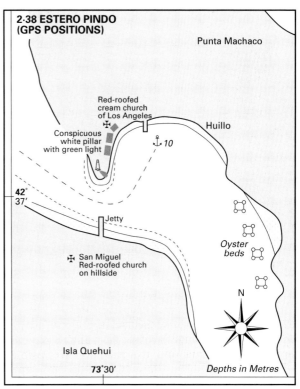

2·38 ESTERO PINDO (GPS POSITIONS)

2·39 Punta Yal

42°40'S 73°40'W

Charts BA *3749*; US *22352*; Chile *7000, 7400*

General

The anchorage is in the S-facing bay SW of Punta Yal. It is a reasonable all-weather anchorage and is a convenient place to stop when heading to or from Castro. Anchor inside the *salmonera* and mussel rafts, limited room. Pleasant walking may be found here.

59

Canal Queilén

The passage through Canal Queilén is straightforward. However where the canal narrows between Punta Yategua and Punta Vilo tidal streams run strongly and can reach 4–5 knots. The stream turns S with the ebb.

2·40 Puerto Queilén

42°54'S 73°30'W

Charts BA *3749*; US *22352*; Chile *7000, 7400, 7432*

General

Puerto Queilén is a small town with several shops, a small hotel, and hospital. Facilities include telephone, fax and post.

Approach

When approaching from the NE keep ¾M off Punta Chomio to avoid off-lying shoals. Punta Queilén has a narrow island lying off it to the SW with a tower (4m). The spit continues some distance SW of the light and is mostly covered at high water.

Anchorage

Anchor in good holding in 12m W of the town jetty, or a little further S between the two piers. There are a large number of fishing boats at anchor and it is very easy to become tangled up with them. A little exposed in W to SW winds and even in strong N winds there is a chop.

It may be possible to anchor in Estero Mechai, immediately NW of Punta Queilén. However this is crowded with fish cages.

Unless it is necessary to stop at Puerto Queilén to provision it is much better to sail an additional 5 miles W and anchor in the peaceful protection of Estero Pailad.

2·41 Estero Pailad

42°52'S 73°36'W

Charts BA *3749*; US *22352*; Chile *7000, 7400*

General

The entrance to this wooded *estero* is easy, wide and deep. A *salmonera* lies on the W side of the channel. At first the *estero* runs between wooded hills, small neat paddocks and low cliffs running by the waterside. After about 1½M the *estero* begins to open out and a pretty yellow church becomes visible on the W shore.

Anchorage

Off the church, good holding in about 8–10m. There is a good anchorage further upstream where the inlet forks into two. Further N it becomes very shallow.

On the other side of the *estero* from the church is a distinctive blue and yellow farmhouse. Next to this house is an old water-driven flourmill. This no longer works but Hector at the house will be pleased to show the visitor inside the mill (*molino de agua*).

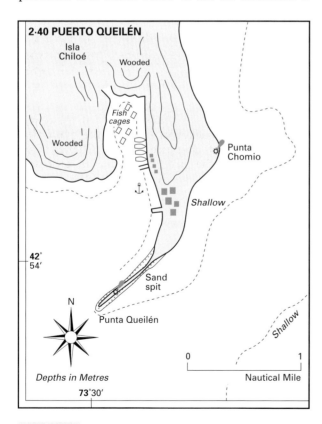

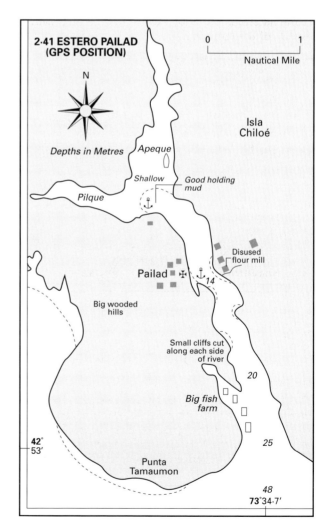

2·42 Chaitén

42°54'S 72°43'W

Charts BA *3749*; US *22352*; Chile *7000, 7400,7421*

General

Wide-open to the W and SW, it is not a good anchorage but possible for a short time in good weather if there is a particular reason to call. There are 3 flights daily to Puerto Montt. Provisions and fuel (from service stations) available in town.

2·43 Estero Huildad

43°04'S 73°31'W

Charts BA *3749*; US *22352*; Chile *7000, 7400, 7431*

General

The coast E of the entrance is shoal. The entrance has 10m, the tidal range is about 6m. The N shore has strong currents. When approaching from the N the light (Estero Huildad Fl.R.5s12·5m6M red GRP tower, 5·5m) is not visible until the yacht is fairly close to the entrance as it is hidden by high land to the NE of it.

Anchorage

Immediately inside the sandy spit and light is a very pretty spot. However it shoals rapidly and currents are strong and irregular. More secure holding, sheltered from N through S to ESE, is to be found immediately to the S of the salmon farm 5 cables due W of the entrance.

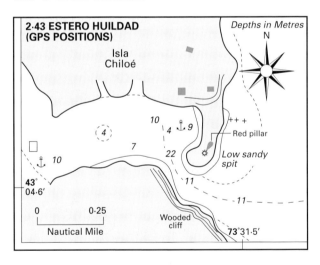

2·44 Puerto Quellón

43°08'S 73°37'W

Charts BA *3749*; US *22352*; Chile *7000, 7400, 7431*

General

Puerto Quellón is a busy fishing port with a population of 8000, which also serves cattle farms and the timber industry. It is open to the S. Shore facilities are limited (it has a restaurant or two) but it is the last convenient place to get fuel before going S.

Approach

Approach through Canal Laitec or Canal Yelcho is straightforward. However, the shortest route when approaching from or exiting to the N is via Canal Chiguao (see sketch 2·45). With justification the American chart states that 'extreme caution is to be used when navigating Canal Chiguao'. Access is on a bearing shown on the chart to enter between a sandbank (which may be shifting) to the S and rocky reef to the N. There is no buoyage to help and the demarcation between deep and shallow water is not easy to see. At springs the E-going current runs across Bajo Chiguao at up to 5 knots so it is easy to be set off course. Once inside Canal Chiguao the leading marks (which appear not to be maintained any longer and are omitted from the light list) low on the N shore, help set a course clear of the inner shallows. Going through Canal Yelcho only adds 5M to the journey and is safer.

Anchorage

With the necessity of a dinghy ride in mind, the easiest place to anchor is just E of the main pier, leaving plenty of clearance for the Chaitén ferry which berths at the pier. An alternative, protected from the S and with good holding, is 6M W at Punta Carmen, in Estero Yaldad. Anchor to the N of a derelict sawmill in 15m or in the next bay to the N. Do not anchor directly off the sawmill, as there are several dangerous wrecks that cover at HW.

Formalities

Check in on Ch 16 and visit the *Capitán del Puerto* opposite the head of the pier.

Facilities

Fuel by can from garages ashore (one fairly close W of the pier).

Water on the W pier.

Fruit and vegetable shop a short distance up the road from the *armada* office.

Some provision shops and butchers.

Market every morning at the head of the main street with range of fresh vegetables and seafood.

Banco de Estado is currently the only bank in town (2001), the ATM will not accept overseas cards.

Communications

Frequent buses and *collectivos* to Castro, Puerto Montt and further afield.

Telephone: Area Code 657. Office 22 de Mayo and Av. Pedro Montt. Internet and telephone opposite Carabineros on Ladrilleros (turn left at the market).

2·45 Bahía Huellonquén

43°10'S 73°32'W

Charts BA *1289*; US *22352*; Chile *7000, 7400, 7431*

General

An alternative anchorage to Quellón can be found in Bahía Huellonquén, on the NE corner of Isla Cailin. This is a large bay but is sufficiently enclosed to provide reasonable all-round protection.

Anchorage

It is deep so it is necessary to anchor NE of the fish farm cages, fairly close to the beach in 12–14m. Holding is questionable and the steep slope makes anchoring precarious. One boat was nearly lost here in a N gale: after dragging, loose netting from abandoned salmon pens fouled the propeller and rudder. The staff of the salmon farm will almost certainly help find a suitable anchorage if requested.

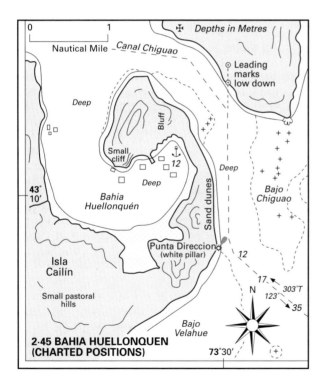

2·46 Isla Cailín, Punta Yelcho

43°12'S 73°35'W

Charts BA *1289*; US *22352*; Chile *7000, 7400, 7431*

General

Situated 5 miles S of the town of Quellón, the long sandy hook on the SW corner of Isla Cailín provides protection from S and SW winds. The anchorage can be approached from the N or from the S. Approaching from the S, keep well clear of the shallow water on the S side of Punta Yelcho.

Anchorage

The best anchorage is close in to the point, on a sandy bottom with excellent holding. On a clear day, there are spectacular views of the four peaks of Monte Yanteles on the mainland. In NW winds several other possible anchorages are available amongst the salmon pens on the E shore of Isla Laitec.

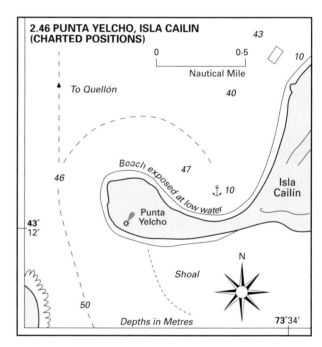

2·47 Puerto San Pedro

43°19'S 73°41'W

Charts BA *1289*; US *22352, 22360*; Chile *7000, 7400, 7431, 7432*

General

Puerto San Pedro is located at the SE tip of Isla Chiloé and makes a good stopping place before crossing the 30 open miles to Melinka.

Anchorage

There are four anchorages near the entrance of Canal San Pedro. The first is off the N shore, near the group of white buildings. The holding is good in 7–8m on a sand bottom. Take care approaching the shore as it shallows rapidly. It is exposed to S and E winds.

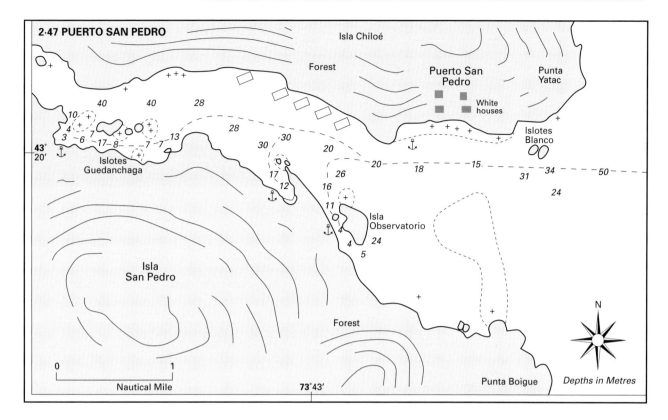

In S winds the second anchorage which is behind Isla Observatorio is preferable. Shorelines are required to hold position.

The third anchorage is behind the long finger of land, on the S side of the canal, 2M from the entrance. It is open to NW winds, with good holding in 10–15m in sand. The entrance is easy and shorelines are not necessary.

The fourth and safest anchorage, used by several yachts, is tucked into the SW corner behind Islotes Guedanchaga. This should be entered at half tide so that the rocks are exposed. Proceed slowly as the rock positions are approximate. This anchorage provides protection from the NW.

2·48 Bahía Tictoc

43°37'S 72°54'W

Charts BA *1288, 1289;* US *22352, 22360;* Chile *7000, 7400, 7422*

General

The area of Bahía Tictoc provides a first class stopping place when crossing the Golfo de Corcovado and has beautiful scenery. There are a number of anchorages, the high surrounding hills can produce squalls and it may be necessary to move around to find shelter. Watering is possible. Good fishing. Recently (Nov 2002) it has been noted that this area is frequently used by the *armada* for live firing excercises.

Approach

The approach from the SW is the most open, passing SE of Isla Redonda and the Colocla group.

Anchorages

The anchorages fall into three groups:

1. **Silva Palma** and **Puerto Tictoc** on the N shore of the outer bay. These are both fair weather anchorages.
2. **Bahía Pescadores** in the N arm of the inner bay and **Puerto Escondido** in the S arm. The very NE end of Bahía Pescadores shallows quickly but there is a deep pool on the W edge where it is possible to anchor with lines ashore. In the S arm, anchor off the settlement, or further S, in appropriate depths. A sand spit marked by stakes extends E in the S part of this arm. At Puerto Escondido the *guarda parques* for Parque Pumalin will almost certainly call you on VHF and invite you to use the heavy mooring off his home just inside the S entrance point.
3. The third possibility is to anchor among the Isla Colocla group in **Puerto Juan Yates**, the W anchorage shown is the most sheltered. If a gale is expected pull very close to shore in the W indentation to escape rachas. The access is straightforward.

   This anchorage saves a 6M journey into the inner bay. There is a penguin colony on Islote Pino. Dolphins swim in the anchorage.

   Note The Chilean chartlet *7422* shows Isla Huepan divided by a small channel from the island immediately to the west. This is incorrect, they are connected by a small isthmus.

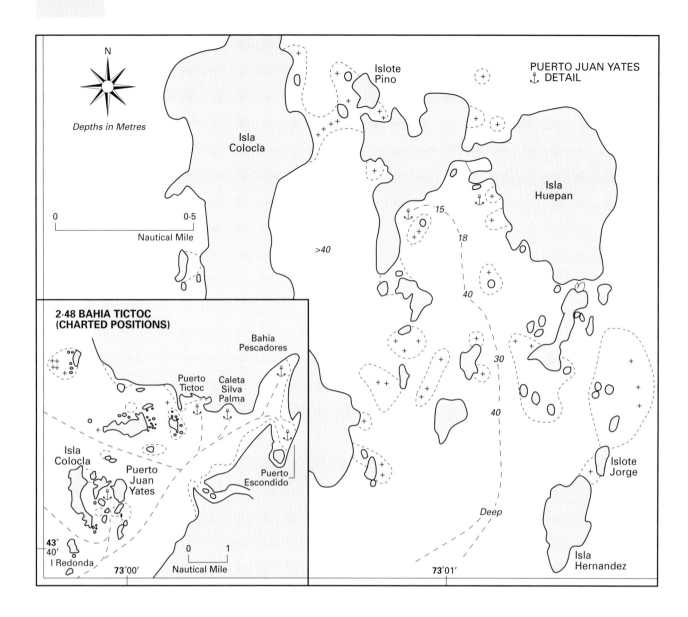

N

Depths in Metres

0   0·5

Nautical Mile

Isla
Colocla

>40

Islote
Pino

PUERTO JUAN YATES
⚓ DETAIL

Isla
Huepan

15

18

40

30

40

Deep

Islote
Jorge

Isla
Hernandez

**2·48 BAHIA TICTOC
(CHARTED POSITIONS)**

Bahia
Pescadores

Puerto
Tictoc

Caleta
Silva
Palma

Isla
Colocla

Puerto
Juan
Yates

Puerto
Escondido

**43°
40'**
I Redonda

73°00'

0   1

Nautical Mile

73°01'

3. S shore of Golfo Corcovado to Laguna San Rafael

General

The Chonos archipelago protects this area from the ocean. It is a huge lump of rock, elevated by the forces that built up the Andes, later eroded by ice and water, then submerged and its crevices flooded by the sea. The archipelago and fjords in this area make for wonderful cruising and are relatively accessible with several good options for obtaining fuel and provisions.

The entire area is too large for one chapter. Chapter 3 covers the inner waterways between Golfo Corcovado and Laguna San Rafael. For the outer part of the archipelago and the Golfo de Penas, see chapter 4. The same overall map has been used in the introduction to chapters 3 and 4 to aid those crossing from one area to the other.

Routes

Possible routes for vessels heading S (or N) through this area:

1. From the S end of Chiloé cross Golfo Corcovado directly to Puerto Melinka. Then go S along Canals Perez Norte & Sur to join Canal Moraleda E of Isla Melchor. Even in bad weather these canales are well protected and there are many good anchorages en route.

    The current flows across Canal Perez to Canal Moraleda as it floods and ebbs from the Pacific and turns N or S in them depending on the easiest route for the water to flow. On any passage the current can therefore flow in both directions. However the current strengths are generally weak and are not a problem except near Puerto Melinka. In the *canales* immediately S and E of Puerto Melinka the current flows S strongly for the last half of the flood and the first half of the ebb, and N on the last half of the ebb and the first half of the flood. At the S end of Perez Sur the flood runs strongly into the canal from Canal Moraleda but after several miles the current becomes weak.

2. From the S end of Golfo Corcovado go directly down Canal Moraleda. Or call at Añihué and then go down Canal Refugio to join up with Canal Moraleda. In calm weather this is straightforward. In poor weather the strong currents of Canal Moraleda can make conditions very unpleasant and it would be better to rejoin Canal Perez Norte via Canal Pihuel.

3. An alternative is to leave Canal Moraleda by Canal Jacaf, go E about Isla Magdalena (the route is not shown on BA Chart *1288*) coming out via Canal Puyuguapi. It is then possible either to rejoin Canal Moraleda or continue S along Canal Ferronave.

4. All routes finish up in Canal Moraleda, which runs into Canal Errázuriz. Canal Errázuriz first passes Canal Darwin and then Canal Chacabuco, which leads to Canal Pulluche and Boca Wickham.

There is exceptionally good cruising and exploration amongst the *canales* and islands to the W of the main channels mentioned, see chapter 4.

Weather

It should always be kept in mind that there will be a strong but usually short-lived SW'ly change following the passage of a front. Fronts pass quickly and one may go to sleep with NW wind and a front approaching and find the SW'ly change occurring at 4–5 in the morning. Therefore a good anchorage is sheltered from N through to SW, assuming that the presence of mountains does not alter the wind direction as it can do quite dramatically especially in Seno Aysén and around Isla Magdalena. Significant winds from the E are rare but do occur and can be strong, however they are usually well forecast.

Fuel

Fuel is always available in Chacabuco at mainland prices. It is almost certainly available in Puerto Aguirre from the fuel station on the quay at higher island prices and may be available in Raul Marin Balmaceda, Melinka and Puyuguapi.

Charts

There are no large scale US charts covering Estuario Elefantes. The small-scale chart is *22370*.

3·1 Rada de Palena

43°45'·2S 72°57'·0W

Charts BA *1288*; US *22360*; Chile *7000, 7400, 7422, 8000*

General

There are several anchorages in Estero Piti-Palena, behind Isla los Leones. After a narrow entrance, the *estero* (inlet) opens out into a bay some 4M long and almost totally shut off from the sea. Brazo Pillán runs N from the NE end of the *estero*. This is well

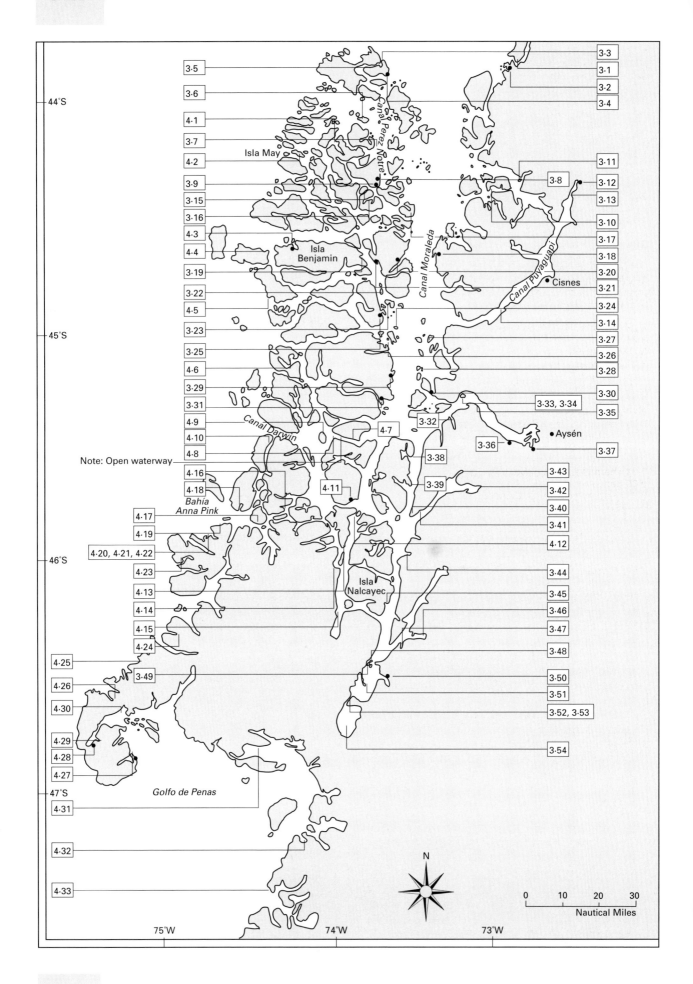

44°S

45°S

46°S

47°S

75°W   74°W   73°W

3·5
3·6
4·1
3·7
4·2
3·9
3·15
3·16
4·3
4·4
3·19
3·22
4·5
3·23
3·25
4·6
3·29
3·31
4·9
4·10
4·8
Note: Open waterway
4·16
4·18
Bahía
Anna Pink
4·17
4·19
4·20, 4·21, 4·22
4·23
4·13
4·14
4·15
4·24
4·25
3·49
4·26
4·30
4·29
4·28
4·27
4·31
4·32
4·33

Isla May

Isla
Benjamin

Canal Darwin

4·7

3·32

4·11

Isla
Nalcayec

Canal Perez Norte

Canal Moraleda

Canal Puyaguapi

• Cisnes

3·36

• Aysén

3·38

3·39

Golfo de Penas

3·3
3·1
3·2
3·4
3·11
3·8
3·12
3·13
3·10
3·17
3·18
3·20
3·21
3·24
3·14
3·27
3·26
3·28
3·30
3·33, 3·34
3·35
3·37
3·43
3·42
3·40
3·41
4·12
3·44
3·45
3·46
3·47
3·48
3·50
3·51
3·52, 3·53
3·54

N

0   10   20   30
Nautical Miles

worth a visit and has a secure anchorage at its head. When navigating within Estero Piti-Palena watch out for shallows which are considerably more extensive than shown on the charts. The mouth of Buta-Palena is inside the sandbank W of Isla los Leones and has a bar. The river Buta-Palena is navigable for about 6 miles. Minimum depth on the bar is 5m but local knowledge is essential. The Szydlowski family has a property on the riverbank and can provide guidance (call *Toninas* on Ch 22 US). It is possible to cross the bar in fairly poor weather due to shelter from the land to the N and the sand spit to the W. Anchorage off the Szydlowski property is safe but uncomfortable if

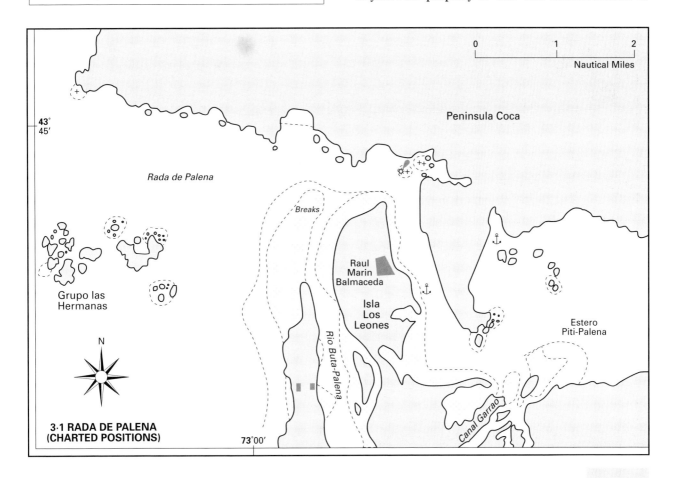

3·1 RADA DE PALENA
(CHARTED POSITIONS)

there is a fresh N wind against the river current. In settled weather this trip is highly recommended.

Approach

Tide streams around Península Coca are strong and can cause tide rips. Enter in settled weather on a rising tide to get help from the current. Swell may break on Barra, the sandbank W of Isla los Leones which extends NW and appears to be extending further each year. Rada Palena light (Fl.G.5s10m5M White and Green GRP Tower 3m, 345°-vis-097°) is opposite the entrance to Piti-Palena. Canal Garrao provides a good route by dinghy from Estero Piti-Palena into the Buta-Palena.

Anchorage

In the N–S stretch between Los Leones and the mainland, with lines ashore. Not all that good in a northerly. Anchoring is also possible off the village to the N of the pier, in the main part of the *estero* and in Brazo Pillán.

Formalities

The village, Raúl Marin Balmaceda, has an *Alcalde de Mar* run by the police *(carabineros)*.

Facilities

Some supplies in the village.

Communications

Ferry service.
Post Office, telephone. 700m airstrip (no scheduled flights in 2001).

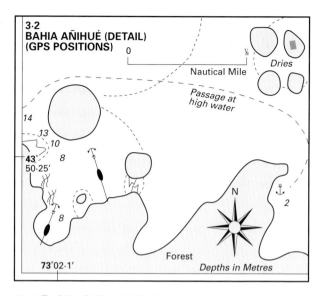

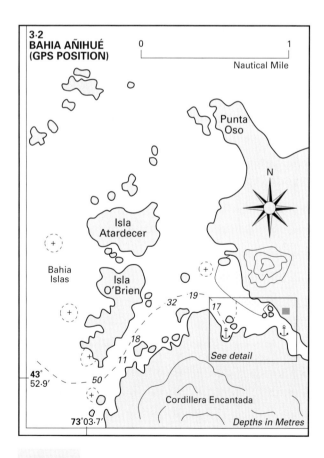

3·2 Bahía Añihué (Bahía Islas)

43°52'·3'S 73°02'·4W

Charts BA *1288*; US *22360*; Chile *7000, 7400, 8000, 8200, 8211*

General

The anchorage is first rate, protected from all winds. The charts show little detail but the access is straightforward as shown on plan 3·2. Once behind Isla O'Brien the shelter is good, even in a NW gale. The American/Chilean family of Juan Carlos, Rachel and Alan Szydlowski, who are keen to meet visiting yachts, owns this area. Juan Carlos is a lynch pin of the SSB Patagonia Cruising Net (8164kHz at 0900 local time) and has assisted in the preparation of this guide and with lobbying for visiting yachtsmen's interests in Santiago. Be assured of a warm welcome and whatever assistance it is within the family's power to give. The Szydlowski family monitor Ch 22 (US) from their houses at Añihué and near Rada de Palena *(Toninas)*. Yachts are welcome with or without VHF contact but would be missing a lot if they did not make contact.

Anchorage

A small secure bay with good holding. Use shorelines. There are other anchorages for the adventurous opposite the house further up the inlet that is navigable near high water. The inner lagoon, reached via this inlet (best to survey the route by dinghy at LW), is an outstanding spot, surrounded by mountains and wildlife with 8m mud and good holding. From the head of this lagoon, Alan Szydlowski has built a trail through the jungle to the slopes of Mt Melimoyu (2,400m).

Passage

Canal Refugio

Canal Refugio, to the S of Añihué, provides a convenient and beautiful route when heading N and S. Wind tends to be funnelled between the mountains on either side with extreme violence so

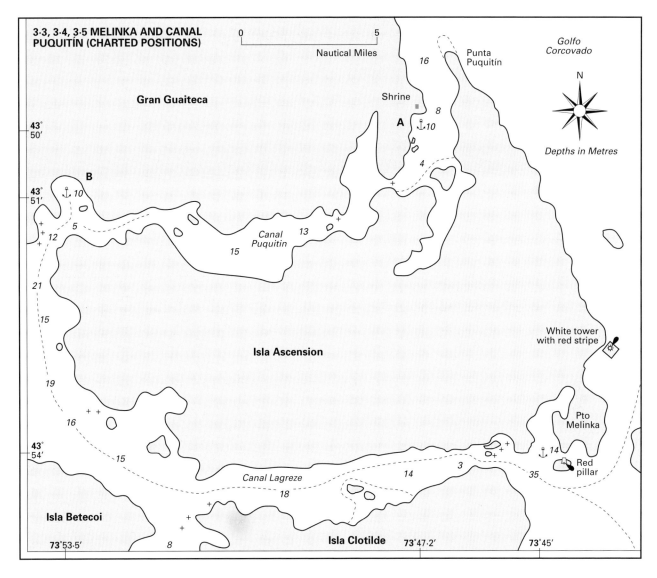

3·3, 3·4, 3·5 MELINKA AND CANAL PUQUITÍN (CHARTED POSITIONS)

the area should be treated with caution. There is an anchorage at Puerto Santo Domingo. This is not recommended other than in very settled conditions. It is wide open to the S *rachas* that blow up the canal following the passage of a front.

3·3 Guaitecas – Isla Ascension – Canal Puquitín NE Anchorage

43°50'S 73°47'W

Charts BA *1288;* US *22360;* Chile *7000, 7400, 8000, 8200, 8300*

General

Just to W of the NE extremity of Isla Ascension is a charming and safe anchorage, sheltered from all weather ('A' on sketch). Entrance is straightforward when approaching from the N. From S or E beware of the shallows that extend well off the N tip of the Isla Ascension. The best shelter is in a tiny cove on Isla Gran Guaiteca, swinging or with lines ashore, 5–6m sand. On the shore is a tiny shrine over the grave of Augustin Manado. Fishermen stop here nearly every day to pray at the shrine and write their

simple prayers for safety and success in their work in the books to be found within. This is an excellent place to await suitable weather for crossing Golfo Corcovado.

Note launches, some quite large, make the passage through Canal Puquitín. One yacht tried it and reported that it was exceedingly tricky.

3·4 Melinka

43°54'S 73°45'W

Charts BA *1289*; US *22360*; Chile *7000, 7400, 8000, 8200, 8300*

General

Puerto Melinka is located on the SE corner of Isla Ascension, at the N end of Canal Perez Norte. There is a light just to the E of the town (Roca Melinka Fl.R.6s6m3M red pillar 5m). The tides are much the same as at Tictoc.

Anchorage

The anchorage is in front of the town, 14m with good holding. It is protected from N winds, but exposed to chop from the S.

Formalities

Reported as a good place to renew a *zarpe*. Check with the *armada* office on arrival, both by radio and by visiting the office. Prior to leaving it is necessary to report the departure time.

Facilities

Emergency repairs are possible.
Water supplies may be limited in summer.
Limited shopping but including a butcher. Freshly smoked fish (*robalo*) at the tin house with a yellow second floor opposite Perfumeria Chiloé, near the fishing boat quay.

Communications

Post office and telephone in town. 900m airstrip (no scheduled flights). Weekly ferry. TV ashore until the electricity is withdrawn early in the evening.

3·5 Guaitecas – Isla Ascension – Canal Puquitín W anchorage

43°51'S 73°53'·5W

Charts BA *1289* US *22360*; Chile *7000, 7400, 8000, 8200, 8300*

Approach

This anchorage is in the waist of the Guiatecas group ('B' on sketch). Approach from the SW between Isla Betecoi and Isla Clotilde. Alternatively approach from Puerto Melinka through Canal Lagreze. The route to clear the shoal area between the N point of Isla Clotilde and Isla Ascension passes very close to the former. From this point the passage through Canal Lagreze is straightforward. Continue round the NW corner of Isla Ascension and the anchorage is in the bay to the N in 10m. A path from the small bay to the W (accessible by dinghy) leads to a beach on Bahía Low.

Note launches, some quite large, make the passage through Canal Puquitín. One yacht tried it and reported that it was exceedingly tricky.

Passage

Canal Moraleda, Canales Perez Norte and Sur

Charts BA *1288*; US *22360*; Chile *8200, 8400*

General

The more obvious route is down Canal Moraleda. However, the preferred route for yachts is down Canales Perez Norte and Perez Sur that avoid the more exposed conditions in Moraleda. Furthermore, the route is more interesting as it winds through the islands.

3·6 Isla Amita

44°05'S 73°53'W

Charts BA *1288*; US *22360*; Chile *7000, 7400, 8000, 8200, 8400*

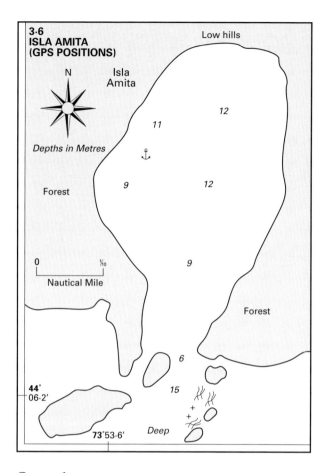

General

The large bay on the S side of Isla Amita provides protection from all directions. The entrance is narrow but well marked by the large islet and three smaller islets lying off the entrance – see plan. When approaching, the two islets shown to the E of the entrance can be difficult to distinguish from the rocky shore behind.

The bay is well sheltered, an excellent and beautiful anchorage. 10–12m, mud.

3·7 Isla Concoto

44°11'·5S 73°48'·5W

Charts BA *1288*; US *22360*; Chile *8000, 8200, 8400*

General

A small bay on the E side has been used to give overnight shelter in a strong N, 8m good holding.

3·8 Isla Valverde – Caleta Tadpole

44°20'S 73°46'W

Charts BA *1288*; US *22360*; Chile *8000, 8200, 8400*

General

Located on the SE corner of Isla Valverde, this *caleta* unofficially named Tadpole provides excellent shelter from all but E winds. Lines ashore were not necessary. Good holding in 7–15m. The small islet shown on the plan is in fact a peninsula at low water. Approach on a SW heading to avoid rocks along the S shore.

3·8
CALETA TADPOLE
(GPS POSITIONS)

Isla Valverde

Forest

Wide stream

44° 20·1'

⚓ 13

N

Forest

0   ⅛

Nautical Mile

Depths in Metres

Canal Perez Norte

73°46'

3·9 Isla Valverde – S Estero

44°20'·5S 73°52'·7W (at the S entrance to the *estero*)
Charts BA *1288*; US *22360*; Chile *8000, 8200, 8400*

General

Known locally as Estero Picalito, this is an example where the charts are misleading. Isla Valverde is in fact two islands completely separated by a N/S canal. The S *estero* has two anchorages, which make good stopping places after or before Canal Skorpio. The N bay is pretty and well sheltered. It can be reached from Estero Picalito by dinghy or from the N by a channel with minimum depth of 3·5m.

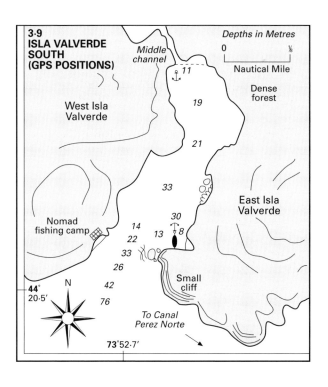

3·9
ISLA VALVERDE
SOUTH
(GPS POSITIONS)

Middle channel

Depths in Metres
0   ⅛
Nautical Mile

⚓ 11

West Isla Valverde

Dense forest

19

21

33

East Isla Valverde

Nomad fishing camp

14
22
13
33
26

30
8

Small cliff

44° 20·5'

N

42

76

To Canal Perez Norte

73°52·7'

Anchorage

Anchor with shorelines near the entrance of the *estero* to the N and E of a small island or at the head of Estero Picalito in 10m, good holding.

Diversion

Canal Jacaf and Canal Puyuguapi

This route is an alternative to passing N or S in Canal Moraleda. It has some interesting anchorages and takes the vessel into the heart of the mountains. There is a highly recommended sophisticated thermal resort at Bahía Dorada, unfortunately their prices are outside the range of many cruisers.

Because of the surrounding mountains the anchorages in this area can be subject to violent *rachas* so they should be chosen with care. Several pretty anchorages have been omitted from the guide because they are suitable for fair weather only. Amongst these is a small bay slightly W of Punta Porvenir. Puerto Cisnes provides access to the road and telecommunications systems but is not a suitable anchorage for yachts.

3·10 Isla Manuel

44°21'S 73°07'W
Charts BA *1288*; US *22360*; Chile *8000, 8200, 8500*

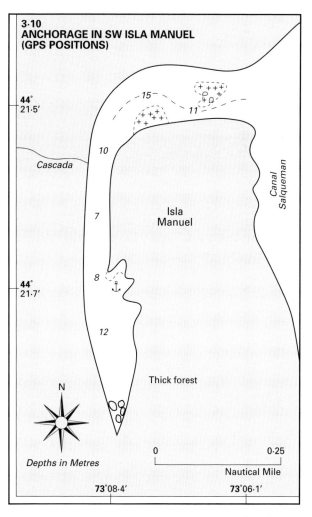

3·10
ANCHORAGE IN SW ISLA MANUEL
(GPS POSITIONS)

44° 21·5'

15
11

10

Cascada

7

Isla Manuel

Canal Salqueman

44° 21·7'

8
⚓

12

N

Thick forest

Depths in Metres

0   0·25

Nautical Mile

73°08·4'   73°06·1'

General

This lies 4 miles to the south of Canal Jacaf at the western end of Canal Salqueman. It is a safe anchorage but subject to severe *rachas*, moor well. The *rachas* appear to be most severe at the S end of the inlet.

Anchorage

A good anchorage may be found parallel to the east shore in a pronounced notch at 44°21'·7S 73°08'·4W (GPS).

3·11 Isla Gemmel

44°19'·25S 72°54'·6W

Charts BA *1288*; US *22360*; Chile *8000, 8500*

General

Isla Gemmel is on Canal Jacaf, E of Isla Manuel and of the rock in the channel, Roca Robinet, and N of Isla Suárez. The anchorage has good protection from N through W to S but is a bit difficult to find. Once in, anchoring and passing lines is done in flat water even in the heaviest winds. Anchor in 10–12m with lines ashore.

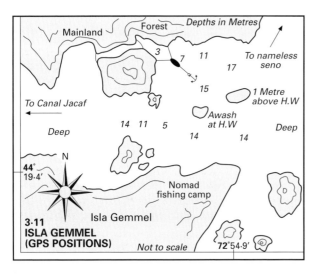

3·12 Puerto Puyuguapi (Puyuhuapi)

44°20'S 72°34'W

Charts BA *1288*; US *22360*; Chile *8000, 8500*

General

Founded in 1935 by Germans settlers, Puerto Puyuguapi at the head of Seno Ventisquero has about 1000 inhabitants and serves a cattle-farming community. Seno Ventisquero (*ventisquero* is glacier) starts at the junction of Canales Jacaf and Puyuguapi, at the NE corner of Isla Magdalena. The town has a sawmill, a famous carpet factory and a small hospital. Try the pier in the NW corner with 5m depth or anchor off. Don't stay the night – there is no protection from the SW; try Bahía Dorada (3·13). Diesel by can, fresh water and some provisions.

3·13 Bahía Dorada (Dorita)

44°24'·5S 72°38'·8W

Charts BA *1288*; US *22360*; Chile *8000, 8500*

General

Bahía Dorada is on the NW shore of Seno Ventisquero (see 3·12 Puyuguapi above). The hotel, Hotel Termas, is a five-star resort hotel with a small marina, thermal pools, floatplanes to fly to the lakes for the fishing and prices to match. The bay is easily entered from the E, N of the two islets which protect it from the *seno* but in poor visibility the bay may be difficult to spot as the point to the N is not obvious. Visiting yachts may use all the facilities (including the laundry); the atmosphere is friendly and informal. Anchoring is difficult because of the depth but a tie-off in the SW corner should be possible in most conditions. Diesel can be purchased. There is a launch service to Puyuguapi airfield, 9km S of that town.

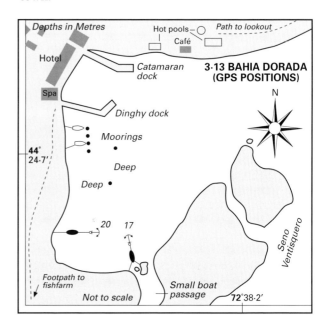

3·14 Isla Magdalena – Caleta Equinoccio

44°52'·5S 73°03'·5W

Charts BA *1288*; US *22371*; Chile *8000, 8500*

General

Caleta Equinoccio (Also known as Caleta Whim and Loca Piel), which has no official name, is an anchorage on Canal Puyuguapi, on the SE side of Isla Magdalena. It provides a snug stopping place when beating N up Canal Puyuguapi against strong head winds. It is perfectly sheltered against winds from the N with good holding. Anchor in 10m plus at the head of the bay but with minimal swinging room.

Equinoccio is the name of Tony Wescott's yacht. In the 1970s Wescott, in *Equinoccio I*, was one of the first Chileans to explore the N *canales*. This was followed by further exploration in the mid 80s when he sailed a Saga 40, *Equinoccio II*, from the UK to Chile.

Continuation

3·15 Canal Skorpios

44°23'S 73°50'W

Charts BA *1288*; US *22360*; Chile *8000, 8200, 8400*

General

The W arm of Canal Skorpios is foul but the E arm, in pleasant weather, makes a delightful short cut between Isla Jéchica and Pen-Davis and saves about 5M.

Entering the E arm from the N depths quickly fall from 50 to 18m as the canal narrows and then to 5–7m as the yacht travels over the first sand bar. Soundings on the plan were taken at half tide and the channel should be taken centrally; the bottom can be clearly seen and there is neither obvious obstruction nor kelp. The canal quickly widens and deepens and is clear.

At the S end of the E arm where it joins up with the W arm is another sand bar. This should be taken centrally; the shallow areas are visible as depths fall to 4–6m, again without kelp. Once the bar is passed the canal quickly deepens to form a wide canal.

At the S end of the main canal, depths fall to a minimum of 10–12m until the canal widens out and Islote Proa is left to starboard.

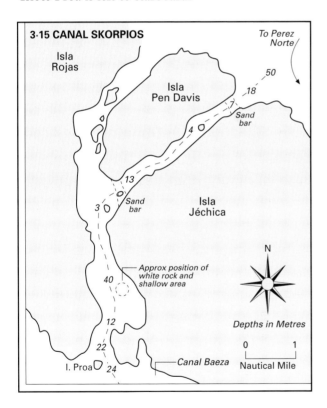

3·16 Isla Jéchica – Pozo Pedregoso

44°23'·7S 73°52'W

Charts BA *1288*; US *22360*; Chile *8000, 8200, 8400*

General

Isla Jéchica is almost bisected from the E by a forked *estero*. The entrance and the W arm of this *estero* are deep and free of dangers with clear passage to Pozo

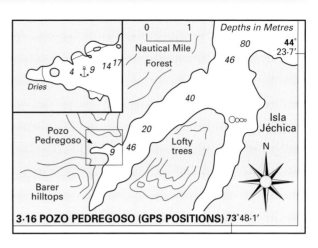

Pedregoso at the SW end of this arm. The depths progressively shelve in this *pozo* with secure anchorage in about 9m. Good all-round shelter. The S arm of the main *estero* is cluttered with islets and is foul.

3·17 Isla Filomena

44°27'S 73°35'W

Charts BA *1288*; US *22360*; Chile *8000, 8200, 8400*

General

There are five anchorages around Isla Filomena, which is privately owned: two in the NW *estero*, two along the SW coast – see plan – and another off the NE coast.

1. Anchorage 1 is likely to be uncomfortable in a SW, otherwise good shelter.
2. Enter anchorage 2 at or near low water. A very secure anchorage.
3. Enter anchorage 3 through the narrow N channel. An extremely secure and safe anchorage, up to 3 boats have used it at one time. GPS position of entrance is 44°28'·1S, 73°38'·4W.

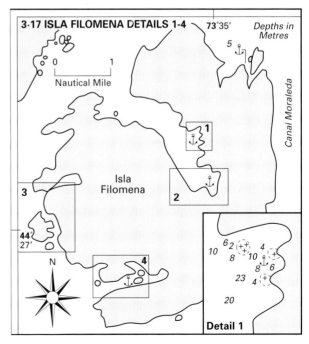

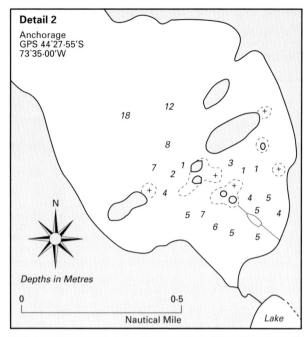

Detail 2

Anchorage
GPS 44°27·55'S
73°35·00'W

Depths in Metres

0   0·5

Nautical Mile

Lake

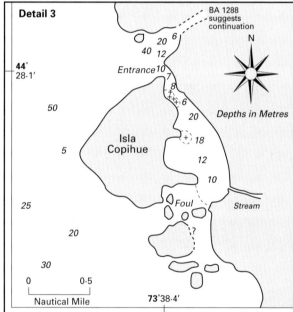

Detail 3

BA 1288
suggests
continuation

44°
28·1'

Entrance

Depths in Metres

Isla
Copihue

Foul

Stream

0   0·5

Nautical Mile

73°38·4'

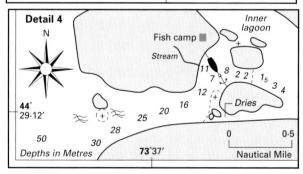

Detail 4

N

*Inner
lagoon*

Fish camp ■

Stream

Dries

44°
29·12'

Depths in Metres   73°37'

0   0·5

Nautical Mile

4. Anchorage 4: the entrance channel to the lagoon has 3·5m at high water. It is less than 20m wide. All channels into the lagoon are tidal rapids and the anchorage is subject to strong tides. Holding is poor on bare rock (a CQR did not hold but a

fisherman's anchor did) and a tie-off is greatly preferable.

5. The other small anchorage is between Isla Filomena and the small island just off the NE coast of Filomena, 44°26'S 73°34'W. Tight space and shorelines necessary but perfectly sheltered. Anchor in about 8m.

3·18 Isla Magdalena – Caleta Calquemán

44°39'S 73°27'W

Charts BA *1288*; US *22371*; Chile *8000, 8200, 8400, 8500*

General

Caleta Calquemán is on the E side of Canal Moraleda and Punta Calquemán (44°38'·5S 73°27'·4W Fl.5s9m7M White GRP tower Red band 4m) is a good landmark to locate the approach. The entrance only opens up when one is close. Hold close to the W shore once abeam of the N end of the island on the E side of the entrance; there is a reef extending N from this island. Anchorage is in the NW corner of the *caleta*, in 9–12m with little swinging room (and it may be crowded with fishermen).

It is possible to leave by an inside passage. Steer towards the 'mainland' (which is in fact Isla Magdalena) keeping well N of the reef described above. Once past this island steer somewhat S of E towards the mainland. As you near the mainland a channel opens up to the SW back into Canal Moraleda. Keep mid-channel.

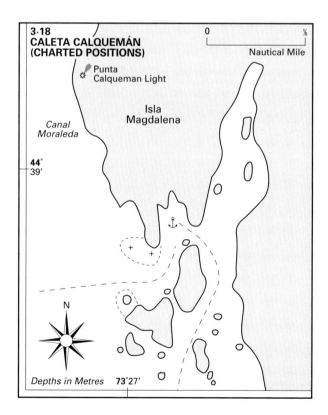

3·18
CALETA CALQUEMÁN
(CHARTED POSITIONS)

0   ⅙

Nautical Mile

Punta
Calqueman Light

Isla
Magdalena

*Canal
Moraleda*

44°
39'

N

Depths in Metres   73°27'

3·19 Isla Benjamin – Estero Arboles Espectrales

44°39'S 73°52'W

Charts BA *1288*; US *22371*; Chile *8000, 8200, 8400*

General

Estero Arboles Espectrales is located on the E side of Isla Benjamin, which is on the W side of Canal Perez Sur. It provides shelter from all except E winds. It is subject to *rachas*, but the holding is

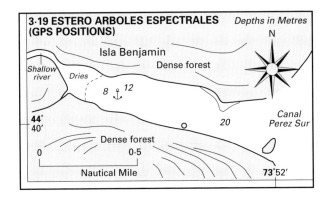

excellent in 6m with a mud bottom. There is a stream at the head of the *caleta* for fresh water. At low water there is a delightful walk for a considerable distance along this stream.

3·20 Isla Cuptana – Puerto Cuptana

44°40'S 73°38'W

Charts BA *1288*; US *22371*; Chile *8000, 8200, 8400, 8412*

General

Tuck in between the main island and the small islets in about 12m. Enclosed, sheltered and good holding. Fisherman's hut on the shore.

3·21 Caleta Ricardo

44°41'·5S 73°46'·5W

Charts BA *1288*; US *22371*; Chile *8000, 8200, 8400*

General

Located on the SW side of Isla Cuptana, 3M E of Punta Nicolas on Isla Benjamin, this unnamed anchorage provides protection from all except S and SE winds. Stay in the centre when entering. The anchorage is in 7m with good holding. The depth shoals quickly at the head near the streams. A good place to obtain fresh water.

3·22 Isla Florencia – Puerto Bueno

44°49'·3S 73°45'·25W

Charts BA *1288*; US *22371*; Chile *8000, 8200, 8400*

General

Puerto Bueno is a perfectly sheltered anchorage tucked into the SE corner of Isla Florencia. Approach from the N or S along Canal Transito (this is deep and clear) or by rounding the N side of Isla Canal from the W and passing S of Islas

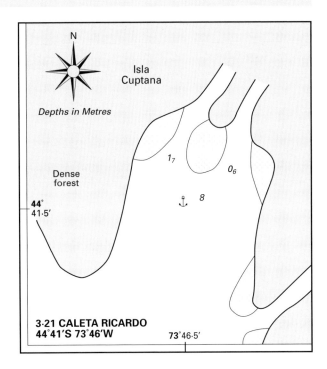

Mauricio and Rameses II. This is also clear and deep although the NW corner of Isla Canal should be given a wide berth.

Approach

Approach the anchorage as shown on the sketch chart. The water remains deep until well into the tiny bay. Although there are rocks and kelp patches, access is straightforward. The anchorage has little swinging room and it is necessary to take a stern line ashore.

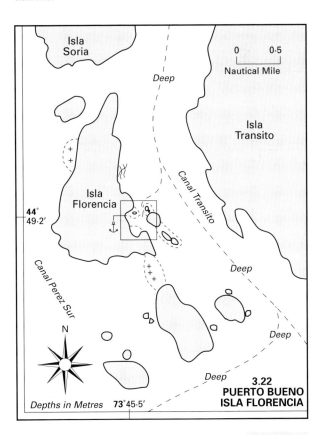

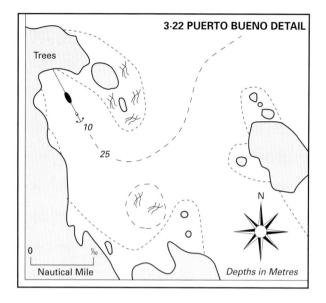

3·22 PUERTO BUENO DETAIL

Trees

10

25

N

0   1/10
Nautical Mile   Depths in Metres

3·23 Isla Canal – Estero Sur

44°52'S 73°42'W

Charts BA *1288*; US *22371*; Chile *8000, 8200, 8400*

General

When entering or exiting Canal Perez Sur at its junction with Canal Moraleda, Estero Sur (it has no official name) on Isla Canal makes an easy and secure stopover. It is well protected from all but S winds and has good holding. A very peaceful place when the wind is blowing outside.

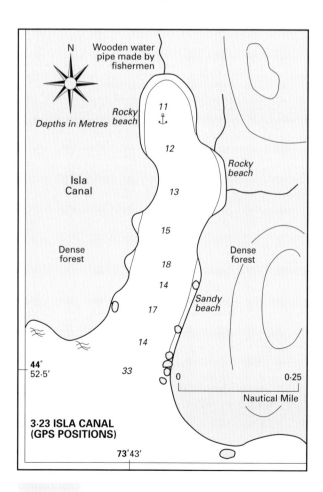

N   Wooden water
            pipe made by
            fishermen

Rocky   11
beach
Depths in Metres

12

Rocky
beach

Isla
Canal   13

15

Dense   18
forest   Dense
                                forest
            14

            17   Sandy
                     beach

            14

44°
52·5'   33   0   0.25
                                     Nautical Mile

3·23 ISLA CANAL
(GPS POSITIONS)

73°43'

If approaching from the S, keep midway between the small island 0·9M to the S and Isla Canal. This small island has a light on its N side (Islote Cervantes Fl.5s6m6M White GRP tower with Red band 3·3m). The entrance is simple and the *estero* is clean. Anchor in about 10m at the head of the *estero*. There is quite a lot of kelp and weed on the bottom although the anchorage is clear of rocks.

3·24 Isla Galverino

44°54'S 73°41'W

Charts BA *1288*; US *22371*; Chile *8000, 8160, 8200*

General

On the E side of the island, the anchorage is well sheltered by tall trees from all winds except from the E. Anchor in about 4m – there is only 2m of water about 60m from the shore. The rocks at the entrance are covered at springs.

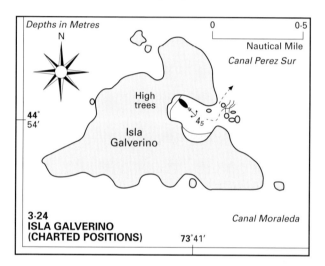

Depths in Metres   0   0.5
N   Nautical Mile
                         Canal Perez Sur

                   High
                   trees

44°   4·5
54'
                   Isla
                   Galverino

3·24   Canal Moraleda
ISLA GALVERINO
(CHARTED POSITIONS)   73°41'

3·25 Isla Teresa – Puerto Lampazo

44°54'·3S 73°46'·0W

Charts BA *1288*; US *22371*; Chile *8000, 8160, 8200*

General

At the SE end of Isla Teresa, the inner part of this *caleta* has silted up to about 1m. However, craft drawing less than 3m might close up to the N shore and obtain shelter from the trees. Anchoring out in 10–15m has good holding but very reduced shelter from the N.

3·26 Isla Tangbac – Puerto Americano

45°02'S 73°37'·5W

Charts BA *1288*; US *22371*; Chile *8000, 8160, 8200, 8621*

General

In the *caleta* between Islas Dar and Tangbac there are two connected anchorages. The outer is open to the SW and has 18m with a rocky bottom. This would only be satisfactory in calm and settled conditions.

Access to the inner bay, La Darsena ('the inner harbour'), is straightforward using the Chilean chart

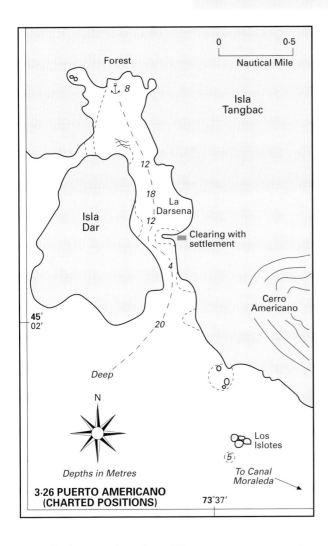

3·26 PUERTO AMERICANO
(CHARTED POSITIONS)

General

This *caleta*, unnamed on the chart, is located on the SE corner of Isla Orestes. There is not sufficient room to swing to an anchor, so a line ashore on the S side is required. It is also reported to be poor holding. The anchorage is very secluded, quiet and well protected, with depths of 6–9m.

3·28 Isla Las Huichas – Puerto Aguirre

45°09'S 73°31'W

Charts BA *1288*; US *22371*; Chile *8000, 8200, 8620, 8621*

General

Puerto Aguirre is a small, pretty, fishing village at the S end of Canal Ferronave. It is an official *armada* post and a yacht calling here must report by radio and personally at the *armada* office. This office will check the *zarpe* and should be advised of the planned time of departure. Sadly, a dinghy was subject to petty vandalism here.

Anchorage

If there is space and permission is asked from the *armada* it is possible to lie alongside the wall for several hours. No charge is made for this. This is particularly useful if picking up fuel.

It is possible to anchor in front of the *armada* building in 12m. However space is tight and there are a number of buoys causing congestion in this tiny bay. There are two better-protected anchorages which are a short dinghy trip, or by foot from Puerto Aguirre. The first, Caleta Poza is just to the N of the village and the other, Estero Copa, is a long narrow inlet about ¾ mile to the N. Both have good

or referring to the plan. The pass appears to be shoaling with about 3m near low water. However at half-tide or higher there is adequate depth and the pass is clear if the path shown is followed. La Darsena is very sheltered and has good holding in mud and sand at the head of the bay. There is a fisherman's camp with two small houses.

3·27 Isla Orestes – Caleta Olea

45°02'S 73°27'W

Charts BA *1288*; US *22371*; Chile *8000, 8200, 8620*

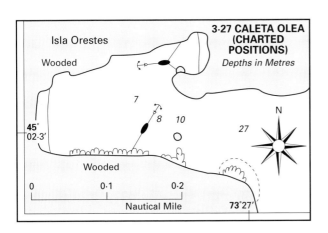

3·27 CALETA OLEA
(CHARTED POSITIONS)
Depths in Metres

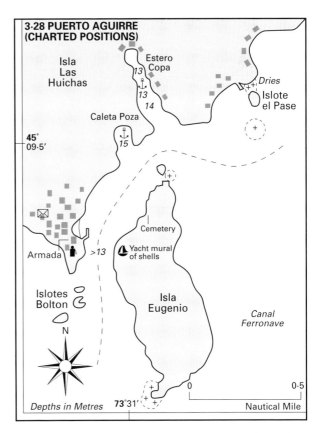

3·28 PUERTO AGUIRRE
(CHARTED POSITIONS)

CHILE

holding. However in strong N winds an uncomfortable swell enters Caleta Poza and Estero Copa is more comfortable.

Facilities

Emergency repairs can be made of a basic kind. There is a hardware store (*ferretería*) and a mechanical workshop (*taller*).
Diesel is available by can or alongside if a space can be found.
Basic provisions can be purchased and there is a surprisingly good fruit shop that is well stocked after the weekly supply ship has called. Prices are reasonable.
There are bars and some restaurants.

Communications

A post office and a Chilexpress office. Small air-strip (mail is handled once a week by air).

3·29 Isla Melchor – Unnamed *estero* and *caleta*

45°11'S 73°42'W

Charts BA *1288*; US *22371*; Chile *8000, 8200, 8600, 8620*

General

A small *estero* that runs E–W on the E coast of Isla Melchor (about 2M south of an inlet named Puerto Atracadero on chart *8200* – there appears to be confusion about names. Anchor at the entrance to the *caleta* on the N side of the *estero* or in the bay just to the W where there are some houses. Holding in sand and pebbles. From the NW of the inner bay there is a passage through to a further bay, accessible by dinghy. In this bay is the home of Carlos Nidal who would welcome a visit.

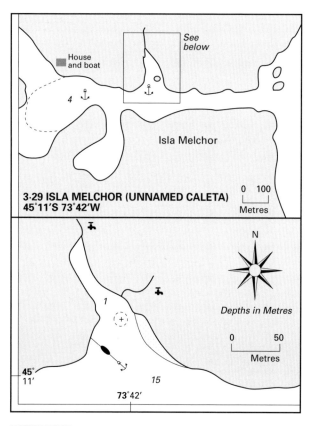

3·30 Península Elisa – Puerto Rosita

45°14'S 73°30'W

Charts BA *1288*; US *22371*; Chile *8000, 8200, 8600, 8620*

General

Puerto Rosita lies 5M S of Puerto Aguirre and is a much more secure and peaceful anchorage than Puerto Aguirre. Anchor in the NE bay where the quality of holding is variable or in the main bay with good holding in about 10–12m. The main bay shelves up gently to its head. There is an excellent stream to replenish water, shown on the plan.

If heading S and W from Rosita beware of the channel between Isla Costa and Punta Alberto on Isla Chaculay which is shoal with minimum depths of 2–3m.

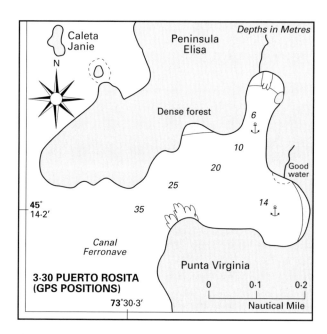

3·31 Isla Melchor – Caleta Sepulcro

45°17'S 73°44'W

Charts BA *1288*; US *22371*; Chile *8000, 8200, 8600, 8620, 8621, 8630*

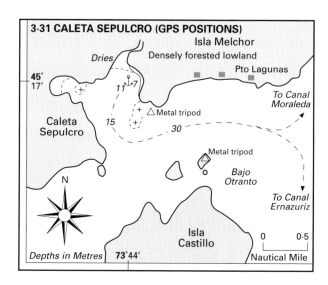

General

On the SE corner of Melchor, inside a big ship anchorage, Puerto Lagunas, and NW of Islas Castillo and Tozzoni. There is a ledge with kelp off Punta Leuquén on the NE side of the entrance. Anchor in about 8m at the head of the NE bay. Excellent holding in sand. Fishermen will sell freshly caught crab (*jaiba*).

Diversion

Seno Aysén

General

Seno Aysén is about 15M long and has its own microclimate, particularly E of Caleta Gato. It is noted for its whirlwinds (*remolinos*) and williwaws (*rachas*). There are several anchorages and two thermal springs. It is easy to be stuck in Chacabuco, the main seaport and ferry terminal for the Aysén Region, waiting for fair weather. Aysén, 15km further up the just navigable river (2·5m depths), may be reached with local knowledge. Annual rainfall is up to three metres. Many yachts have used Chacabuco as a stop for provisioning and visa renewal (via Coihaique).

3·32 Seno Aysén – Estero Sangra

45°21'S 73°19'·5W
Charts BA *1288*; US *22371*; Chile *8000, 8600, 8610, 8620*

General

This long estuary 1 mile SE of Isla Colorada has no name on the Chilean chart, but is in fact called Estero Sangra. It provides wonderful shelter in most attractive surroundings.

Anchorage

There are many possible anchorage spots in the estuary, according to wind conditions. Beware of lines to the shore from the salmon cages. The anchorage shown in the sketch plan detail is completely landlocked and well protected. It is difficult to see from the approach as it is very narrow. Favour the E entrance around the islet, keeping mid channel, and the E side within the pool, but not too close to the shore. In 2001 this anchorage was reported to be blocked off by a rope from shore to shore, this may not be permanent.

3·33 Seno Aysén – Islas Cinco Hermanos

45°15'·5S 73°16'W
Charts BA *1288*; US *22371*; Chile *8000, 8600, 8610*

General

This pretty anchorage lies at the N end of the most W island in the group. The approach is straightforward from the W passing mid-way between the main island and the small islet to its N. Anchor in 4m in sand with good holding. It is a fair weather anchorage, open to the NW. There may be others within the group. If the wind shifts NW anchor off Puerto Perez or go to Caleta Gato.

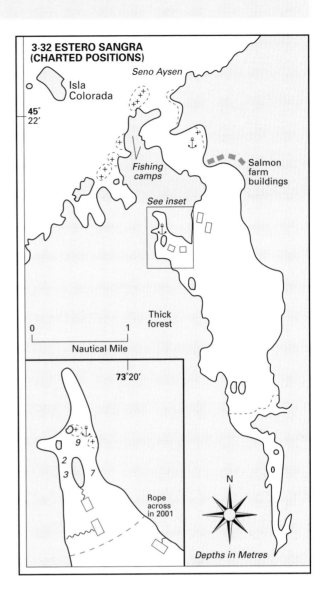

3·34 Thermal springs of Seno Aysén

There are two *termas* (hot springs) that can be visited in good weather.

1. **Terma E of Puerto Perez**

   This *terma* lies NE of Las Islas Cinco Hermanos in GPS position 45°14'·6S 73°12'W. When approaching the area a huge, quarry-like landfall marks the approximate location. A *salmonera* is now moored in the best position but there are several other *termas* in the immediate vicinity that are worth a visit. The hot springs emerge at sea level and warm the sea in the immediate vicinity. When close, the final location of the *termas* can be seen by steam rising from the sea. There are no hot inland pools. Anchor very close to the shore in 13m and take a shoreline.

2. **Terma Chiconal, Punta Tortuga**

   E of Punta Tortuga, near a small jetty in the NW corner of the bay, lies a large salmon farm with several buildings. The *termas* are several hundred metres behind these buildings. The *termas* are private and belong to Pesca Chile. Yachts have visited after obtaining advance permission (at least 24 hours notice is required as the pools have to be filled). This should be done at the main office in Chacabuco of Pesca Chile. ☎ (67) 351121. Anchoring is difficult and very near the shore adjacent to the pier in about 14m. The bottom shelves very steeply. Take a stern line to the end of the pier. Yachts may be invited to tie up to a moored salmon pen. The staff at the *salmonera* will point out the route to the *termas*, which lies along a raised wooden boardwalk. This wanders through pretty alpine meadows until 5 small pools are found in ferny dells in the forest. The water in each pool is at a different regulated temperature. It is well worth the effort of reaching these *termas* as they are exquisite.

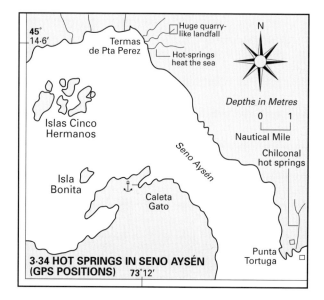

3·34 HOT SPRINGS IN SENO AYSÉN (GPS POSITIONS)

3·35 Seno Aysén – Caleta Gato

45°18'S 73°12'W

Charts BA *1288*; US *22371*; Chile *8000, 8600, 8610*

General

This beautiful anchorage is on the S side of Seno Aysén just E of Punta Angosta. It is an excellent stopping place *en route* to Chacabuco. Anchor in the centre off the beach in about 4m, good holding in mud. Either swing or take shorelines. Do not go too close to the beach as it shoals rapidly. Good water can be taken from the stream in the SE corner at the head of the bay. The *caleta* is best shown on BA chart *1288*. Bad *rachas* have been experienced here but the anchorage has served many yachts well when conditions are bad in the main channel.

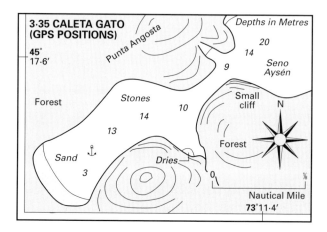

3·35 CALETA GATO (GPS POSITIONS)

3·36 Seno Aysén – Punta Camello

45°27'S 72°59'·5W

Charts BA *1288*; US *22371*; Chile *8000, 8600, 8610*

General

This anchorage underneath Punta Camello, on the S side of Aysén, provides good protection from the W but is subject to *rachas*. The holding is good in 10m on sand at the head of the bay. Beware of the rock in the centre of the entrance. Caleta Dagny, on the W side of Punta Camello, may provide better shelter. The safe position is on a private buoy belonging to Admiral (ret) Jorge Sepulveda. Permission should be sought on Ch 16 from the caretaker or the Sepulvedas (who speak Spanish, English and Norwegian). It is possible to anchor inshore of the mooring buoy.

3·37 Seno Aysén – Puerto Chacabuco

45°28'S 72°49'W

Charts BA *1288*; US *22371*; Chile *8000, 8600, 8610, 8611*

Tides
HW −0244hrs on Bahía Orange. To enter Ensenada Baja at half tide there was a minimum clearance of 3m from sea surface.

General

Bahía Chacabuco is a working port. The main bay is exposed to the winds, which are frequently very strong and gust from all directions. It can be very wet. Ensenada Baja, behind Península Fontaine, has

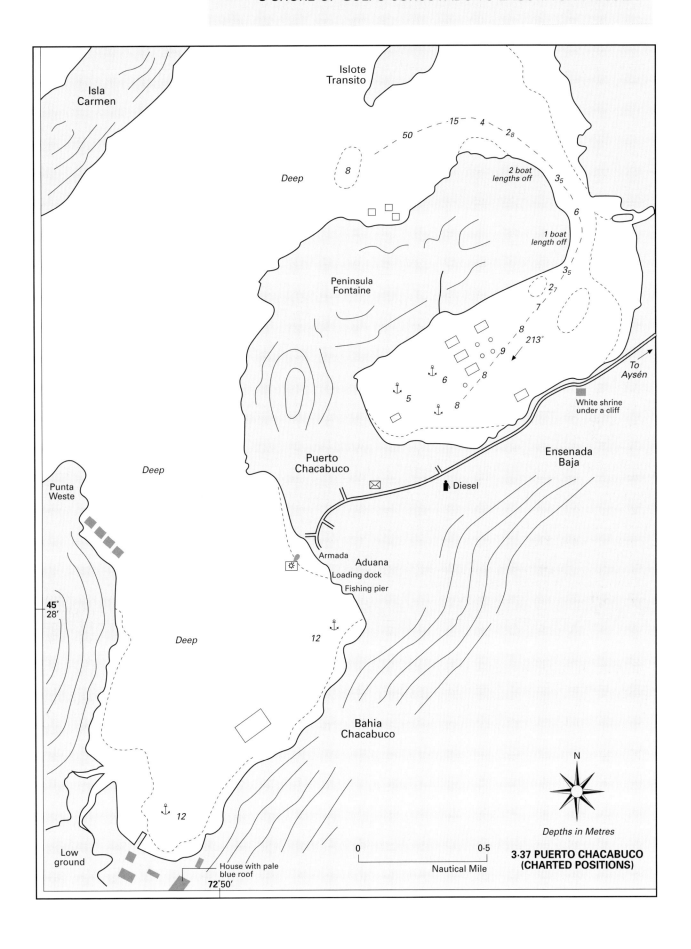

Isla
Carmen

Islote
Transito

50   15   4
                2₈
Deep

8

2 boat
lengths off   3₅

6

1 boat
length off

Peninsula
Fontaine   3₅

2₇

7

8

9   213°

6   To
                    Aysén

5   8

8

White shrine
under a cliff

Puerto
Chacabuco   ✉   ⬛ Diesel   Ensenada
                                            Baja

Deep

Punta
Weste

Armada   Aduana
          Loading dock
          Fishing pier

45°
28'

⚓

Deep   12

Bahia
Chacabuco

N

⚓ 12

Depths in Metres

Low
ground

0   0·5

House with pale
blue roof   Nautical Mile   **3·37 PUERTO CHACABUCO
                                        (CHARTED POSITIONS)**

72°50'

better protection but even there the gusts are fierce. It is possible to be trapped inside by the weather for several days. Apart from that hazard, Chacabuco is a good place for a crew change via the airfield at Balmaceda (Coihaique) which is reached by minibus. The town of Aysén is nearby and has a fair run of shops, banks etc. Further afield, Coihaique provides excellent shopping. The boat can be left here for a trip via Coihaique to Chile Chico and thence to Los Antiguos in Argentina (to renew visas). The inland country is beautiful and an incredible contrast to the coast. In 2001 several crews had problems with the international police at the border crossings of Balmaceda and Coihaique Alto. The police wished to impose a minimum time outside the country before re-entry and seemed to regard frequent border crossing with suspicion. No similar difficulties have been reported to the editor at any other location in Chile.

Approach

The approach is straightforward, passing S of Isla Carmen.

Anchorages

Ensenada Baja is secure but windy and has very good holding indeed (tested by many different yachts in all conditions). Detailed sailing directions, to be read in conjunction with the plan, are as follows. Enter or leave above half tide: Approach mid-channel between Isla Transito and Península Fontaine. As the entrance opens up, bear round to starboard and head for a position about two boat lengths off the Fontaine shore. Follow this shoreline round, closing to about one boat length off at the E end of Fontaine. Depths will drop to 2–3m but keep in to the Fontaine shore to avoid the drying patch off the mainland shore. When a course of about 213° can be made to the SW end of the harbour, follow it and anchor beyond the salmon pens in 4–7m. The surrounding scenery is spectacular but the fish-processing plants in Chacabuco can be smelly when the wind blows from them.

In Bahía Chacabuco itself, yachts are allowed alongside the jetty subject to shipping movements. This is useful for a quick stop but it is very expensive. It is probably better to go alongside the fishing pier. This is very busy with boats coming and going but a yacht will be allowed to lie temporarily alongside the fishing boats on the outside wall of the fishing jetty. Report to the small office there. This is useful for a crew change or to take on a water hose. The pier master may make a small charge for this.

There are two possibilities for anchoring in the bay. The first, in the E corner near the *armada* and fishing pier, with poor holding and strong *rachas* is only useful for a short stop. The second is in the S corner of the bay in front of a collection of agricultural buildings and a large farmhouse with a pale blue roof. Anchor in 10–12m of water, 100–150m N of a small jetty. It would be wise to use 2 anchors in tandem, but the holding is good in silt.

Large commercial catamarans anchor in this area between trips to Laguna San Rafael.

It is possible to reach Aysén by yacht with local advice.

Formalities

Check with the *Capitanía del Puerto*. It is necessary to report to the *armada* by calling Chacabuco radio and by visiting the office. A new *zarpe* will be issued on departure. Should a visitor's visa be nearing its expiry date, it can be renewed in Puerto Aysén or by a trip across the border.

Facilities

Diesel is available by can at Ensenada Baja.
Water on the piers in Chacabuco but by can at Ensenada Baja.
Provisions available in Aysén, much better in Coihaique.
Banco de Crédito, Av. Prat, or Banco de; Chile (both in Aysén), for automatic teller machines.
Laundry (expensive) at Oska, Sgto. Aldea 1221

Communications

Buses every 20 minutes to Aysén and more than 6 times a day from Aysén to Coihaique (67km), whence buses to the rest of Chile and to Argentina.
Airports at Aysén and Balmaceda, the later being served by frequent connections to Puerto Montt and Santiago. Navimag ferry services to Puerto Montt.
Telephone: Area code 67; several *centros de llamados*.
Excellent internet facility on the Plaza de Armas.

Continuation

3·38 Isla Traiguén – Caleta Christiane

45°31'S 73°35'W
Charts BA *1288*; US *22371*; Chile *8000, 8600*

General

Caleta Christiane is the N-most indentation on the E side of Isla Traiguén with good shelter from N and W. Anchor in about 13m, mud and sand. Fishermen lie parallel to the shore with lines out to the S shore, right at the head of the bay, and an anchor to hold the boat offshore.

3·39 Isla Traiguén – Estero Colonia Grande

45°38'·1S 73°35'·8W
Charts BA *1288*; Chile *8000, 8600*

General

This large *estero* is not named on the charts, but is called Estero Colonia Grande by the fishermen from Puerto Chacabuco. It lies a third of the way up Canal Costa and is a good place to shelter in strong N winds as well as being peaceful and beautiful. The approach is clear of dangers and by passing close to the W of the small island on the plan, the rock (that covers) is easily avoided.

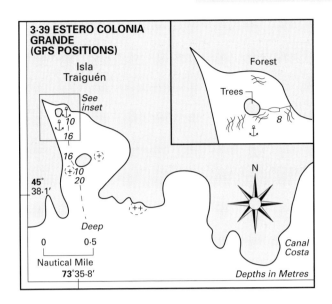

3·39 ESTERO COLONIA GRANDE (GPS POSITIONS)

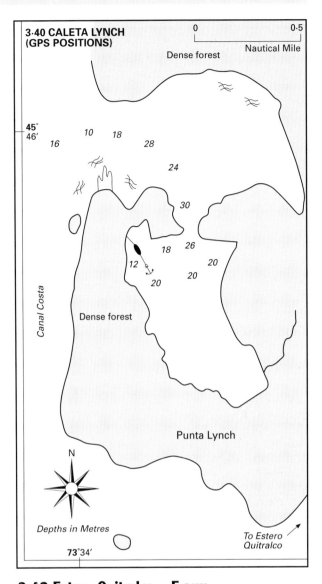

3·40 CALETA LYNCH (GPS POSITIONS)

3·40 Canal Costa – Caleta Lynch

45°46'·7S 73°34'W

Charts BA *1288*; US *22371*; Chile *8000, 8600*

General

Caleta Lynch, situated just N of Punta Lynch, is an outstanding anchorage, the best choice along Canal Costa. Enter just N of the centre line to the first bay. Entry is simple and deep but the depths become shallower in the S part of the entrance. The outer entrance should be entered mid-channel to avoid kelp on the S side. Once inside the outer bay there is immediate shelter from winds blowing strongly in Canal Costa. Hold to the starboard (W) shore on the way in to the inner pool as there is a rock off the E side of the inner entrance. Anchor in the NW corner of the inner pool where there is perfect shelter for several yachts.

Canal Costa

At the S end of Canal Costa there is an uncharted rock 100m WNW of the islet NE of Isla Raimapu. On the E side of Isla Raimapu just N of Isla Raimapu (Fl.5s9m7M White GRP tower with Red band 4m) there are sea lion and red-legged shag colonies.

Diversion
Estero Quitralco

3·41 Estero Quitralco – Caleta Descanso

45°46'S 73°31'W

Charts BA *1288*; US *22371*; Chile *8000, 8600*

General

This bay, which lies 2 miles NE of Punta Lynch, in Estero Quitralco, provides perfect shelter from strong N winds. Access is straightforward. Good holding in 6m.

3·42 Estero Quitralco – E arm

45°35'·5S 73°15'·2W

Charts BA *1288*; US *22371*; Chile *8000, 8600*

General

Estero Quitralco is a huge estuary visited regularly by the cruise ships, *Skorpios 1, 2* and *3*, which sail from Puerto Montt to Laguna San Rafael. The ships stop at the *termas* on the N shore of the main, E, arm of the *estero*. Between ship visits, especially in winter when there is no tourist activity, the caretaker may make visiting yachts welcome and give permission to use the *termas*.

Anchorage

Permission may be obtained for temporary mooring to the dock or buoys (do not obstruct them if a ship is expected). Secure mooring to shore on the peninsula to the south as shown in the sketch plan.

3·43 Estero Quitralco – N Arm

45°35'·5S 73°15'·2W (GPS*)

Charts BA *1288*; US *22371*; Chile *8000, 8600*

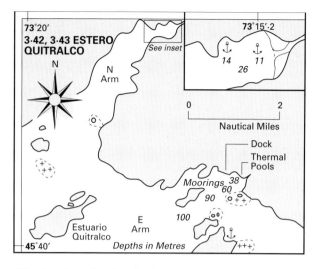

The land at the head of the N arm, extending for many kilometres, is owned by the Wescott family, based in Santiago. Tony Wescott and his brother, Michael have sailed the *canales* for years. Contact Tony Wescott via the Valdivia Yacht Club for permission to visit the ranch.

From the anchorage proceed by dinghy at half tide, or higher, up the River Maullín. The countryside opens out into a beautiful level valley surrounded by huge mountains. After about a mile the buildings of the ranch are visible. You will be made welcome. Towing a spinner while travelling up the river will almost certainly catch a large trout or salmon.

Anchorage

Anchor at the head of the arm. The bay is very deep (25m) but shoals very rapidly, almost vertically, where the River Maullín enters the bay. The best anchorage is probably tied off fore and aft in the small bay in the NW corner.

Continuation

3·44 Estuario Elefantes – Puerto Bonito

45°56'·35S 73°34'·25W
Charts BA *1288*; Chile *8000, 8600*

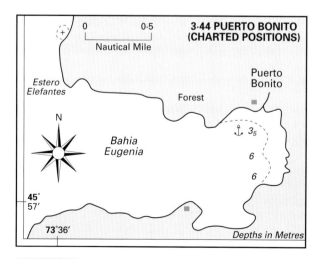

General

At the N end of Elefantes and on the E side, it is well sheltered despite its open appearance. There is protection from N and W winds in the N arm of the bay. The bottom is even and mud. There is a sawmill ashore.

3·45 Isla Nalcayec – Estero Odger

46°09'S 73°43'·5W 46°08'·81S 73°42'·79W (GPS)
Charts BA *1288*; Chile *8000, 8900*

General

Estero Odger is a significant indent on the E side of Isla Nalcayec and is named on Chile *8900*. Several boats have reported this location to be peaceful and secure when the weather outside is atrocious. Anchor at the head of the bay in as shallow water as is suitable, good holding (and an interesting dinghy trip beyond). Along the SW shore, in 8m with lines

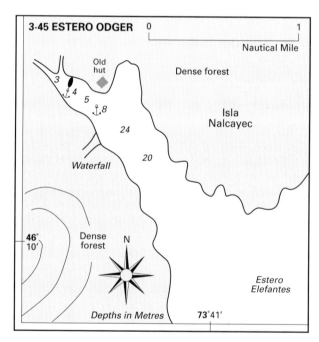

to the trees, it is possible to collect water from the falls. There are deep coves inside the entrance on the NE shore where it is possible to lie up whilst waiting for the tide in Elefantes.

3·46 Estero Cupquelan – Bahía Exploradores

46°17'·7S 73°31'·5W
Charts BA *1288*; Chile *8000, 8900*

General

Bahía Exploradores is the second, N, bay on the E side of Estero Cupquelan (Francisco on BA chart *1288*). One of the reasons for anchoring here is to explore the 20M Río Exploradores by dinghy and to catch salmon. However, in the anchorage behind the spit (9m) there is a current which may make the ship lie stern to the wind though otherwise it is described as a good, sheltered, anchorage.

3·47 Estero Cupquelan – Caleta Primera

46°19'·5S 73°36'W
Charts BA *1288*; Chile *8000, 8900*

General

Caleta Primera is the first bay on the E shore of Estero Cupquelan (Francisco on BA chart *1288*). The entrance is easy, deep and clean. Even in strong N winds it is possible to tuck up into the E corner near a prominent stream. In this position the yacht is protected from any swell entering the bay. Holding is excellent in mud but a shoreline should be taken to protect the yacht from swinging in case the wind shifts to the S. Buoy the anchor as there are submerged trees.

This is a spectacular anchorage with vertical waterfalls on the mountains above the anchorage. In addition it is possible to enter by dinghy the second secluded large bay, which lies in a valley surrounded by tall peaks; it is a fine and sheltered place to explore.

3·48 Paso Quesahuén

46°24'S 73°45'W
Charts BA *1288*; Chile *8000, 8660*
Tides
HW is +45 mins on Bahía Orange

General

The strait is about 300m wide, the stream reaches 5–7kts at springs and it can be most uncomfortable. Take into account wind and tide conditions and take it around slack water. Approach from the NE, favour the Isla Leonor side and pass N of Islote Pelado (Fl.R.5s8m5M Red GRP tower 342°-vis-295°).

3·49 Golfo Elefantes – Bahía Quesahuén

46°24'S 73°47'W
Charts BA *1288*; Chile *8000, 8660*

General

Known also as Bahía Sisquelan, this bay lies between the mainland and a number of small islets and rocky outcrops just S of Paso Quesahuén. It provides a safe overnight anchorage, or a useful place to wait for a fair tide before tackling the San Rafael Glacier, in an area where there are few alternatives.

Approach

The area should be approached with caution as the strong tidal streams that run in Paso Quesahuén affect it. There are two entrances to the bay: one immediately S of Isla Leonor, the other S of the first prominent islet.

Anchorage

Once inside, a yacht can anchor in the N or S part of the bay, depending on the wind. The N anchorage shown provides good shelter from passing fronts. Good holding but not a particularly attractive spot. Water is available from a catchment point in the stream just to the left of the house. Take great care if going S beyond the sawmill and disused pier as there is a reef which dries at half tide about one third of the way from the disused pier to the islet in the centre of the S end of the bay.

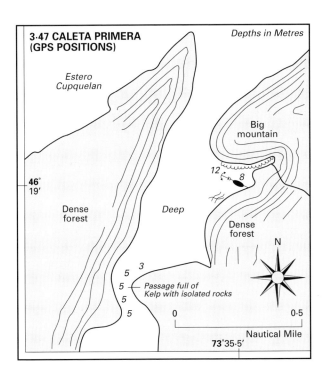

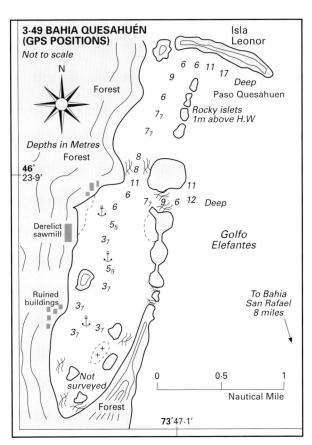

3·50 Golfo Elefantes – Caleta Gualas

46°28'·5S 73°45'·5W

Charts BA *1288*; Chile *8000, 8660*

General

Recommended for fair weather only, this spot is protected from the N but not from the W. Anchor in 8m behind Punta Huidobro. If caught in the *caleta* by a southerly, anchoring is possible off a pebble beach E of Punta García in the S half of the bay, 8m.

3·51 Golfo Elefantes – Bahía Islotes Ruiz

46°30'·7S 73°51'W

Charts BA *1288*; Chile *8000, 8660*

General

Lying approximately 1M NW of Punta Leopardos, this small bay on the W coast of Elefantes may provide a useful anchorage for yachts going to or from Laguna San Rafael. It is easily identified by the three small islets lying offshore. It can be entered from the N or the E through a narrow channel between the islets and the mainland. Well protected from the S, some shelter from the N is provided by the islets. Holding is good in mud.

3·52 Río Témpanos

46°32'S 74°50'·6W

Río Témpanos emerges from the SW shore of Bahía San Rafael. Its entrance is deep (18m) but very narrow, between the islets off Punta Leopardo and

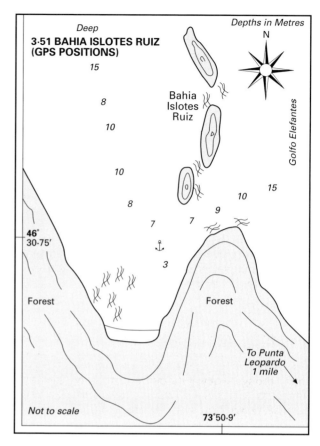

Bahía San Rafael light (Fl(3)9s7m6M White GRP tower, red band, 015°-vis-314°). There is a steep-to spit extending N from the light and there can be a

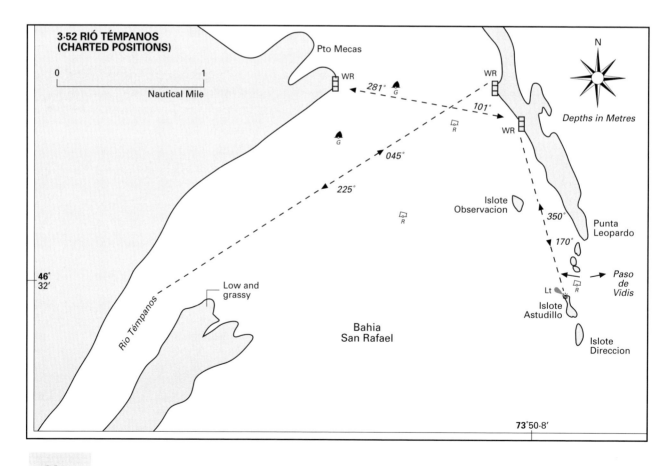

strong current at the entrance. Enter at the beginning of the flood when the ice is being pushed back. See plan, which indicates the marks not shown on Chile 8660 in the atlas. Favour the N side. Minimum depth 5–6m over one shoal patch up river.

3·53 Río de los Patos

46°33'·62S 73°56'·18W (GPS)

Charts BA *1288*; Chile *8000, 8660*

Río de los Patos is on the W side of Río Témpanos and easily missed when being swept along by the current. There is plenty of water in the entrance (GPS co-ordinates 46°33'·62S 73°56'·18W); inside, the depth at first falls to 3m (at low water) but increases to 5m. Quarter of a mile upstream, past three or four moored tour barges, is a large round pool where the river turns back on itself.

Anchorage

There are several possible anchorages, however, between approximately November and May the tour barges will be in regular use and should not be obstructed. The pool is a good anchorage, 5m in mud, though a few bits of ice drift in on the tide. The bottom is foul with sunken tree trunks; it would be wise to buoy the anchor here.

3·54 Laguna San Rafael

46°40'S 73°55'W

Charts BA *1288*; Chile *8000, 8660*

General

Cruise boats regularly visit the *laguna*. There is generally plenty of ice in the lagoon, along with dolphins, penguins and sea lions. Río Lucac, which runs within half a mile of the S shore, joins Río San Tadeo that emerges in Bahía San Quentín, about 15M away on the S side of Península Taitao.

Approach

Up Río Témpanos – see the approach to Río de los Patos.

Anchorage

In settled weather it is possible to anchor within the lagoon. There are many small bays with adequate depth to anchor. However care needs to be taken of floating ice as bergy bits can be sizeable. For example anchor in the NE bay for a N wind and off the S shore for a S wind. The alternative is to make a day visit to the Laguna and then return to Río de los Patos, Bahía Sisquelan or to Caleta Gualas.

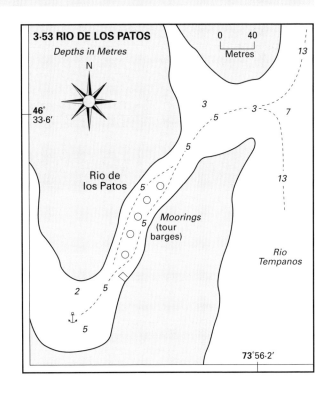

4. Isla Chaffers to Golfo de Penas

General

This section covers the W side of the Chonos archipelago, links from the *canales* on the E side of the archipelago to the Pacific, the outside passage to Golfo de Penas and anchorages on the N and E sides of that Gulf.

There is excellent cruising and exploring to be found in the *canales* running N to S in this region. The *canales* to the N of Canal Darwin are not well charted, so should be approached with caution and in settled weather. These provide good alternative routes to those described in Chapter 3. An interesting cruise to Laguna San Rafael could include a passage one way via the eastern channels and the other via the outer islands.

There are also numerous ways to reach the Pacific Ocean. Those heading to or from Cabo Ráper and the Golfo de Penas will almost certainly want to reach the ocean via Canal Pulluche, Boca Wickham and Bahía Anna Pink. However, the seaward approach to Canal Darwin is more straightforward than the approach to Canal Pulluche and may be preferable if coming from the S in poor visibility. Puerto Yates (see below) is a sheltered anchorage 5 miles from the entrance.

Vessels wishing to reach Golfo de Penas from Estero Elefantes often first return to Canal Chacabuco. It is also possible to reach Canal Pulluche from Estero Elefantes by Canal Tuahuencayec, Estero Barros Arana and thence via Canal Chacabuco or via Canal Carrera del Diablo (on the west side of Isla Fitzroy) and Canal Alejandro.

Charts

There are no large scale US charts S of Península Skyring.

4·1 Isla Chaffers, Bahía Totorore

Charted Pos. 44°10'S 74°03'·5W.
Charts BA *1288*; Chile *8000, 8200*

General

This is on the NW side of Isla Chaffers. The entrance is opposite Isla Goicolea. The anchorage is in the N arm of a long inlet running SE. It provides a good stopover if going N or S. This anchorage was recommended by Gerry Clark (*Totorore*) shortly before he disappeared in the S Ocean and is referred to in his book *The Totorore Voyage*.

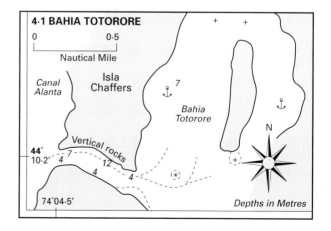

4·1 BAHIA TOTORORE

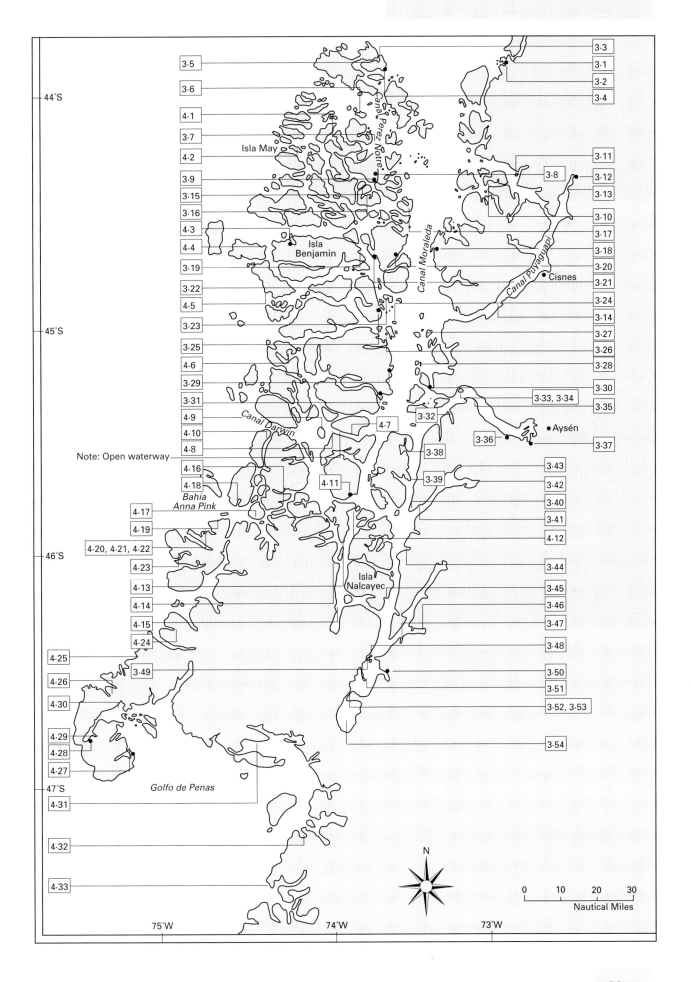

Approach

The entrance from Canal Alanta is straightforward through a narrow but deep cut in the rocks. Stick to the N side. The shallow water is where the channel opens into the inlet. Turn N into a bay that is split into two parts by a small island. Beware the covering rock between the inner entrance and the S tip of the island. (Shown on the charts.)

Anchorage

Anchor either side of the island. The holding on the W side is good but the E anchorage would probably be preferable in a strong southerly.

4·2 Isla May

Charted Pos. 44°13'·5S 74°15'W.
Charts BA *1288*; Chile *8000, 8200*

General

The anchorage is on the E side of Isla May inside a small islet.

Note This and the next three anchorages were used by Gerry Clark aboard *Totorore* (11·1m LOA and 1·3m draught) and reported to be good. They almost certainly offer good protection for vessels travelling between Isla Chaffers and Isla Kent, a passage that should only be undertaken with caution and in fair weather. Vessels planning to use them should ensure that there is time to reach Isla Chaffers or Isla Kent if the selected anchorage proves untenable.

4·3 Puerto Robalo

Charted Pos. 44°38'S 74°17'·5W.
Charts BA *1288*; Chile *8000, 8200*

General

According to Gerry Clark, who had local information and the Chilean chart, Puerto Robalo is the bay at the NW end of Isla Benjamin, to the SE of Grupo Elvirita. This is not in agreement with the Admiralty Pilot, which states that Robalo is on the N side of Isla Stokes. Clark found this to be a secure anchorage and made the dinghy trip up the shallow, fast-running river to the lake shown on the chart.

Note the canal between Isla Level and Isla Izaza is not passable and has a least depth of 0·6m.

4·4 Isla Stokes – Caleta Parmiento

Charted Pos. 44°40'S 74°27'W
Charts BA *1288*; Chile *8000, 8200*

General

Located halfway down the east side of the island. See note for 4·2.

4·5 Isla Rowlett

Charted Pos 44°25'·5S 74°50'·5W
Charts BA *1288*; Chile *8000, 8200*

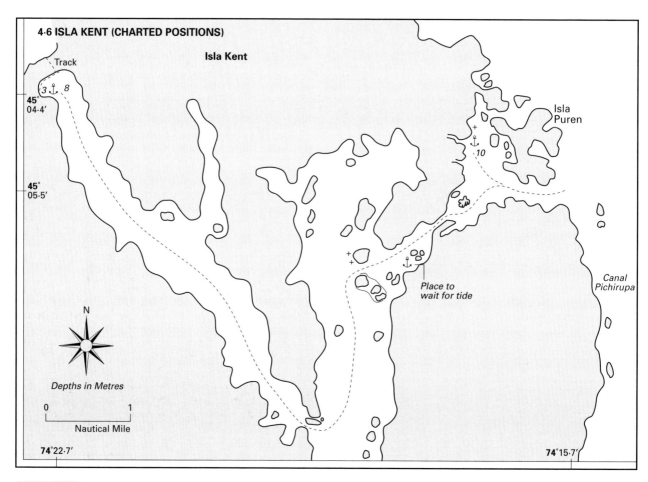

4·6 ISLA KENT (CHARTED POSITIONS)

General

A bay on the SW corner of the island, sheltered from the S by a small island. Described as a delightfully sheltered haven, this bay has also been recommended by *Caipir*, a 13m yacht from Puerto Montt.

4·6 Isla Kent

45°05'·5S 74°15'·7W (Entrance)
Charts BA *1288*; Chile *8000, 8160, 8161, 8200*
Tides
Slack HW Puerto Americano −0100hr, LW same as Puerto Americano.

General

Isla Kent offers several anchorages. The most attractive and deservedly popular is at the head of the NW arm of the inner lagoon, this offers excellent walking. Others are suitable for awaiting a tide to enter or leave the lagoon. Enter the inner lagoon at slack water (the time appears to be uncertain so it is wise to arrive early and observe conditions) the tidal stream in the narrow part of the entrance exceeds 7 knots and turbulent water can make rock spotting very difficult.

Approach

Puerto María Isabel, the outer anchorage, is straightforward to enter using Chilean Chart *8161*. Though the *puerto* is deep, an anchorage can be found in 8–10m on the W side. Beware of several uncharted rocks.

To visit the inner lagoon, pass through the outer narrows, avoiding a charted rock about 300m to the NE, which covers at HW. Once past these narrows there is a temporary anchorage off the shore on the SE side. From here pass slowly, keeping a good lookout, between the two islets shown. There are several uncharted rocks in this area. Once inside the lagoon the passage to the top of the NW arm is straightforward.

Anchorage

At the head of the NW arm in 3–8m, mud. Excellent protection. On the N shore there is a path, marked by bottles left hanging from a tree by crews visiting yachts that leads across the isthmus to a glorious white sandy beach.

4·7 Isla Quemada – Caleta Morgane

45°25'·5S 73°58'·5W
Charts BA *1288*; US *22371*; Chile *8000, 8630*

General

This is a pretty anchorage when passing through Canal Darwin. It lies on the S coast of Isla Quemada, with a river at its head. Good holding in sand. Beware the rocky shallows.

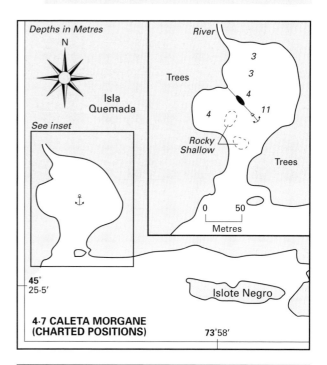

4·7 CALETA MORGANE (CHARTED POSITIONS)

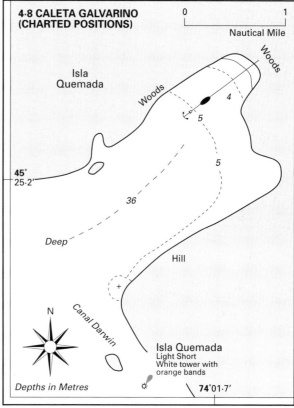

4·8 CALETA GALVARINO (CHARTED POSITIONS)

4·8 Isla Quemada – Caleta Galvarino

45°25'S 74°02'W
Charts BA *1288*; US *22371*; Chile *8000, 8630*

General

Galvarino is located at the W end of the S coast of Isla Quemada, 10 miles in from the E entrance to Canal Darwin. There is a light near the E entrance. It is somewhat exposed to the S and SW. It is best to anchor as close to the head of the bay as possible with a line ashore. The bottom is sand, but the holding is reported to be only fair.

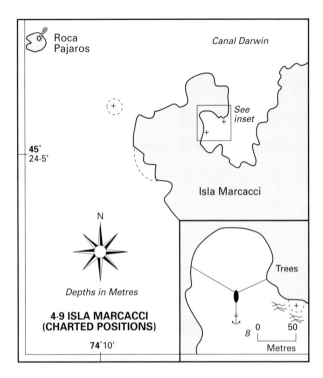

4·9 Isla Marcacci

45°24'S 74°09'W
Charts BA *1288*; US *22371*; Chile *8000, 8630*

General

The anchorage lies on the NW corner of Isla Marcacci, well sheltered from all winds. Anchor in about 8m with lines to trees. There are sea lions and otters in the anchorage but plastic rubbish on shore.

4·10 Isla Rivero – Puerto Yates

45°28'S 74°24'W
Charts BA *1288*; US *22371*; Chile *8000, 8632, 8700*

General

Puerto Yates is a good place to wait prior to exiting Canal Darwin or a place to rest after a long offshore passage from the S. It is located 3 miles down Canal Williams, on the W side of Isla Rivero. The entrance is easy to find, even under radar. The holding is good on a sand bottom in 14m on the E side and 5m in the bay on Isla Garrido.

4·11 Isla Humos – Caleta Jacqueline

45°44'S 73°57'W
Charts BA *1288*; US *22371*; Chile *8000, 8640*

General

Caleta Jacqueline is the unnamed *caleta* shown at the extreme W end of Bahía Harchy, 4M W of Punta Harchy and at the S mid-point of Isla Humos. The entrance is easily identifiable from the E by the pale coloured beach just S of the entrance. Although the bay appears to be open to the E, the shelter is better than it looks because it is possible to tuck around the point to the N. There is considerable kelp in the bay that may be by-passed. Either anchor where shown, 6m in good holding, or

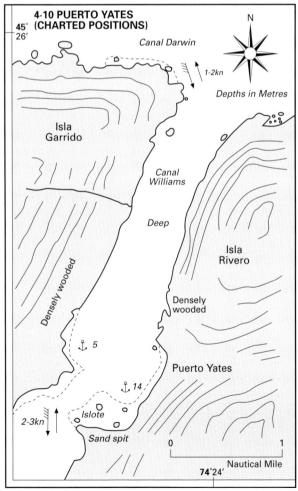

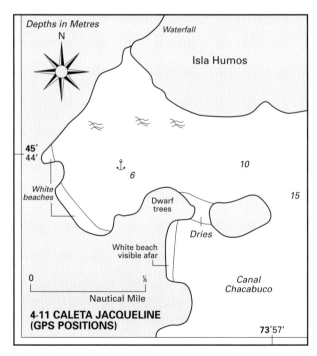

go to the waterfall with a line ashore which may be more sheltered. There are often small pieces of pumice on the beaches and in the surrounding waters. Fishermen consider this the most secure anchorage in this sector.

4·12 Canals Errázuriz and Chacabuco – Caleta Charlotte

45°46'S 73°53'W

Charts BA *1288*; US *22371*; Chile *8000, 8640*

General

This unnamed *caleta* has been nicknamed Charlotte after the daughter of Oscar Prochelle, who discovered this anchorage. Approach from the N via the small canal between Isla Fitzroy and Isla Piusco. There is a rock shown on the sketch plan but it is well marked by kelp. The rest of the canal is free of dangers. Anchor in the small bay, 6m, sand. The bay is very sheltered even when strong winds are blowing from the N.

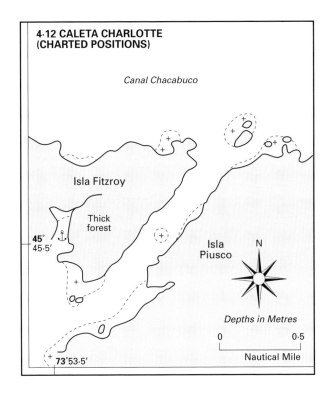

4·13 Estuario Barros Arana – Caleta San Patricio

45°55'·2S 73°58'·5W (position on chart *8900*)
45°55'·2'S 73°57'·9W (GPS)

Charts BA *1288*; Chile *8000, 8900*

Tides

HW Bahía Orange –0100hr

General

(No official name is known, in the Mantellero guide it is named Pozo Mark.) On the S of Isla Fitzroy, it is the first bay having rounded the S tip from Estuario Barros Arana. The approach is through

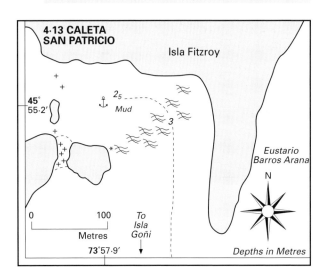

kelp, which may hide as yet unreported rocks, proceed with care.

Anchorage

There is room for vessels up to about 15m to anchor and swing safely behind the island or to take a line ashore. This is an exceptionally beautiful and secure anchorage.

A very narrow channel with 2·5m at HWS leads S of the rock to the W of the anchorage, to a landlocked inner bay, well worth a short dinghy trip. A hole could be found in which to anchor. There is a bay immediately to the W of the *caleta* that is much used by *jaiva* (crab) fishermen; this is well protected, but shallow.

4·14 Península de Taitao – Caleta Diablo

46°01'·4S 74°00'·3W (Chart 8900)
46°01'·1S 73°59'·7W (GPS)

Charts BA *1288*; Chile *8000, 8900*

General

First noted by Gerry Clark aboard *Totorore* and explored in detail by Hans and Eva Kolbeck of the

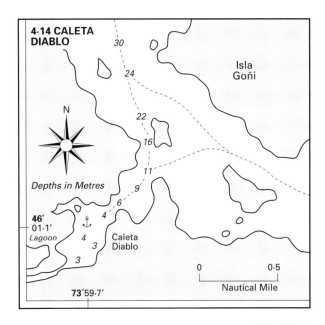

German yacht *Finte*, this is a useful anchorage if passing through Carrera del Diablo (see below). The entrance is narrow and shallow but passable with care for vessels of up to 2m draught. Once inside, holding is very good in mud and sand. The anchorage may be exposed to strong winds but should be secure. The row and walk to the inner lagoon, via a stepped *cascada* in the SW corner of the bay, is most attractive.

4·15 Península de Taitao – Estuario Thompson – Bahía Oz

46°08'·5S 73°59'·8W (position on chart 8900)
Charts BA *1288*; Chile *8000, 8900*

General

This bay has no name on the chart and has been called after Oz Robinson, the editor of the first edition of this guide. It is on Península Taitao opposite Isla San José, a beautiful inlet providing very good shelter from NE through W to SE. Anchor in the river mouth, 8–10m, excellent holding. Other spots are available but deeper.

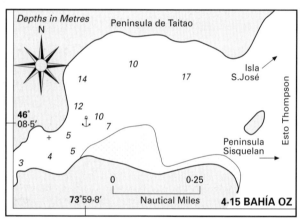

Passage

Carrera del Diablo

45°49'S 74°06'W
Charts Chile *8460, 8800*

This translates as Devil's Racetrack and gives a good idea of what the conditions are like when the tide is running at its maximum. The canal permits vessels to make a passage north or south to Laguna San Rafael without covering the same ground twice. It is also a short cut between the *laguna* and Bahía Anna Pink. Many vessels have traversed the passage safely even with full current, which may exceed eight knots. It would be wise to go through at slack water, if only to spare the skipper's nerves. The only dangers reported so far appear to be shown on Chile Chart *8640*. Keeping to midstream is the recommended course. The tide tables give an offset of: Puerto Montt +0100hr for HW and LW at nearby Canal Pulluche. Different reports have given conflicting times for slack water so a vessel should aim to arrive well before HW or LW and observe local conditions. There are sheltered temporary anchorages at either end.

4·16 Isla Rivero – Estero Balladares

45°44'S 74°21'W
Charts BA *1288*; US *22371*; Chile *8000, 8640*

General

Estero Balladares is a long fjord off Canal Pulluche. It is very important to move with a favourable tidal current in Canal Pulluche as the flood tide in this area can run up to 4 knots. Balladares is a good place to wait for a fair tide. The two streams on the N side have good drinking water. The W stream has many pink Coicopihue (*Philesia magellanica*) beside it. The Coicopihue is also called Copihue chilote

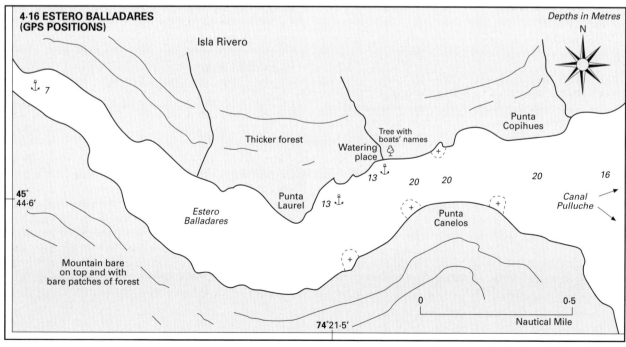

and Copihue de cordillera because of its close resemblance to the Copihue. The latter is the national flower of Chile and is found between Valparaíso and Osorno. It was named after Josephine Tascher de la Pagérie, an enthusiastic patron of gardening and wife of Napoleon Bonaparte. Aguada, the E stream, was a watering point for ships.

Anchorage

Good shelter and holding off the N shore in about 10m. Subject to strong *rachas*. Some protection from these can be gained by tucking in behind the headland of Punta Laurel. In settled weather it is possible to anchor at the head of Estero Balladares which is very beautiful. Holding in very soft mud in about 7m.

Several vessels have reported that this is a windy and uncomfortable anchorage. The nearby bay on the S coast of Isla Prieta (GPS 45°48'S, 73°23'·4W) provides much better shelter in all conditions with room to swing or tie up as desired.

4·17 Isla Guerrero

45°48'·9S 74°31'·7W

Charts BA *1288*; US *22371*; Chile *8000, 8700, 8710*

General

On the S coast of Isla Guerrero, about 2·5 miles WNW of Isla Ricardo light (45°49'·4S 74°28'·1W Fl(4)12s7m4M White GRP tower Red band 4m) and Punta Wickham bearing 202° approximately 1·5 miles away. Open to the SE but otherwise good shelter.

Anchorage

Use lines ashore in SW corner. Tide sweeps into the bay on the flood and it is possible that some swell might too if it is rough outside.

4·18 Isla Clemente – Puerto Millabú

45°44'S 74°38'W

Charts BA *1288*; US *22371*; Chile *8000, 8700, 8710, 8711*

General

Estero Clemente is the long fjord running into the S end of Isla Clemente. The Isla is easily identified on the N side of Bahía Anna Pink as it is an island of large barren mountains dominated by Monte Haddington. Puerto Millabú, at the head of Estero Clemente is a beautiful harbour with sandy beaches and a spectacular waterfall, Cascada Salmón. The bay, a shallow indentation, is in front of some old tent posts below a saddle in the hills. A good place to wait for the weather but subject to *rachas*. Good fishing.

Approach

On the E side, the area S of Punta Salida is shallow with half a dozen small islands. The deep water lies W of the southmost, Isla Picnic, which has a pole beacon.

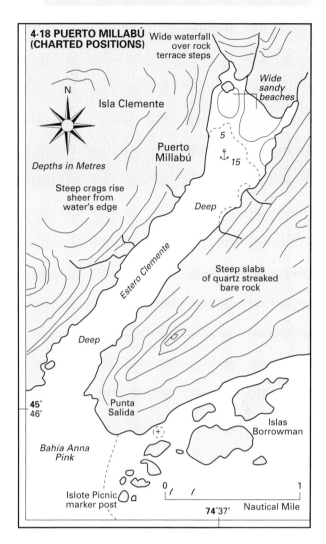

Anchorage

The holding is good in about 15m at the head of the bay. Anchor on the W side off a small beach with a large off-lying rock. It can be squally so take a line ashore. Watch out for shallows in the delta of Río Casma on the NE side. A bay half way up the W side has also been recommended.

Boca Wickham

The state of the sea breaking on Punta Wickham (45°50'S 74°33'W) gives a good idea of conditions in Bahía Anna Pink and beyond. Estero Goñi looks like an obvious anchorage, but the entrance is in fact blocked by foul ground.

Historical note: the name Bahía Anna Pink derives from the *Anna*, a 400-ton 3-masted barque, a supply ship, part of Lord Anson's 1741 fleet sent to capture a Spanish treasure fleet in the Pacific. Having had a rough passage around the Horn and being in imminent danger of shipwreck, the *Anna* had the fortune to discover Puerto Refugio and there recover from scurvy and refit the ship for the voyage. Many names hereabouts recall the ships and men of that expedition that fell upon this coast.

4·19 Channel between Isla Larga and Península Taitao

45°48'·5S 72°42'W

Charts BA *1288*; US *22371*; Chile *8000, 8700, 8710*

General

Small armada vessels regularly use the channel between Isla Larga, Isla Dirección and the mainland. It is a good choice for small craft going with the tide as it avoids some of the swell entering Bahía Anna Pink. Care should be taken at the W end of Isla Larga as rocks extend out from the SW end of the island and from the headland on the mainland opposite. Keep mid-channel to avoid these dangers.

Passage

It is about 72M from Isla Inchemó (45°48'·4S 74°58'·4W Fl.10s32m14M White concrete tower, Red band 4m 231°-vis-118°) to Cabo Ráper (see below) and a further 20M to the first possible anchorage in the Golfo Tres Montes. From Ráper to Isla San Pedro is about 72M. This coast is exposed to the ocean and the return to large ocean swells may be a surprise to crews accustomed to the waters of the channels. The coast is poorly charted and a good lookout should be kept for water breaking on uncharted reefs.

Puerto Refugio area

45°52'S 74°48'W

Charts BA *1288*; US *22371*; Chile *8000, 8700, 8710*

General

The Puerto Refugio area is a spectacular amphitheatre formed by big mountains with steep, barren slab faces. Several hard climbs have been made on these slabs, notably by the crew of the British yacht, *Pelagic*. There are several anchorages in this area. One of these, Caleta Canaveral has proved to be dangerous in strong winds and is not recommended or described. Puerto Refugio itself does not afford much protection.

4·20 Caleta Lobato

45°52'S 74°46'W

General

Caleta Lobato runs off to the NE of Puerto Refugio.

Approach and anchorage

The entrance to Puerto Refugio and then on to Caleta Lobato is between the rocks SW of Punta Stripe and Isla Hyatt. Considerable care has to be taken as there are many rocks and islands in the area. There is a good anchorage in 12m at the head of the *caleta*. This has proved secure in very severe gales from NW to SW, though it is subject to *rachas*.

4·21 Caleta Perrita

45°53'·6S 74°50'·8W

General

At the head of the unnamed *caleta* on the E side of Península Gallegos. The entrance is to the S of the island in the centre of the *caleta*.

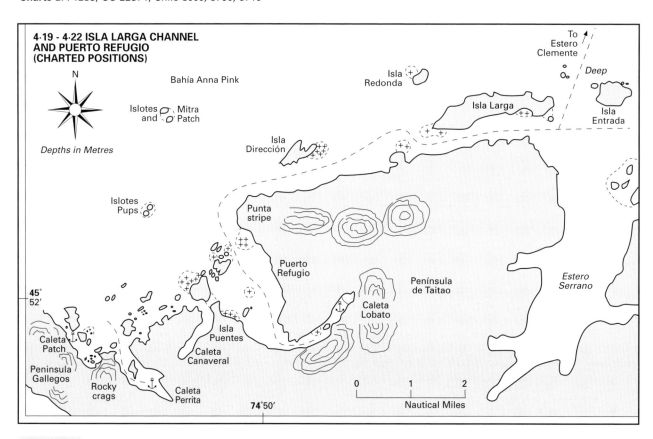

4·22 Caleta Patch

45°53'S 74°52'W

General

The third anchorage recommended in the Puerto Refugio area is Caleta Patch. Although recommended by fishermen it is more exposed than the other anchorages.

4·23 Península Skyring – Seno Pico Paico

45°58'·5S 75°02'·5W (Entrance)
Charts BA *1288*; Chile *8000, 8700, 8800*

Approach

The name originates with local fishermen and probably refers to anchorage B. This *seno* is not named on the charts; it is immediately to the N of Seno Burns and might be considered as the N arm of that *seno* except that its entrance is separate. The entrance is clean although it would be subject to swell if a big sea were running. Once inside there are two arms, both of which are navigable with ease.

Anchorages

A. 45°58'·1S 74°59'·6W (GPS) The recommended anchorage is at the head of the W arm. This is considered safe with good holding but may be subject to *rachas*.
B. 45°57'·6S 74°58'·8W (GPS). The NE entrance point of the W arm has an islet off it. There is a wooded anchorage inside the island with fishermen's lines. The bay looks open but is surprisingly sheltered. The bottom is rock so a fisherman anchor might be advisable, along with lines ashore. Fishermen use this spot frequently and will make visiting yachts very welcome.
C. An alternative anchorage has been recommended at the head of the E arm, no other details are available. On the S side of this arm is a *cascada* from which water can be collected with ease.

4·24 Península de Taitao – Caleta Gato

46°17'·5S 75°03'W
Charts BA *1287, 1288*; Chile *8000, 8800*

General

Although the bay appears on the chart to be open to the W, it offers better shelter than might be supposed because the islands and headlands at the mouth close if off considerably. Swell does not seem to penetrate and in a strong W, the fetch within the bay might be more of a problem than swell from the sea outside. When approaching, the island NW of the entrance appears to be about one mile further W than shown on chart *8800*, at approximately 75°05'·75W by GPS. The SW entrance point has visible rocks off it with breakers but a mid-channel course is free from dangers.

Anchorage

Half way up the bay on the N shore there is a point with a small notch behind it with a sheltered anchorage in 6m, mud and shingle, with lines ashore.

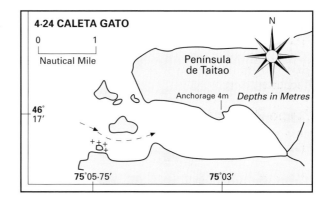

4·25 Caleta Cliff

46°26'·5S 75°19'·0W 46°25'·4S 75°20'·6W (GPS – entrance)
Charts BA *1287, 1288*; Chile *8000, 8800*

General

Several vessels have reported this to be a secure and pretty anchorage. Plenty of space and good shelter where shown.

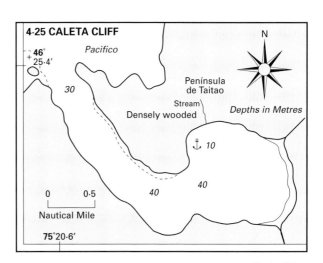

4·26 Península de Taitao – Bahía San Andres – Caleta Suárez

46°37'·4S 75°27'W

Charts BA *1287*; Chile *8000, 8800, 8112*

General

Bahía San Andres is a very good place to wait for the weather when crossing the Golfo de Penas from the N, or to go to after crossing from the S. The *bahía* can be approached in bad weather and, with the help of radar, landfall can be made safely, even in thick fog. Once in the bay there is some shelter and Islote Cono gives more protection. Caleta Suarez is much used by local offshore fishermen, who advise against using Caleta Monono. The most notable feature is Monte Cono at 488 metres, an impressive spike of old volcanic core. (Darwin climbed Monte Cono on his trip through this area.)

Approach and Anchorage

The *caleta* lies 2·5M up Estero Cono. It is a small bay behind a narrow wooded spit at the SE end of the *estero*. The approach is easy with deep water right to the edge of the spit.

Anchorage

Anchor in about 12m in mud and take stern lines ashore (or use the lines that fishermen have rigged). Protection is perfect from N winds and in strong S winds extra lines from the bow can be set up. Water

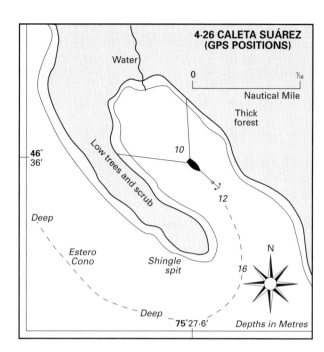

may be collected from the stream at the head of this bay. The only disadvantage of the anchorage is that it can be a long slog to windward to get back to open water.

While waiting for good weather it is possible to walk the length of the E shore. Where the *caleta* begins to open out, near a rock pinnacle, there is a large rock pool, good for a swim on a warm day. In addition there is a shallow inner lagoon with a lovely sandy beach at the head of the *caleta*. The whole area is excellent for sea and woodland birds: buff necked ibis, black oystercatchers, ashy-headed and upland geese on the beach and steamer ducks, blue-eyed shags, and magellanic penguins on the water. The woodland edges reveal the green-backed firecrown, beautiful hummingbirds and flocks of noisy austral blackbirds. The flora at the edge of the forest is reminiscent of an English garden with many familiar species such as hebe, fuchsia, pernettya and gunnera, the giant rhubarb, all growing in wild and natural profusion.

Passage

Cabo Ráper

Cabo Ráper, (46°49'·3S 75°37'·3W Fl.5s61m17M White round concrete tower and building 14m 331°-vis-175°) lies between Bahía San Andres and Puerto Barroso. Ráper should be called on channel 16. They will provide a weather forecast *(pronostico)* for the Golfo de Penas.

Golfo de Tres Montes

The anchorages are listed clockwise from Puerto Barroso.

Warning

To the E of Golfo de Tres Montes, NW of Caleta Mala, at 46°49'·5S 074°48'·0W on the BA chart, is an attractive looking inlet. This has been

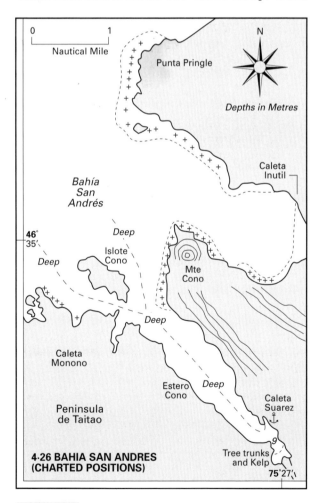

investigated and found to have a shallow bar at the entrance. Even if it were possible to enter, a swell developing from the SW could trap a vessel here for months. It should be avoided.

4·27 Puerto Barroso

46°49'S 75°17'W

Charts BA *1287;* Chile *8000, 8800, 8810, 9000*

General

Puerto Barroso is a good place to stop when travelling S to N. Anchor in the outer bay in mud or rock or proceed to the inner bay passing N of Isla Block as shown on the sketch plan. The rock shown in the channel, NW of the Isla Block, is in mid channel and should be passed by staying very close to the N side of the channel. Both locations provide good holding and shelter.

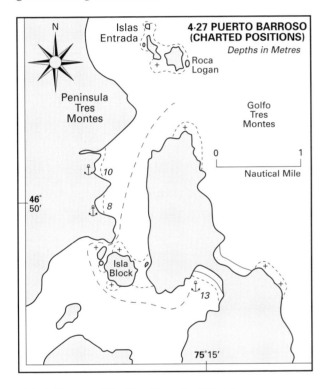

4·28 Estero Slight – Puerto Slight

46°48'S 75°34'W

Charts BA *1287;* Chile *8000, 8800, 8810, 8112, 9000*

General

Much kelp reported off the pier (*muelle*), exposed to the N and holding is possible but not good. Nevertheless this is a useful fair weather anchorage to visit the light, an interesting and scenic walk. The *armada* maintains a presence here and there are thermal springs at 40°C. About a two and a half mile hike to Cabo Ráper.

4·29 Estero Slight – Caleta Buena

46°46'·5S 75°30'W

Charts BA *1287;* Chile *8000, 8800, 8810, 8112, 9000*

General

A deep inlet with reasonable shelter. Quiet, if drawn in close to the shore with stern lines to the trees, in the inner NE arm between the tree side and the gravel bank below the waterfall. The S arm has good holding but may be disturbed by *rachas*. This anchorage has been reported as poor in very strong NW winds. Better shelter may be found at 46°44'·61S 75°32'·2W (GPS) in a bay shown on chart *8810.*

4·30 Seno Hoppner – Pozo Omega

46°40'S 75°25'·5W

Charts BA *1287;* Chile *8000, 8800, 8810, 9000*

General

Named Omega because of its shape, it has moderate shelter except from the SE. Favour the E shore on entering. Some protection from the SE can be obtained by tucking in behind the spit that extends from the W shore at the entrance. Sand and pebble bottom. Strong N winds tend to funnel down the anchorage into the *pozo*, in such conditions the bay mentioned in 4·29 might be the best choice.

Nearby is the barren island Islote Amarillo with a large bird colony: an interesting place to view wildlife. A ledge extends 100m from the island on the SE side and the currents can be strong. On the shoreline between the *pozo* and Amarillo are very hot springs with the possibility of a daytime anchorage, depending on the weather.

Passage

Crossing the Golfo de Penas

Charts BA *1287;* Chile *8800, 9000*

General

It is about 67M from Cabo Ráper to Isla San Pedro across the Gulf of Penas, which has a reputation for bad weather and deserves considerable respect. The bay is shallow and frequently subjected to cross swells that can kick up a very nasty sea. The most logical timing of a crossing from N to S is to leave Bahía San Andres shortly after the passage of a warm front with the wind veering from the N to NW though this may be accompanied by rain and poor visibility. But a light SW wind can give good conditions for a N–S crossing. The trip should be timed so as to arrive at the entrance of the Messier Canal in daylight; though it is five miles wide, there is considerable foul ground to the NW of San Pedro light and an error in navigation could be disastrous. If the tide is ebbing out of the canal, the seas in the entrance can be very confused. The crossing from S to N is usually less of a problem as long as it is timed for a period of W to SW winds and there is the alternative of Canal Darwin if Bahía Anna Pink looks difficult.

There are a number of anchorages in the immediate area of the entrance of the Messier Canal. Puerto Escondido between Isla Wager and Isla Schröder, Caleta Ideal and Caleta Chica at the SW corner of Isla Schröder, Puerto Francisco on the E side of the entrance in Seno Baker, and Caleta Hale on Isla Orlebar 17 miles S of San Pedro light. Both Ráper and San Pedro will give forecasts if asked and will also advise on local conditions.

If time permits or the weather is too unsettled for the direct crossing there is an excellent stop at Puerto San Salvador.

4·31 Bahía San Quentín

46°50'S 74°30'W

Charts BA *1287*; Chile *8000, 8800, 8820, 9000*

General

The sight of the Andes to the E of Bahía San Quentín has been described as one of the most spectacular views of the region. Possible anchorages are mentioned in the pilot, none appear to be all-weather locations. These anchorages are Caleta San Tomás (46°52'S 74°25'W) and Caleta Barrancos (46°51'S 74°29'W) on the N shore of Pen. Forelius and open to the N; Puerto Covadonga (46°46'·5S 74°36'W) in the NW part and open to the S. A fourth, Puerto Esmeralda or Seno Escondido off the NW shore of Península Forelius at 46°49'5S 74°36'·6W, has not been recommended. The only anchorage that has been reported as secure lies at 46°44'·39S 74°30'·01W (by GPS), in Seno Aldunate near Puerto Angamos. If working N and it has been found advisable to pass through Canal Cheap, one of the Bahía San Quentín anchorages may provide respite. The area provides an opportunity for further exploration and the editor would welcome further information.

4·32 Puerto San Salvador

47°12'·5S 74°17'·5W (BA Chart) 47°11'·6S 074°14'·9W (GPS)

Charts BA *1287*; Chile *8000, 8800, 9000*

General

This inlet lies near the S end of Canal Cheap and is just within the SW entrance point of Seno Jesuitas (which in itself would be worth further investigation). It is a valuable stopping point for boats coasting around the Golfo de Penas.

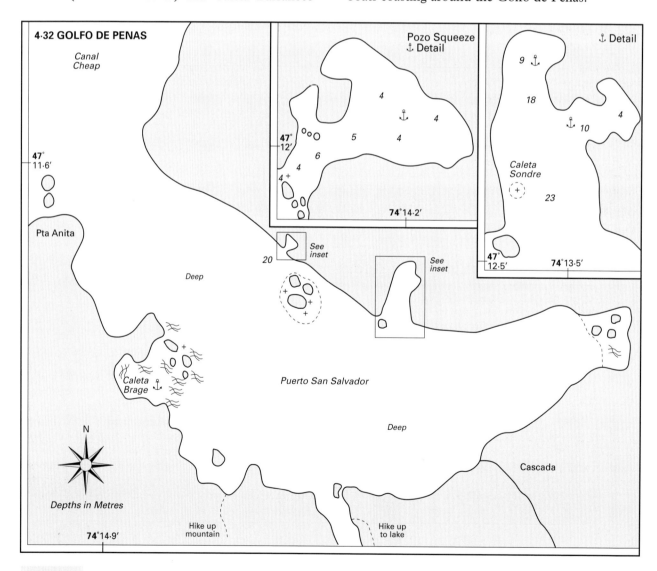

Anchorage

Three good anchorages have been reported:

4.32a Caleta Brage

47°12'·7S 74°14'·9W (GPS)

Named after the Norwegian grandson of Bjørn Bratlie, who first described it, the *caleta* is tucked in behind a projecting headland and islets on the SW shore. Good holding in sand, stern lines recommended unless the weather is settled.

4.32b Caleta Sondre

47°12'·3S 74°13'·5W (GPS)

Named after Bratlie's other grandson, this lies at the head of a horseshoe bay, not shown on charts, on the N shore approximately ¼ mile W of NE corner of the main bay. Excellent shelter and holding in 10m, mud, with lines ashore.

4.32c Pozo Squeeze

47°12'·0S 74°14'·2W (GPS)

Approach

Very narrow (less than 10m), hence the name, stay to west side, watch from the bow for the underwater obstructing rocks to the east. Minimum depth 3m. See plan detail.

Anchorage

Anchor in 4m in mud. Total protection and room for two boats to swing. Once in the pond the depths are even. Very secluded.

4.33 Caleta Clark

47°27'·7S, 74°28'·4W (On BA *1287*)
47°26'·7S, 74°27'·2W (GPS)
Charts BA *1287*; Chile *8000, 8800, 9000*

General

This anchorage and several others mentioned earlier in this guide were documented by New Zealand ornithologist and accomplished high latitude small boat sailor, the late Gerry Clark of *Totorore* who did much work in these waters.

Approach

The *caleta* is the SW arm of an inlet on the SW side of an unnamed estuary to the W of Cape Machado. The approach from Boca Canalas is straightforward. It is possible to pass inside the small island on the W side of the entrance.

Anchorage

In the SW arm, 3m in mud near the centre of a shallow bay, protection from all directions. Though the wind may blow strongly here, the absence of high ground makes *rachas* unlikely. There are probably several other anchorages in the vicinity.

5. Golfo de Penas to Puerto Simpson

Caution – Charts

There are no large-scale US charts covering this section. The small-scale chart is *22395*.

Note Alternative route between Golfo de Penas and S end of Canal Messier.

The recent publication of Chile charts *9600* and *9700* simplifies navigation through Canales Fallos and Adelberto. This passage was made in November 2002 by the North American yacht *Eelyos*. The skipper of *Eelyos* reports that this route is acceptable to the *armada* and is sometimes used by the Navimag ferries. Details of three anchorages are given at the end of the chapter.

The entrance to Canal Messier

The entrance is marked by Isla San Pedro light (47°41'·9S 74°51'·8W on Chile *9300*, Fl.7·5s 39m16M White GRP tower, red band, 8m. 124°-vis-328° Ch 16 c/s *CBS* Aero RC. Weather forecasts).

Four anchorages are noted at the entrance, three on the W side and the fourth, reckoned to be the best, on the E. The first three have good radio communication with San Pedro; communication from the fourth may be hampered by the land.

5·1 Isla Wager – Puerto Escondido

47°45'·4S 74°55'·2W
Charts BA *1287*; Chile *9000, 9100, 9300, 9311*

General

Between Isla Schröder and Isla Wager. The entrance is very narrow and not to be attempted in poor visibility. 10m, mud, good shelter.

5·2 Isla Schröder – Caleta Ideal

47°45'·5S 74°53'·5W (Chart *9300* and GPS agree)
Charts BA *1287*; Chile *9000, 9300*

General

Chart *9300* shows the approach and entrance well. It is easy to enter and a good place to end or start a *Golfo* crossing. It has shelter from the N but is open to the S, though fairly well protected from the SW.

Anchorage

In the lagoon according to anticipated wind direction. The bottom is said to be rocky but several yachts have reported good holding in bad weather.

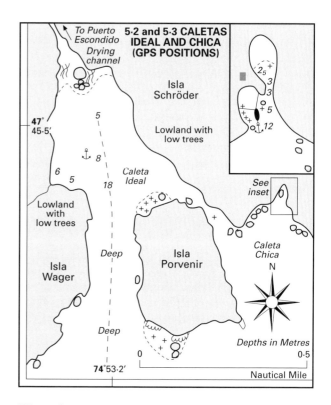

Water from a stream in SW corner.

It is possible to take a dinghy up to the head of the bay and with a short portage pass over into Estero Escondido. 1M further N, Laguna Byron can be entered by dinghy through some narrow passes. This *laguna* gives the impression of a secret place and is quite delightful. Isla Wager is the island where Wager of Anson's fleet was shipwrecked in 1741. This is a great adventure story and is well told in two books: *Byron of the Wager* by Peter Shankland – published by Collins 1975 and *The Wager Mutiny* by S W C Pack – published by Alvin Redman Ltd 1964.

5·3 Isla Schröder – Caleta Chica

47°45'·8S 74°52'·7W
Charts BA *1287*; Chile *9000, 9300*

General

Caleta Chica is an open bay. However there is a small nook in the N corner where it is possible to anchor in 12m, abeam of the rocks, and to take lines ashore. There is a lot of kelp. This nook is well protected except from the SSE. Good shelter has

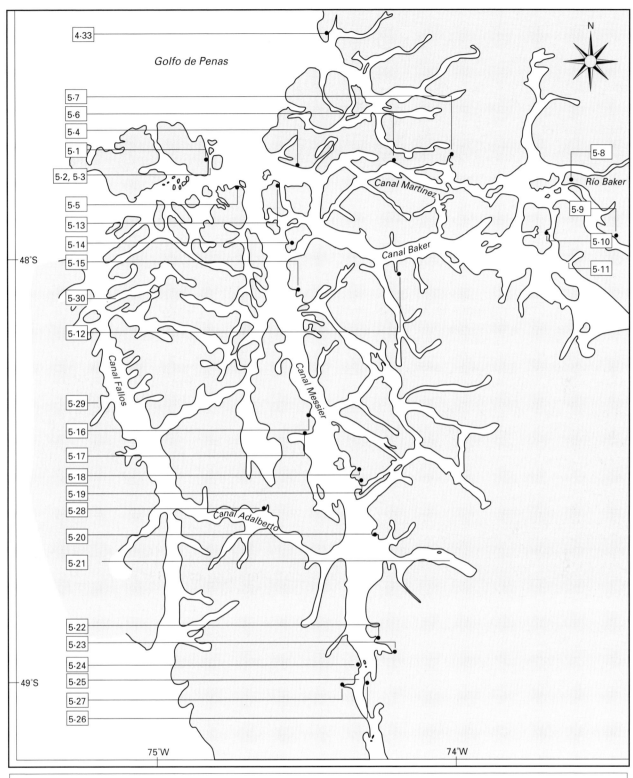

5·1   Isla Wager – Puerto Escondido
5·2   Isla Schröder – Caleta Ideal
5·3   Isla Schröder – Caleta Chica
5·4   Península Fresia – Puerto Francisco
5·5   Isla Penguin – Caleta Austral
5·6   Canal Martinez – Caleta Feliz
5·7   Canal Martinez – Puerto Merino Jarpa
5·8   Río Baker – Caleta Tortel
5·9   Estero Mitchell – Puerto Yungay
5·10 Isla Alberto Vargas – Puerto Contreras
5·11 Estero Montenegro
5·12 Canal Baker – Puerto Cueri-Cueri

5·13 Isla Zealous – Cala Ardevora
5·14 Isla Orlebar – Caleta Hale
5·15 Península Swett – Puerto Island
5·16 Isla Little Wellington – Caleta Point Lay
5·17 Isla Little Wellington – Abra Cuthbert
5·18 Isla Farquhar – Caleta Connor
5·19 Isla Farquhar – Caleta Lenga
5·20 Caleta Ivonne
5·21 Seno Iceberg
5·22 Bahía Libertá – Caleta Vittorio and Bahía Halt

5·23 Bahía Libertá – Puerto Gray
5·24 Isla Wellington – Caleta Hoskyn
5·25 Angostura Inglesa
5·26 Caleta Lucas
5·27 Puerto Simpson
5·28 Canal Adalberto – Isla Little Wellington – Estero Eelyos
5·29 Canal Fallos – Isla Campana – Seno Mac Vicar NW arm
5·30 Canal Falos – Seno Nuestra Señora – Isla Jungfrauen – Caleta Virgen

been obtained here in 50kt N winds, whilst 200m out in the bay there was white water. The yacht can be moored with lines rigged from bow and stern. There is a fisherman's hut on the shore with heaps of mussels (*cholgas*) nearby. Spider crabs and otters have been seen.

Seno Baker

5·4 Península Fresia – Puerto Francisco

47°45'·5S 74°34'W (Chart *9300* and GPS are in agreement)
Charts BA *1287*; Chile *9000, 9100, 9118, 9300*

General
Puerto Francisco is on the N side of Seno Baker, up a narrow channel from the outer bay with two very tight turns.

Approach
The charted position is inaccurate in the detailed plan given on *9118*. The entrance is immediately E of a prominent conical-shaped hill along the S shore of Península Fresia. The entrance is unencumbered. The passageway to the inner lagoon is narrow and is tree-lined but deep enough (minimum 3·5m in the first narrows and 4·5m in the second). Vessels up to 20m overall, 5m beam and 3m draft should be able to manage the channel without difficulty. Do not leave on a strong ebb or with a strong following wind, either of which will cause trouble at the corners.

Anchorage
The surrounding land is low and well covered in trees so there is little chance of *rachas*. Inside the basin, depths are consistent and the bottom is strong mud. There are a number of small coves around the shore. The best anchorage is in the NW corner of the inner lagoon with lines ashore. There is another attractive 'lines ashore' position in the bay on the W side between the two narrow cuts. NW winds blow strongly across the inner lagoon so the possibilities on the E side are rather exposed. Tying in close ashore may be safest but may also bring flying insects.

If in a hurry to moor, shelter can be found tying off to trees in the wide part of the channel but this blocks the entrance and bugs could be a nuisance.

5·5 Isla Penguin – Caleta Austral

47°48'·2S 74°47'W
Charts BA *1287*; Chile *9000, 9300, 9311*

The anchorage between Isla Penguin and Isla Juan Stuven provides good shelter from S winds but beware of an easterly blowing down Canal Baker when this anchorage can become untenable. It is an easy anchorage to make for after crossing the Gulf of Penas from N to S. If exiting into Canal Messier through Paso Tate, stay close to the S shore of Isla Penguin. The pass is full of kelp but with someone on the bow it is possible to wend a way through.

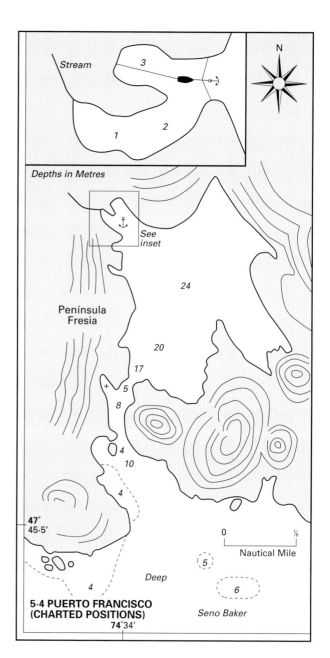

5·4 PUERTO FRANCISCO (CHARTED POSITIONS)

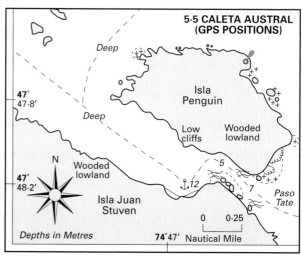

5·5 CALETA AUSTRAL (GPS POSITIONS)

Diversion

Río Baker

Charts BA *1287*; Chile *9100*

General

The diversion from Canal Messier through Canal Martinez or Canal Baker is very rarely visited by yachts. However it contains magnificent scenery, good anchorages and the possibility of making crew changes here. Chart *9100*, though a new edition, was first published in 1901 and positions disagree considerably with GPS.

The Carretera Austral (Chile's major project to extend the link from Puerto Montt to the S extreme of the country by a mixture of ferry links and new roads, without having to make major detours into Argentina) has now extended as far S as Puerto Yungay on the Río Bravo. There is a great deal to explore in this area. The following anchorages have been visited:

5·6 Canal Martinez – Caleta Feliz

47°47'S 74°16'·5W
Charts BA *1287*; Chile *9000, 9100*

General

This unnamed narrow inlet, to the E of Punta Graciela has been described by the crew of yacht *Felice* as one of the most beautiful they have visited and they named it Caleta Feliz. The entrance is narrow but clear of dangers. Anchor in about 10m.

5·7 Canal Martinez – Puerto Merino Jarpa

47°48'S 74°03'·5W
Charts BA *287*; Chile *9100, 9118*

General

On the mainland NE of Isla Irene, Merino Jarpa is an inlet with a straightforward entrance and waist leading to an inner cove. At the waist, keep to the W as there are rocks off the E shore. In the inner cove there are depths of about 11m but anchor in 7m near the end with lines to trees.

5·8 Río Baker – Caleta Tortel

47°50'·5S 73°35'W
Charts BA *1287*; Chile *9000, 9100*

Approach

The ranges shown on the chart are no longer in use. There is a light on Pta. Mancilla (Caleta Tortel Fl.G.5s36m5M G GRP tower).

General

The village of Tortel lies on the W side of Caleta Tortel, near the mouth of the Río Baker. In recent years investment has been made to develop this small village so that today there is a small airstrip, new wooden boardwalks around the village, post office and telephones.

It is possible to take a dinghy with a powerful outboard up the Río Baker (the Río Baker is said to discharge more water into the sea than any other river in Chile). It is also possible to travel down the Río Baker from near Cochrane by inflatable craft on one of the commercially run river trips.

Anchorage

The sketch plan shows two anchorages. The N position is best for using anchor and lines and is a convenient distance from the village. The second anchorage is in the central bay by the N pier, which is used by the *carabineros* launch. Anchor well out in deep water and take a line to the pier. The S pier is used for loading lumber and is no good for going alongside. Poor holding.

Facilities

There are a few shops and gas can be obtained. Diesel is available from the new EMAZA store, which is well stocked with the basics.

Communications

There is a regular ferry to Los Vagabundos (economic, 4 hours) to link up with the bus service that travels to Cochrane three times a week (Sundays, Tuesdays and Thursdays, 3 hours).

Flights – It is possible to buy a ticket at the post office for the weekly flight on a Wednesday from Tortel to Cochrane. It is also possible to charter a flight but this is expensive.

Post office and telephones.

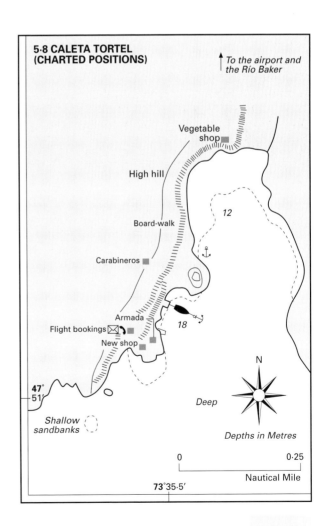

5·8 CALETA TORTEL (CHARTED POSITIONS)

5·9 Estero Mitchell – Puerto Yungay

47°59'S 73°25'·5W
Charts BA *1287*; Chile *9000, 9100*

General

Puerto Yungay is at the current S limit of the Carretera Austral. There is a small military base here and a village is to be developed. The military are helpful and have given assistance with mechanical problems and, if asked, may give individuals a lift along the road to La Vagabundos.

Anchor in an open bay, sheltered from the N in variable depths (4m or more).

5·10 Isla Alberto Vargas – Puerto Contreras

47°58'S 73°42'W (47°55'·5S 73°49'·1W GPS*)
Charts BA *1287*; Chile *9000, 9100*

General

A very secure anchorage with good holding in 5 to 12m. The inner bay has a bar at its entrance, which is too shallow to cross.

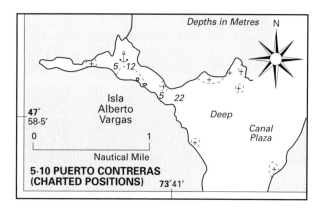

5·10 PUERTO CONTRERAS (CHARTED POSITIONS)

5·11 Estero Montenegro

48·S 73°38'·5W
Charts BA *1287*; Chile *9000, 9100*

General

Estero Montenegro is deep with easy access. A well-protected anchorage can be found beyond the low tree covered delta, close to the river mouth, in about 4–6m. Approach the delta on a SE heading. There are rocks off the end of the delta and off the opposite shore but the central passage is clear of dangers.

5·12 Canal Baker – Puerto Cueri-Cueri

48°01'S 74°15'·5W (47°59'·4S 74°12'·3W GPS*)
Charts BA *1287*; Chile *9000, 9100, 9118*

General

Roughly halfway between Canal Messier and Tortel on the S shore of Canal Baker. It is popular with those making the passage. The anchorage, which is 1·5M up at the head of the *caleta* in 10–13m, mud, is reputed to be free from squalls but the BA *Pilot* notes heavy overfalls and a strong in-going tide in northerlies of F5 or more. There are three shoal patches inshore along the SW coast at the head.

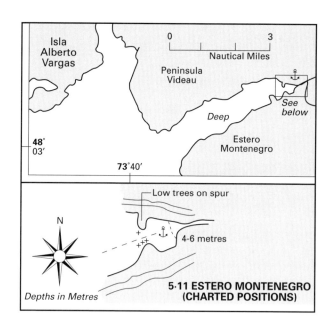

5·11 ESTERO MONTENEGRO (CHARTED POSITIONS)

Continuation

5·13 Isla Zealous – Caleta Ardevora

47°49'·1S 74°37'·5W (Chart *9300* and GPS agree)
Charts BA *1287*; Chile *9000, 9100, 9300*

General

Isla Zealous is on the E side of Canal Messier and this *caleta*, which has no official name, is on its E side, off Canal Cronje that leads S from Canal Baker. Kelp marks either side of the channel, which has 7m in the middle. Once through the second narrows, depths increase to over 20m.

Anchorage

The small *caleta* in the NW corner is recommended. With dramatic high cliffs all around it can be squally in the main bay but the anchorage remained calm. Good holding. Stream for watering. There is also an anchorage in 5m in the indentation between the two narrows on the N side of the entrance channel.

5·14 Isla Orlebar – Caleta Hale

47°56'S 74°36'W (Chart *9300* and GPS agree)
Charts BA *1287*; Chile *9000, 9100, 9300, 9331*

General

The anchorage is in the small bay on the N side of Caleta Hale. Well sheltered from the N but open to the SSW. There is kelp at the entrance with a depth of about 5m. Water at the beach at low tide. There is a pretty little waterfall about 50m up the stream.

5·15 Península Swett – Puerto Island

48°03'S 74°35'·3W (Chart *9300* and GPS agree)
Charts BA *1287*; Chile *9000, 9100, 9300, 9331*

General

Puerto Island is on the E side of Canal Messier, 23 miles from San Pedro Lighthouse. The most secure approach is midway between Punta Fleuriais and

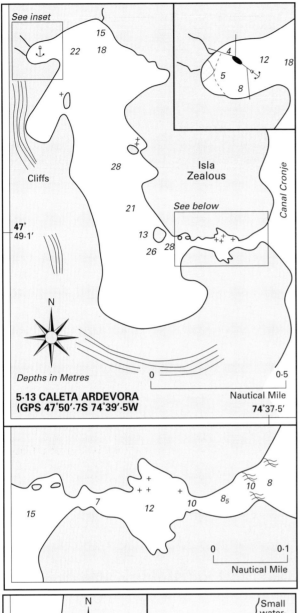

5·13 CALETA ARDEVORA
(GPS 47°50'·7S 74°39'·5W

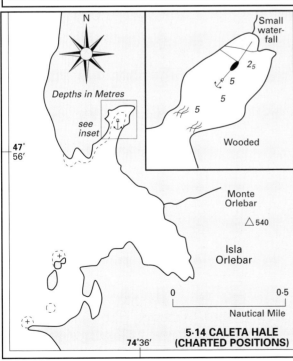

5·14 CALETA HALE
(CHARTED POSITIONS)

Isla Phipps. Many of the hazards between this island and the E shore are covered at high water. It has good all-round protection except from strong SW winds. In these winds the islands and rocks at the entrance to the bay provide some shelter but a swell enters and the security of the large *armada* buoy at the head is very welcome. Yachts can anchor nearby but further in, on a mud bottom, 12m. At the very head there is a picturesque waterfall, good for showers and laundry. The shores are thickly wooded.

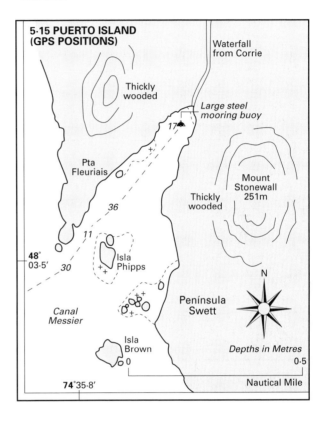

5·16 Isla Little Wellington – Caleta Point Lay

48°21'·2S 74°32'·5W (Chart *9300* and GPS agree)
Charts BA *1287*; Chile *9000, 9100, 9300, 9400*

General
Caleta Point Lay lies behind the long finger of land on the E shore of Península Negra. The first part of the main bay is clear but level with a small island halfway down. It is necessary to pass close to a large flat rock on the starboard to avoid shallow water and kelp to port. Once level with this rock, turn to port to avoid a large rock that is covered at high water. It is marked by surrounding kelp. Past this dog-leg the *caleta* is clear right to its end.

Anchorage
Anchor in about 12m in Butler Cove with good mud holding or moor with shore lines in the small nook at the head of the bay. Punta Wetherall to the S gives initial protection from SSW winds and the bay is well sheltered. It would be excellent in N winds.

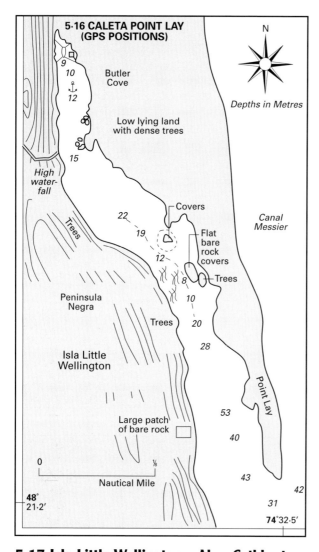

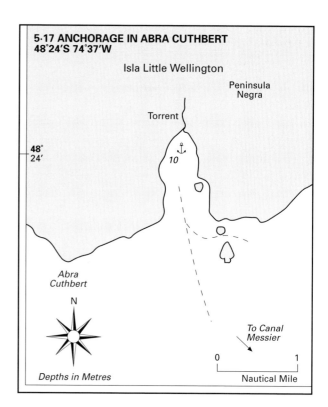

5·17 Isla Little Wellington – Abra Cuthbert

48°24'S 74°35'·2W (Chart *9400*)
Charts BA *1287*; Chile *9000, 9400*

General

The anchorage is in an unnamed *caleta* on the N side of Abra Cuthbert. Anchor at the head in about 10m. It is an attractive place but it is not a good place to stop in bad weather. The terrain is rugged and bare and there is a risk of *rachas*.

5·18 Isla Farquhar – Caleta Connor

48°29'·8S 74°24'·1W (Chart *9400*)
Charts BA *1287*; Chile *9000, 9331, 9400*

General

On the W side of Isla Farquhar, the entrance to Caleta Connor is wide and clean.

Anchorage

The best anchorage is in a small shallow cove in the NE corner with one or two lines ashore. It is sheltered from all winds, with good holding in strong mud. Beware of the rock off the SW point of the cove. It is also possible to anchor in 18m in mid-channel with good holding in mud. The river at the head of Caleta Connor runs quite strongly after heavy rainfall. On the point SW of the cove is a tall tree on which there are a number of name signs of visiting yachts.

5·19 Isla Farquhar – Caleta Lenga

48°31'·2S 74°21'·5W (Chart *9400*)
Charts BA *1287*; Chile *9000, 9400*

General

Named Caleta Lenga, after the cat aboard *Morgane*, the owners of which first reported the anchorage. This is a small bay about half a mile to the W of Caleta White Kelp in Bahía Lión. It provides shelter from winds between W and N. Anchorage is at the head of the bay in 18m with two lines ashore, in front of the small waterfall.

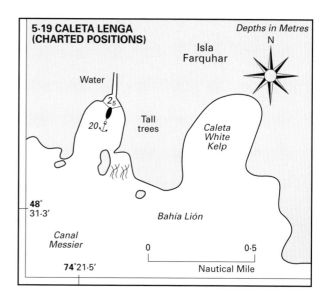

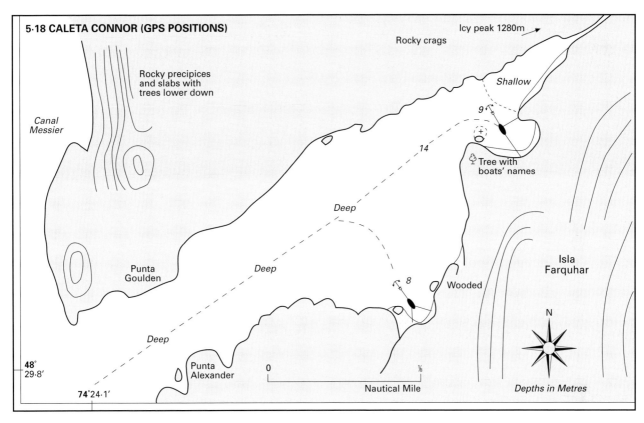

5·18 CALETA CONNOR (GPS POSITIONS)

5·20 Caleta Ivonne

48°39'·8S 74°19'W (Chart *9400*)

Charts BA *1287*; Chile *9000, 9400*

General

Unnamed on the charts, Caleta Ivonne is on the E side of the Canal Messier, N of Isla Launch and under the S point of Punta Estación. Punta Estación has a rock off it, awash at high water. Ivonne has two

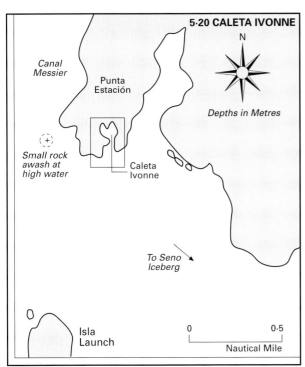

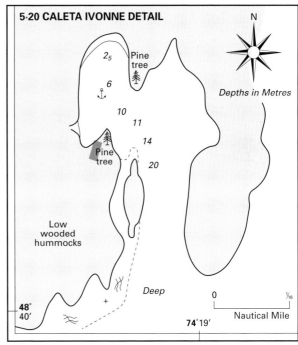

5·20 CALETA IVONNE DETAIL

bays; the anchorage is in the W bay, which has a narrow but clean entrance. It is a very well protected and secure anchorage. Anchor in 5–10m, mud, with a line astern or take shore lines straight across the bay. The water is glacial melt water. It is a good stopping place prior to a trip up Seno Iceberg.

Diversion

5·21 Seno Iceberg

48°44'S 74°18'W

Charts BA *1287*; Chile *9000, 9400*

On the E side of the Canal Messier, Seno Iceberg leads to a spectacular glacier which frequently calves, sending bergy bits and brash down the *seno*. Calving can cause large waves and it is wise to keep about a mile away from the glacier face. The point on the NW shore a mile from the glacier face has two rocks about 200m off it. They may be covered at high water and at other times and in certain lights look like bergy bits. They are easily and safely avoided by keeping to the centre line of the *seno*.

On both shores, three miles or so to the W of the glacier, there are various nooks where a boat might shelter from bad weather and drifting ice but remaining overnight would be a doubtful proposition. As shown on the sketch plan, there is an anchorage to the N of the glacier in 12m, E of the waterfall, the current from which keeps most of the ice away. From the waterfall it is possible to hike to the glacier. Depending upon the wind, crew might have to remain on board to cope with a shift in the ice and fend off bergy bits.

An anchorage, possibly the same as that refered to above, has been reported on the north side, GPS position 48°44'·9N, 74°05'·14W. Depths of 5–7m, good holding in mud and plenty of trees for attaching lines to shore. Protected from all but E winds. From this anchorage the glacier is in view, 3 miles to the east.

Shelter for the night may possibly be found in the *ensenada* on the E side of Punta Yelcho, at the S entrance to Seno Iceberg. It has not been explored but appears to have good opportunities for tying up to trees. If this proves an illusion, the nearest places are Caleta Ivonne to the N and Bahía Halt to the S.

Continuation

In 1868 the Italian corvette *Magenta* sailed these waters and the zone N of Angostura Inglesa is full of names of interest in the context of Italian toponymy: Bahía Libertá, Isla Vittorio, Isla Lamarmora, Isla Cavour, Bahía Magenta, Bahía Solferino. There are three possible anchorages on the E side of Canal Messier in Bahía Libertá, about 5M N of Angostura Inglés. In descending order of merit they are Caleta Vittorio, Bahía Halt and Puerto Gray.

5·22 Bahía Libertá – Caleta Vittorio and Bahía Halt

48°54'·4S 74°21'·3W

Charts BA *1286*; Chile *9000, 9400, 9510, 9511*

General

Positions on chart *9510* are inaccurate but agree with GPS on *9400* and *9511*. Isla Vittorio, at the NW entrance to Bahía Libertá, is separated from the mainland by a non-navigable passage.

Anchorages

Caleta Vittorio is a very beautiful anchorage and a good place to wait for a favourable tide. It is protected from all winds. Entrance to the anchorage is around the SE corner of Isla Vittorio. The bottom is mud, 18m. Shallower depths seem to have rocky bottom but it is also possible to moor in the nook at

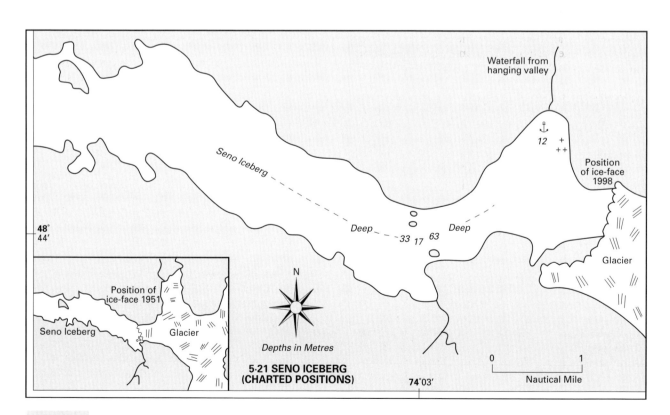

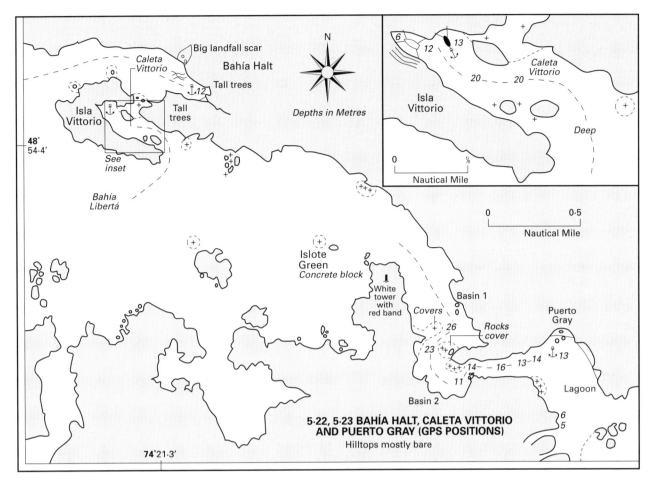

5·22, 5·23 BAHÍA HALT, CALETA VITTORIO AND PUERTO GRAY (GPS POSITIONS)
Hilltops mostly bare

the W end of the *caleta* with a four-point tie off, well sheltered by the large trees. Access is easy and there is all-round protection.

Bahía Halt is approached from the N side of Isla Vittorio. Favour the N side of the channel to stay clear of the shallow areas off the N shore of Isla Vittorio. The anchorage is at the E end (see sketch plan) with lines ashore. This anchorage would not be protected in NW and W winds.

5·23 Bahía Libertá – Puerto Gray

48°54'·1S 74°20'·9W
Charts BA *1286*; Chile *9000, 9400, 9511*

General
Puerto Gray is some 2·5M E of Caleta Vittorio and lies behind an unnamed headland running S to N with a light (listed as Bahía Libertá 48°55'·1S 74°19'·5W Fl.5s28m8M White GRP tower, red band 8m. 024°-vis-334°).

There are three basins. The first is shown on chart *9511* as the anchorage of Puerto Gray. It lies on the E side of the headland, N of Roca Talisman. It is sheltered but has depths of 20–30m and is not a practical anchorage for a small boat. The second basin, also deep (18–20m), is entered by a narrow passage to the E and then S of Roca Talisman. Rocks lie off the point to the S. This is a very difficult entrance. All the rocks on either side of the passage are hidden except for an hour or so either

side of low water. When covered they are very difficult to see and it would be very easy to run up onto them. The best time to enter the pass is at low water. Beyond that, another narrow but simple passage with a minimum depth of 11m and no kelp leads to a fresh water lagoon.

Anchorage
Anchor in 10–15m, mud, very sheltered. Presumably a boat lying here for a few days would lose its barnacles and weed, if it has any.

5·24 Isla Wellington – Caleta Hoskyn

48°56'·3S 74°24'·6W (9400)
Charts BA *1286*; Chile *9000, 9470, 9510, 9541*

General
Caleta Hoskyn is immediately N of Angostura Inglesa, round the S side of Isla Lamarmora and on the W side of the passage. It is recommended as a good waiting place for the tide in the narrows.

5·25 Angostura Inglesa

48°59'S 74°27'W
Charts BA *1286*; Chile *9000, 9400, 9510*

General
According to the Hydrographic Office, the N-going stream begins about HW+45mins, the S-going stream at LW+45mins. However, the timing of slack

water may vary by as much as an hour and when northerlies have been blowing, the S-going stream may continue up to two hours after HW, leaving a very short time for the N-going stream to run. In extreme conditions, when the wind has been pushing the tide, the streams may reach 6–8kt. In reasonable wind conditions the rate rarely exceeds 1–2 knots and at slack water is almost negligible.

It's best to pass at slack water. The narrows are well marked with range markers and port and starboard markers (which look much the same as light marks). In most parts there is plenty of room for a ship to pass a yacht and if a ship is seen approaching, there is adequate space to hold back until it has passed.

Formalities

Regulations for big ships are given below. In practice the full protocol is only followed by cruise liners and large freighters and providing small ships notify Puerto Edén on VHF Ch 16 before entering there should be no problem. Puerto Edén notifies the passage of a large vessel on Ch 16.

a. The International Regulations for Preventing Collisions at Sea apply, except that N-bound traffic has priority.
b. Vessels should give advance notice of passage.
c. From one hour before passage a continuous listening watch should be maintained and a general call made every ten minutes giving the vessels ETA at Isla Medio Canal (48°59'S 74°27'W), her position vis-à-vis a conspicuous feature and current weather.
d. On sighting another vessel, contact should be established on Ch 16.
e. Between Isla Kitt and Islote Entrada two ships are not allowed abeam of each other.
f. If S-bound, a vessel should sound a prolonged blast at Islote Entrada and if a reply is heard, wait for the N-bound vessel to pass. A second prolonged blast should be sounded at Isla Disraeli.
g. If N-bound, a vessel should sound a prolonged blast at Isla Kitt and at Islote Zealous.

5·26 Caleta Lucas

48°59'·5S 74°24'·5W (9400)
Charts BA *1286*; Chile *9000, 9400, 9510*

General

On the E side of the channel, entered by a narrow channel with 7m (and kelp) SE of Isla Chinnock. This is another anchorage recommended for those going N as a waiting place for the tide in the Angostura. The bottom is very fine mud, 15m, but good holding after the anchor has settled.

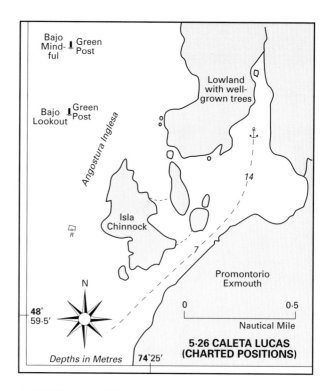

5·26 CALETA LUCAS (CHARTED POSITIONS)

5·27 Puerto Simpson

49°01'S 74°31'W
Charts BA *1286*; Chile *9000, 9400*

General

On the W side of the channel. The N side of the entrance, Punta Roberto, has off-lying rocks. There are various possible anchoring places in 8–10m, mud, good holding. A good place to wait for the tide without going back to Puerto Edén, if going N.

Alternative route

Canales Adalberto and Fallos

Canals Adalberto and Fallos are reasonably well charted in the *Atlas Hidrográfico* and have lights or markers on many prominent headlands. Navimag ships use these canals as an alternate route to Canal Messier. Aside from the three anchorages described below, several other *senos*, *esteros* and *caletas* appear to offer suitable refuge to a cruising yacht.

5·28 Canal Adalberto – Isla Little Wellington – Estero Eelyos

48°36'·87S 74°40'·65W (GPS)
Charts Chile *9000, 9400, 9700, 9800*

General

This unnamed *estero* on Isla Little Wellington is nearly one mile long. It is entered from the N side of Canal Adalberto.

Approach

Entry is gained by keeping the small island (prominent from afar) to the west. From there the long, narrow entrance shoals to 7m and then quickly deepens once inside.

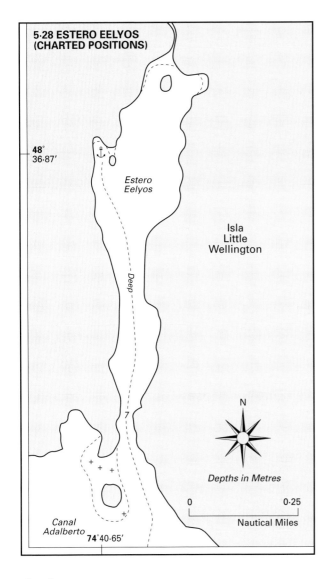

5·28 ESTERO EELYOS (CHARTED POSITIONS)

Anchorage

The anchorage *Eelyos* used was on the W shore of the basin, in 6m, rocky. There is adequate room to swing at anchor in the basin or to take lines ashore. The anchorage in the southern end of the basin is untested, however soundings showed adequate depth. Excellent protection from all winds, but it seems that the whole area may be subject to *rachas* blowing down from the surrounding mountains.

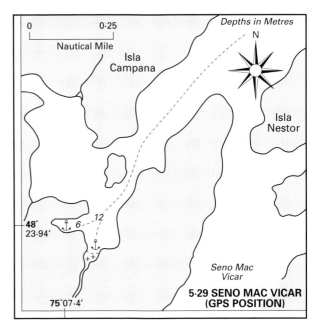

5·29 SENO MAC VICAR (GPS POSITION)

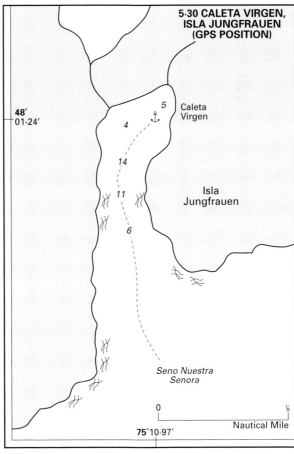

5·30 CALETA VIRGEN, ISLA JUNGFRAUEN (GPS POSITION)

Anchorage

There is a nook in the NW corner, the entrance to which is marked by a low, small island. Anchor in 7m, mud, with two lines ashore off the stern. Good protection from the N and W, but fetch from within the *estero* itself could make the anchorage uncomfortable in E and S winds. There are other possible anchorages in the *estero*.

5·29 Canal Fallos – Isla Campana – Seno Mac Vicar, NW arm

48°23'·94S 75°07'·40W GPS
Charts Chile *9000, 9700*

General

A beautiful spot, there are several anchorages available to anyone wishing to explore.

Approach

Enter the *seno* and pass to the N of both Isla Nestor and the point immediately W of Nestor. A small island mid-channel should then be passed to SE. Once clear of the island, a basin that offers two very suitable anchorages appears.

5·30 Canal Fallos – Seno Nuestra Señora – Isla Jungfrauen – Caleta Virgen

48°01'·24S 75°10'·97W (GPS)

Charts Chile *9000, 9600, 9700*

General

Eelyos used this anchorage while waiting for suitable weather for a S to N crossing of the Golfo de Penas. It is located approximately 1·5M inside Seno Nuestra Señora along its N shore.

Approach and anchorage

Entrance is open and straightforward, although there is a 6m shoal with kelp near the mouth. Once inside there are only a few patches of kelp. Anchor in the NE corner near the stream in 5–7m, mud and sand. Lines may be taken ashore. There is limited protection from southerly winds and seas, well protected from other directions.

Note A maze of islands separates the northern end of Canales Fallos and Messier. These were navigated, with difficulty, by the New Zealand research yacht Totorore. A safe route is not known to the editor, it is not even certain that Paso Suroeste is navigable.

6. Puerto Edén to Canal Sarmiento

Charts

There are no large-scale US charts for this section. The small scale charts are *22395* and *22420*.

Older Chilean charts (beware of confusing a new edition, which may be based on very old information and cartography, with a new publication generally based on up-to-date information) show considerable variation in lat. and long. Charts *9400* and *9500* have been published recently and positions plotted on these charts are close to reported GPS positions.

6·1 Puerto Edén

49°08'S 74°25'W (*9400*)

Charts BA *1286*; Chile *9000, 9400, 9510, 9511*

General

Different charts put Puerto Edén in different places but as it is at the N end and on the W side of Paso del Indio, in a bay some two miles from N to S lying behind islands, it is easy to find. Several small bays in the vicinity provide shelter. The place has wonderful views and friendly and helpful people. There is talk of extending the pier and adding facilities for visitors.

Approach

Call the *capitania* on the approach. If not stopping at Edén, he should be called anyway.

Anchorage

For formalities, anchor off the *armada* in the position shown on the sketch chart. It is a prominent blue building with a white roof. If the *armada* buoy is unoccupied, it might be used but ask first. However, the holding in this area is good and it will probably be more convenient to swing to an anchor since if using the buoy it is necessary to deploy a stern anchor to stop the yacht riding down on the buoy when the wind drops. At the village, holding is moderate in mud, rock and kelp. There is a convenient, but decrepit, pier with a least-depth of 1·7m alongside.

Warning

An overhead cable crossing the entrance (not shown on the charts in the atlas) now closes Caleta Malacca.

Formalities

The *zarpe* must be checked. In fine weather the *capitania* (in the *armada* station) may be reached by

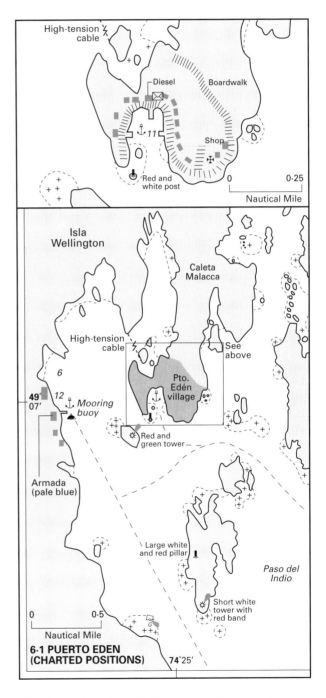

6·1 PUERTO EDEN (CHARTED POSITIONS)

dinghy and outboard from the village anchorage. Several boats have been directed to anchor off the village and been visited there by the friendly *armada* official who returns the *zarpe* and only requires radio

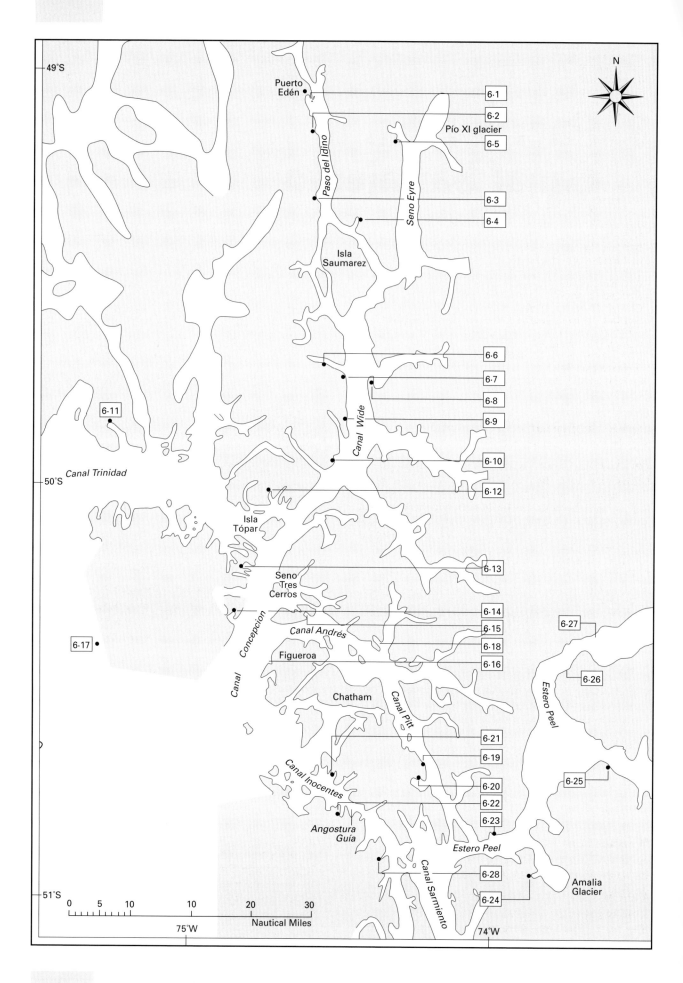

49°S

Puerto
Edén

6·1

6·2

Pío XI glacier

6·5

Paso del Idino

Seno Eyre

6·3

6·4

Isla
Saumarez

6·6

6·7

6·8

Canal Wide

6·9

6·10

6·11

6·12

Canal Trinidad

50°S

Isla
Tópar

6·13

Seno
Tres
Cerros

6·14

Canal Andrés

6·15

6·17

6·18

Canal Concepcion

Figueroa

6·16

6·27

Chatham

Canal Pitt

Estero Peel

6·26

6·21

6·19

Canal Inocentes

6·20

6·25

6·22

6·23

Angostura
Guía

Estero Peel

Amalia
Glacier

Canal Sarmiento

6·28

6·24

51°S

0   5   10   10   20   30

Nautical Miles

75°W

74°W

notification of departure. Such courtesies may vary with changes in personnel.

Facilities

Diesel is available through EMAZA, Empresa Abastecimiento Zonas Aisladas. It is in barrels and may need filtering. To be sure of obtaining diesel it would be wise to give notice of your impending arrival and likely needs two weeks in advance. An *armada* post to the N or S may be able to assist with this. There is an official post office at which stamps may be bought but despatch and delivery of mail through this office is unreliable. Showers may be available ashore: ask the *armada*.

Bread may be baked on request at the blue house, third left from the Police Station. Fresh *centollas* and sometimes fish may be available. Fresh supplies are sometimes available after the ferry calls. There are several stores in the settlement, if one cannot supply an item another may have it. To the E, round a headland and past the Church, is a store with limited supplies and, sometimes, frozen meat. Beyond it may be found a restaurant, La Barquita, prior booking is required.

Communications

The Navimag ferry, running between Puerto Montt and Puerto Natales, calls twice a week, once going S and once going N. Schedules vary but will probably have been discovered already when meeting the ferry in the canals.

6·2 Puerto Río Frío

49°12'S 74°24'W 49°12'·9S 74°24'·9W (GPS at entrance)
Charts BA *1286*; Chile *9000, 9400, 9500, 9510*

General

This bay is easily entered. Anchor in the N bay in about 5m. The anchorage is very well protected and the holding is good.

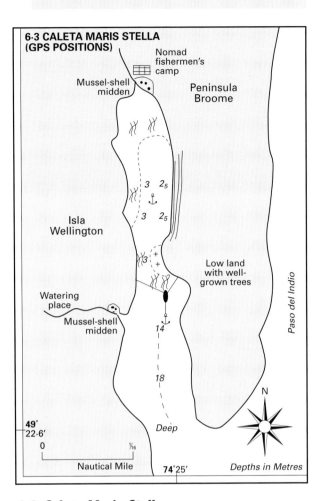

6·3 Caleta Maris Stella

49°22'·6S 74°25'W (*9500*)
Charts BA *1286*; Chile *9000, 9500, 9510*

General

The *caleta* lies on the W side of Paso del Indio, at the junction of Canales Escape and Grappler, behind Península Broome. It has a clear approach. It is open to the S but otherwise has very good shelter.

Anchorage

Anchor in about 14m just S of the kelp-strewn narrows with shore lines to the point of the narrows. A yacht drawing less than 2m may go to the inner bay which is both pretty and tranquil. By tying to trees on the E shore, all round shelter can be obtained.

Alternative routes

Isla Saumarez can be passed on either side. The W side has, from N to S, Canal Escape and Paso del Abismo and its parallel, Paso Piloto Pardo; on the E side is Canal Grappler, with an anchorage at Puerto Grappler, and Canal Icy. Paso del Abismo is one-way S and Paso Piloto Pardo is one-way N. Canales Grappler and Icy are two-way.

Pasos del Abismo and **Piloto Pardo** may only be passed in daylight. Many waterfalls come into them and there are coves that may give temporary shelter from the winds that, in unsettled weather, blow very strongly either up or down the channel. The passage is fairly dramatic and good visibility is advisable.

Canales Grappler and **Icy** are an easier passage. Canal Grappler has wider views, with a waterfall on either side and if visibility is good, there are grand views of the mountains from Canal Icy.

6·4 Puerto Grappler

49°25'S 74°18'·5W (on *9500*)
Charts BA *1286*; Chile *9000, 9500, 9530, 9531*

General

The entrance to Grappler is wide and clean. Although Grappler provides protection from all winds, and is oriented from the S to the NE, its E side is very steep and high and may be prone to *rachas* in strong NW winds. Grappler is a good stopping place on the route S and also for those planning a trip up Seno Eyre to view the spectacular Pío XI glacier.

Anchorage

The anchorage is to the N of Islote Diamante in 6m, mud with good holding.

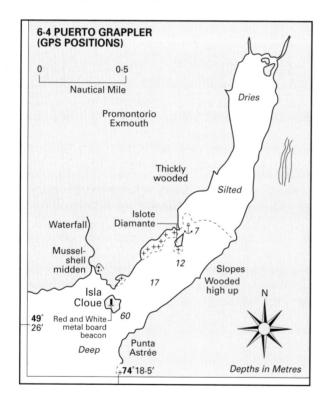

and one of the most spectacular glaciers of the Patagonian Ice Cap. The glacier is advancing and its face is further S than is shown on the charts. There is considerable ice in the *seno*. On a clear day the views of Mount Fitzroy and Mount Piramide (3000m+) beyond the glacier are spectacular.

Anchorages

In 1997 ice blocked the entrance to Seno Exmouth which runs off to the SE and might otherwise provide anchorage.

Good anchorages have been found in the bay 1M NW of Islote Genaro, in about 5m, mud, with excellent holding. A W wind and the flow of water down Bahía Elizabeth keep icebergs out of the anchorage. There is another anchorage on the E side of the bay, 1·5 miles NNW of Punta Micalvi, which has good protection from all quarters. It is in a notch with a shingle beach immediately NE of the islet which closes off the W side of a little *caleta*, 4m, mud and kelp. A waterfall lies on the E side of the *caleta*. This *caleta* is not immune to ice but the outflow from the waterfall and tucking in well behind the islet as described should minimise the problem except in a strong S wind. The Islotes Mardones can be left to port going N though there is a 5m patch between them and Punta Micalvi.

Another possible anchorage in Seno Eyre is amongst the group of islands about halfway up its W side.

Diversion

6·5 Seno Eyre – Bahía Elizabeth

49°15'S 74°05'W
Charts BA *1286*; Chile *9000, 9500, 9520*

General

In settled conditions it is worth making a diversion to the head of Seno Eyre to view Pío XI, the largest

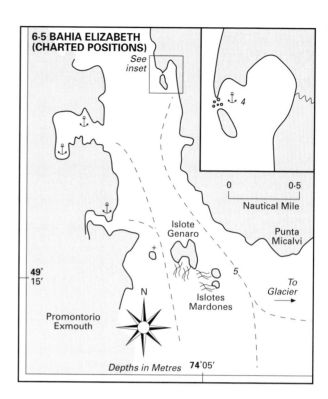

Continuation
Canal Wide

6·6 Seno Antrim – Caletas Elena and Nassi Bal

49°46'S 74°24'W

Charts BA *1286*; Chile *9000, 9500, 9541, 10000*

General

These *caletas* are in Seno Antrim, on the W side of Canal Wide. Caleta Nassi Bal is a tiny uncharted inlet on the S shore of Antrim about a mile from the entrance. It is about 30m wide. Lie to an anchor at the head of the inlet in 6m, sand, with two stern lines. It is said to be a good alternative to Elena, which may be more easily discovered.

Caleta Elena, on Chile *9541*, is deep (30m+ once inside) but the SE point, Punta Choros, is foul to the NW up to the middle of the entrance; favour the N shore. Yachts have moored here with stern lines ashore.

6·7 Seno Antrim – Caleta Sandy

49°47'S 74°24'W

Charts BA *1286*; Chile *9000, 9500, 9541, 10000*

General

Caleta Sandy is on the W side of Canal Wide, just S of Seno Antrim and well illustrated on Chile chart *9541*. The *caleta* has two possible anchorages, with protection from the N on the N shore and from the S, on the S shore. The N anchorage has a shoal patch (4m) to its S that can be circumnavigated. The S anchorage has a rock to the NW that can be observed and avoided. Anchoring depths are in 10m or less, rock and sand, with stern lines ashore.

6·8 Estero Ringdove – Caletas Richmond and Chacabuco

49°47'·8S 74°18'·6W

Charts BA *1286*; Chile *9000, 9500, 9541, 10000, 10300*

General

There are three anchorages in a very pleasant setting on the E side of Punta Hyacinth, at the entrance to Estero Ringdove. All provide good protection from NW and SW winds. The area was important for mussel fishing and there are large piles of shells around the shores but the problem of *marea roja* has significantly reduced the business.

Anchorage

The most secure anchorage is to moor between Isla Rosa and the mainland as shown in the small insert chart. This anchorage is well protected and with stern and bow shorelines it is very secure. The holding is mud at Caleta Richmond, anchor off the beach in about 14m with two lines off the stern. This anchorage is too deep to anchor in the middle without lines ashore. Caleta Chacabuco, half a mile S of Rosa Island, is also deep and requires lines ashore.

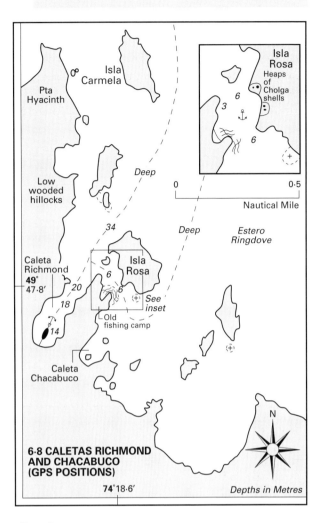

6·8 CALETAS RICHMOND AND CHACABUCO (GPS POSITIONS)

Depths in Metres

Caution

E winds, especially in the autumn, bring much ice down the E-leading Senos Penguin, Europa and Andrés, blocking them and sometimes even blocking Seno Wide at the narrows with Isla Tópar.

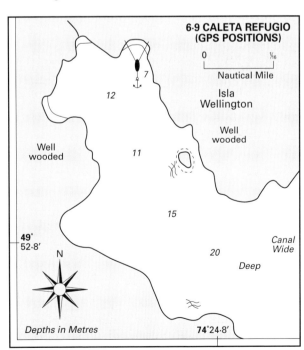

6·9 CALETA REFUGIO (GPS POSITIONS)

Depths in Metres

119

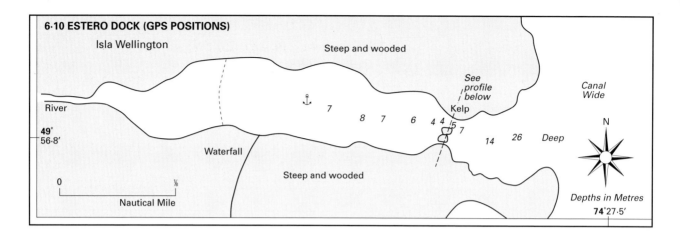

6·10 ESTERO DOCK (GPS POSITIONS)

6·9 Isla Wellington – Caleta Refugio

49°52'·8S 74°24'·8W (*9500* – entrance)
Charts BA *1286*; Chile *9000, 9500, 10000, 10300, 10310*

General

1½M N of Punta Camerón, Caleta Refugio is a well-protected anchorage surrounded by low land and well developed woodland. The approach is easy and a secure anchorage can be taken at the N end of the bay, in 7m swinging or with shorelines. This *caleta* is deservedly popular with many yachts. There is a good walk from the stream at the N end to Estero Gage. Several sheltered anchorages are available in Estero Gage (Chile *9541*).

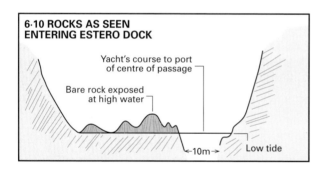

6·10 ROCKS AS SEEN ENTERING ESTERO DOCK

6·10 Isla Wellington – Estero Dock

49°56'·8S 74°27'·5W (*9500* agrees with GPS)
Charts BA *1286*; Chile *9000, 9500, 10000, 10300, 10310*

General

Estero Dock is a pretty anchorage (with otters) on the SE side of Isla Wellington and is easily identified from the E. In strong S and N winds with white horses in Canal Wide, the *estero* has been reported calm. The entrance is very narrow but straightforward. At the entrance pass keep to the N side, passing N of the large bare rock in the S two-thirds of this narrow pass. Depths fall to about 3·5m but the bottom is sandy and the rocks on either side can be seen through the clear water. Once past the rock depths increase to 7m. Good holding.

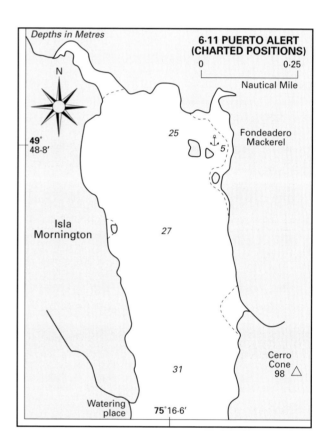

6·11 PUERTO ALERT (CHARTED POSITIONS)

Golfo Trinidad

6·11 Isla Mornington – Puerto Alert

49°53'S 75°13'·5W The GPS position of the entrance is 49°52'S 75°14'W; the head of the inlet is 49°48'S 75°17'W.
Charts BA *1286*; Chile *9000, 10000, 10200, 10211*

General

If entering or leaving the Pacific through the Golfo Trinidad, there is a very snug and beautiful anchorage at the far NE corner of Puerto Alert, shown on chart *10212* as Fondeadero Mackerel. The anchorage is in 3–5m and is well sheltered by a group of small islands. The stream at the N end of the bay is good for laundry and fresh water.

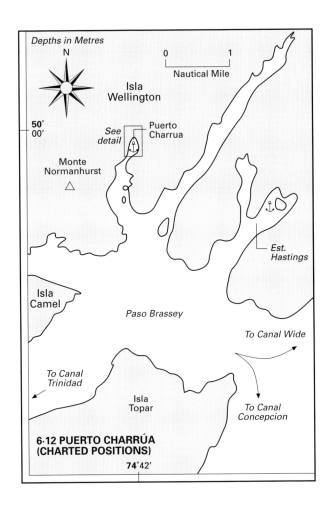

6·12 PUERTO CHARRÚA
(CHARTED POSITIONS)

74°42'

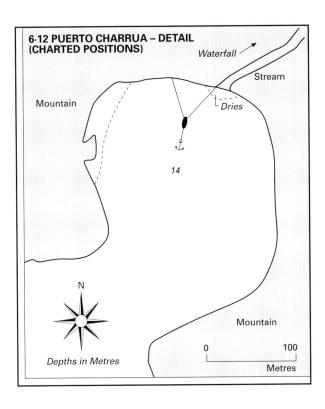

6·12 PUERTO CHARRUA – DETAIL
(CHARTED POSITIONS)

Paso Brassey

6·12 Puerto Charrúa

50°02'S 74°42'W
Charts BA *1286*; Chile *9000, 10000, 10200, 10300*

General

Paso Brassey leads N of Isla Tópar between Canales Wide and Trinidad. Puerto Charrúa is on its N side with precipitous Monte Normanhurst, 625m, on its W shore. Anchorage is found in 14m or less, close to the 130m waterfall – it is worth a stop if only to see that magnificent waterfall. The high cliffs all around add to the splendour of the anchorage but also produce gusts when the wind is between NW and NE. Get lines ashore. An anchorage has also been reported on the W side of the upper end of Estero Hastings.

Isla Tópar to Isla Brinkley

Isla Tópar is at the junction of Trinidad and Wide. Isla Brinkley is about 110M S at the junction of Canal Sarmiento and Estrecho de Collingwood.

Alternatives

See BA Charts *1282, 1286* and Chilean Chart *10000*.

Isla Tópar to Estero Peel

The alternatives of Canales Concepción, Inocentes, Angostura Guía and Canal Sarmiento on the one hand and, on the other, Canal Andrés and Canal Pitt, now lie ahead of the S-bound vessel. The former is the main route and has some known anchorages. The latter is more liable to ice up; see Isla Chatham. Both connect with Estero Peel, which is a suggested diversion.

The usual SW wind can kick up nasty seas in Canal Concepción for the 30M stretch until well inside the entrance to Canal Inocentes. Canal Pitt offers a much more sheltered route down into Estero Peel, at which point there is a choice of anchorages: Villarrica to the E (if going to the Peel Glacier), or Bueno to the W and then S in Canal Sarmiento.

Canales Concepción, Inocentes, Angostura Guía and Sarmiento

6·13 Isla Stratford – Bahía Tom

50°11'·65S 74°49'·20W (*10300*)
Charts BA *1286*; Chile *10000, 10300, 10325*

General

This is an excellent well-sheltered anchorage protected from all winds. The surrounding countryside is low, and the trees provide protection even in very strong winds.

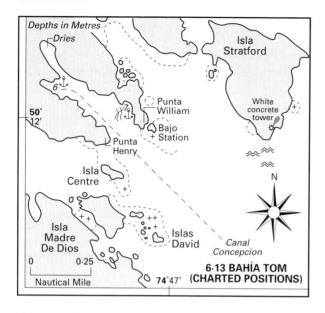

6·13 BAHÍA TOM (CHARTED POSITIONS)

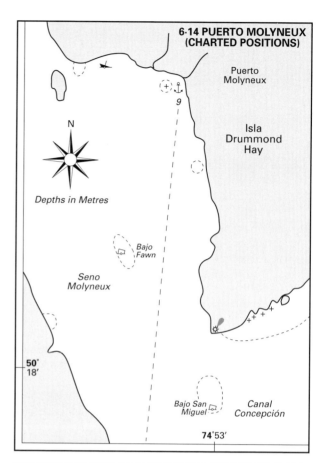

6·14 PUERTO MOLYNEUX (CHARTED POSITIONS)

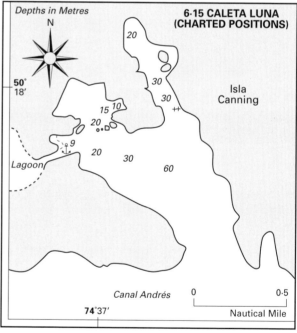

6·15 CALETA LUNA (CHARTED POSITIONS)

Approach and anchorage

There are a number of possible anchorages in the area. A favoured one is at the very head of an indentation between Punta Henry and Punta William. The bearing into the bay is approximately 290°. The entrance is clean but favour the centre or the port side of the channel as there are a couple of rocks with kelp at the head. The GPS co-ordinates of the anchorage are 50°11'·6S 74°49'·4W. The notch itself is about 50m wide. Use a three-point mooring, two lines off the stern and one off the bow in about 6m of water. Do not attempt to go into the starboard channel at the head of the bay as it dries at low tide.

6·14 Isla Drummond Hay – Puerto Molyneux

50°17'S 74°53'W (Chile *10300* is correct)
Charts BA *1286*; Chile *10000, 10300*

General

Going N against a NW wind in Canal Concepción can be difficult and the anchorage in Seno Molyneux is a useful stopping place if it is not possible to reach Bahía Tom, 10M further N. It is in the bay immediately N of Punta San Miguel (Fl.5s6m8M white GRP tower, Red band 4m). Molyneux is not a great anchorage but it is protected from the NW wind. Anchor in 10m close to an exposed rock on a rocky bottom. Mud has been reported at a depth of 30–35m.

6·15 Isla Canning – Caleta Luna

50°18'S 74°37'W
Charts BA *1286*; Chile *10000, 10300*

General

This is a sizeable bay on the SE corner of Isla Canning on Canal Andrés. Because of its size and depth, it probably wouldn't be the best place in bad weather but it is good enough in reasonable conditions.

Anchorage

The bay has two arms, one to the W and one to the NW. The NW arm is deep but there are a couple of bays where a yacht could moor close in.

In the S corner of the W arm there is a narrow gut to an inner lagoon. Anchor in 7m, bow or stern into the flow through the gut with lines ashore. There is a strong outflow from the lagoon on the ebb and a

Flamingos, Atacama *Becky Trafford*

El Niño brought many pelicans to Valdivia
fish market in 1998
Below Sooty sheerwaters (*sardellas*) fishing
for sardines in Bahía Corral
Ian and Maggy Staples

Kingfisher (*Martin pescador*) frequently
seen in the anchorages of the canals

Palafitos from the anchorage – Castro Chiloé
Ian and Maggy Staples

The church in Pailad from the anchorage – Chiloé *Ian and Maggy Staples*

Volcan Corcovado from Canal
Chiguao, leaving from Puerto
Quellón, Chiloé
Ian and Maggy Staples

Left Looking towards the mainland from Puerto Juan Yates, Bahía Tic Toc *Ian and Maggy Staples*

Above Estero Pailad *John Clothier*

Church on Quinchao Island
John Clothier

Puerto Montt. Lancha Vela – the traditional sailing craft around Chiloe; few remain *Andrew O'Grady*

Left Chacabuco: Ensenada Bahía the foreground, and Bahía Chacabuco behind
Seno Aysen looking towards Chacabuco *John Clothier*

Below Isla Amita *John Clothier*

Above Hot springs go into the sea in Seno Aysen – Termas de Puerto Perez
Ian and Maggy Staples

Cabo Tres Montes *John Clothier*

Whisky is readily available in Chile – so is ice *Andrew O'Grady*

Above Puerto Edén *Ian and Maggy Staples*

Monte Cono, Bahía San Andres *Ian and Maggy Staples*

Top Caleta Maris Stella, a heap of *cholga* (giant mussel shells) where they used to be smoked – now quiet because of the *marea roja Ian and Maggy Staples*

Above Huge cliffs in Canal Grappler *Ian and Maggy Staples*

Top Estero Gage - *Baleena* lies in perfect shelter.*Andrew O'Grady*

Above Looking out of the entrance of Estero Dock – in the morning there was ice right up to the entrance and across Canal Wide *Ian and Maggy Staples*

p Looking out of Caleta Millabu, Isola
emente, in the morning
n and Maggy Staples
bove Exploring the entrance to Caleta
eokita, Puerto Profundo *Ian and Maggy
aples*

Estero las Montañas – condor
Andrew O'Grady

Top Estero las Montañas – unnamed glacier   *Andrew O'Grady*
Above Estero las Montañas – the vessel's bow wave is the only thing that disturbs
the stillness. Mountains are reflected in the still water   *Andrew O'Grady*

Magellan Strait – Western end *John Clothier*

Below Cape Horn seen from the east with the Swedish-French yacht *Baltazar Andrew O'Grady*

Teokita and *Solieman* in Caleta Angosto *Ian and Maggy Staples*

Looking back to Paso Shag from the north *Ian and Maggy Staples*

Looking out from Caleta Cushion, Isla
Chair *Ian and Maggy Staples*

Right Caleta Olla. NW Beagle
Channel *Jeremy Burnett*

Caleta Mediodia – Bahía Romanche *Ian and Maggy Staples*

Canal Beagle *John Clothier*

Brazo Noroeste, Caleta Olla – note that the *caleta* is still yet
there are white caps outside *Andrew O'Grady*

Beagle: Puerto
...s. *Micalvi* is in the
...let at the bottom
...he picture
... *O'Grady*

... *left* Brazo Noroeste,
...squero Romanche
... *O'Grady*

Above Brazo Noroeste,
Canal Beagle looking west
Jeremy Burdett

Shaman has a
closer look at
an iceberg
Rob Johnson

The peaks of Torres
del Paine seen from
Ultima Esperanza
Rob Johnson

weak inflow on the flood. The gut is impassable to yachts but is possible in a dinghy, and the lagoon, which is more or less fresh water, is interesting to explore.

There may be other anchorages in the W arm.

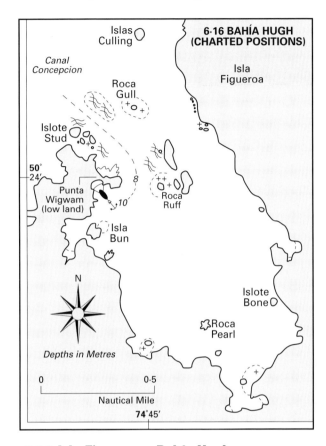

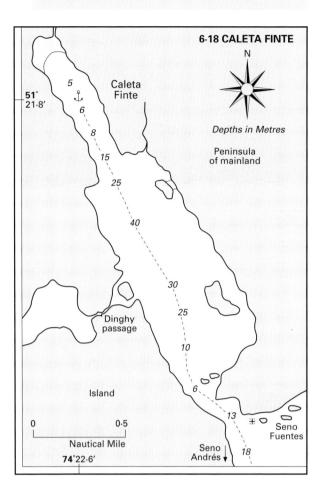

6·16 Isla Figueroa – Bahía Hugh

50°24'S 74°45'W

Charts BA *1286*; Chile *10000, 10300, 10325*

General

Bahía Hugh lies on the NW coast of Isla Figueroa on the E side of Canal Concepción.

Anchorage

Although it is open to the NW, there is shelter in the bay on the W side, 10m or less, mud. Good holding with shore lines. The bottom at the head of the inlet is rocky.

Diversion
Canal Oeste Isla Guarello

6·17 Bahía Corbeta Papudo

50°22'S 75°20'W

Chart BA *1286*; Chile *10000, 10330*

General

This anchorage is included as it is the only place for miles and miles where a yacht may get assistance if necessary. It is a huge limestone quarry with a resident community of miners. The limestone is

shipped to the steel works in Concepción. The mine is at the N end of Isla Guarello, which is at the W end of Canal Oeste. Anchor close-to in 10–16m. The few yachts that have visited this community have been made very welcome.

Continuation
Seno Tres Cerros: Canal Concepción to Canales Andrés and Pitt

Charts BA *1286*; Chile *10300*

This *seno* provides a more direct route between Canales Concepcíon and Pitt, but is unsounded. Several vessels have transited without incident. A least depth of 30m and an average depth of 70-100m was found on an alignment of 120-300° mag from just off Cape Clanricarde and the SE shore of the unnamed island about 4 miles NE of Isla Canning. At the mouth of the unnamed *seno* running NE from Seno Tres Cerros about 2 miles SE of Cape Clanricarde there is a small *caleta* with a fish camp which provides good shelter, company and information.

Canal Andrés and Canal Pitt

6·18 Seno Fuentes – Caleta Finte

50°21'·8S 74°22'·6W
Charts BA *1286*; Chile *10000, 10300*

General

The anchorage is at the head of an unnamed inlet, 1·75M long, entered from the SW end of Seno Fuentes. The unnamed island NE of Islas Kentish forms the SW side of the first part of the inlet. The passage around the N of the unnamed island is not suitable for yachts but passable for dinghies.

Anchorage

At the head of the inlet, in 5m, good holding in sand and mud. The *caleta* has been reported as mirror calm with 35 knots NW blowing outside. No reports are available for other conditions but the size of trees along the shoreline suggests that the *caleta* is sheltered from most winds.

6·19 Isla Chatham – Steamer Duck Lagoon

50°38'S 74°15'W
Charts BA *1286*; Chile *10000, 10300, 10350*

General

Steamer Duck Lagoon has no official name. It is an alternative to Estero Plainsong with a more straightforward entrance, though the entrance may be rough in very strong NW winds.

Anchorage

The entrance is clean. The preferred cove is on the W side (the cove on the E side has inadequate depths). Holding is good and perfect shelter with N gales has been reported. Use lines to pull as close in to the N and W shores as possible. Abundant wildlife includes otters and steamer ducks in the lagoon and condors on the rocky hills above the anchorage.

6·20 Isla Chatham – Estero Plainsong

50°41'·5S 74°13'W
Charts BA *1286*; Chile *10000, 10350*

General

This is a useful anchorage half way along the W side of Canal Pitt, at the entrance of an unnamed *estero* running NW and almost bisecting the island. The *estero* is studded with islands and rocks, and anchorage can be chosen according to conditions.

Approach and anchorage

There are several ways of getting into the *estero*. From the N, it can be entered through a passage between Isla Chatham and the next island to the S, keeping closer to the latter. There is an underwater rock immediately to the E of the kelp patch beyond the visible rocks (see sketch).

After passing mid-channel between the next two points, turn to starboard holding the shore close on the starboard side. Ahead there is an 8m pool with good shelter. There is an alternative approach from the S between the unnamed island and the islets to its W.

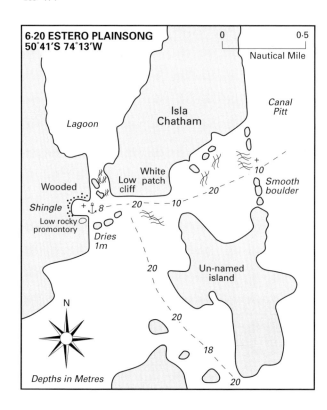

Canal Pitt – S End

The channel between Isla Peel and Isla Chatham is navigable, with depths averaging 40m in mid-channel.

Canal Inocentes

6·21 Isla Chatham – Caleta Paroquet

50°40'S 74°33'W

Charts BA *1286*; Chile *10000, 10340, 10341*

General

Caleta Paroquet is a first-class anchorage protected from all winds. It is on the W side of Isla Chatham, 3M E of the light on the SW extremity of Isla Juan, Punta Don (Fl.5s10m7M white GRP tower, red band 6m. 325°-vis-150°) and E of Islotes Long. The land is low and wooded and the entrance has a whitish cliff on the E side of the approach.

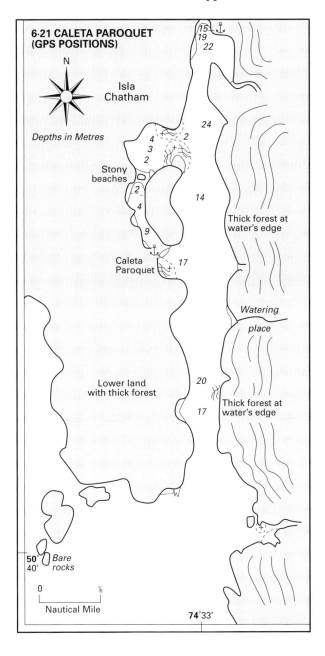

6·21 CALETA PAROQUET (GPS POSITIONS)

Anchorage

Half way up the *caleta* there is a península which looks like an island as it is approached from the S. A very secure mooring can be made between this and the main island with bow and stern lines. It is also possible to tuck well up into this narrow cut; the overhanging trees on either side provide perfect shelter. Another choice would be to anchor right at the head of the *caleta*. It is deep close to the shore but anchoring is possible in 14m, with shorelines.

6·22 Isla Hanover – Caleta Rayo

50°45'S 74°32'·5W

Charts BA *1286*; Chile *10000, 10340, 10341*

General

Caleta Rayo is on Isla Hanover just W of Punta Porpoise. A mooring has been taken between two islands on the W shore in 4·8m (low tide) with three lines ashore. A report states that the detailed chart *10341* is inaccurate and adds that it blew hard for 12 hours with the barometer at 986hPa. There is a large seal colony.

Angostura Guía

Charts BA *1286, 1282*; Chile *10000, 10340*

Tides

The flood tide runs south. HW and LW, Orange bay –0225hrs.

General

Angostura Guía is described by Roth as 'a wonderful mountainous narrows, (with) *cañons*, ravines and domes. It seemed unbelievable to be sailing at sea level with such scenery around us'. It is about 6M long and connects Canal Inocentes with Canal Sarmiento. Estero Peel joins Canal Sarmiento S of Angostura Guía.

Formalities

Commercial vessels have to give one hours notice of passage and whilst on passage call every 10 minutes on 500kHz or Ch 16. Vessels sighting each other should establish contact on Ch 16.

Overtaking or passing a vessel going in the opposite direction is forbidden between Punta Porpoise and Isla Escala light at the S end, a 4M stretch. S-going vessels should wait for those going N. It is fairly easy for a yacht listening out on Ch 16 to be fully aware of the position of vessels in transit through Angostura Guía. Unless visibility is poor a vessel is also easily seen and there is plenty of room to take avoiding action. The Chilean pilots all speak English and will respond to a vessel calling them.

Alternatives

Peel to Tópar

A N-bound vessel may care to consider the alternative route between Estero Peel and Isla Tópar mentioned above (following 6·12 Puerto Charrúa.)

Diversion
Estero Peel

Charts BA *1282, 1286*; Chile *10000, 10350*
Neither of the two BA charts is adequate.

General

Estero Peel runs E from Canal Sarmiento at 50°52'S for about 15 miles before turning NNE for a further 30 miles. Estero Peel has a number of glaciers running down from the Patagonian ice cap. These include those at the head of Estero Amalia, Estero Asia, Estero Calvo and finally those right at the head of Estero Peel itself. Ventisquero Calvo was the route chosen by Tilman when he crossed the Patagonian ice cap in 1954. A number of anchorages are listed below which have been used with caution by yachts. A fall-back plan should be considered in relation to each of these anchorages, should they be blocked or the weather turn foul. The estero may be blocked by ice in winter.

6·23 Península Wilcock – Caleta Villarrica

50°50'S 74°00'·5W
Charts BA *1282, 1286*; Chile *10000, 10350*

General

Located on the N side of Estero Peel, this anchorage was recommended by *Andromeda*, a 20m German boat. There is a distinctive cone-shaped hill to the E of the entrance. The entrance to the basin is narrow

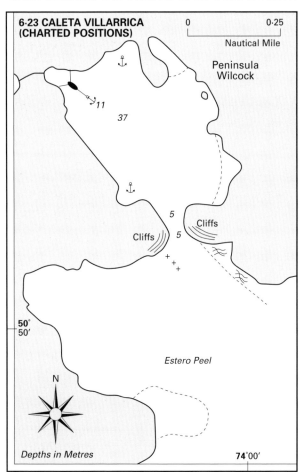

(25m) but clean. Avoid the rocks and shingle running SE from the W entrance point. The entrance is subject to *rachas*. Inside is a peaceful, totally protected anchorage.

Anchorage

Anchor in the SW corner with two stern lines to the shore, in the notch on the N shore of the bay, or swing to anchor in the N part of the bay.

The whole bay is subject to *rachas* but holding is good and several boats have reported a safe stay in periods of bad weather.

6·24 Estero Amalia – Caleta Amalia

50°56'S 73°51'W
Charts BA *1282, 1286*; Chile *10000, 10350*

General

Caleta Amalia is across the *estero* from the glacier. The entrance is clear, but beware of the rock off the S side of the island as it is covered at high tide. Depths are around 6m between the island and the S shore, though isolated shallower patches have been reported – proceed with extreme caution. Past the island, the depths increase and are about 30m almost to the head of the bay.

Anchorage

There is an anchorage with good holding in sandy mud in 10m off the notch in the SW end of the island. This position has a fine view of the glacier. The face of the glacier is comparatively low so the ice in the immediate area is mostly small bergy bits. If the entrance to Amalia happens to be blocked by ice, as it was when Tilman was there, there is the indentation he used at 50°54'·76S 73°50'·45W (by GPS).

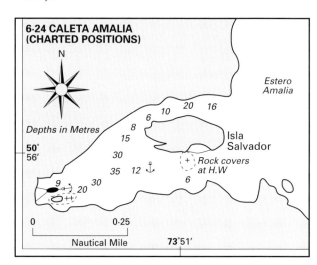

6·25 Estero Calvo – Caleta Pelagic

50°38'·23S 73°38'·67W (GPS and chart *10350*)
Charts BA *1282, 1286*; Chile *10000, 10350*

General

Estero Calvo is halfway up the N arm of Peel and is off the E side of BA chart *1286* (which here wrongly

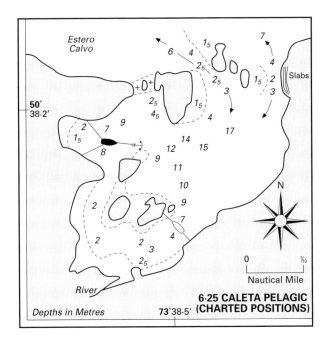

Estero Calvo

Slabs

River

Depths in Metres

6·25 CALETA PELAGIC (CHARTED POSITIONS)

Nautical Mile

50° 38·2'

73°38·5'

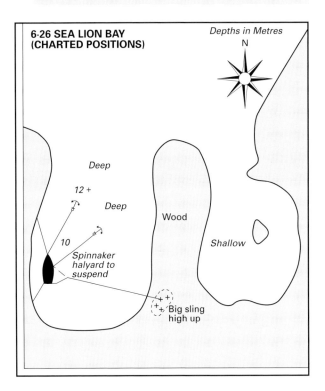

6·26 SEA LION BAY (CHARTED POSITIONS)

Depths in Metres

Deep

Deep

Wood

Shallow

Spinnaker halyard to suspend

Big sling high up

labels Estero Peel as Estero Asia). It is about 23M from Isla Peel. The *caleta* is on the S side of the entrance of Estero Calvo. Its entrance is between rocks, is narrow and may be blocked by grounded bergy bits. To enter by the E track shown on the plan keep close to the E shore – about 3m from the slab shore. The better entrance is further to the W as shown on the sketch plan. It is worth having a fall-back anchorage in case this *caleta* is blocked by ice.

6·26 Sea Lion Bay

50°30'·5S 73°43'W

Charts BA *1282, 1286*; Chile *10000, 10350*

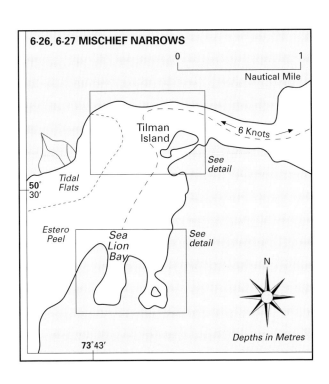

6·26, 6·27 MISCHIEF NARROWS

Nautical Mile

Tilman Island

See detail

Tidal Flats

Estero Peel

Sea Lion Bay

See detail

50° 30'

73°43'

Depths in Metres

General

Sea Lion Bay lies just before Mischief Narrows. The plan shows the system used by *Pelagic* to keep their shorelines high up and under tension so that the line stayed clear of the ice. *Pelagic* described this anchorage as 'dodgy'.

It may be possible for a shallow draught, or lifting keel vessel to enter the shallow E bay at high water and 'bottom out' at low water. This may be a more secure long term anchorage as it would be less threatened by ice.

6·27 Angostura Mischief (Mischief Narrows)

50°29'·5S 73°42'·5W

Charts BA *1282, 1286*; Chile *10000, 10350*

General

The Chilean chart names this pass Mischief after Tilman's *Mischief* which was run aground here while Tilman was busy crossing the icecap. Tilman quotes Procter, who was in charge of the yacht. Having accepted they were firmly aground he wrote: 'For one thing we had reason to be grateful – the reef kept off the bigger bergs which had been careering down stream, spinning and breaking up with thunderous roars just before reaching us as they grounded on the edge of the reef.'

Pelagic recommends going through the narrows at slack water. The current runs strongly at 6 knots. Do this at low water so that the shoal area along the shore can be gauged. Bergy bits run aground on the shoal area. This passage may be better in a dinghy with a powerful outboard. The mountain scenery above the narrows is spectacular.

127

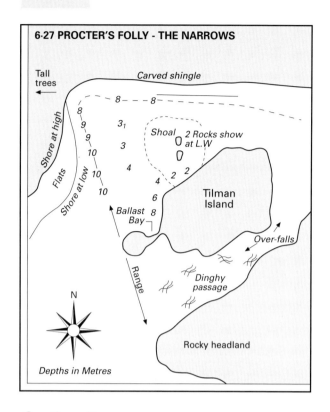

6·27 PROCTER'S FOLLY - THE NARROWS

Tall trees

Carved shingle

Shore at high

Flats

Shore at low

8 — — 8 — — — 8

8

9

9

9

3₁

3

Shoal 2 Rocks show at L.W

10

10

10

4

4

2

2

6

Tilman Island

Ballast Bay 8

Range

Over-falls

Dinghy passage

N

Rocky headland

Depths in Metres

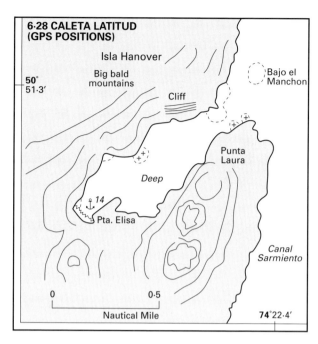

6·28 CALETA LATITUD (GPS POSITIONS)

Isla Hanover

50°
51·3′

Big bald mountains

Cliff

Bajo el Manchon

Punta Laura

Deep

14

Pta. Elisa

Canal Sarmiento

0   0·5

Nautical Mile

74°22·4′

Continuation

6·28 Isla Hanover – Caleta Latitud

50°51′·3S 74°22′·4W (*10340*)

Charts BA *1282, 1286*; Chile *10000, 10340, 10511*

General

This *caleta* is on Isla Hanover at the W side of Canal Sarmiento and just N of the entrance to Estero Peel. Although it appears to be a useful place to stop *en route* to the Amalia Glacier, it is not recommended. Winds gust into the bay and NW gusts fan out and make all shores a lee shore. The possible anchorage is in 15m at the head of the bay and very long lines (100m) would be needed to provide a measure of security.

7. Canal Sarmiento to Puerto Natales and to Islote Fairway

This chapter covers the leg of the *canales* north of Estrecho de Magallanes (Straits of Magallan). Two diversions are described following on from Seno Union and lead into the Andes.

Canal Sarmiento

Charts BA charts do not cover the area E of 73°20'W. Large-scale US charts only cover the S part of this section. The small-scale chart is *22420*

7·1 Puerto Bueno

50°59'7S 74°13'·4W (10500)

Charts BA *1286, 1282*; Chile *10000, 10500, 10511*

General

Puerto Bueno lies on the E side of Canal Sarmiento near the junction with Estero Peel. The entrance is clean and wide to the S of Islote Pounds (Fl.5s18m7M white GRP tower, red band 6m, obscured by Isla Hoskins, 156°-vis-144°). The NW passage between Islote Pounds and Isla Hoskins Sur has Roca Hecate in the middle and foul ground off Hoskins. Go S about Isla Pounds.

Anchorage

Anchorage can be taken close to the shore at either end of the bay, depending on the winds, in 10–15m. At high water it is possible to take the dinghy right up to the base of the waterfall and fill water containers without getting out of the dinghy. From the beach near the waterfall there is an easy walk on small animal trails up to the lake. There are *centollas* (King Crab) in the bay. Puerto Bueno was where Sarmiento spent some time 400 years ago waiting for Drake to pass by – but Drake went into the Pacific through the Estrecho de Magallanes. There is little vegetation here, the wind blows strongly and it is not an attractive place, however it is a reasonable option if an anchorage is required.

7·2 Puerto Mayne

51°19'S 74°05'W (*10500*)

Charts BA *1282*; Chile *10000, 10500, 10511*

General

Puerto Mayne, on Isla Evans, is an impressive bay surrounded with barren hills and edged with trees and shrubs. It has several opportunities for anchoring. The entrance is about 100m wide, but clean.

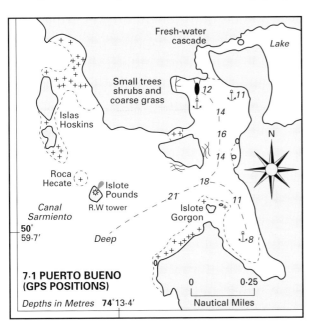

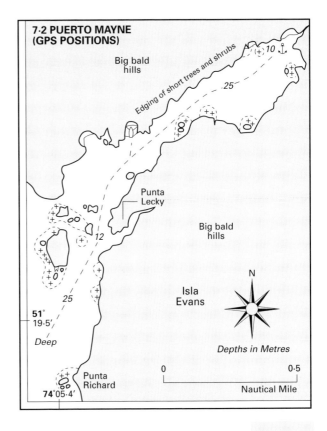

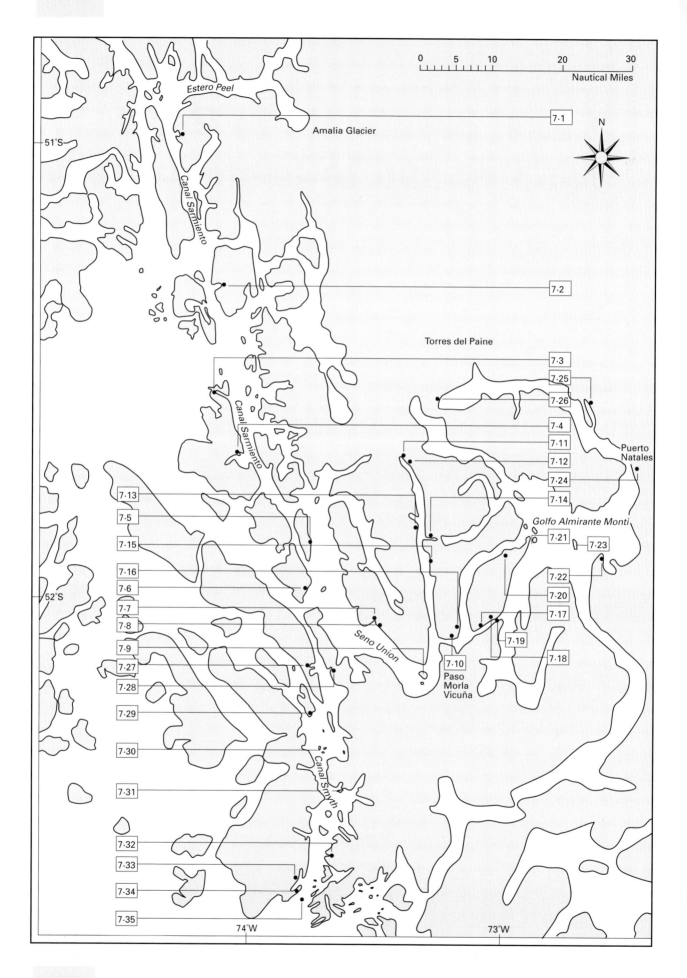

Estero Peel

Amalia Glacier

Canal Sarmiento

7·1

N

51°S

7·2

Torres del Paine

7·3

7·25

7·26

Canal Sarmiento

7·4

7·11

7·12

Puerto
Natales

7·24

7·14

7·13

Golfo Almirante Monti

7·5

7·21

7·23

7·15

7·16

7·22

7·6

7·20

52°S

7·7

7·17

7·8

Seno Union

7·19

7·9

7·18

7·27

7·10

7·28

Paso
Morla
Vicuña

7·29

7·30

Canal Smyth

7·31

7·32

7·33

7·34

7·35

74°W

73°W

0 5 10 20 30
Nautical Miles

Anchorage

There is good holding at the head of the bay in 10m, mud bottom. Lines ashore are advisable as the bay is subject to gusts and *rachas*. Another well recommended spot is the small bay just before the narrows, in 3m at low tide. This is a four point tree-tie.

7·3 Isla Piazzi – Caleta Moonlight Shadow

51°34'·4S 74°01'·8W (*10500*)

Charts BA *1282*; Chile *10000, 10500*

General

Caleta Moonlight Shadow cuts deep through the low-lying land at the N end of Isla Piazzi. It is a very secure and sheltered anchorage and there is little danger of *rachas*. The entrance is a little hard to find; GPS appears to be in agreement with the newly published chart *10500*. The entrance is relatively narrow. Pass to the S of the group of rocks and small *islotes* on the N side of the entrance. There are long strands of kelp in it but these can be threaded through and the area is soon passed. The depths in the narrows are about 8m and then quickly increase to 15–20m. The *caleta* continues deep with no dangers mid-channel for a mile up to the anchorage.

Anchorage

The first position (51°33'·7S 74°04'·6W by GPS) is where shown to the S of the tiny península. Anchor in 7m and take shorelines. A more secure position is in a nook immediately to the SW, sheltered by tall trees. Depth in this anchorage is about 3m shoaling. There is a less well sheltered anchorage in the next bay, with adequate swinging room in about 12m, soft mud. Access is through a pass about 10m wide with minimum depth of 6m, clear of kelp in its centre.

From either anchorage it is a short distance by dinghy to the head of the *caleta*. From there it is a very pleasant walk through the shore-side scrub and out onto moor-like vegetation. When the high point

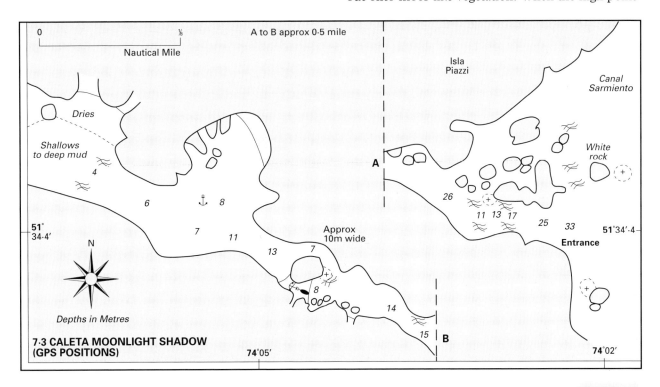

7·3 CALETA MOONLIGHT SHADOW (GPS POSITIONS)

is reached after about half a mile there is a magnificent view over the Pacific.

7·4 Isla Piazzi – Caleta Balandra

51°42'S 74°00'W
Charts BA *1282*; Chile *10000, 10500, 10511, 10700*

General

Travelling S, Caleta Balandra on Isla Piazzi is a logical stopping place after a 45-mile run from Puerto Bueno or a visit to the Amalia Glacier. It is located on the N shore at the entrance to Abra Lecky's Retreat, itself a bay about 1·5M deep. There are two *caletas*, Caleta Ocasión is rocky and exposed, the more sheltered, Caleta Balandra, runs to the W off Caleta Ocasión.

Approach and anchorage

There is a lot of kelp and a shallow spot in the entrance to Balandra but it is deeper inside with 4–5m off the N shore. Anchor in the middle of the bay in 6m, good holding in sand and mud. Lines can be taken ashore.

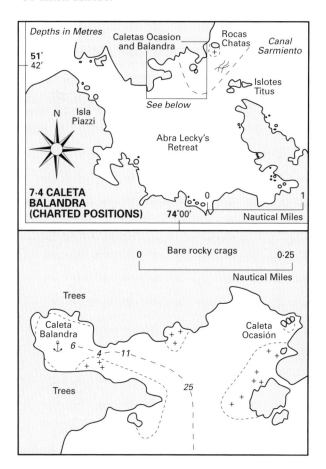

Estrecho de Collingwood

7·5 Isla Newton – Caleta Columbine

51°52'·4S 73°42'·4W
Charts BA *1282*; Chile *10000, 10700*

General

On Isla Newton, as well as being a tide station Caleta Columbine provides good shelter from N and W winds but is open to SE winds. The entrance is clean and wide but beware of the rocky shelf that extends out from the E point, marked by kelp. Although the entrance to the *caleta* is clean there is considerable kelp as the head of the bay is approached. It is necessary to thread through and anchor among this. The anchorage is off the beach in 6m, sand and mud. There may be some effect from the wake of passing ships.

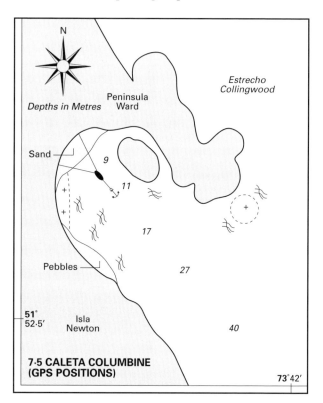

7·6 Isla Hunter – Caleta Victoria

52°00'S 73°45'W 52°00'·20S 73°43'·44W (GPS)
Charts BA *1282*; Chile *10000, 10700*

General

This *caleta* is not named on the chart, but seems to be known by the name of the pass on which it is located. It provides protection from all winds. Although the entrance is open to the SE, it is unlikely that any swell or wind from that direction would be a serious problem in the anchorage. The bay is subject to very strong NW winds, though it is safe in those conditions.

Approach

The entrance is clean as long as it is approached on a course around 300°, with care taken to avoid the

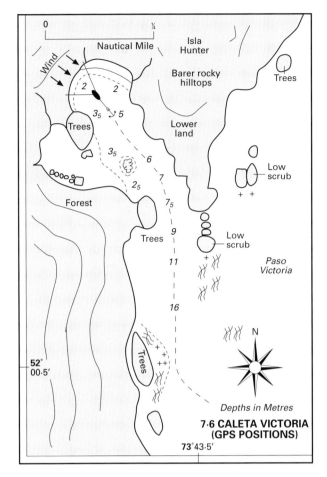

7·6 CALETA VICTORIA (GPS POSITIONS)

7·7 Península Las Montañas – Puerto Fontaine

52°04'S 73°27'·5W (*10640*)

Charts BA *1282*; Chile *10000, 10600, 10640, 10643, 10700*

General

Puerto Fontaine is not a good, but a possible, anchorage on the NE shore of Seno Union, opposite Cabo Año Nuevo. It is sheltered either side of N but poor in S to SE winds. Río Bermudez comes in at the N shore; anchor outside it in 5–10m but go carefully towards the river mouth as it forms banks. Away from the *río*, it is deep and very difficult to tie a line ashore.

Laguna Adelaide, fresh water, has depths of 10–12m and it may be possible to get to it up Río Bermudez by keeping to the E shore. It is very narrow and it would be necessary first to explore by dinghy. There is a waterfall.

7·8 Península Las Montañas – Surgidero Allard

52°04'S 73°26'W

Charts BA *1282* Chile *10000, 10600, 10640, 10712*

General

Surgidero Allard is on the N side of Seno Union immediately to the SE of Puerto Fontaine. It provides good shelter from W winds, though it is exposed to S winds. The holding is good on a sand bottom.

rocks and kelp that extend a considerable distance out from the islands that are the S protection to the *caleta*. The entrance is 10m deep and inside it shoals to 4–5m. There is a large rock in the middle, shown on the sketch plan, which may cover at high water. The water is clear and the extent of this rock can be seen under the water. The bottom of the *caleta* is kelp-covered initially but becomes clear beyond the rock.

Anchorage

Good holding in silt. Shore lines are required as there is insufficient room to swing when fishing vessels also want to moor. The most important mooring line is one taken to the NW corner of the bay, from which direction come very strong *rachas*. It is much used by fishing boats from Puerto Natales, which congregate mainly near the shore immediately W of the anchor symbol.

Seno Union

This *seno* lies to the east of the direct route N or S and leads into the Cordillera de los Andes and to two possible diversions.

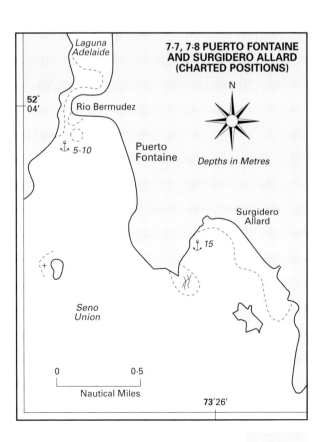

7·7, 7·8 PUERTO FONTAINE AND SURGIDERO ALLARD (CHARTED POSITIONS)

7·9 Isla Jamie

52°10'9S 73°17'·1W (*10640*
Charts BA *630*; Chile *10000, 10600, 10640*

General

The bay on the SE side of Isla Jamie offers excellent protection from all directions except E. Holding off the beach is good in sand and this spot was almost calm in a 35 knot NW. Better shelter may be found where the fishermen have permanent lines on the S side of the cove.

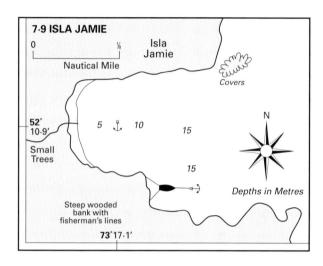

7·10 Paso Morla Vicuña
(unnamed *caleta* on N shore)

52°06'S 73°12'W (GPS agrees with Chile *10640*)
Charts BA *630*; Chile *10000, 10600, 10640*

General

This is a secure anchorage, useful if awaiting suitable tidal or weather conditions before undertaking the diversions below. It is located behind a promontory giving shelter from the W. Fishermen have left lines in the trees marking the spot. Anchor in 10m with lines ashore.

Diversion 1
Estero Las Montañas

Charts BA *630*; Chile *10000, 10600, 10640*

General

This *estero* is about 30M long and takes the traveller into the heart of the Andes with spectacular mountain scenery. Many glaciers fall from the Cordillera Sarmiento, several reaching the sea and easily accessible by dinghy. The charts provide little detail but there are several anchorages. In 2001 the yachts *Balaena* or *Flanneur* visited all the anchorages described. Many other possibilities were observed especially on the W shore behind small promontories.

The *estero* has a reputation for fierce *rachas* in N winds. Despite this there is a substantial amount of well-developed vegetation especially on the W

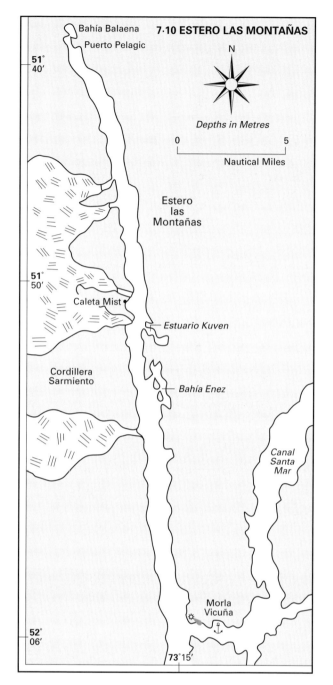

shore, which would suggest that good shelter may be found close to shore when the wind is fierce in open water. Also, because it is in the rain shadow, the weather here tends to be better than to the W of Cordillera Sarmiento, especially at the N end. This area is so spectacular that it is well worth waiting for an opportunity to visit. The anchorages at Paso Morla Vicuña or Isla Jamie are both suitable places to sit out a strong N wind.

All the anchorages are believed to be secure in strong winds. The editor would appreciate more information and reports on conditions experienced. Names given to the anchorages are those of vessels cruising in Patagonia in 2001, as local names are not known.

7·11 Bahía Balaena

51°38'·9S 73°23'·3W (GPS)
Charts BA *630*; Chile *10000, 10600*

General

This is a large shallow bay at the very head of the *estero*. It is well sheltered from the S but could be uncomfortable in a strong N, in which case moving to Puerto Pelagic (7·12) would be the best option. Anchor where shown in 10m, sand and mud, steeply shoaling. It may well be possible to anchor in the area marked unexplored, however the water is opaque due to glacial silt and this makes exploration a little difficult.

From the NE corner of the bay it is possible to climb the mountainside heading N. There are wonderful views of a hidden valley, lakes, rivers and mountains. If the walk is continued above the level of vegetation to the head of the valley there is a magnificent view of the most S glacier of the Campo de Hielo Sur calving into a lake.

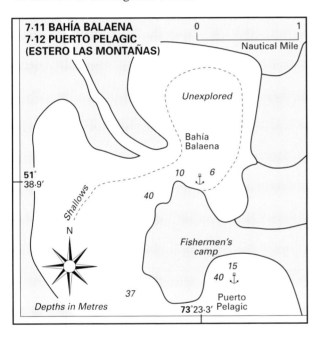

7·12 Puerto Pelagic

51°39'·3S 73°22'·8W (GPS)
Charts BA *630*; Chile *10000, 10600*

General

This is believed to be the most secure spot in the *estero* in N winds. It is obviously well used by fishermen and the presence of large trees indicates good shelter. The bottom shelves rapidly from 40m to the shore, the gradient is greatest off the fishing camp at the W end of the beach. Anchor in 15m with lines pulled well in to the shore.

7·13 Caleta Mist

51°51'·2S 73°19'W (GPS)
Charts BA *630*; Chile *10000, 10600*

General

Large trees and a fishing camp suggest that this *caleta* is well sheltered from the N. A projection about ½M to the S may provide a degree of protection from this direction. Anchor in 15m in sand and pull close to the beach with lines. From here it is a short row to the entrance of a 1M-long *estero* leading to a glacier. This *estero* is particularly spectacular because the sides rise almost vertically to several thousand feet and there are two glaciers that calve over the mountainside with impressive avalanches of ice. There is also a large colony of cormorants.

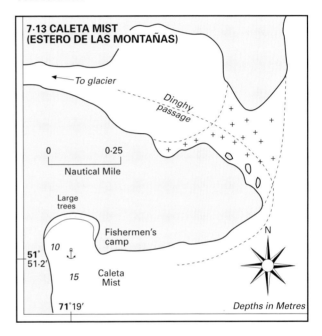

7·14 Estuario Kuven

51°52'·4S 73°17'·4W (GPS Entrance)
Charts BA *630*; Chile *10000, 10600*

General

This is a large estuary with moderate depths and good holding.

Anchorage

There are several good positions. The northern anchorage shown has plenty of room to swing in 4m sand and mud and gives excellent views across the *estero*, however it may be exposed in bad weather. It is thought that the best spot in strong N winds could be the innermost anchorage with a line to the N shore.

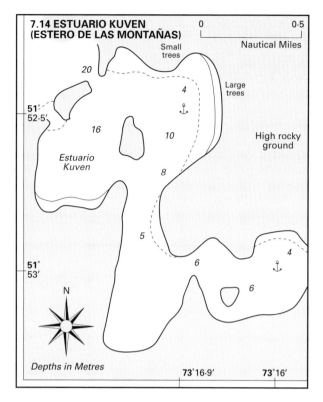

7.14 ESTUARIO KUVEN (ESTERO DE LAS MONTAÑAS)

Small trees
20
4
Large trees
51° 52·5′
16
10
High rocky ground
Estuario Kuven
8
51° 53′
5
4
6
N
6
Depths in Metres
73°16·9′   73°16′
0   0·5   Nautical Miles

7·15 Islas and Bahía Enez

51°55′S 73°17′W (GPS)
Charts BA *630*; Chile *10000, 10600*

General

Two anchorages have been used. Caleta Flanneur is easy to enter but with no shelter from the south. A tour of the inner bay showed that there are other possibilities at the N and S ends.

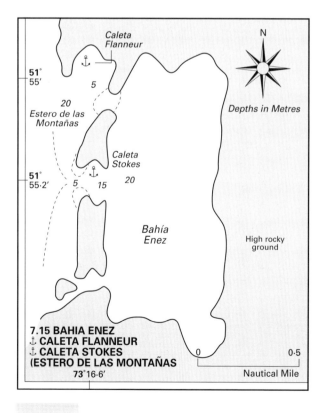

Caleta Flanneur
N
51° 55′
5
20
Estero de las Montañas
Depths in Metres
Caleta Stokes
51° 55·2′
5   15
20
Bahía Enez
High rocky ground
7.15 BAHIA ENEZ
⚓ **CALETA FLANNEUR**
⚓ **CALETA STOKES**
(ESTERO DE LAS MONTAÑAS
73°16·6′
0   0·5   Nautical Mile

7·15a Caleta Flanneur

51°55′S 73°17′W (GPS)
Charts BA *630*; Chile *10000, 10600*

General

There are two large fishermen's camps here with good holding in 5m. In strong winds better shelter will be found by pulling close to shore.

7·15b Caleta Stokes

51°55′·2S 73°16′·6W (GPS)
Charts BA *630*; Chile *10000, 10600*

General

The entrance is a little tricky between two sandbanks (GPS co-ordinates of entrance 51°55′·2S 73°16′·7W). However the water is clear and there is a little kelp to mark the banks. There is 5m in the entrance that deepens within and provides good access to the inner bay.

Anchorage

Holding here is superb in 4m in thick mud. Vegetation is sparse so it may be windy but as there is no high ground in the immediate vicinity winds may be steady.

Diversion 2
Seno Union and Golfo Almirante Montt to Seno Ultima Esperanza via Puerto Natales

Charts BA *1282*; Chile *10600*

General

Puerto Natales is a long detour for yachts *en route* S or N. Along the route there are several secure anchorages. Puerto Natales itself is a fairly marginal anchorage but nearby Puerto Consuelo in Seno Eberhardt is excellent and larger vessels with a powerful tender will find Puerto La Forest, opposite Puerto Natales to be safe and convenient. The passage is spectacular and Puerto Natales is an excellent place for a crew change, to visit the Torres del Paine and to provision.

It is also possible to sail NW from Puerto Natales up Seno Ultima Esperanza. The inner parts of this *seno* offer fantastic views of and access to mountains and glaciers. It is a national park and takes the yacht very close to Torres del Paine. Tourism is being developed with 70,000 tourists visiting the Torres del Paine each year.

Leaving Canal Collingwood, take the route through Seno Union, along Canal Morla Vicuña, either through Canal White or Canal Kirke and then cross Golfo Almirante Montt passing W of Isla Focus. The route passes through the Andes and is one of the most spectacular waterways in Chile. Although it is possible to reach Natales in one day, the necessity to transit the narrows in Canal Kirke at slack water or the occurrence of strong winds on the E side of the Andes often means a two-day trip.

Canal Kirke is shorter with fewer obstacles; but Canal White is more spectacular.

7·16 Puerto Condell

52°04'·4S 73°08'·7W (10640)
Charts BA *630*; Chile *10600, 10640, 10641*

General

At the S entrance of Canal Santa Maria which leads to Canal White. It is a bay wide open to the S. The anchorage is close to the beach just W of the S side of Isla Margarita. Anchor in 6m in sand. The anchorage provides protection from the N. A little susceptible to *rachas*.

Canal Kirke

7·17 Isla Diego Portales – Caleta Cascada

52°04'·7S 73°04'·8W (*10640*)
Charts Chile *10600, 10640, 10641*

General

Caleta Cascada is a reasonable anchorage before Canal Kirke. The entrance is easy and clear from the SW. Anchor in about 12m. Good holding. The bay is protected from the W, N and E.

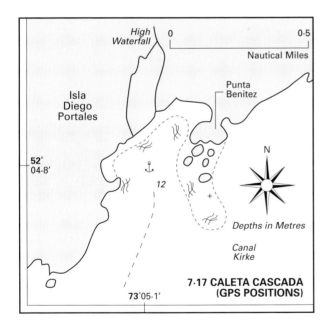

7·17 CALETA CASCADA (GPS POSITIONS)

7·18 Isla Diego Portales – Caleta Espinosa

52°04'·3S 73°03'·5W
Charts Chile *10600, 10640, 10641*

General

Caleta Espinosa is about 1·5M from the SW end of Canal Kirke and half way to Angostura Kirke. The bays on both sides of the island have been visited; they are both deep (20m plus) and neither were inviting as an anchorage. If waiting some hours for the tide, Caleta Cascada would be better.

7·19 Angostura Kirke

52°03'S 73°00'·7W
Charts Chile *10650, 10641*

General

Canal Kirke is a narrow pass draining the huge *esteros* that run 30 miles N and S from Puerto Natales. As a result, tidal streams can run at 8–10kts in the narrows and at times more than this. Both the *armada* and local fishermen treat the pass with respect and traverse it at slack water. Times of slack water can vary by as much as an hour compared to published times. The time of low water is more reliable and the stand is longer than at high water. At slack water in calm conditions the traverse of the pass is straightforward with a 1–2kts current and little sign of disturbance on the water. It is probably wise to arrive at the pass a short time before slack water and commence the traverse with the current running weakly counter to the yacht's direction. This would allow the yacht to hang back if conditions are not right and then go through dead on slack.

When moving E, after passing Isla Medio Canal it may be wise to head up towards Punta Escoben, about 039°, in order to identify the leading marks. These are two posts with orange triangles and white borders, on the W shore 400m N of Isla Medio Canal. The line, 090° or 270°, leads between Punta Restinga and Isla Merino.

Anchorage may be found at Caleta Zorro at the E end of Kirke (see plan). This bay is clear and deep to its head if entered on a central line. It would be possible to anchor close to the head in about 14m and take shore lines, or to tie to the shore near the S entrance, where fishermen have fixed tyres to make a mooring point. Caleta Zorro is open to the W.

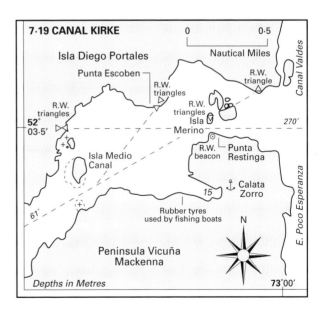

7·19 CANAL KIRKE

Canal White

Charts Chile *10600, 10631*

General

The approach to Canal White, along Canal Santa Maria, gives spectacular mountain views. Canal White presents no serious obstacles. Currents are said to be strong at springs and every attempt should be made to pass at slack water. From the hills above Caleta Chandler it is possible to observe the times of slack.

7·20 Caleta Chandler, Canal White

51°54'·65S 72°59'·5W (GPS in anchorage)
Charts Chile *10600, 10631*

General

This small inlet is situated just before the canal and offers excellent protection. There is room for vessels up to 16m, though manoeuvring in the narrow entrance is awkward. Strong gusts blow SW up Caleta Chandler, therefore it is important to pull well into the small indentation by taking lines ashore. Once in, it is a very good anchorage and the walking is excellent with close-up sightings of condors possible.

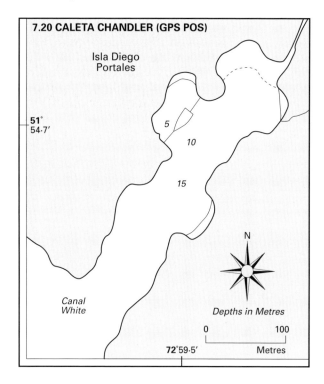

Canal Valdes

7·21 Isla Diego Portales – Bahía Easter

51°53'·5S 72°53'W (*10631*)
Charts Chile *10600, 10631*

General

Bahía Easter is at the NE end of Isla Diego Portales, behind Islas Lavaqui, about 1·5M S of the N entrance to Canal White. It has good shelter in depths of 11m, sand. There are shallows in the middle of the entrance and round the N edge of the bay. Favour the W shore on entering.

Golfo Almirante Montt

7·22 Bahía Desengaño – Puerto Lastarria

51°55'·4S 72°36'W
Charts Chile *10600, 10643*

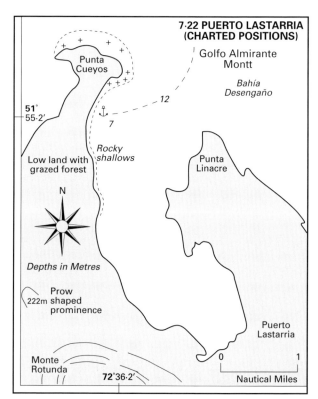

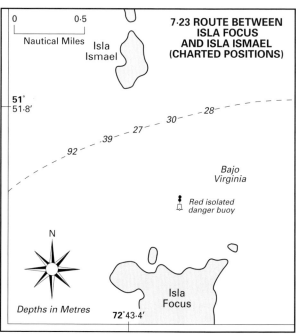

General

Located 15 miles S of Puerto Natales, Puerto Lastarria is a large open bay, which provides good shelter from W to NW winds behind the low land on its W side. The holding is very good in heavy clay about 8m, close along the W shore. In strong S wind the bay is sufficiently large for the anchorage to become fairly choppy. In these conditions better shelter may be found at the SE corner of the bay.

7·23 Passage between Isla Ismael and Isla Focus

Charts Chile *10600*

General

The route between these two islands taken by all fishing boats and the Navimag ferry is to pass about half a mile S of Isla Ismael, as shown on the plan. There is a minimum depth of about 27m if this line is followed.

7·24 Puerto Natales

51°44'S 72°31'W (*10600*)
Charts Chile *10600, 10610, 10611*
Port communications
VHF Ch 16 c/s *CBW*

General

The anchorage in front of town is totally exposed to the strong NW and W winds that blow regularly, particularly in the afternoon. Winds can change from calm to gale force with no warning. Natales is the principal town of the area serving sheep and cattle farms and the timber industry. Founded in 1912, it has a population of 19,000 and has a strong

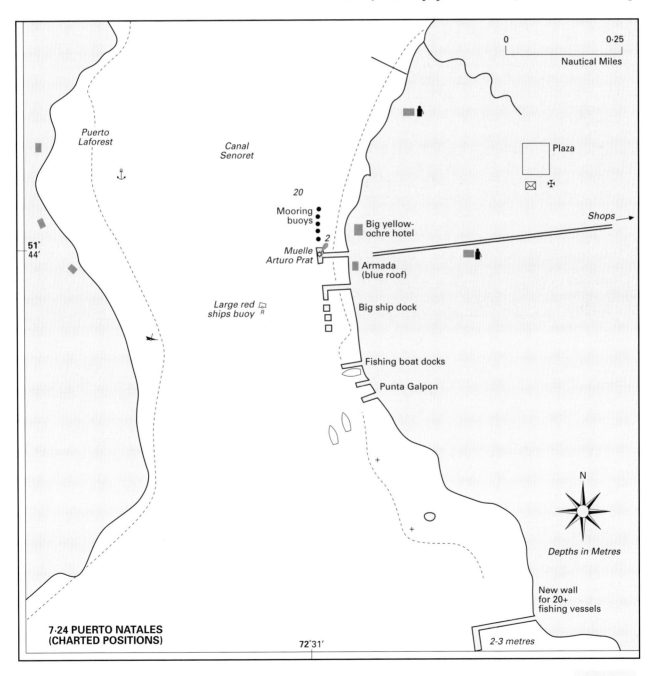

7·24 PUERTO NATALES
(CHARTED POSITIONS)

summer tourist industry, supported by hotels, restaurants and transport facilities; it is the centre for excursions to the glaciers and Parque Nacional Torres del Paine.

Anchorage

Anchorage is possible but not recommended off the rock-fringed shore just to the N of a group of local mooring buoys. Anchor in 10m or less, mud and sand, open to the N. The bottom shelves very quickly. The anchorage is on a shallow shelf that extends less than a tenth of a mile off the shore. The port captain is not happy with yachts staying at anchor without crew on board as yachts have dragged ashore. It may be possible to tie up to one of the buoys. They are owned by two local men, one of whom, Konrado Alvares, owns the gaff-rigged schooner, the *Penguin*, built in 1907 in the UK and used until recently as the government launch in the Falklands. Even if permission is given to use a mooring it is wise to set one or two anchors to the NW as extra security. When the Navimag ferry arrives, it may go beyond the ship terminal dock, turn in Canal Senoret and then, with a line to the large red shipping buoy, go alongside.

It is possible to tie within the shelter of a new concrete fishing boat pier to the S of town (see Chile *10611*). Depth here is barely 2m, a little more outside the pier, which lacks shelter. Call *terminal pesquero* for permission. There is a small charge, hot showers included. The terminal staff will arrange for a truck to call with fuel. This pier is very secure from the strongest winds when moored within.

It is possible to anchor on the shore opposite Puerto Natales at Puerto Laforest to obtain good protection from the N and W winds, but the strong winds can make it almost impossible to travel by dinghy across the ¾M stretch between this anchorage and Puerto Natales.

Vessels of less than 2m draught planning to stay for any time are advised to use Puerto Consuelo (7·25).

Formalities

The *capitanía* is a blue-roofed building between the main shipping pier and Muelle Arturo Prat.

There are immigration authorities in Puerto Natales who can authorise a 3-month extension to a visa. Alternatively, it is only about 1 hour by bus to Río Turbio, an unattractive coal-mining town across the Argentinian border. Buses run mainly morning and evening; it is possible to take a bus late afternoon and return the same evening with a fresh stamp in the passport.

Facilities

The nearest diesel pump is on the corner of Bulnes and Militar, two blocks in from the Capitanía. It is also possible to fill up with diesel alongside the *terminal pesquero* from a mobile truck; ask at the office for details.
Water from the pier.
Supermarkets on Bulnes, 3rd and 10th blocks.
Excellent fresh fruit and vegetable shops.

Hardware and general spares available.
Laundry at Lavandería Papaguyao, Bulnes 518; Tienda Milodon, Bulnes.
Dentist Dr. Nelson Zuniga, whose clinic is conveniently located on one of the streets surrounding the main square.

Communications

Air: Ladeco, Bulnes 530.
Buses to Punta Arenas, Puerto Montt, Argentina.
Car hire: If renting a car, be sure the spare tyre is in good condition as the road to Torres del Paine is unpaved.
Telephone: Area code 61. Office Eberhardt 417.
Internet: many places offer connections.

7·25 Seno Eberhardt – Puerto Consuelo

51°36'·4S 72°39'·5W
Charts Chile *10600, 10610*

General

About 8 miles N of Puerto Natales, Seno Eberhardt provides excellent security in the prevailing W winds, though these do tend to be funnelled down the *seno* with great force. Enter on the rising tide in settled conditions.

It is a marvellous place for hiking and viewing the spectacular mountain ranges to the N and W. There are a number of interesting species of birds in the area including flamingos, coots, owls and condors. This is a good spot from which to make longer visits to Puerto Natales or the surrounding area.

The grandfather of the present owners founded Estancia Consuelo. He was a seaman who came from Germany in search of suitable land to set up as a sheep farmer. After failing to find land in the Falklands or Argentine Patagonia he rowed up to Ultima Esperanza in an open boat. For him it was the 'last hope'. The *estancia* prospered but recently has had a chequered history and with the current slump in wool and mutton prices looks to tourism for the future.

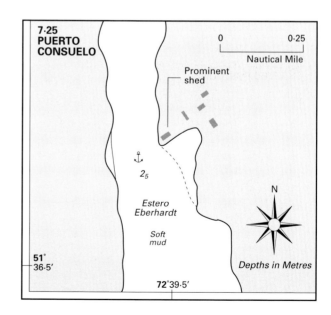

Anchorage

Very secure anchorage in 2·5m mud can be found at Punta Cajon (slightly to the north of the symbol shown on Chile *10610*) near the Eberhardt homestead (Estancia Consuelo). In 2001 it was possible to get a lift to town and an inexpensive taxi back. Several vessels have been left here for a week or more in complete safety. The *estero* may freeze in mid-winter.

7·26 Seno Ultima Esperanza – Lago Azul

Charts Chile *10600, 10610*

General

Chilean chart *10610* gives the details of entering the *seno*. This is the most difficult part. Stay mid-channel for the first part of the *seno* above the narrows.

Anchorage

1. (See plan) Anchorages can be found at the W end of the *seno* in one of the three bays NE of the river entrance to the Blue Lagoon. All are deep and require shore lines. Tie off to the trees with the yacht tucked in very close to shore.

   There is a good dinghy trip into the Blue Lagoon. The quiet river mouth is too shallow for a yacht.

2. Previously the tourist pier at Río Serrano provided a good option when not in use by boats, which come from Puerto Natales with day-trippers. In 2001 this was in bad repair and considered unsafe.

3. In a small bay NW of the delta of the mouth of the Río Serrano a new hostel has been built. The hostel has a good pier but with only 1·7m depth. Anchor in 20m E of the pier (GPS 51°24'·9S 73°05'·7W). The bay is open to the S and the SW.

It is possible to travel right up the Río Serrano with a well-powered dinghy. The navigation is difficult as the current is strong and the glacier meltwater makes it impossible to see the bottom. Take care of the sandbanks in the middle of the river. Branches also add a risk to the inflatable. There is only one necessary portage of about 30m and the dinghy can get right up to Lago del Toro. Tourist companies in Puerto Natales make organised trips in large inflatables along the full length of this river. There is an *estancia* about 2 hours up the river, where two big rivers meet. From here it is possible to hire horses to take a very pleasant excursion up into the mountains. The *estancia* offers lodgings.

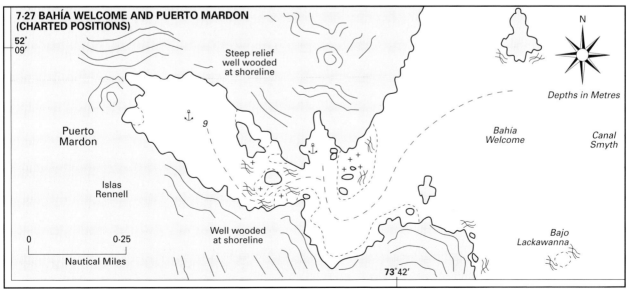

Continuation

Isla Brinkley to Isla Tamar

The route winds S through Paso Victoria to Canal Smyth merging in to Estrecho Magallanes at Isla Tamar.

Canal Smyth

7·27 Islas Rennell – Bahía Welcome – Puerto Mardon

52°09'·5S 73°42'·6W

Charts BA *1282*; Chile *10000, 10700, 10712*

General

On the W side of Canal Smyth, the outer anchorage is sheltered from all winds. The inner anchorage (Puerto Mardon) is attractive but should only be used in settled weather as it is subject to strong *rachas*.

Approach and anchorage

The outer anchorage is the small *caleta* on the N side of the entrance. It is secure and frequently used by fishermen. Anchor in 5m with lines to shore near the fishing camp.

Puerto Mardon has rocks obstructing the channel but with a careful lookout a safe entrance can be made with 4m at low water. Pass close S of the exposed rock in the entrance and then steer towards the S shore. The dangers are clearly marked by thick kelp. The anchorage is in the centre of the basin in 10m, with good holding. The very high hills that surround the anchorage make it prone to *rachas*, though none were experienced when it was blowing 30 knots from the NW. There is a good stream for water at the head of the bay.

7·28 Península Zach – Bahías Isthmus and Mallet

52°10'S 73°37'·5W

Charts BA *1282* Chile *10000, 10700, 10712*

General

Coming from the N, it is easy to spot this anchorage at the S end of Península Zach, as there is a tall and rusty, red iron beacon on the N point. The entrance route is marked with a green buoy and further in by a second green buoy (unlit, numbers 2066 & 2068 in Chile light list) both of which should be left to port. Large ships anchor in this area, but yachts can continue on to Bahía Mallet that is on the E side at the head of Bahía Isthmus. The basin shallows in the SE part.

Anchorage

The anchorage is in 10m, mud. Boats have experienced *rachas* in this basin. The problem at the head of Bahía Isthmus is that the isthmus itself causes air turbulence, which adds to the usual *rachas* caused by the high ground.

An alternative is to anchor where shown on the

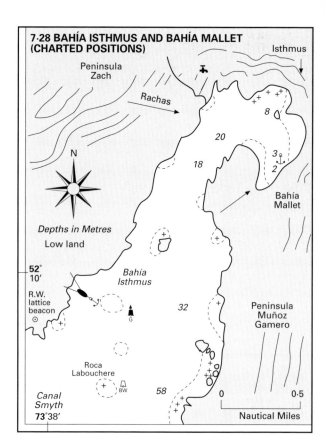

7·28 BAHÍA ISTHMUS AND BAHÍA MALLET (CHARTED POSITIONS)

plan near the entrance to Bahía Isthmus but this spot has poor holding in kelp and rock. The surrounding land is low and less subject to *rachas*. There is a portage to Seno Union if anyone feels like a hike and good hiking on the surrounding hills. On a clear day Mount Burney (1760m) can be seen to the SE.

7·29 Isla Baverstock – Bahía Fortuna

52°15'S 73°42'W

Charts BA *1282, 631*; Chile *10000, 10700*

General

On the E side of Isla Baverstock and 7M from Bahía Isthmus, it has protection from the N and W. It is not recommended for a night stop but has a waterfall if tanks are low. The entrance has Islote Low on its NE side and two other rocks just SE of Low.

7·30 Islas Otter

52°22'·4S 73°40'W

Charts BA *1282, 1281, 631*; US *22405*; Chile *10000, 11111*

General

Islas Otter are a group of islands in Canal Smyth between Isla Pedro Montt and Península Muñoz Gamero. On a N bound trip, the shelter amongst these islands provides good protection from the NW winds. The bay is open to winds from the SW. Caleta Otter is on the S side of Isla Campbell and approached from the SW, between Islas Cunningham and Bedwell. The anchorage is close

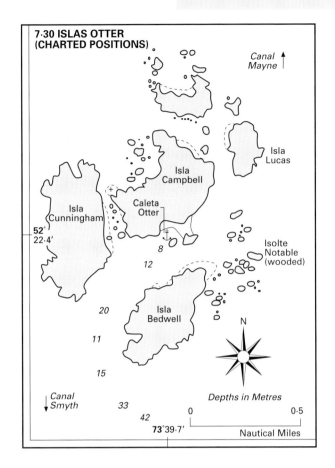

7·30 ISLAS OTTER (CHARTED POSITIONS)

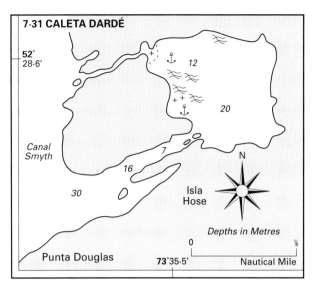

7·31 CALETA DARDÉ

to the shore underneath Isla Campbell, in mud. It is also possible to anchor on the E side of the peninsula on the E side of Caleta Otter. This peninsula covers at high tide.

7·31 Isleta Hose – Caleta Dardé

52°28'·5S 73°35'·3W 52°28'·9S,73°35'·7W (GPS – entrance)
Charts BA *1282, 631*; US *22405*; Chile *10000, 11111*

General

Caleta Dardé, named after those who first described it, is on the SW side of the waist of Isla Hose. The entrance to the *caleta* is obstructed by a small unnamed island and can be a little difficult to see. The channel on the NW side of this small island is not passable. The channel on its SW side is narrow, 8m depth, with room enough to dodge the kelp-marked rocks if care is taken.

Anchorage

Anchor in the NW corner of the *caleta* or, with lines, to a shallow bay on the NE face of the small island in 10m. The bottom comes up quickly and there are two rocks close to the latter position. The *caleta* is well sheltered in strong winds from NW to SW.

7·32 Caleta Burgoyne

52°37'·5S 73°39'W
Charts BA *1282, 1281, 631*; US *22404*; Chile *10000, 11112*

General

On the S part of Península Muñoz Gamero, the entrance to Caleta Burgoyne is immediately S of Cabo Walker (Fl(3)9s12m7M White GRP tower, red band 4m. 035°-vis-188°). The middle of the entrance is clear but within, there is a rock marked by a black and white buoy, which should be left to port. Keep in the middle until a small point and two rocks have been passed to port, then make cautiously towards the bay on the N shore; the bottom comes up quickly. Anchor off in 10–15m, mud, with lines ashore. In strong W or SW winds the small bay on the W side of the main bay would be a good alternative anchorage.

Caleta Burgoyne is a good place to wait for weather in Paso Tamar, 15M to the S, and is well within range of Islote Fairway on Ch 16.

7·33 Isla Manuel Rodriguez – Puerto Profundo

52°41'·05S 73°45'·41W
Charts BA *1282, 1281, 631*; US *22404*; Chile *10000, 11100, 11112*

General

Puerto Profundo, towards the SE end of Isla Manuel Rodriguez, is an excellent stopping place before entering or after leaving the Estrecho de Magallanes. It is an intricate system of waterways amongst low-lying land, and provides excellent shelter from all winds.

Approach and anchorage

The entrance to Puerto Profundo is wide and clean, but favour the S side to avoid two rocks to the SE of Isla Carreta. The main harbour is deep, but there is a large *armada* buoy at 52°40'·7S 73°46'·0W (GPS) to which a yacht may moor with bow and stern line, or with bow line and a long line to the shore from the stern. From here it is possible to reach Fairway

143

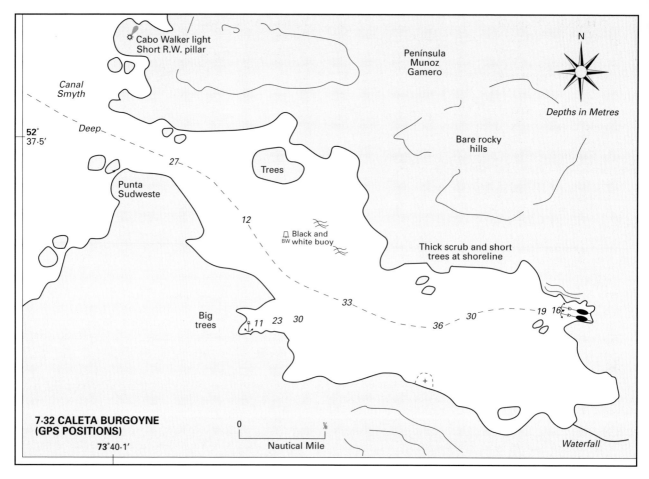

7·32 CALETA BURGOYNE (GPS POSITIONS)

Light on VHF to report your position and obtain a current weather forecast. There is also an anchorage between Isla Carreta and the long, thin island to its NW. Enter from the NE. Good walking on Isla Carreta. Two bays with good shelter have been reported opposite and northwest of Isla Carreta.

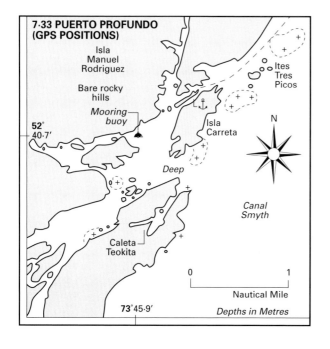

7·33 PUERTO PROFUNDO (GPS POSITIONS)

7·34 Puerto Profundo – Caleta Teokita

52°41'·2S 73°45'·2W

Charts BA *1282, 1281, 631*; US *22404*; Chile *10000, 11100, 11112*

General

The approach to Caleta Teokita, an otherwise unnamed *caleta*, is in the S arm of the entrance to Puerto Profundo. The entrance is narrow but is easily negotiated. There is kelp either side of the entrance but the route in is clear. The *caleta* is surrounded by low-lying hills so that there is little risk of *rachas*, however the wind blows very strongly here. Proceed to the head of the *caleta* as shown on the chart and anchor in mud in about 6m with shorelines. It is possible to anchor very close to the beach at the head of the creek so that the yacht is tucked well under the trees. Caleta Teokita provides better shelter than Puerto Profundo does.

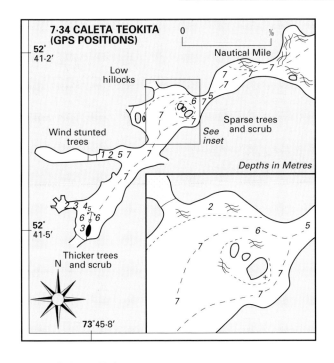

against large rubber tyres against the N shore of Islote Fairway. Approach either from the W or via the narrow passage between the *islote* and the small *islote* to its N. It would be wise only to consider this in settled weather, though the island is spared the heavier seas of the straits.

7.35 Islote Fairway

52°43'·8S 73°46'·3W (*11100*)

Charts BA *1282, 1281, 631*; US *22404, 22412*; Chile *10000, 11100, 11112, 11120*

Light

1480 **Islote Fairway** Fl.5s39m19M White tower, orange bands 5·5m 268°-vis-266°. VHF Ch16 c/s *CBM4*

General

This lighthouse has a well-deserved reputation for friendly keepers. Many yachts have been welcomed for a social call at the light. It is possible to moor

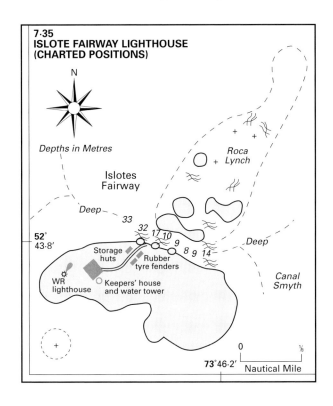

8. Estrecho de Magallanes, Tamar to Dungeness

8·1 Isla Tamar – Caleta Rachas

52°54'S 73°48'W

Charts BA *1281, 1282, 631*; US *22412*; Chile *11000, 11100, 11120*

General

Caleta Rachas is on the E side of Isla Tamar. This is not a good anchorage as it is exposed to severe *rachas* and should only be used in settled weather or as a last resort. The route inside the island, though tricky, provides a sheltered short cut.

Approach

From the N, the approach around the NE corner of Isla Tamar, Paso Roda, is difficult to identify. The entrance lies between Rochas Izquierda, and Punta Grup. Great care is needed, as the channel is very narrow. Rocks seaward of the Rochas Izquierda need to be avoided. If coming from the N, hold close to the islet with the marker on it, judging distance off by the kelp. As the island comes abeam there is a barrier of kelp ahead and you should turn sharply to starboard around the marker island in order to leave the kelp and Rocas Derechas (awash) to port. From that point in to the anchorage the route is then straightforward, though the cove has several offshore islets, the Islotes Cleto. The passage lies between them and Tamar.

The S entrance is more open.

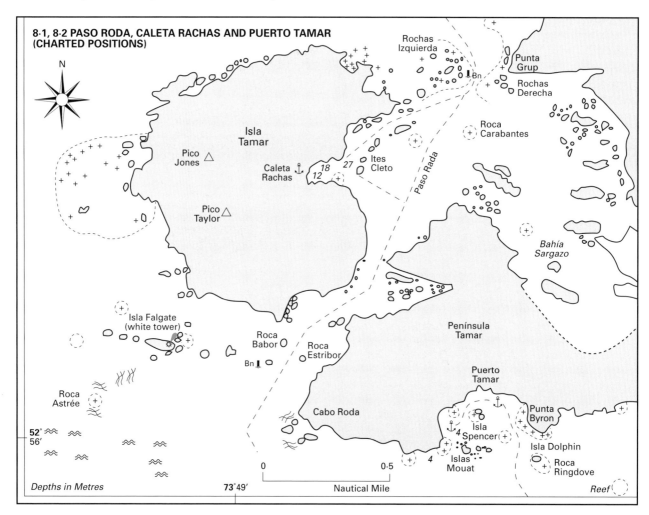

8·1, 8·2 PASO RODA, CALETA RACHAS AND PUERTO TAMAR (CHARTED POSITIONS)

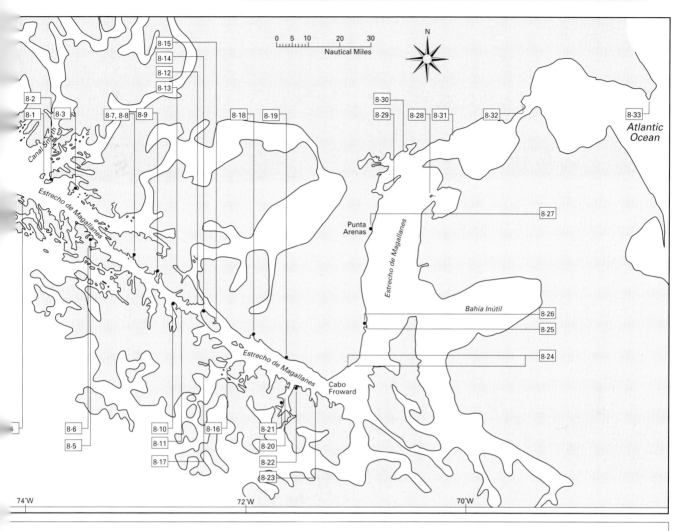

Anchorage

One anchorage lies at the head of the *caleta*, in about 12m. Alternatively anchor in a notch on the N shore with the W end of the most W of Islotes Cleto bearing 133°, use an anchor and lines ashore.

8·2 Península Tamar – Puerto Tamar

52°56'S 73°46'W

Charts BA *1281 631*; US *22412*; Chile *11000, 11100, 11200, 11131*

General

The S side of Península Tamar has shelter from the NW but is subject to *rachas*. Approach Puerto Tamar with the most E Islet of Islas Mouat in line with the prominent white mark visible on the shore. When S of the W end of Punta Byron head N to pass W of Isla Dolphin and the E of the shoal patch, which is clearly marked by kelp. Then proceed to

147

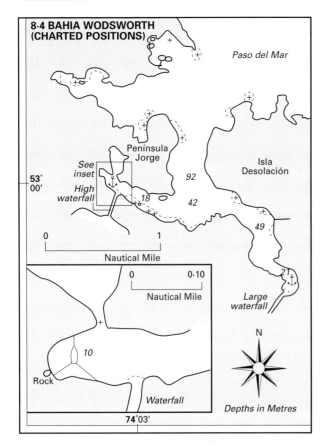

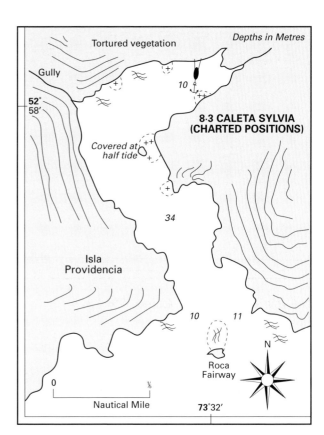

anchor E of Isla Spencer off the beach in 5–11m depths.

Paso Largo

8·3 Isla Providencia – Caleta Sylvia

52°58'S 73°32'W

Charts BA *1281, 631* US *22412*; Chile *11000, 11200, 11212*

General

Caleta Sylvia is on the SE side of Isla Providencia and has a hook to the NE. The gully at the NW corner funnels the wind and *rachas* can be strong. The rock at the entrance can be passed either side. Go up to the NE corner and get lines to the trees on the N shore with anchors off, 10m. The tormented vegetation in Caleta Sylvia shows this to be a wild place. It is an anchorage only for use in an emergency though one large yacht reported it to be very good and calm with 40 knots NW blowing outside.

8·4 Isla Desolación – Bahía Wodsworth

52°59'S 74°01'W

Charts BA *1281, 631*; US *22412*; Chile *10000, 11000, 11100, 11114*

General

Wodsworth, on Isla Desolación, is easy to find as the 100m waterfall that falls into the bay is visible from the N side of the straits 20 miles away. Bahía Felix Light (Fl.15s30m21M White round metal tower with red bands and building, 14m 122°-vis-294°) is

about a mile to the N. The entrance is wide and clean, and there are no dangers in the bay. There are two possible spots to anchor, in the NW corner, close W of the waterfall, or at the end of the E bay, both with lines ashore. The anchorages are well sheltered and very beautiful.

8·5 Isla Desolación – Puerto Angosto

53°13'S 73°20'W

Charts BA *1281, 887*; US *22412*; Chile *11000, 11200, 11212*

General

On the SE part of Isla Desolación (called Isla Jacques on charts BA *1281* and; Chile *11212*), Puerto Angosto is where Joshua Slocum received what he described as a 'Fuegian autograph', a shower of arrows. The anchorage has strong *rachas* and a rocky bottom. The entrance is wide, but be careful of the rock off the islands on the N shore. Once in the entrance there is immediate shelter from strong W winds. There are a number of anchorages.

1. Fishermen tie up against the wall where shown on the sketch plan.
2. In the small bay S of Punta Hoy 53°13'·2S 73°21'·8W (GPS). It is possible to take a 4-point line tie-off ashore as well as set anchors. This anchorage is subject to gusts but is secure.
3. At the head of the bay near the waterfall with lines ashore: for yachts drawing less than 2m and for fair weather.

Caleta Mostyn provides much better shelter than Puerto Angosto.

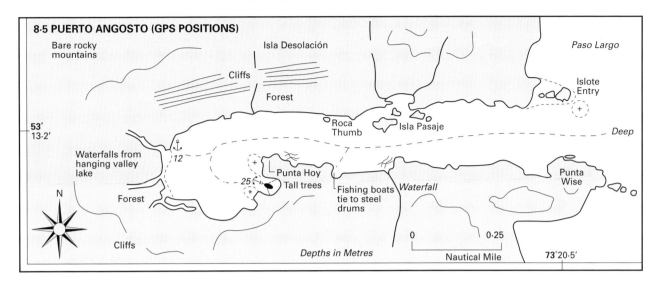

8·5 PUERTO ANGOSTO (GPS POSITIONS)

8·6 Isla Desolación – Caleta Mostyn

53°16'S 73°22'W

Charts BA *1281, 887*; US *22415*; Chile *11000, 11200*

General

Caleta Mostyn is the N-most arm at the head of Estero Cormorant on Isla Desolación. It is a small bay with a narrow entrance marked by two islets on the port side when entering and is to be found by following the N shore of Cormorant. It has good shelter, once within, but may be exposed to S winds.

Anchorage

Anchor in the NW corner in 10m, mud on rock but good holding, and take a line to a sturdy tree. Several vessels have reported shelter here with strong winds (especially NW gales) in the strait.

8·7 Península Córdova – Caleta Playa Parda

53°19'S 73°01'W (*11312*)

Charts BA *1281, 887*; US *22415;* Chile *11000, 11200, 11312, 11700*

General

Caleta Playa Parda is one mile ENE of Isla Shelter, at the E side of the entrance to Estero Playa Parda.

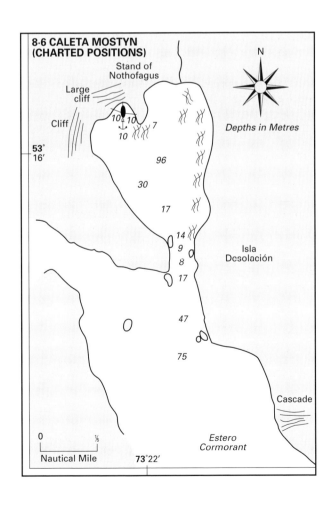

8·6 CALETA MOSTYN (CHARTED POSITIONS)

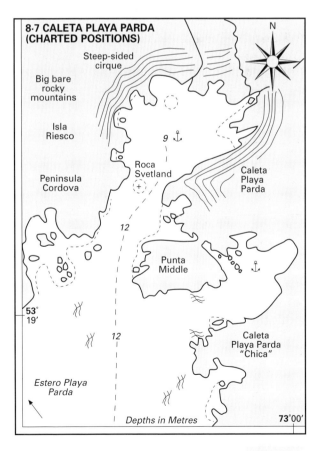

8·7 CALETA PLAYA PARDA (CHARTED POSITIONS)

149

The scenery is spectacular; there is good holding and room to swing.

Approach and anchorage

Go into the N basin (leave Roca Svetland, in the middle of the channel, to port), 10m mud. Some patches of soft mud but good holding in the centre of the *caleta* with the waterfall bearing 080°. Sheltered from the SW but subject to severe *rachas* in NW, when Caleta Playa Parda Chica is a better anchorage for small vessels. Estero Playa Parda, a long inlet about a mile to the W of Caleta Playa Parda, is mentioned in *Mantellero's Guide* as being used by fishermen.

8·8 Caleta Playa Parda Chica

53°18'·70S 73°00'·01W (GPS)

Charts BA *1281, 887*; US *22415*; Chile *11000, 11200, 11312, 11700*

General

For small vessels, less than 13m, a better alternative to Playa Parda is Playa Parda Chica, a small bay well protected from W and NW winds, which offers protection from the SW when the even smaller bay in the NW corner is used. It is possible to take lines ashore. As the surrounding hills are lower than those of Playa Parda and are well wooded, there is less risk of *rachas*. The entrance appears clear and by keeping fairly close to the kelp of the N shore there is a depth of 6–7m. This may be the best small boat anchorage in this stretch of the strait.

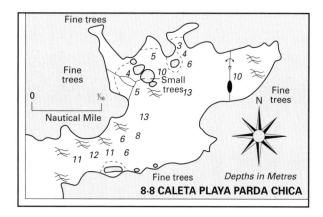

8·8 CALETA PLAYA PARDA CHICA

8·9 Península Córdova – Caleta Notch

53°24'S 72°49'W

Charts BA *1281, 887*; US *22415*; Chile *11000, 11200, 11311, 11700*

General

Caleta Notch is about halfway along Península Córdova and is one of the more spectacular anchorages in this area. If you have a copy of the discontinued BA chart *547*, use it.

Approach

The entrance is narrow but clean, keeping well clear of the rocks on the N side of the entrance off Isla Collins. It has shelter from all winds and good

holding but it has severe *rachas*. Do not try to enter at night. When passing to the E of Isla Westley the rock lying off this island can be avoided by lining up the whitish patch on the shore to the N with the cairn above it.

Anchorage

In the inner basin there are several possible anchorages in 3·5 to 11m, hard mud. However in severe weather there is no one place that gives complete security as the *rachas* tend to come from many directions. Several boats have found it preferable to anchor in 7–8m, off a waterfall on the west shore, at the N end of the basin. There is an excellent notch for a small boat, often used by fishermen, just inside the entrance on the port side. The bottom is rocky so four lines ashore may be needed. A climb up the hill on the N side gives a good view of the conditions in the straits.

Paso Tortuoso

Paso Tortuoso (twisted and devious pass) has earned its name (see Tilman) and most yachts try to get past as quickly as possible.

8·10 Isla Spider

53°31'·4S 72°40'·4W

Charts BA *1281, 554, 887*; US *22415*; Chile *11000, 11200, 11230, 11700*

General

Isla Spider is at the NW corner of Península Ulloa.

Approach

When coming from NE along the SE side of Isla Spider, pass the small island, then anchor in 12m and back in between Isla Spider and the S side of the small island, put lines ashore. Further in the depth is 3m and there is lots of dead kelp on the bottom. It is open to NE, though the kelp bar probably reduces the swell. Fishing boats use this anchorage and strongly recommend it. There is evidence of a temporary fishing camp on the shore.

8·11 Península Ulloa – Bahía Butler

53°34'·5S 72°34'W

Charts BA *1281, 554, 887*; US *22415*; Chile *11000, 11200, 11230*

General

Once a yacht on its way W through Paso Tortuoso has passed Cabo Crosstides it is a further 18 miles to Caleta Notch. Tilman used Bahía Butler and found good shelter on the W side anchoring in about 7m some 20m from the shore. Holding is mud on rock.

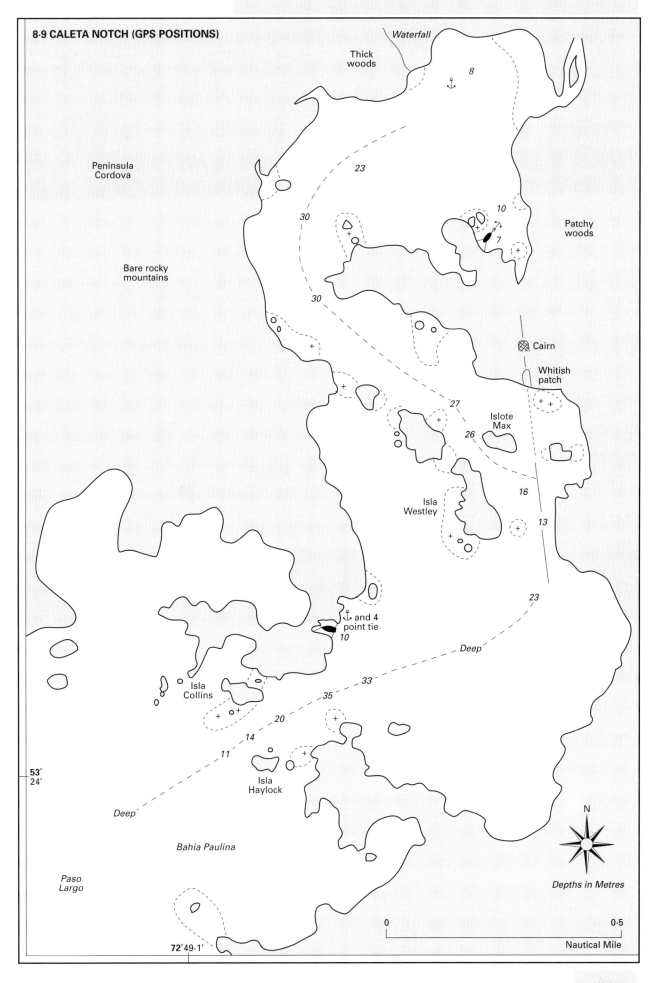

8·9 CALETA NOTCH (GPS POSITIONS)

Waterfall

Thick
woods

8

Peninsula
Cordova

23

30

10

Patchy
woods

7

Bare rocky
mountains

30

Cairn

Whitish
patch

27

Islote
Max

26

16

Isla
Westley

13

23

⚓ and 4
point tie

10

Deep

33

35

Isla
Collins

20

14

11

Isla
Haylock

Deep

53°
24'

Bahia Paulina

N

Paso
Largo

Depths in Metres

0   0·5

72°49·1'

Nautical Mile

151

8·12 Península Córdova – Bahía Borja

53°32'S 72°30'W

Charts BA *1281, 887*; US *22415*; Chile *11000, 11200, 11230, 11300, 11311, 11700*

General

On the N of Paso Tortuoso on Península Córdova, Bahía Borja faces SE but is sheltered between SW and N. The bottom is clay with good holding. It can have strong winds and *rachas* – the BA pilot remarks on very fierce squalls at times – but apparently seas remain low. The best anchorage is on the E side at the head of the bay with lines ashore. Names of previous visiting ships are inscribed on the E shore.

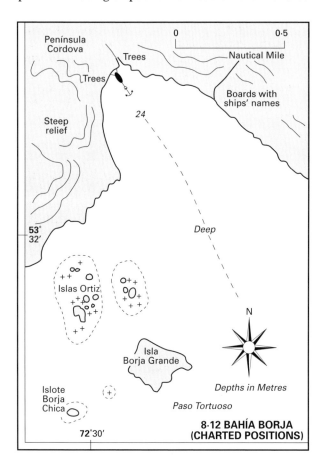

8·13 Estero Cóndor – Puerto Cóndor

53°21'S 72°38'W

Charts BA *1281, 887*; US *22415*; Chile *11000, 11200, 11230, 11700*

General

Puerto Cóndor is at the head of Estero Cóndor, off Canal Jerónimo. There is no point in going up to it unless you are 'collecting anchorages'. The anchorages are either in the bay N of Isla Dagnino or in Ensenada Llanza. In either place get lines ashore. Lago de la Botella is fresh and accessible by portage.

Continuation
Paso Inglés

8·14 Isla Carlos III – Bahía Tilly

53°34'S 72°23'W

Charts BA *1281, 554, 887*; US *22415*; Chile *11000, 11230, 11311*

General

Bahía Tilly is on the N side of Isla Carlos III. It is subject to squalls but is a fairly sheltered stopping place in Paso Tortuoso.

Anchorage

Go to the inner basin, zigzag between the rocks, and tie up across the narrow end of the bay, lines out ahead and astern to the shores or anchor in 18–20m, mud and kelp, with lines ashore. Several yachts have anchored on the W side of the entrance where

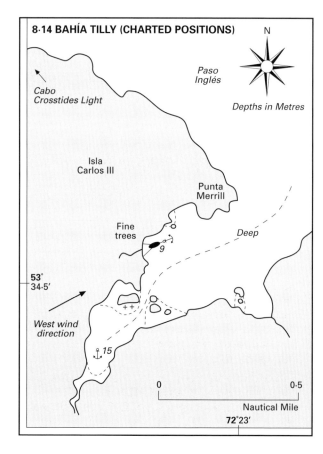

Diversion
Canal Jerónimo to Puerto Cóndor

Canal Jerónimo runs NE from Isla Carlos III. The streams are fairly regular and run up to 8kts N and 6kts S in the narrows. Slack water lasts about 20 minutes at high water and 10 minutes at low water.

shown, an anchorage also used by fishermen. The holding is good. From this anchorage it is possible to see conditions in Paso Inglés.

8·15 Isla Carlos III – Bahía Mussel

53°36'·4S 72°17'·7W

Charts BA *1281, 554, 887*; US *22415*; Chile *11230, 11311*

General

Bahía Mussel is on the NE side of Isla Carlos II and has a view of Paso Inglés. The passage W along Paso Inglés can be difficult and Bahía Mussel is a useful stopping point. The bay is large and there are many anchoring possibilities. The anchorage shown is in 5m with good holding with shorelines. It is reported to be relatively calm in strong winds with *rachas* outside. An attractive spot with woodland and large trees.

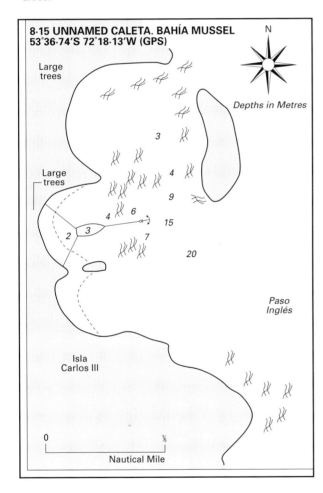

Diversion

There are three principal routes connecting Estrecho de Magallanes, E of Paso Inglés, and Canal Cockburn. They are:

1. **Canal Barbara**

   From Cabo Edgeworth at the N entrance to Canal Barbara to Canal Cockburn, at 72°W, via Canal Barbara, is about 40M. Canal Barbara is an impressive canal and, of the three routes,

finishes in the most westerly position along Canal Magdalena. However, it has several disadvantages. The pilotage is fairly complicated. The canal is quite open and can be subject to *rachas*, especially if there is N in the wind when it gusts down from Península Bowles. Finally there are very few identifiable anchorages if the weather deteriorates en route. Canal Barbara is used regularly by fishing boats.

2. **Seno Pedro and Canal Acwalisnan**

   From Cabo Edgeworth to Canal Cockburn at 72°W, via Seno Pedro and Canal Acwalisnan, is about 58M. This is much the easiest route of the three. Canal Acwalisnan is well protected and the narrows at Paso O'Ryan are straightforward at slack water. This route is used a lot by local fishing boats. They call Paso O'Ryan 'La corriente de San Pedro'. Neither Canal Barbara nor Canal Acwalisnan are approved routes for a yacht's *zarpe*. It is hoped that this will change as they offer a more sheltered and therefore safer passage.

3. **Canal Magdalena – Canal Cockburn**

   From Cabo Edgeworth to Canal Cockburn at 72°W, via Canal Magdalena, is about 100M. This is currently the only approved route. It is quite tough and keeps the yacht in relatively unprotected canals for a long way. On the positive side there are well-documented anchorages along the way to break the passage.

The three routes are considered below (Magdalena/Cockburn in chapter 9).

8·16 Canal Barbara

Charts BA *554*; US *22425*; Chile *11300, 12400*

Tides

At the N end of Canal Barbara the flood stream runs S from Estrecho de Magallanes. The timing through Paso Shag is important as the current can run at 7 knots with tide rips and eddies. Even near slack water the current still runs quite strongly through the pass but in calm weather this is not problematic. However BA Pilot NP6 states that the passage 'is not considered safe during SW winds'. vessels are recommended to wait for an improvement in the weather. Note that the S-going tidal stream divides at Isla Wet and the N-going stream divides at Isla Alcayaga; in both cases the main stream flows through Paso Shag.

Slack tide is between 0115hrs and 0150hrs after slack tide at Punta Arenas. *Note*: the time of slack water varies with weather conditions and barometric pressure. When travelling N it is a good idea to arrive just before high slack water so as to be pushed through the Pass and still have a fair current when travelling N to join Estrecho de Magallanes. At this time the current in the W part of the Paso runs at about 2 knots near spring tide. When exiting, W of Isla Wet the current runs at 4 knots with eddies and tide rips. In calm weather this does not give a problem transiting with the current but it would be difficult to make progress if travelling against it.

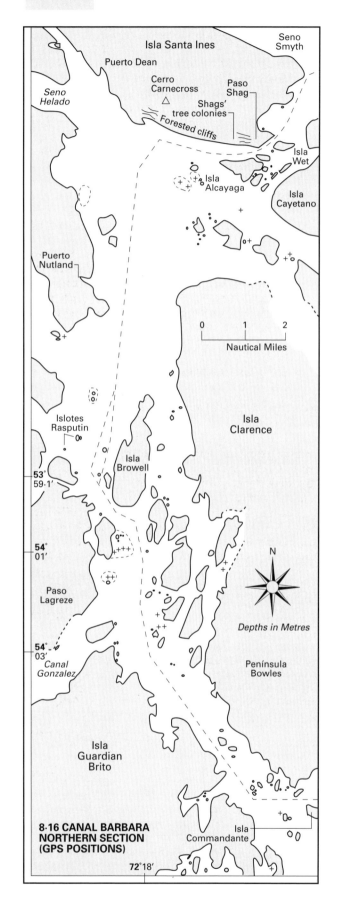

Isla Santa Ines

Puerto Dean

Seno Smyth

Cerro Carnecross

Paso Shag

Seno Helado

Shags' tree colonies

Forested cliffs

Isla Wet

Isla Alcayaga

Isla Cayetano

Puerto Nutland

Isla Clarence

Islotes Rasputin

Isla Browell

0   1   2

Nautical Miles

53° 59·1'

54° 01'

Paso Lagreze

N

54° 03'

Canal Gonzalez

Depths in Metres

Península Bowles

Isla Guardian Brito

8·16 CANAL BARBARA NORTHERN SECTION (GPS POSITIONS)

Isla Commandante

72°18'

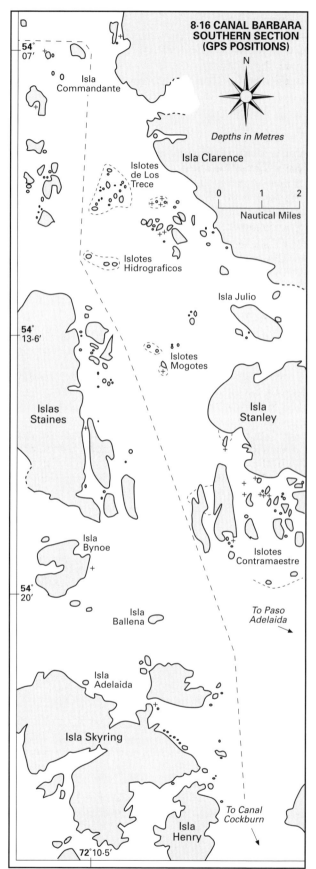

8·16 CANAL BARBARA SOUTHERN SECTION (GPS POSITIONS)

N

Depths in Metres

54° 07'

Isla Commandante

Isla Clarence

Islotes de Los Trece

0   1   2

Nautical Miles

Islotes Hidrograficos

Isla Julio

54° 13·6'

Islotes Mogotes

Islas Staines

Isla Stanley

Isla Bynoe

Islotes Contramaestre

54° 20'

Isla Ballena

To Paso Adelaida

Isla Adelaida

Isla Skyring

To Canal Cockburn

Isla Henry

72°10·5'

General

Canal Barbara is a wide waterway with many islands and shoal areas to complicate the route. The sketch plan shows the route that has been used by yachts and is the one described in BA *Pilot NP6*. The route has been described N to S. Yachts have travelled in both directions through Canal Barbara. However, the principal advantage of this route is realised when travelling S to N as the yacht gains access to Estrecho de Magallanes at the most W point. The S passage may be made in one day. Paso Shag can be transited early in the morning but the N passage may take two days as it is often necessary to wait for favourable tidal conditions in Paso Shag. The route is as follows:

a. Pass E of Cabo Edgeworth, avoiding its off-lying shoals, and head for Isla Wet, staying fairly close to the E coast of Isla Santa Ines after passing the entrance to Ensenada Smyth and take care of an E-going set when approaching Isla Wet.

b. Paso Shag runs between Isla Alcayaga and Isla Santa Ines, which is steep-to. At the NE end, the entrance lies between Isla Wet and Isla Santa Ines. The pass is about 1½ miles long and has a least width of about 200m. The passage throughout lies along the middle of the canal. At the SE end there may be the odd ice floe coming from the glaciers at the head of Seno Helado.

There are numerous shags sitting in the trees on Isla Santa Ines – hence the name of the pass. In the Canal W of Isla Wet there is a profusion of wildlife fishing in the disturbed waters, including families of seals, and much bird life.

(Local fisherman advised one yacht to use the alternative N entrance: Canal San Miguel. In these narrows the tidal streams are said to be weaker than in Paso Shag.)

c. If going N, Puerto Nutland (8·16) makes a good stopping place to wait for slack water to transit Paso Shag. Take care of an E-going set when approaching Isla Alcayaga.

d. The passage to E of the headland after passing Puerto Nutland is deep. Make down the W side of Isla Browell, keeping E of the small group of drying rocks shown on the sketch and passing through Angostura Sur between Isla Browell and Isla Santa Ines. S of Isla Browell the tidal current is strong at 1–2kts with small eddies.

e. Then follow the NE coast of Isla Guardian Brito for 4M. Pass S of the small islands off the S shore of Península Bowles and E of Isla Commandante. This area can be subject to stronger winds caused by the mountains of Península Bowles and wind funnelling down the large, unnamed *estero* to the NE.

f. Turn S and follow a mid-canal course W of the Grupo de los Trece, Islotes Hidrograficos and Islotes Mogotes. Pass between Isla Staines and Isla Stanley and W of Islotes Contramaestre.

g. S of Islotes Contramaestre, Canal Barbara can be left via Paso Sur, Paso Aguila or by Paso Adelaide. They are all deep and clear of dangers. Puerto Niemann (9·10) in Canal Adelaide is a good anchorage from which to finish or start the passage through Canal Barbara

Anchorages in Canal Barbara

The documented anchorages are 8·17 Puerto Nutland at the N end and 9·9 Caleta Parmelia, 9·10 Puerto Niemann and 9·11 Caleta Tarmac at its S end. There are no obvious secure anchorages along the main length of the canal and the land is barren and windswept.

The bay (GPS position 54°06'·2S 72°15'W) on the NE coast of Isla Guardian Brito has been used and found to provide protection from W to S winds. It is not recommended. When strong winds blow down the canal from the N, they funnel into this bay making it untenable.

Puerto Dean (53°50'S 72°20'W) is reported to be a good anchorage with better shelter than suggested

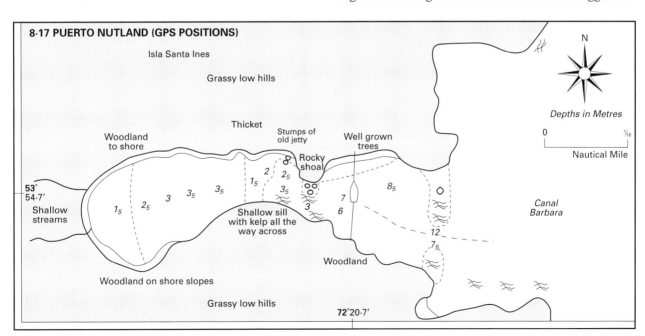

8·17 PUERTO NUTLAND (GPS POSITIONS)

Isla Santa Ines

Grassy low hills

Thicket

Woodland to shore

Stumps of old jetty

Well grown trees

Rocky shoal

Depths in Metres

0   ¹⁄₁₆

Nautical Mile

53° 54·7'

Shallow streams

Shallow sill with kelp all the way across

Canal Barbara

Woodland

Woodland on shore slopes

Grassy low hills

72°20·7'

CHILE

on the chart. Holding in about 10m in sand.

Seno Helado has also been visited. There is shallow water at the entrance to the *seno* where the moraine was deposited but the shallow areas are well marked by kelp. Beyond this area the *seno* is deep. A shallow indentation on the S side of the *seno* provided a good anchorage with lines ashore. There are extensive glaciers from which ice continually falls and drifts down the *seno*.

8·17 Isla Santa Ines – Puerto Nutland

53°54'S 72°20'W 53°54'·69S 72°20'·73W (GPS)
Charts BA *1201*; US *22425*; Chile *11000, 11300, 12400*

General
Puerto Nutland is on Isla Santa Ines about 6M SW of the S end of Paso Shag. It provides good shelter from all but E winds. The indicated anchorage is in 6m on a mud bottom with shorelines. The anchorage is fairly near the entrance to the bay. It would be possible to anchor beyond the rocky shoal in about 3m just S of the remains of an old jetty but beyond this there is a bar and the depths shoal quickly further into the bay.

Continuation

8·18 Bahía Fortescue – Caleta Gallant

53°42'S 72°00'W 53°41'·33S 72°00'·06W (GPS)
Charts BA *1281*; US *22425*; Chile *11300, 11312*

General
Caleta Gallant is situated in the inner part of Bahía Fortescue on Península Brunswick, NE of Islas Charles. It is behind Isla Wigwam which has shoal water on its E side. From the earliest days, Bahía Fortescue has provided shelter for sailing ships travelling W up the straits. It is shown on charts

from the 1700s.

Approach
The entrance to Bahía Fortescue is wide and unencumbered and there is a light on the W shore, 1450 Fortescue (Fl(3)9s19m6M White GRP tower, red band 4m 240°-vis-070°). The entrance to Caleta Gallant is rather narrow and shallow, with a least depth of around 6m.

Anchorage
The best anchorage is as close as possible to the N side of Isla Wigwam in about 6m on a sand bottom. A build up of dead kelp has been a problem on occasion but once the anchor has found a place the holding is good in strong mud. Yachts that have anchored further N than this have experienced *rachas* coming down the valley at the head of the bay. It is also possible to tuck up into the NW corner of Bahía Fortescue under the protection of tall trees on the shore. This is well protected from winds from the W and NW and is calm even when fresh winds are blowing outside.

Paso Froward

8·19 Península Brunswick – Bahía Wood

53°49'S 71°37'W
Charts BA *1281*; US *22425*; Chile *11300, 11432, 12400*
Tides
Bahía Wood is Punta Arenas +0120hrs for both HW and LW.

General
On Península Brunswick under Cabo Holland, Bahía Wood provides shelter from winds from the N through to the SW. Care should be taken to avoid the foul ground extending 200m off the SE end of Cabo Holland, with Roca Esk awash at its edge. The holding in the bay is good in 4–5m with a bottom of sand and stones. Swell does enter the bay during strong W winds and it would be better to use a different anchorage in unsettled weather.

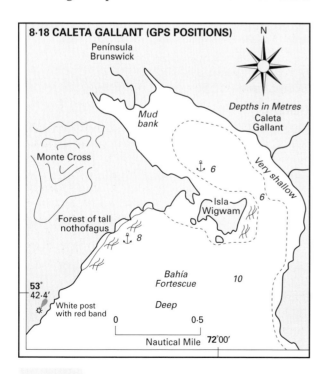

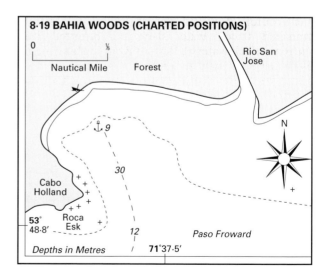

8·20 Canal Acwalisnan

Charts BA *554*; US *22425*; Chile *11300, 12400*

General

Canal Acwalisnan, which leads S from Canal Pedro, provides a much shorter route between Estrecho de Magallanes and Canal Cockburn than the approved commercial traffic route using Canal Magdalena. Local fisherman prefer it over Canal Barbara because it can be transited in one day. Acwalisnan is narrow and winding and is therefore more sheltered than Magdalena where strong SW winds can kick up a nasty head sea. The thick woodland that grows high up the sides of the mountains along Canal Acwalisnan indicates that it is sheltered. Despite the fact that it is not an approved route it is the one most frequently chosen by yachtsmen. This deviation from the *zarpe* is taken on grounds of safety when adverse weather makes the open waters of Canal Magdalena unsafe. It would be wise to document such deviations and the reason for taking them in the ship's log.

There is no detailed chart of Canales Pedro and Acwalisnan. Along the centre track there are no dangers and depths range between 100–120m. Coming from the N, the first obstacle is the pass leading from Canal Pedro into Canal Acwalisnan ('Northern Narrows' on the sketch plan). There is a wooded island in the middle that should be left to port. This island is not immediately obvious when approaching from the N as it looks like part of the hill behind. However as it is approached the continuation of the canal becomes obvious. The GPS position at the point marked on the exploded view on the sketch plan is 54°05'·50S 71°36'·8W.

The next obstacle is Paso O'Ryan 'La corriente de San Pedro to the fishermen'. This pass is narrow and shallow and as a result tidal streams can run at up to 8 knots. The flood tide runs S from Estrecho de Magallanes into Seno Pedro and from the S northwards into Canal Acwalisnan at more or less the same time. A passage timed to catch slack high water at Paso O'Ryan will give the yacht a fair tide down the north or south section depending upon her route. However yachts have successfully transited at low water slack and reported little current. Slack water at Paso O'Ryan is about Bahía Woods +0100 hour. Close to slack water at springs the current runs at about 2 knots, with some eddies, but the current soon helps push the yacht clear of the narrows.

After exiting Canal Acwalisnan head for the W end of Isla Sccbrock and pass between Seebrock and the end of Isla Clarence, keeping along the Isla Clarence shore to avoid the extensive foul ground on the NW end of Isla Seebrock. Bahía Millicent (9·8) on Isla Clarence, opposite to the S entrance to the canal, is a convenient anchorage if it is rough in Canal Cockburn.

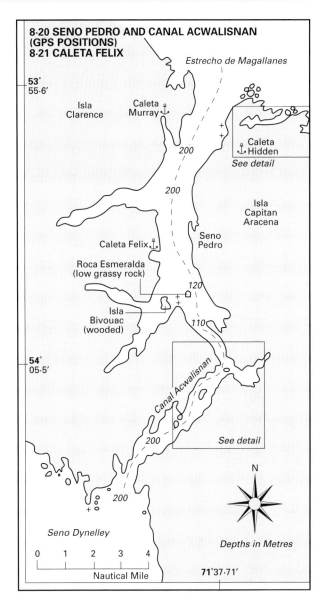

8·21 Canal Acwalisnan – Seno Pedro – Caleta Felix

54°01'·3S 71°41'·4W (GPS)
Charts BA *554*; US *22425*; Chile *11300, 12400*

General

This attractive anchorage is named after the youngest crew member of the French yacht *Cauane*, who investigated it. It is much favoured by fishermen who find it secure all through winter. The head is a curved sandy beach 100m long and very shallow up to about 100m off. There is a river mouth at the N end of the beach and a dinghy can go a little way up, even at LW. An attractive valley runs west from the *caleta*. Big trees surround the anchorage giving good protection from *rachas*.

Approach

Caleta Felix lies about 5M to the S of the entrance to Seno San Pedro on the W side of the channel, between Ensenadas Wilson and Elsa. It is shown on Chile *11300* but absent from other charts. The

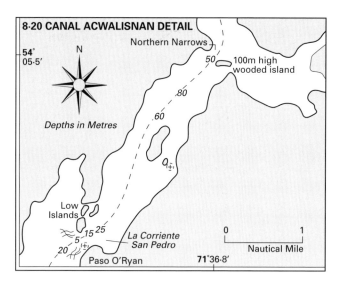

8·20 CANAL ACWALISNAN DETAIL

Northern Narrows

54° 05·5'

N

50 — 100m high wooded island

.80

.60

Depths in Metres

Low Islands

.15 .25

5

20

La Corriente San Pedro

Paso O'Ryan

0 — 1 Nautical Mile

71°36·8'

entrance is clear and only visible at the last moment. The *caleta* is about 150m wide and 300m long with some kelp in the northeast part.

Anchorage

Fishing boats tie to a rope strung across the *caleta* from N to S and secured to large trees. They move along the rope, according to wind direction, to obtain the best protection, staying as close to shore as possible. Visiting yachts will be welcome to do the same though it is recommended that an anchor is also set mid-bay in about 12m, sand. This anchorage was perfectly calm with WNW 35 to 45 in Estrecho de Magallanes.

There is a good hike on the hills to the N from where there is a panorama of the strait and Cabo Froward.

Several yachts have used Caleta Murray, about 4M to the north, near the W entrance of the canal. It may be subject to the funnelling of strong NW winds.

8·22 Isla Capitán Aracena – Caleta Hidden

53°56'·9S 71°34'·2W

Charts BA *1281*; US *22425*; Chile *11300, 12400*

General

Boats travelling N or S through Canal Acwalisnan often use this anchorage. The entrance is about 1·5M E of the entrance to Seno Pedro and is marked by a small group of rocky islets E of its entrance. The GPS position of the entrance is 53°56'·6S 71°33'·5W. The Caleta is a 0·75M long slot with a wider basin at its head.

Anchorage

The small notch on the S side of this passage provides an anchorage protected from all but E winds but it is more secure to continue to the head of the bay, leaving the rock shown to port. Depths fall here but there are no dangers in the centre of this pass and it is clear of kelp. At the head of the bay there are a number of secure anchorages, the best probably being the most W bay with good holding and shore lines.

8·23 Isla Capitán Aracena – Caleta Cascada

53°58'S 71°31'W

Charts BA *1281*; US *22425*; Chile *11300, 12400*

General

The entrance to Cascada is a little narrow but quite clean. The bay is sheltered from all winds. Anchor in 18m at the head of the bay. There is also a small bay on the E side of the entrance with 10m depth in the middle and two stony beaches on the E side. Cormorants nest on the W entrance of the *caleta*. There is good hiking beside the stream leading to the waterfall.

Cabo Froward

At Cabo Froward, the most S point of the mainland, the Estrecho de Magallanes turn N via Paso del Hambre and the various narrows to Dungeness and the Atlantic. The main shipping route to Puerto Williams, via Magdalena and the Beagle Channels goes S from this point and is considered below.

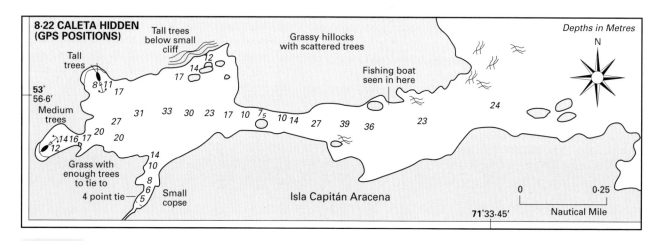

8·22 CALETA HIDDEN (GPS POSITIONS)

Tall trees below small cliff

Grassy hillocks with scattered trees

Depths in Metres

N

Tall trees

12

14

17

Fishing boat seen in here

53° 56·6'

8 11 17

Medium trees

31 33 30 23 17 10 7 5 10 14 27 39 36 23

24

27

20

20

14 16 17 20

12

Grass with enough trees to tie to

14 10

8 6 5

Small copse

4 point tie

Isla Capitán Aracena

71°33·45'

0 — 0·25 Nautical Mile

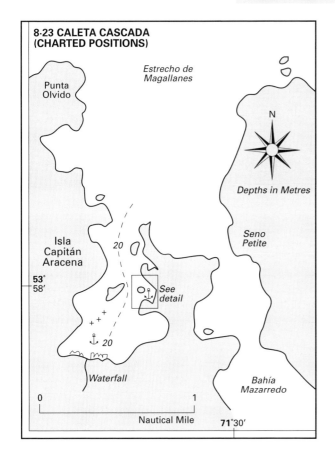

8·23 CALETA CASCADA
(CHARTED POSITIONS)

Estrecho de Magallanes

Punta Olvido

N

Depths in Metres

Isla Capitán Aracena

20

Seno Petite

53° 58'

See detail

20

Waterfall

Bahía Mazarredo

0   Nautical Mile   1

71°30'

The characteristics of Cabo Froward light at 53°53'·7S 71°18'·6W are Fl(3)9s21m6M White concrete tower, red band 3m 276°-vis-126°.

Cabo Froward to Dungeness

Paso del Hambre

General

Between Cabo Froward and Punta Arenas two groups of bays afford some protection if caught by westerlies. There is no protection from E winds except at Bahía Porvenir on Tierra del Fuego (chart Chile *11421*). Porvenir is limited to a draught of about 1·7m at low water and a tortuous entrance.

Between Punta Arenas and Punta Dungeness there are two narrows to be negotiated, Segunda Angostura and Primera Angostura. E bound vessels are advised to be off the entrance to Segunda Angostura as the E-going stream is starting, which the BA *Pilot* states is about 0230hrs before high water at Cabo de Hornos. W bound vessels are advised to be off the NE approach of Primera Angostura just before the SW stream starts, 0230hrs after high water at Cabo de Hornos.

8·24 Península Brunswick – Bahías San Nicolás, Bougainville and del Cañon

Around 53°50'S 71°02'W

Charts BA *1281*; US *22425*; Chile *11000, 11300, 11400, 11432*

General

Bahía San Nicolás Anchor inside Islote Sanchez and the W point in sand and mud. There is a little pier and a sawmill.

Bahía Bougainville Used by fishermen and sealers. Tuck well in, stern to trees. There is a fresh water rivulet.

Bahía del Cañon Depths of 7–10m within the headlands.

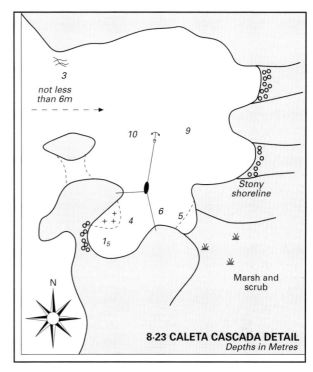

3
not less than 6m

10   9

Stony shoreline

6   5

4

1·5

Marsh and scrub

N

8·23 CALETA CASCADA DETAIL
Depths in Metres

8·25 Península Brunswick – Bahía San Juan de las Posesion

53°39'S 70°55'W

Charts BA *1281*; Chile *11000, 11300, 11400, 11431*

General

Bahía San Juan de las Posesion is a possible day stop for visiting Fuerte Bulnes, a replica of Chile's first settlement on the strait (1843). Before then sailing vessels knew the bay as Puerto del Hambre or Port Famine, a confusion maintained on earlier editions of the charts (it is correctly named on Chile *11300* and *11400*). The white cross (*cruz blanca*) on the chart marks the grave of Pringle Stokes in the *cemeterio ingles*. Captain Stokes was the first commander of HMS *Beagle* during the Philip Parker King expedition that charted the strait and other parts during 1826–1830. Anchor on the NE side of the bay under the fort.

8·26 Península Brunswick – Bahía Mansa (Puerto del Hambre)

53°36'·6S 70° 55'·5W (*11432*)

Charts BA *1281*; Chile *11300, 11400* (This is marked on detail plan *11432* but the detail is dangerously inaccurate.)

General

Just over 30M S of Punta Arenas, Bahía Mansa offers much better shelter to small yachts. There is road and public transport access to the city. For a vessel under 14m it is probably better to avoid Punta Arenas and use this anchorage.

Approach

Bahía Mansa is the third and longest of three bays to the N of the Santa Ana Península, between the point where a Chilean flag flies to mark the site of Puerto del Hambre, the ill fated Spanish settlement of 1583 and Punta Askew to the E. The Bahía Carreras chartlet on Chile *11432*, showing a shallow bay, is incorrect. There are houses at the head of Bahía Mansa with fishing boats crowding the shore or anchored close in.

Anchorage

Anchor in 8–10m and take a line through the kelp to a tree on the W shore. Leave the E side free for fishing boats to come and go. The anchorage is subject to swell. There are rental cabins in the small bay to the W. It is possible to hike over to the Santa Ana península and Fuerte Bulnes.

Facilities

There are no facilities at Bahía Mansa but frequent

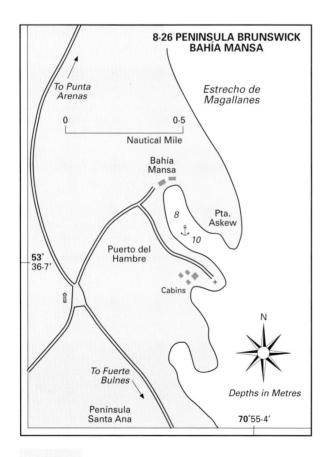

buses and *fletes* (pickup trucks for hire) run to and from Punta Arenas and are quite used to transporting large amounts of provisions and fuel.

8·27 Península Brunswick – Punta Arenas

53°10'S 70°54'W

Charts BA *554, 1281, 1694;* US *22482;* Chile *11000, 11400, 11411*

Port communications

VHF Ch16, 09, 14 c/s *CBM25* ☎ 22 10 01

General

The face of Punta Arenas, the capital of the region, has changed under the influence of oil revenues from the Estrecho Magallanes. The population is about 100,000. It still serves the extensive sheep farming industry. Some of the large establishments of former sheep barons have been converted into museums or *monumentos nacionales*.

There are many restaurants and hotels to suit all pockets. There are two museums but diversion for the tourist consists largely of visiting national parks, such as the penguin colony on Isla Magdalena, Torres del Paine, the waterways or very expensive expeditions to Chilean Antarctica.

Berthing

Inquire on Ch 16. There is no anchorage as such in Punta Arenas, only an open roadstead. It is possible to shelter by rafting against fishing boats or other vessels tied to the docks but damage during strong winds, particularly from the E, can be substantial. An E wind at Punta Arenas is unlikely but very dangerous when it blows and vessels are advised to leave if one is forecast. A number of very uncomfortable workboat moorings, sometimes vacant, have been laid near the pier; consult the harbourmaster.

Facilities

Shipyard ASMAR (Astillero y Maestranzas de la Armada) for major repairs.

Fuel, water, electricity may all be obtained at the Muelle Fiscal.

Supermarkets: There are many large and well-stocked supermarkets, the best being a taxi journey from the docks. A supermarket just to the N of the main pier will deliver to the pier.

There is a good fish market in the centre of town. Public market: Mercado Municipal, Chiloé 600 near Mexicana.

Laundry: Autoservicio O'Higgins 969.

British Consulate Calle Sarmiento 780 (PO Box 237, Punta Arenas) ☎ 24 81 00 and 22 24 75. *Fax 56 61 22 22 51* Ext 108. There are also Consulates for Argentina and Germany.

Communications

Bus to Santiago, Valdivia, Puerto Montt, Puerto Natales and to Argentina (Río Gallegos and Ushuaia). Frequent air services provided by four national airlines to Puerto Montt and Santiago, to Puerto Williams and weekly to the Falkland Islands.

DAP airlines fly to Puerto Williams every day except Sunday in summer, and on Tuesdays, Thursdays and Saturdays in winter.

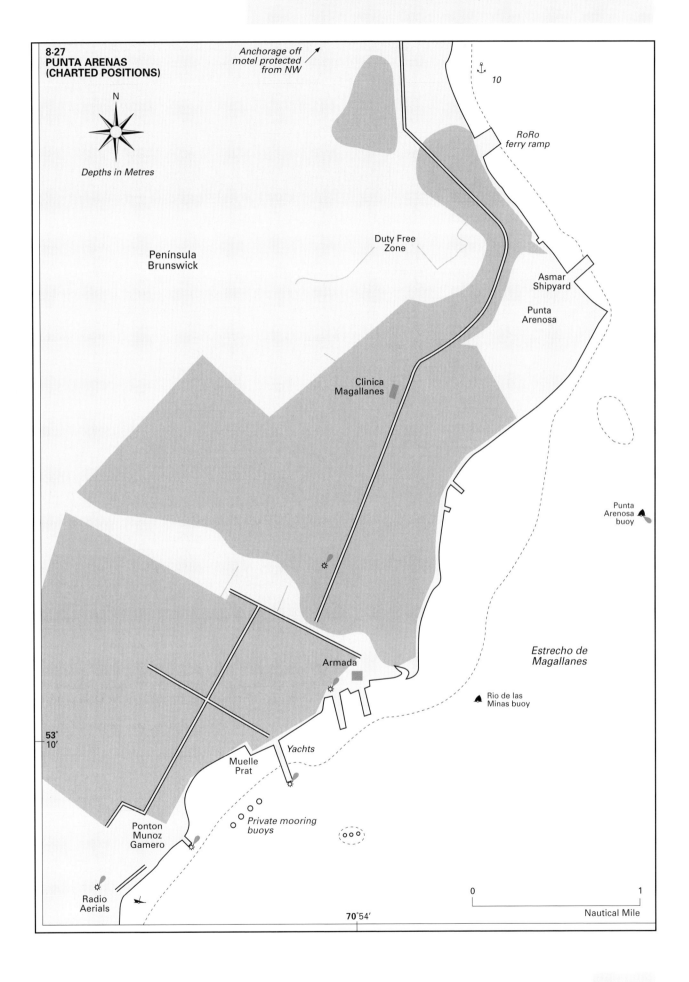

8·27
PUNTA ARENAS
(CHARTED POSITIONS)

N

Depths in Metres

Anchorage off motel protected from NW

10

RoRo ferry ramp

Duty Free Zone

Península Brunswick

Asmar Shipyard

Punta Arenosa

Clinica Magallanes

Punta Arenosa buoy

Estrecho de Magallanes

Armada

Rio de las Minas buoy

53° 10′

Yachts

Muelle Prat

Private mooring buoys

Ponton Munoz Gamero

0   1

Nautical Mile

Radio Aerials

70°54′

Car hire: Automóvil Club de Chile, Avis, Budget, Hertz and others.
Ferry to Porvenir.
Telephone: Area code 61. CTC Plaza Muñoz Gamero, ENTEL Chile, Lautaro Navarro 941.

Canal Nuevo

8·28 Bahía Gente Grande – Isla Contramaestre

52°57'S 70°21'W
Charts BA *554, 1281, 1694*; US *22481*; Chile *11000,11400, 11500, 11530*

General

Isla Contramaestre is at the entrance to Bahía Gente Grande on Tierra del Fuego. The anchorage is just round the SW corner, Punta Baja, strong mud 5m. Shelter from SW.

8·29 Isla Isabel – Surgidero Punta Alfredo

52°51'·5S 70°38'·5W
Charts BA *554, 1281,1694*; US *22481*; Chile *11000, 11500*

General

This is an anchorage along the NW coast of Isla Isabel, about 1·5M from the NE end of the island. It is opposite a pronounced ravine. Good holding in 14m or less.

8·30 Bahía Whitsand

52°43'S 70°37'W
Charts BA *554, 1281, 1694*; US *22481*; Chile *11000, 11500*

General

Good shelter from wind if N of SW. Close up to the shore according to draught.

8·31 Bahía Gregorio

52°36'S 70°06'W
Charts BA 554; Chile 11000, 11500

General

The anchorage at Punta Sara in the NW corner of Bahía Gregorio is well sheltered from the W but quite shallow.

8·32 Punta Delgada

52°27' S 69°32'W
Charts BA *554*; Chile *11000, 11500, 11600*

General

The anchorage, which is E of Punta Delgada, is well sheltered from the W and has been used by the *armada* to check incoming yachts.

8·33 Punta Dungeness

52°24'S 68°26'W
Charts BA *554, 3107*; US *22471*; Chile *11000, 11600*

General

It is possible to anchor either side of Punta Dungeness. The tidal stream does not affect the W anchorage. Neither side has protection from the S. A Chilean reporting station has been established here.

Note All vessels passing through Argentine territorial waters are required to report to Cabo Vírgenes Naval Station Ch 16, 67.

9. Cabo Froward to Brazo Noroeste

Note: Chile chart *1201*, which covers much of this area, has been renumbered *12400*.

Canal Magdalena

9·1 Isla Capitán Aracena – Caleta Beaubasin

54°04'·9S 71°03'·3W

Charts BA *554, 1373*; US *22425*; Chile *11000, 11300, 12400*

General

Beaubasin is a very attractive, snug little anchorage on the NW entrance to Canal Magdalena. It provides a welcome refuge on a northbound passage if there are strong W winds blowing down the Estrecho de Magallanes. There is a sill at the narrows with a least depth of 5m at low water. The anchorage is in 9m, mud and kelp, with lines ashore.

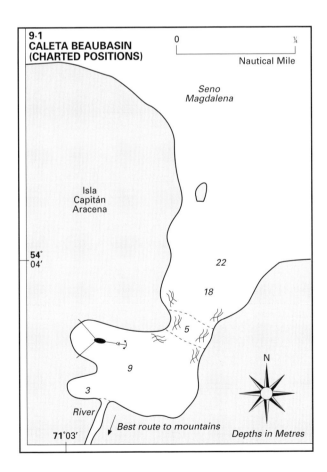

There is a little stream on the S side for fresh water or laundry. There are said to be *centollas* in the bay.

9·2 Isla Capitán Aracena – Puerto Hope

54°07'·3S 70°59'·9W

Charts BA *554, 1373*; US *22425*; Chile *11000, 11300, 11431, 12400*

General

At the N end of Canal Magdalena, Puerto Hope has a shoal patch with kelp on the N side of the entrance; favour the S shore. The inner basin is well protected from outside winds but has a reputation for *rachas*. Anchor in 9m in the centre, mud. Good hiking on clean rock in the surrounding hills.

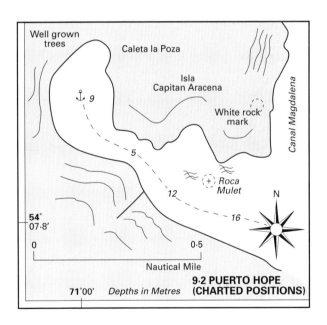

9·3 Isla Capitán Aracena – Bahía Morris

54°15'S 70°58'W

Charts BA *554, 1373*; US *22425*; Chile *11000, 12400, 12421*

General

Also known as Puerto Sholl, Bahía Morris is half way along the E coast of Isla Capitán Aracena almost opposite Seno Keats. Big ship pilots describe it as the best anchorage in either Canal Magdalena or Canal Cockburn but yachtsmen have labelled it as for emergencies only, probably because the wind

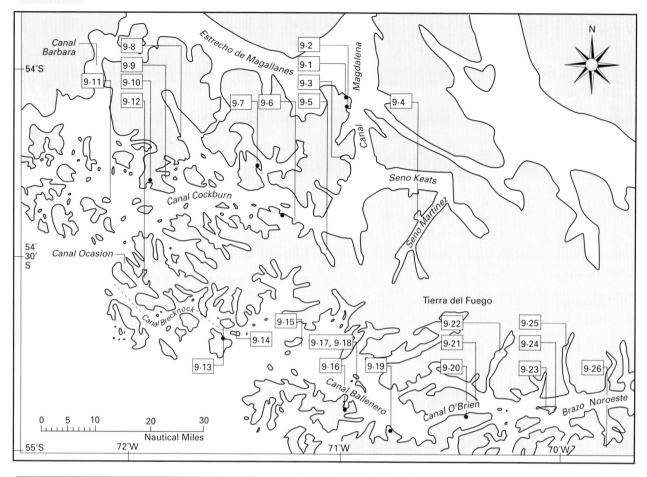

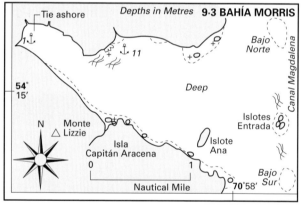

9·1   Isla Capitán Aracena – Caleta Beaubasin
9·2   Isla Capitán Aracena – Puerto Hope
9·3   Isla Capitán Aracena – Bahía Morris
9·4   Tierra del Fuego – Seno Martinez – Caleta
      Escandello
9·5   Tierra del Fuego – Caleta Chico
9·6   Tierra del Fuego – Puerto King
9·7   Isla Diego – Puerto Soffía
9·8   Isla Clarence – Bahía Millicent
9·9   Isla Clarence – Caleta Parmelia
9·10 Isla Clarence – Puerto Niemann
9·11 Isla Adelaida – Caleta Tarmac
9·12 Península Brecknock – Caleta Brecknock
9·13 Isla Brecknock – Puerto Paso Aguirre
9·14 Paso Aguirre – Isla Macias
9·15 Islas Burnt – Caleta Ancha
9·16 Isla Stewart – Caleta Fanny
9·17 Islas del Medio – Pozo Marit
9·18 Islas del Medio – Caleta Frog
9·19 Isla Londonderry – Puerto Engaño
9·20 Isla Londonderry – Puerto Fortuna
9·21 Isla O'Brien – Caleta Emelita
9·22 Canal Pomar – Seno Ventisquero
9·23 Isla Chair – Caleta Sur
9·24 Isla Chair – Caleta Cushion
9·25 Seno Garibaldi
9·26 Bahía Tres Brazos

blowing up Canal Magdalena comes in to the bay.

There are two anchorages in Bahía Morris. The most obvious is at the very head of the inner bay, with lines ashore. At times of strong W winds, very powerful *rachas* blow down from the surrounding steep mountains. In such conditions, it is better to anchor off the beach and low-lying land on the N side as shown on the sketch plan. The *rachas* still reached there occasionally but the holding is very good in mud and stones.

Diversion – Seno Martinez

9·4 Tierra del Fuego – Seno Martinez – Caleta Escandallo

54°26'S 70°41'W
Charts BA *554, 1373*; US *22425*; Chile *11000, 12400*

General

Seno Keats leads E off Canal Magdalena and then turns S into Seno Martinez, which leads to Caleta Escandallo, about 32M from the entrance of Seno Keats. In Caleta Escandallo there is good shelter from the W and SW with sandy bays in the two corners. It has a high ridge of mountains surrounding it so *rachas* may be expected.

Continuation

Junction of Canal Magdalena and Canal Cockburn

Canal Cockburn

9·5 Tierra del Fuego – Caleta Chico

54°28'S 71°08'W
Charts BA *554, 1373*; US *22425*; Chile *11000, 12400*

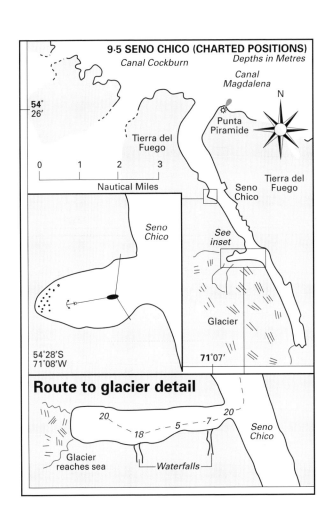

General

About 4M down Seno Chico is an inlet running to the W. At the head of this inlet is a spectacular glacier that is well worth a visit. About one and a half miles to the N of this inlet there is a small notch, which, with lines ashore is an excellent sheltered anchorage. The sides are very steep, but there are trees to tie off to. There is a fast flowing stream at the head of the bay for an easy supply of fresh water.

9·6 Tierra del Fuego – Puerto King

54°24'·7S 71°14'·2W (by chart)
Charts BA *554, 1373*; US *22425*; Chile *11000, 12400*

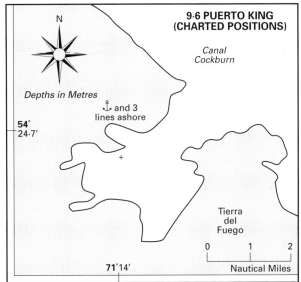

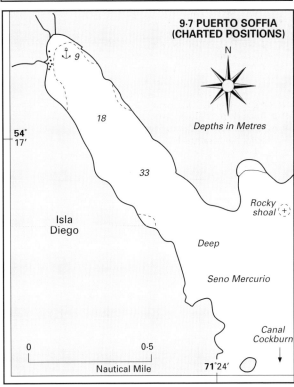

General

Do not confuse the anchorage with Isla King lying about two miles to the NW of the bay and clearly shown on Chile *12400*. The anchorage provides excellent shelter to a vessel battling down Canal Cockburn against the prevailing W winds.

9·7 Isla Diego – Puerto Soffía

54°16'S 71°26'W
Charts BA *554, 1373*; US *22425*; Chile *12400, 12421*

General

The entrance to this long, deep bay is wide and clean. The anchorage at the head in 9m, mud, stone and sand bottom, provides excellent shelter from all winds but is subject to severe *rachas*.

9·8 Isla Clarence – Bahía Millicent

54°12'·5S 71°47'W
Charts BA *554*; Chile *12400*

General

This *caleta*, regularly used by fishermen, provides excellent all weather shelter in a cove lying in the NW corner of the S bay.

Anchorage

Use lines to pull in close under the large trees. There is a lot of kelp in the anchorage but the bottom appears to be mud alone and provides excellent holding.

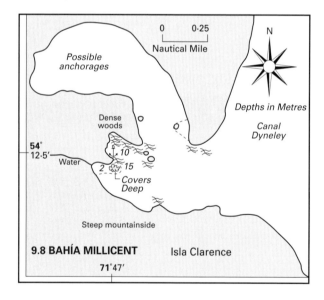

9·9 Isla Clarence – Caleta Parmelia

54°18'S 71°51'·4W
Charts BA *554*; US *22425*; Chile *12400*

General

This unnamed *caleta* was used by the yacht *Parmelia* after they found an uncomfortable swell entering nearby Caleta Louis. Other reports state that in strong westerlies, with the wind howling down Seno Duntze, access to Caleta Parmelia is difficult.

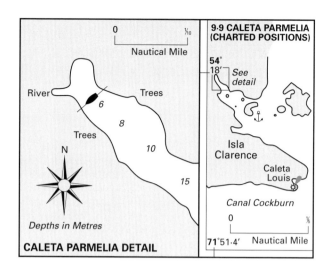

The *caleta* on the SE corner of Isla Clarence (Caleta Louis in the previous edition of this guide) just north of Seno Duntze (54°24'·6S 71°47'·8W Fl(3)9s8m6M White GRP tower red bands 3·3m) has been omitted because it is subject to swell from canal Cockburn and several better anchorages are available in the vicinity.

Approach and Anchorage

There is ample depth all the way up to the anchorage. Once inside there is protection from winds from all directions. The *caleta* is narrow enough to tie fore and aft across it with plenty of places to secure to. The bottom is mud. Another anchorage (GPS 54°18'·7S 71°49'·9W) is in the bay on the E of the half-moon-shaped island shown on the sketch.

9·10 Isla Clarence – Puerto Niemann

54°20'S 71°55'W 54°18'·9S 71°54'·3W (GPS)
Charts BA *554*; US *22425*; Chile *12400*

General

Puerto Niemann is a large harbour on the S side of Isla Clarence (see plan). It contains two anchorages, the N one being well protected. The entrance is straightforward, deep with no off-lying hazards.

Anchorage

The N nook is tucked in below trees, the kelp is fairly close to the shore and does not pose a problem, and once shore lines are fixed it is peaceful. The nook on the W side of the large island in Puerto Niemann is also secure but winds are reported to blow quite strongly between here and the main island. Vessels that have tried anchoring in the main bay have dragged in severe *rachas*.

9·11 Isla Adelaida – Caleta Tarmac

54°22'S 72°05'W
Charts BA *554*; US *22425*; Chile *12400*

General

Located on the NE side of Isla Adelaida, Tarmac is the N-most of two indentations on the NE side of

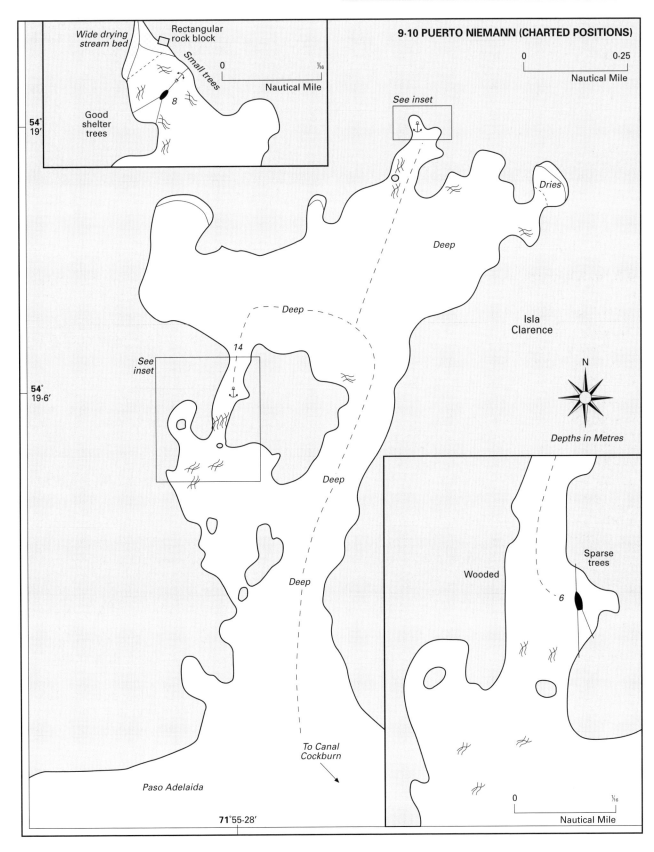

9·10 PUERTO NIEMANN (CHARTED POSITIONS)

Isla Adelaida. It is well-sheltered from the prevailing W winds and two small islets give some protection from the E.

Anchorage

There is considerable kelp in the bay. The holding is poor in 12m on a rocky bottom (hence the name Tarmac). Take lines ashore.

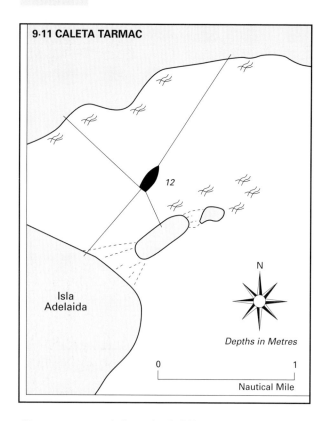

9·11 CALETA TARMAC

Isla Adelaida

N

Depths in Metres

0   1
Nautical Mile

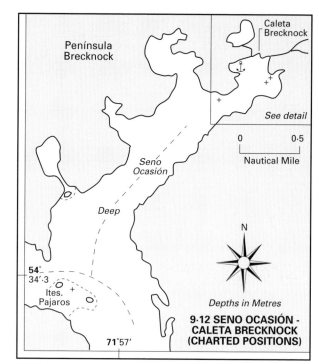

Península Brecknock

Caleta Brecknock

See detail

0   0·5
Nautical Mile

Seno Ocasión

Deep

N

54° 34'·3

Ites. Pajaros

Depths in Metres

9·12 SENO OCASIÓN - CALETA BRECKNOCK (CHARTED POSITIONS)

71°57'

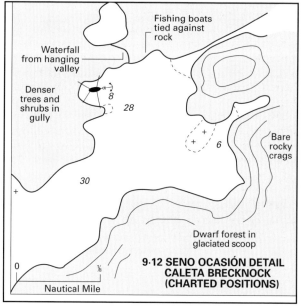

Fishing boats tied against rock

Waterfall from hanging valley

Denser trees and shrubs in gully

28

Bare rocky crags

30

Dwarf forest in glaciated scoop

9·12 SENO OCASIÓN DETAIL CALETA BRECKNOCK (CHARTED POSITIONS)

0   ½
Nautical Mile

Note some vessels have had difficulty in locating this anchorage but have reported a narrow *caleta* with the frame of a fishing hut at its head, open to the NE but still providing some protection from that direction, due to kelp at the entrance .

Canal Ocasión

54°32'·7S 71°54'·5W

Charts BA *554*; US *22425*; Chile *12310, 12400, 12600, 12711*

General

Canal Ocasión leads between Canal Cockburn and Canal Brecknock, running NE of Isla Aguirre. If taken, it avoids the rough seas outside and is the route taken by fishing boats and small ships. Seno Ocasión, leading to Caleta Brecknock, runs off Canal Ocasión.

9·12 Península Brecknock – Caleta Brecknock

54°34'·3S 71°57'W

Charts BA *554*; US *22425*; Chile *12400, 12600, 12711*

General

Caleta Brecknock is 1·5M up Seno Ocasión and is a justifiably popular anchorage. The surrounding hills and cliffs are spectacular and there is excellent hiking on the exposed glaciated rock. From the anchorage it is possible to scramble to the top of the mountain overlooking the anchorage. There have been reports of boats having trouble with *rachas* here whilst anchoring but once tucked back into the notch the yacht should be protected.

Anchorage

The safest anchorage is in the NW corner, in a well-protected notch, with four lines ashore. To the E of the waterfall there are truck tyres secured along the cliffs and small boats can go alongside to collect water in fine weather only. Do not use this position in strong winds and watch out for trees snagging in the rigging.

Canal Brecknock

9·13 Isla Brecknock – Puerto Paso Aguirre

54°41'·35S 71°32'·7W (GPS)

Charts BA *554*; US *22425*; Chile *12400, 12600, 12711*

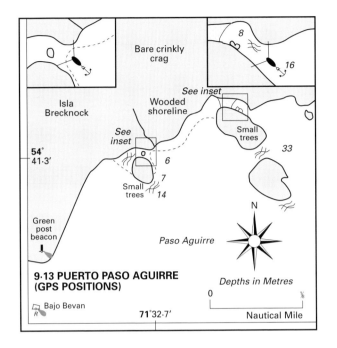

9·13 PUERTO PASO AGUIRRE (GPS POSITIONS)

Depths in Metres

0 ⅛

Nautical Mile

71°32·7'

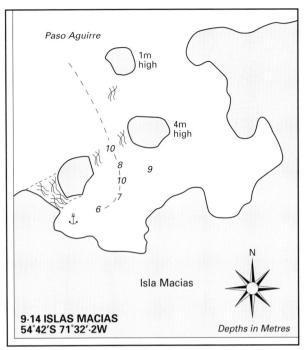

9·14 ISLAS MACIAS
54°42'S 71°32'·2W

Depths in Metres

General

There are two anchorages shown on the sketch plan, both providing excellent protection, the one to the W being particularly well protected. This anchorage is right up in the corner shown on the sketch. The depth falls to about 3m and care needs to be taken, as there are rocky areas close in with less water over them. Close in would be very tight for a yacht more than 12–13m long. The anchorage is almost always occupied by fishing boats and it is possible to tie up with them and to take shorelines. The fishermen are very polite and will happily offer the visitor sea urchins (*erizos*). Delicious but an acquired taste; the eggs are consumed raw with a squeeze of lemon. A box of wine is a good exchange.

The E anchorage has quite a lot of kelp close in but it is possible to anchor clear of the kelp, in about 10m, and to take shorelines.

9·14 Paso Aguirre – Isla Macias

54°42'S 71°32'·2W

Charts BA *554*; US *22425*; Chile *12400, 12600, 12711*

General

This is a regularly used anchorage by yachts and by small fishing boats from Punta Arenas. The anchorage lies in the obvious bay on the N side of Isla Macias. Anchor with lines in about 7m against the W shore. A well-protected anchorage.

Canal Ballenero

9·15 Isla Burnt – Caleta Ancha

54°44'S 71°12'W

Charts BA *554*; US *22425, 22418*; Chile *12400, 12600, 12711*

General

Caleta Ancha is on the SE side of Isla Burnt. Anchor near the waterfall with a line astern. The bottom is rock but said to be good holding.

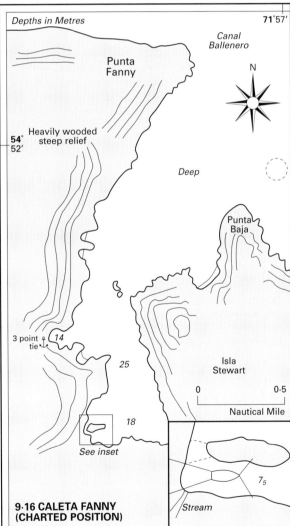

9·16 CALETA FANNY (CHARTED POSITION)

9·16 Isla Stewart – Caleta Fanny

54°53'S 70°58'W

Charts BA *554, 1373*; US *22425, 22418*; Chile *12400, 12600, 12713, 12800*

General

Caleta Fanny is at the NE end of Isla Stewart. As there is foul ground off Punta Baja it is better to favour the W shore of the approach.

Anchorage

The first anchorage is in 15m; rock and kelp, with a three point tie to white painted rocks on the shore in a small cove on the W side of the long indentation. There is considerable kelp along the sides of the cove. It is surrounded by steep hills and subject to strong *rachas* particularly during W winds. The second anchorage is in the SW corner of Puerto Fanny taking a 4-point tie between the small island and the main shore. There is kelp but the depth is 7·5m.

9·17 Islas del Medio – Pozo Marit

54°49'S 70°57'·2W

Charts BA *554, 1373*; US *22425, 22418*; Chile *12600, 12800*

General

This *caleta*, in the Islas del Medio, was named for Marit Asdahl of the Norwegian yacht *Kuven*. It is well known to local fishermen and provides good shelter. The wind may blow with great force here but, as there are no mountains nearby, it is steady.

Approach and Anchorage

The entrance is narrow with 4·5m between banks of kelp. Once inside, space is limited but there is room for a yacht to anchor in 3m, mud, with lines to the W shore.

9·18 Islas del Medio – Caleta Frog

54°49'S 70°57'W

Charts BA *554, 1373*; US *22425, 22418*; Chile *12600, 12800*

General

This unnamed *caleta* (Caleta Frog) is in the Islas del Medio that lie between Isla Stewart and Isla O'Brien. The anchorage is at the NW end of the largest island, Isla Grande, off which there is a maze of little islets and shoals.

Approach

There are two routes into the anchorage. The approach from the N is narrow but is well sheltered from W winds. This entrance has considerable kelp fringing it and a least depth of 4·5m. However, especially as it is sheltered, it is fairly straightforward picking a way through this kelp. The approach from the W is wider but has the disadvantage that it is W facing.

Anchorage

A secure 4-point tie can be made between the islands and holding is good in soft mud. It is well protected from winds from all directions. In strong

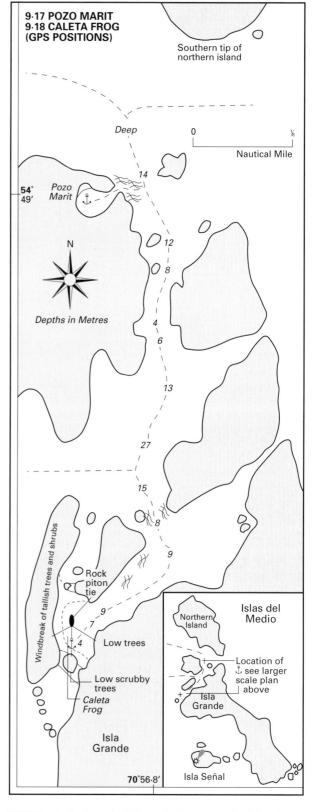

WSW winds the wind funnels between the islands so that the security of lines is reassuring. This anchorage is a good alternative to Puerto Fanny. The surrounding islands are relatively low-lying and it is not subject to the *rachas* that may be found in the latter.

9·19 Isla Londonderry – Puerto Engaño

54°56'·9S 70°46'·6W
Charts BA *554,1373*; US *22425, 22418*; Chile *12700, 12800*

General

Puerto Engaño is on Isla Londonderry, towards the E end of Canal Ballenero. The anchorage itself is in Caleta Silva in the SW corner of Puerto Engaño. The entrance is open. There is a beacon on the N point of the entrance. The holding is excellent in 8m, sand bottom, and there is water available from a stream at the head of the bay. It is also possible to anchor and take shorelines.

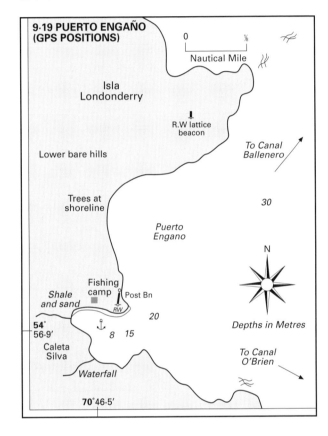

Canal O'Brien

Report by VHF to the nearby *armada* station at Timbales. If you are approaching from the W they will be expecting to hear from you.

9·20 Isla Londonderry – Puerto Fortuna

54°53'S 70°26'W 54°54'·45S 70°26'·10W (GPS)
Charts BA *554, 1373*; US *22418*; Chile *12700, 12713, 12720, 12800*

General

Puerto Fortuna on Canal O'Brien provides good protection from winds from the NW through to the E. However Caleta Emelita or Caleta Lagunas, well charted and on the opposite, N shore of the canal, are better alternatives.

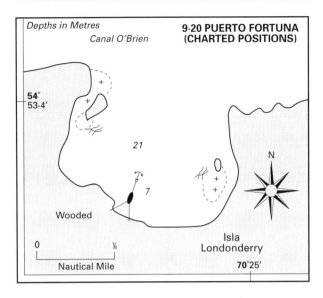

Anchorage

The holding is good in mud, but unfortunately the anchorage is very deep, more than 20m. There is ample swinging room if anchored in the middle of the bay but a more secure position can be found in the S part of the bay anchoring in about 7m and tying close into the shore. This position gives better protection than the chart suggests.

9·21 Isla O'Brien – Caleta Emelita

54°52'·9S 70°22'·9W (GPS)
Charts BA *554, 1373*; US *22418*; Chile *12700, 12720, 12800*

General

Caleta Emelita, at the end of Isla O'Brien, is best approached from the S, from which direction there are no dangers. The channel inside the islets to the NE is passable but needs a good lookout. This little cove provides excellent shelter from all but the E, either swinging or with lines ashore, it is used by fishermen. Holding is good in 12m. A second small cove is available just to the N of the channel inside the islets.

9·22 Canal Pomar – Seno Ventisquero

54°51'S 70°19'·5W
Charts BA *554, 1373*; US *22418*; Chile *12700, 12800*

General

This glacier lies at the junction of the W end of Canal Beagle and Canal Pomar. The moraine at the entrance to the *seno* is shallow with a depth of 5–7m. At the first narrows, shown on detail 2, pass about 50m from the wooded spur. There is a depth of 5–7m. Bergy bits are usually aground on the moraine at this point.

Anchorage

The best anchorage is shown in detail 1. This is a particularly lovely spot with well-developed trees that appear never to have felt a breath of wind. While it is calm here with a N gale blowing in the *seno*, there is a risk of ice blowing into the anchorage with a S wind.

171

CHILE

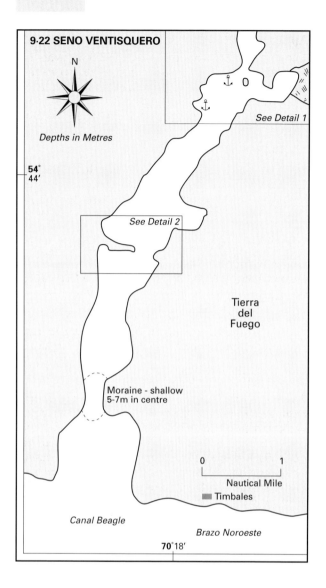

9·22 SENO VENTISQUERO

N

Depths in Metres

54°
44′

See Detail 2

Tierra
del
Fuego

Moraine - shallow
5-7m in centre

0   1

Nautical Mile
▪ Timbales

Canal Beagle

Brazo Noroeste

70°18′

See Detail 1

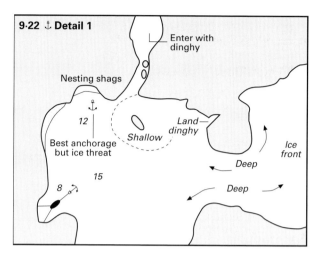

9·22 ⚓ Detail 1

Enter with
dinghy

Nesting shags

12

Best anchorage
but ice threat

Shallow

Land
dinghy

Ice
front

Deep

8

15

Deep

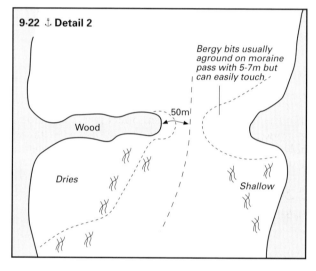

9·22 ⚓ Detail 2

Bergy bits usually
aground on moraine
pass with 5-7m but
can easily touch.

50m

Wood

Dries

Shallow

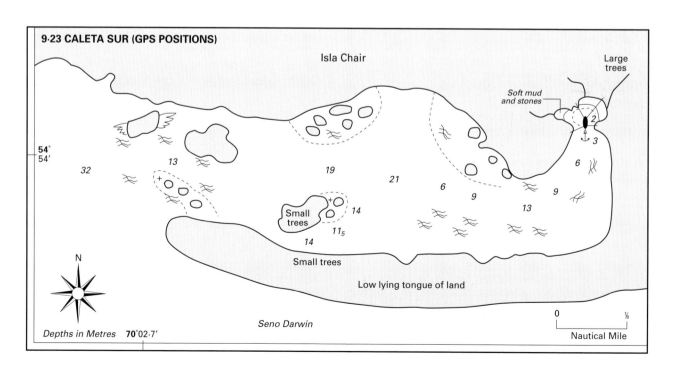

9·23 CALETA SUR (GPS POSITIONS)

Isla Chair

Large
trees

Soft mud
and stones

2

3

54°
54′

32

13

19

21

6

6

9

9

13

6

+

Small
trees

14

11₅

14

Small trees

Low lying tongue of land

N

Seno Darwin

Depths in Metres   **70°02·7′**

0   ⅛

Nautical Mile

In settled weather it is possible to enter the basin at the NE end and drift close to the ice front.

9·23 Isla Chair – Caleta Sur

54°54'S 70°02'·7W (GPS)

Charts BA *554, 1373*; US *22418*; Chile *12700, 12800*

General

Caleta Sur is deep within the bay on the SE side of Isla Chair. Caleta Cushion (9·24) is preferred as the approach is sheltered from all prevailing winds, whilst the approach to Caleta Sur faces these winds and in heavy weather it may be difficult to distinguish the kelp in the outer bay.

Approach

The entrance looks difficult, but is actually quite straightforward. There is quite a lot of kelp in the bay, which helps mark the safe route, clear of rocks. Depths in this inner bay fall from about 7m to 2m near its head.

Anchorage

The bottom is very soft mud and the yacht can sit partly in the mud at low water when snuggled up into the bay. The inner basin offers protection from all winds while the outer basin provides protection only from E winds and therefore is of limited value as the prevailing winds are W.

9·24 Isla Chair – Caleta Cushion

54°53'·9S 70°00'·6W (GPS)

Charts BA *554, 1373*; US *22418*; Chile *12700, 12800*

General

The second anchorage on Isla Chair, nicknamed Cushion, provides excellent shelter from the W winds that are prevalent in the Beagle Canal. Caleta Cushion is on the E end of the island.

Approach

The approach is from the large outer bay, which is deep and wide, and provides immediate protection from all but S and E winds. The anchorage is situated in the small bay behind the island in the S part of the bay. The approach leaving the island to port is easy.

Anchorage

Holding is good, and tall trees which provide excellent protection and tie-off points for a 4-point mooring, surround the bay. Fishermen occasionally use the bay.

9·25 Seno Garibaldi

54°50'S 69°56'W (*13111*)

Charts BA *554, 1373*; US *22418*; Chile *12700, 12800, 13111*

General

The entrance to Seno Garibaldi is at the W end of the Brazo Noroeste of Canal Beagle. The *seno* runs N–S and has three glaciers running into it at the N end.

Anchorage

There is an anchorage at the entrance on the W side immediately behind the point, 10m sand and mud, protected from the W. Puerto Garibaldi, about five miles in on the W side, provides some protection between NW and SW. The anchorage is in about 18m, sand and mud. In the N, there is an anchorage S of a small island, but with a high risk of ice. The view of the glaciers from the top of the island is remarkable. It is usually possible to sail right up to the face of the main glacier.

Warning

When the wind is fresh, it howls down Seno Garibaldi with great ferocity. The first two anchorages are open and provide negligible protection and although there is some shelter to the S of the island there are far better anchorages within a few miles of the entrance to Seno Garibaldi, at Isla Chair, for example.

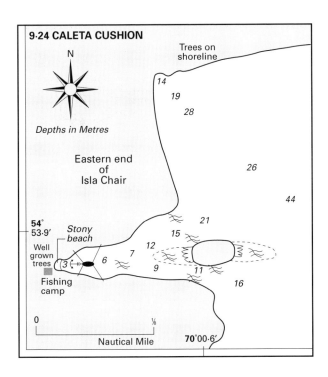

9·24 CALETA CUSHION

N

Trees on shoreline

Depths in Metres

14
19
28

Eastern end of Isla Chair

26

44

54°
53·9'

Stony beach

21
15

Well grown trees

3
6
7
12
9
11
16

Fishing camp

0 ⅛

Nautical Mile 70°00·6'

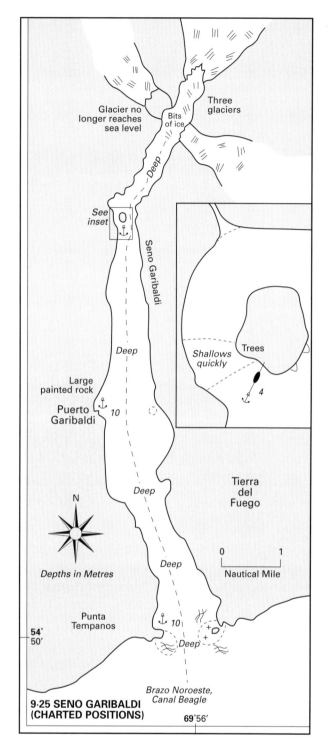

9.25 SENO GARIBALDI (CHARTED POSITIONS)

Brazo Noroeste, Canal Beagle

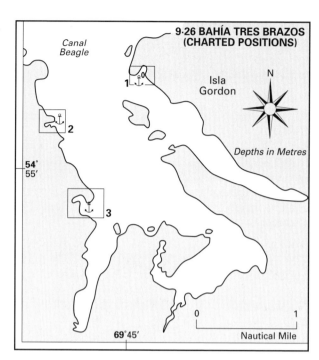

Canal Beagle – Brazo Noroeste

Caution In this area several anchorages are prohibited, as are Canal Murray and Paso Goree. Yachts entering Canal Murray will be towed out of the canal by an *armada* vessel in an unceremonious way and taken to Puerto Williams. There is no question but that this is a prohibited route.

9.26 Bahía Tres Brazos

54°53'S 69°46'W

Charts BA *554*; US *22418*; Chile *12700, 12800*

General

This is a large bay on the S side of Brazo Noroeste, opposite Ventisquero España. Considerable discrepancies have been observed between charts and GPS positions in this area.

The bay has many potential anchorages; the three shown on the plan have been used and found to be secure.

Anchorage

1. This is open to the SW. When mooring pull close into the shore for the maximum protection.
2. *Caleta Julia* (54°54'·66S 69°47'·10W GPS) About 1·5M S of the entrance, behind the first point on the W side. It appears no more than a bay on Chile chart *12700*, but opens up into a sheltered pool where a boat can tie from shore to shore. The *caleta* is used by fisherman and may be blocked by lines tied across the entrance. This is an exceptional anchorage and is good for all winds.
3. *Pozo Cauane* is at GPS 54°56'·7S 69°46'·1W (on Chile chart *12700*, 54°55'·5S 69°46'·5W), in an unnamed *caleta* about 2·5M further S from Caleta Julia. Once around the point to the S of the entrance, hold to the starboard shore, leave a visible rock to starboard and follow the 'river' round to port. Depths in the narrow part of the entrance have to be judged by eye. The pool at the head is very well sheltered from all quarters. There is anchorage in 2–5m with lines ashore. Besides excellent shelter and convenient fresh water, the *caleta* is in a lovely setting and has good hiking on the high ground above.

Another *caleta* in the NW corner of the SW Brazo has also been suggested but not examined.

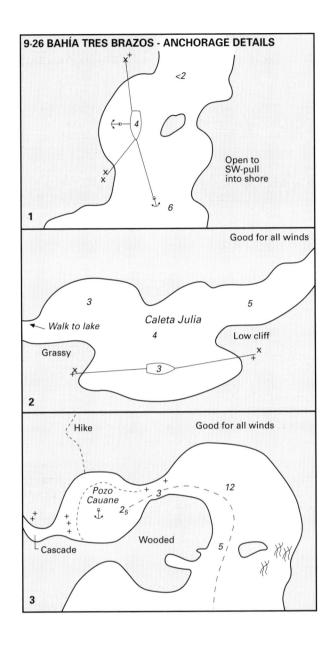

9·26 BAHÍA TRES BRAZOS - ANCHORAGE DETAILS

1

<2

4

Open to
SW-pull
into shore

6

2

Good for all winds

3

5

Caleta Julia

Walk to lake

4

Low cliff

Grassy

3

3

Hike

Good for all winds

Pozo Cauane

3

12

2·5

Wooded

5

Cascade

10. Brazo Noroeste to Cape Horn and Isla de los Estados

For the cruiser, this area is very different from other parts of Chile. The climate in the E part of the Canal Beagle is much warmer and drier than to the N and W, while to the S of Isla Navarino the waters are more exposed and anchorages less well protected. Perhaps the greatest contrast is in the attitude of the *armada*. Rules and regulations that are applied with a light touch in other areas are rigidly enforced here. For instance only a few waterways and anchorages are approved for use by yachts. Paper work must be correct, light dues will be collected and requests for examination of safety equipment and insurance documentation are not unusual. Radio schedules must be kept; failure to do so may result in a search being mounted after as few as three days.

The *armada* has several observation posts that will call passing yachts requesting the yacht's name, flag, number of people on board etc. The posts are at: Timbales – Canal O'Brien; Punta Yamana – five

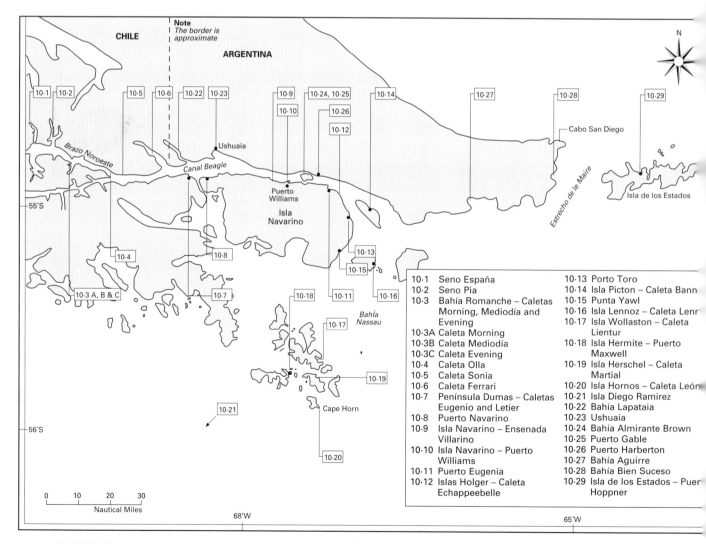

10·1	Seno España	10·13 Porto Toro
10·2	Seno Pia	10·14 Isla Picton – Caleta Bann
10·3	Bahía Romanche – Caletas	10·15 Punta Yawl
	Morning, Mediodía and	10·16 Isla Lennoz – Caleta Lenr
	Evening	10·17 Isla Wollaston – Caleta
10·3A	Caleta Morning	Lientur
10·3B	Caleta Mediodía	10·18 Isla Hermite – Puerto
10·3C	Caleta Evening	Maxwell
10·4	Caleta Olla	10·19 Isla Herschel – Caleta
10·5	Caleta Sonia	Martial
10·6	Caleta Ferrari	10·20 Isla Hornos – Caleta León
10·7	Península Dumas – Caletas	10·21 Isla Diego Ramirez
	Eugenio and Letier	10·22 Bahía Lapataia
10·8	Puerto Navarino	10·23 Ushuaia
10·9	Isla Navarino – Ensenada	10·24 Bahía Almirante Brown
	Villarino	10·25 Puerto Gable
10·10	Isla Navarino – Puerto	10·26 Puerto Harberton
	Williams	10·27 Bahía Aguirre
10·11	Puerto Eugenia	10·28 Bahía Bien Suceso
10·12	Islas Holger – Caleta	10·29 Isla de los Estados – Puer
	Echappeebelle	Hoppner

miles to the E of Caleta Olla; Canal Murray – N entrance; Puerto Navarino (NW corner of Isla Navarino); Puerto Toro (on the E side of Isla Navarino); Isla Snipe; Caleta Lennox (Isla Lennox): Carlos (Isla Nueva); Wollaston Radio (on the N of Isla Wollaston); Cape Horn.

Control of yachts is carried out with the usual polite efficiency and courtesy that is typical of the Chilean authorities. With the exception of Canal Murray, which is totally out of bounds to foreign

vessels, it is accepted that alternative routes and anchorages can be used if necessary for the ship's safety. In practice this means that one should not apply for non-approved places on your *zarpe* or when reporting your departure by radio. If the reasons are good, such as a strong headwind, permission will generally be granted following a request by VHF when nearby. There appears to be a process of opening up new areas to visitors, however it is very slow. Approved anchorages in

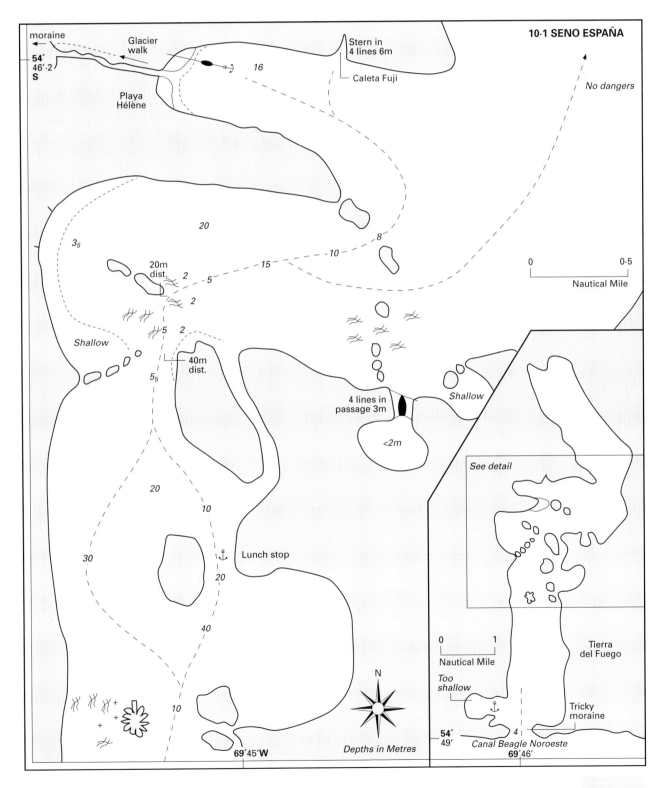

10·1 SENO ESPAÑA

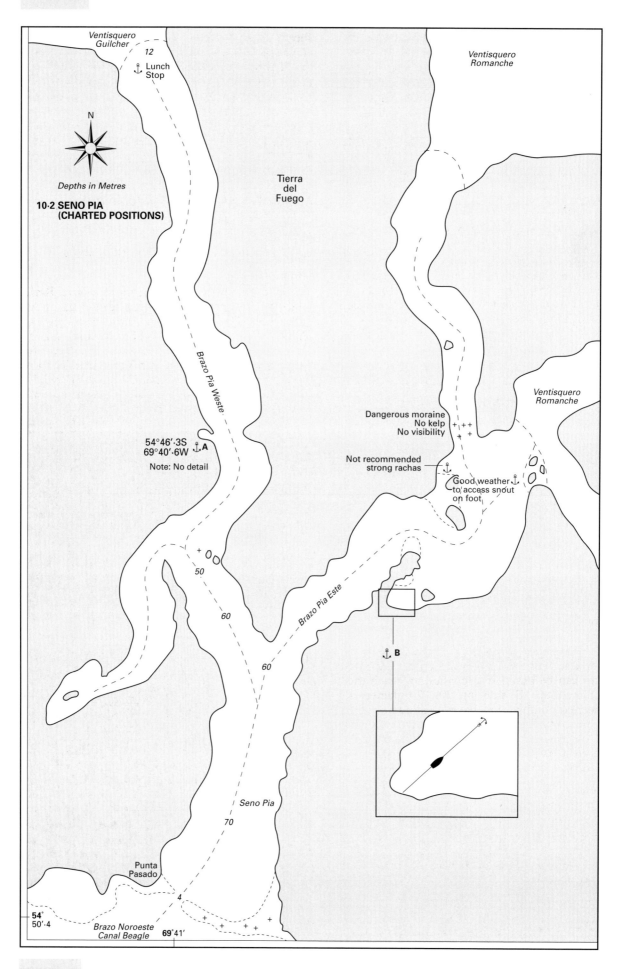

Ventisquero
Guilcher

12

⚓ Lunch
Stop

N

Depths in Metres

**10·2 SENO PIA
(CHARTED POSITIONS)**

Ventisquero
Romanche

Tierra
del
Fuego

Brazo Pia Weste

54°46'·3S ⚓ A
69°40'·6W
Note: No detail

Ventisquero
Romanche

Dangerous moraine
No kelp
No visibility

Not recommended
strong rachas ⚓

Good weather ⚓
to access snout
on foot

50

60

+ O

Brazo Pia Este

60

⚓ B

Seno Pia

70

Punta
Pasado

4

54°
50'·4

*Brazo Noroeste
Canal Beagle*

69°41'

2001/2 were as follows, but may be subject to change:

Bahía Romanche, Caleta Olla, Caleta Sonia, Puerto Navarino, Puerto Williams, Puerto Toro, Caleta Banner (Isla Picton), Caleta Lennox, Caleta Martial, Caleta León (Isla Hornos).

10·1 Seno España

54°49'S 69°46'·5W

Charts BA *554*; US *22418*; Chile *12700, 12800*

General

This is a difficult Seno with a tricky moraine at the entrance that has plenty of kelp and depths of 2m. Enter centrally, close to HW. Once inside there are a number of anchorages, though all, perhaps with the exception of Playa Hélène, are regularly threatened by ice. The passage of the shallows shown in the detailed sketch is difficult because the water is opaque due to glacial run off and the currents are very strong. On a clear day it is possible to see the dangers from aloft.

Anchorage

At Playa Hélène (GPS 54°46'·2S 69°45'·1W) the bottom shelves steeply. It is possible to anchor in 16–20m with lines to trees on the beach. A bowline can also be taken to the N shore for extra security. From a position about 20m to the N of the stream a track leads through the bush to a small lake and moraine below the glacier. From here there is a track that runs behind some rocky outcrops up to the S flank of the glacier. This walk is highly recommended.

10·2 Seno Pia

54°50'·4S 69°41'W (entrance chart *13113* agrees with GPS)

Charts BA *554*; US *22418*; Chile *12700, 12800, 13113*

General

A beautiful *seno* leading N into Cordillera Darwin from Brazo Noroeste, 'the avenue of the glaciers'. It is well protected though it would become uncomfortable with a wind blowing up the *seno* and the *caletas* can be gusty. It is possible to reach the glacier faces (the E side of the W glacier is recommended) and yachts have anchored at the head of Brazo Pia Weste in 12m off the stone beach between the two glaciers. Some people have made this trip by dinghy, however it could be extremely nasty should the wind freshen.

Entrance

There is a 12m bar at the entrance to the *seno* and a shoal area off the W shore clearly marked by kelp. A reef extends off the E shore to a prominent white rock with two smaller rocks close together further off-shore. Enter about 400m W of these two rocks; the bar has no kelp.

Anchorage

Anchorage A shown on the plan is at 54°46'·3S 69°40'·65W (GPS and Chile *13113*). There is a

shoal patch on the S side of the *caleta* where a river comes out and depths are generally greater towards the N shore. Anchor in 4m, good holding, but put lines ashore as it is squally. There is invariably ice in the *seno*, it does sometimes come in to the *caleta* and may block the entrance.

As Anchorage B is reported to be very good, the other anchorages indicated in the sketch of the E arm are only recommended for short stays in fair weather.

10·3 Bahía Romanche – Caletas Morning, Mediodía and Evening

54°55'S 69°29'W

Charts BA *554, 1373*; US *22418*; Chile *12700, 12800*

General

The entrance to this bay is on the S side of Brazo Noroeste immediately opposite the spectacular Romanche Glacier. This glacier is retreating quite rapidly and there is a huge waterfall running from the base of the glacier into tide water. There are three good anchorages in Bahía Romanche. The bay itself is surprisingly well sheltered from the strong W winds that can blow down Brazo Noroeste of Canal Beagle. These anchorages are:

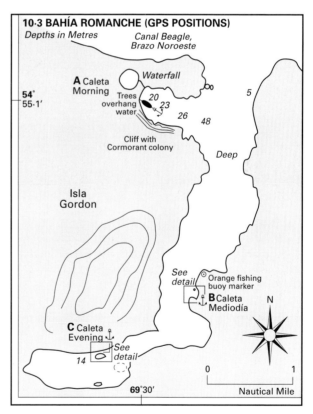

10·3A Caleta Morning

54°55'S 69°30'W

General

Situated at the entrance and on the W side of Bahía Romanche, Caleta Morning provides all round protection and is generally free from *rachas*. The entrance is wide and clean apart from a rock close to the S shore. The anchorage has good holding in 18m at the head of the bay. There are also rings set into the rocks underneath the cliffs at the SW corner which could be used for a stern-to tie. These cliffs are a nesting site for blue-eyed cormorants and condors have also been seen amongst the nests.

10·3B Caleta Mediodía

54°57'·1S 69°28'·9W

General

This is the most secure anchorage in Bahía Romanche. Fishermen use it and orange fishing buoys have been tied to trees to mark its position. There is just turning room inside the bay but it would be better to drop anchor and back in before taking 4 shorelines.

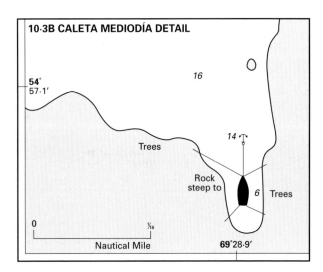

10·3C Caleta Evening

54°57'·8S 69°30'·8W

General

Different charts give the location of Caleta Evening in different positions. However the plan shows a secure anchorage between a small island and thick woodland on the N shore. This anchorage is better

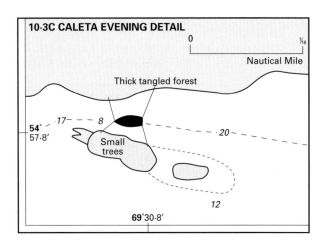

protected than it would appear but could be a little exposed in W gale conditions. An anchorage has been reported at the head of the SW arm.

10·4 Caleta Olla

54°56'S 69°08'W

Charts BA *554, 1373*; US 2*2418, 22430*; Chile *12700, 12800, 13113, 13200*

General

Caleta Olla (cooking pot) is on the N side of Brazo Noroeste. It is about 400m in diameter and is sheltered except from the SE. The bay has perfect protection due to the tall trees that grow along its W side.

Anchorage

Anchor in 14m and then use shore lines to pull close to the beach in about 6m. In this position winds can howl overhead and the anchorage, close in, is windless. Holding is excellent on a sand bottom.

Charter boats often stop here. There is excellent hiking. A trail follows the stream at the NW end of the beach, leads through the swamp, goes up beside a large waterfall and on to high ground where there is a wonderful view of both the Italia and Hollandia glaciers – 2 hours' (plus) walk each way. A second trail follows the river to the NE side of the bay and leads to high ground overlooking the Hollandia glacier. There is a small Indian midden off the beach, and a wide variety of wildflowers. There are many *guanaco* trails on the shore.

Report by VHF to the nearby *armada* station at Punta Yamana.

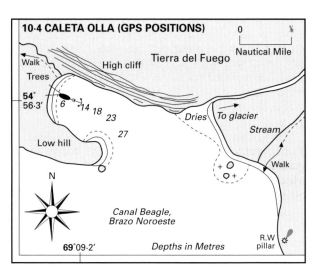

Canal Beagle – Main Channel

10·5 Caleta Sonia

54°58'S 69°01'W

Charts BA *554, 1373*; US *22430*; Chile *13200*

General

Caleta Sonia is just E of Punta Yamana (Fl.12s13m7M white concrete tower, red band 5m 265°-vis-095°).

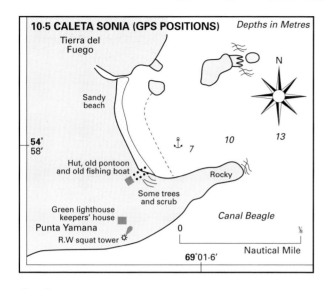

10·5 CALETA SONIA (GPS POSITIONS) *Depths in Metres*

Tierra del Fuego

Sandy beach

54° 58'

Hut, old pontoon and old fishing boat

Rocky

Some trees and scrub

Green lighthouse keepers' house

Punta Yamana

R.W squat tower

Canal Beagle

0   ⅛
Nautical Mile

69°01·6'

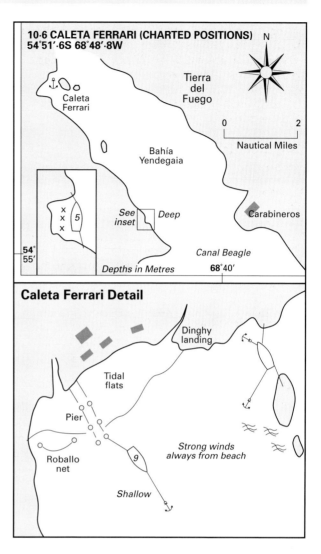

10·6 CALETA FERRARI (CHARTED POSITIONS)
54°51'·6S 68°48'·8W

Caleta Ferrari

Tierra del Fuego

Bahía Yendegaia

0   2
Nautical Miles

See inset

Deep

Carabineros

Canal Beagle

54° 55'

Depths in Metres   68°40'

Caleta Ferrari Detail

Dinghy landing

Tidal flats

Pier

Roballo net

Shallow

Strong winds always from beach

Anchorage

After rounding the headland leave the small group of islets/rocks to starboard and anchor close to the beach in 15m or less, excellent holding in sand and mud. Shore lines can be taken to trees or the remains of an old pier. This anchorage would give good protection from the W but is probably gusty when winds are from the N. In poor conditions Caleta Olla would make a more secure stopping place. The Yamana *armada* post is located here.

10·6 Caleta Ferrari

54°51'S 68°48'W 54°51'·37S 68°49'·01W (GPS)
Charts BA *554, 1373*; US *22430*; Chile *13200*

General

Caleta Ferrari is on the NW of Bahía Yendegaia, which is on the N side of Canal Beagle. The wind usually blows strongly from the beach. For additional security it is possible to set an anchor out from the pier and take bow and stern lines to the S shore and a further stern line to the pier. The anchorage between the small island and mainland is good.

Caleta Ferrari is the home of Estancia Yendegaia. The caretaker (2001) may supply horses and guiding to the exceptional area, including a glacier which comes down to the pasture. There is excellent hiking in the surrounding mountains. Centolla crab can be caught in the bay behind the islands in 30m of water.

10·7 Península Dumas – Caletas Eugenio and Letier

54°56'S 68°27'W
Charts BA *554*; US *22430*; Chile *13100, 13131, 13200*

General

These anchorages lie on the NE corner of Península Dumas (Isla Hoste), at the junction of Canal Beagle and Canal Murray. The access is straightforward and they give good protection from all winds except from the E and SE. Eugenio is better than Letier. Anchor in 5–8m with shorelines.

Passage

International frontier

The border in the Beagle Canal has been subject to dispute. The Chileans are particularly sensitive about activity in the area. As yachts cannot move between anchorages on either side of the canal with complete freedom, the following text follows the Chilean shore and then describes Argentinian anchorages at the end.

10·8 Puerto Navarino

54°55'·4S 68°19'·3W
Charts BA *554, 1373*; US *22430*; Chile *13100, 13131, 13200*

General

Puerto Navarino is 26M W of Puerto Williams and almost exactly half way between Puerto Williams and Caleta Olla, the latter being the best anchorage at the E end of Brazo Noroeste, Canal Beagle. It is a good stopping point, especially when travelling W against the prevailing winds. Puerto Navarino has a small *armada* station that will make the visiting yacht welcome.

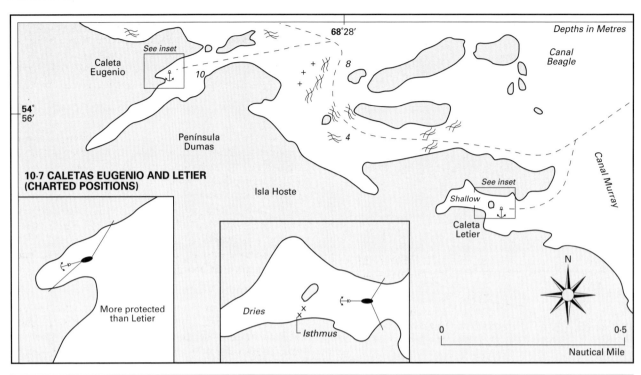

10·7 CALETAS EUGENIO AND LETIER
(CHARTED POSITIONS)

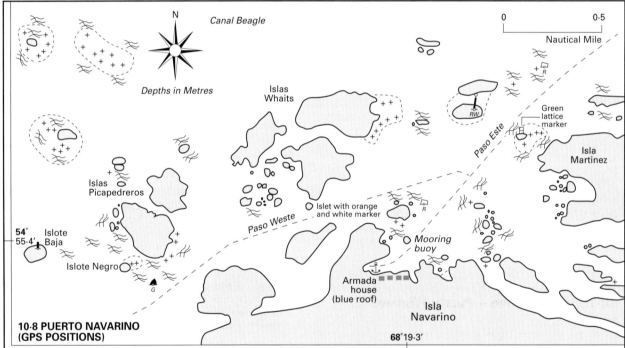

10·8 PUERTO NAVARINO
(GPS POSITIONS)

Approaches

The passage from E or W is straightforward and is well shown on Chilean chart, *13131*. The channels are well buoyed with the buoyage direction (red right returning) leading into the harbour (which means that the buoyage is in opposite directions in Paso Weste and Este).

Anchorage

By calling *Navarino Radio*, permission can be obtained to use the rather exposed *armada* buoy. Use a stern anchor (in about 20m) to hold the yacht clear of the buoy in case the wind drops. A more sheltered alternative is to anchor in about 7m close to the small jetty in front of the *armada* building and take a shore-line to this jetty. In strong winds the most sheltered option is to anchor, facing W, with lines to rocks ashore, in the shallow inlet to the W of the buildings. The mud is very soft and holding is excellent.

Formalities

In 2002 it was said that Puerto Navarino was about to become a port of entry and exit. If this is so it will considerably simplify travel between Chilean waters and Ushuaia, in Argentina. However, check that this

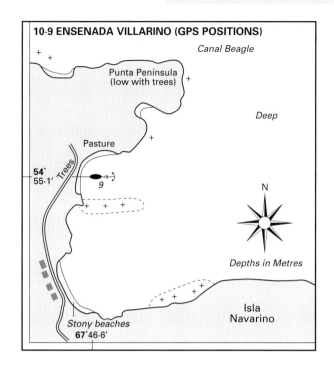

10·9 ENSENADA VILLARINO (GPS POSITIONS)

Canal Beagle

Punta Península
(low with trees)

Deep

Pasture

54°
55·1'

Trees

9

N

Depths in Metres

Stony beaches
67°46·6'

Isla
Navarino

service is available before attempting to complete formalities, as the border here is sensitive.

10·9 Isla Navarino – Ensenada Villarino

54°55'·2S 67°46'W

Charts BA *554, 1373*; US *22430*; Chile *13100, 13200*

General

This anchorage is only 6M W of Puerto Williams but it is useful if travelling late in the day and an easy stopping place is required. It is a peaceful place to stop.

Anchorage

The entrance is straightforward and the bay is well protected from all but E winds. There is good holding in about 12m with a shoreline. When E winds blow in this area they are generally light but a swell does enter this bay if the wind swings round to this direction.

10·10 Isla Navarino – Puerto Williams

54°56'S 67°37'W

Charts BA *554, 1373*; US *22430*; Chile *13100, 13142, 13200*

Port communications
Ch 16, 09, 14. c/s *CBW*
☎ 62 10 90 *Fax* 62 10 41

General

The town is a naval base and is controlled by the *armada*. It is also the Chilean administrative centre for the Antarctic. The principal civilian occupation is fishing for *centolla* crabs; there is a packing plant near Puerto Williams.

Approach

Call on VHF in advance and give an ETA. The *armada* and Immigration will visit the yacht when at Micalvi.

Banco Herradura extends 1·2M N of Punta Gusano (Fl(3)R.9s10m3M red GRP tower 5·5m) at the end of Península Zañartu which shelters Puerto Williams from the W. It is safe to pass about 75m to the N of the red tower with 2·5m water, unless there is a big swell.

Berthing

Go to the Club de Yates at the Micalvi, a retired munitions carrier, in Seno Lauta. The approach to the Micalvi is a channel with shallow water on either side (5m or less) and there is limited turning room. Charges were US$5 per day in 2001. It would be hard to find a more secure berth than this one, less than 100M to the N of Cape Horn. Alternatively request permission to anchor in the river NW of Micalvi in 4–6m or tie to the large mooring buoy there (a smaller charge will still be levied).

Formalities

Puerto Williams is a port of entry, arrivals and departures are processed at any hour with great efficiency. A written application for the *zarpe* is expected. If coming from the E with the intention of continuing to the W, it may be best to go first to Ushuaia to stock up and then return to Puerto Williams for the *zarpe*. A small buoyage and light fee will be collected from all vessels.

Facilities

Diesel from COPEC in cans.
Propane available through the *armada*.
Water alongside Micalvi.
Supermarket: run by the *armada*, most basic supplies are available.
Bank which will accept credit cards and provide cash.
Shopping: limited and expensive
Laundry can be taken to the *armada* lavandería, which is on the same street as the Port Captain's office.
Cafetería at the local bakery.
Hot showers and toilets are available on the Micalvi.
The bar on the Micalvi serves lunch on Sundays (excellent empanadas) – a very friendly club.
The *armada* has extensive repair facilities and appears to be delighted to assist with essential work.
There are several small restaurants, a reasonably priced pension and a hotel a couple of miles W of the town that serves excellent meals.
The Museo Martín Gusinde, close to the yacht club, is worth a visit.

Tourism

There is good hiking around Puerto Williams. A trail starts just to the S of the prominent Virgin Mary statue that is reached by following the road winding up the E coast of the inlet and turning left at the first junction and continuing a short distance to a park on the right hand side. It leads to the top of Cerro Bandera (Flag Hill) with magnificent views up the valley in front of Les Dientes, and also of the Woolastons and Cape Horn. The trail is marked by paint splashes on the occasional tree, and there and back takes about 6 hours. From the top of Cerro Bandera, there is also a 5-day hike which takes you to Les Dientes, the impressive spiked mountain range that can be seen from the Micalvi. Near the beginning of the walk to Cerro Bandera there is a less well marked route

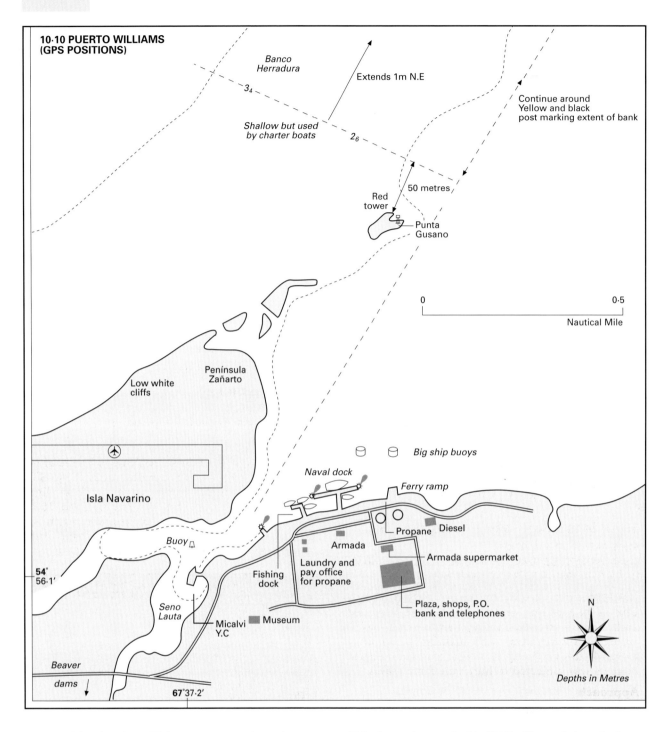

10·10 PUERTO WILLIAMS (GPS POSITIONS)

Banco Herradura

Extends 1m N.E

3₄

Shallow but used by charter boats

2₆

Continue around Yellow and black post marking extent of bank

50 metres

Red tower

Punta Gusano

0   0·5

Nautical Mile

Península Zañarto

Low white cliffs

Big ship buoys

Naval dock

Ferry ramp

Isla Navarino

Buoy

Propane   Diesel

Armada

Armada supermarket

Fishing dock

Laundry and pay office for propane

Plaza, shops, P.O. bank and telephones

54° 56·1'

Seno Lauta

Micalvi Y.C   Museum

N

Beaver dams

Depths in Metres

67°37·2'

---

alongside the river. This passes some large beaver dams and eventually leads to open country at the foot of Los Dientes.

Communications

Flights to Punta Arenas, daily in summer, less frequent in winter; flights are often blocked by bad weather. Advance booking is necessary, office in the plaza.

Ferry to Punta Arenas every week.

There is no public transport between Puerto Williams and Ushuaia. A passage on a charter yacht may be possible; the going rate in 2001 was US$50. Flights can occasionally be arranged with the aero club in Ushuaia. There is a small travel and tour business in the plaza that may be able to assist.

Telephone: Area code 61. CTC office and also telephone in the shopping centre.

Internet: one of the telephone providers also has an internet connection. The connection is slow but reasonable out of office hours.

Chile – the Far E and S
Isla Navarino

10·11 Puerto Eugenia

54°56'S 67°17'W

Charts BA *1373*; US *22430*; Chile *13200, 13300, 13322*

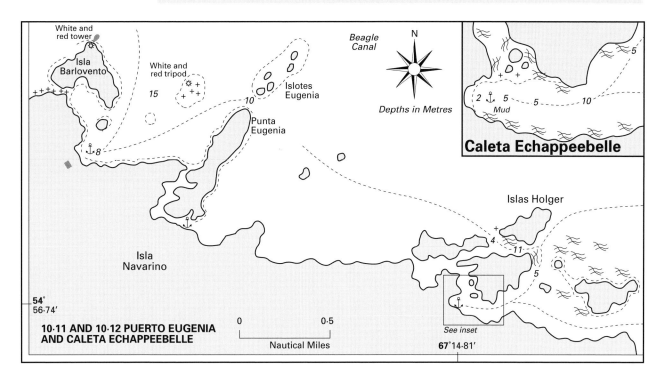

10·11 AND 10·12 PUERTO EUGENIA AND CALETA ECHAPPEEBELLE

Caleta Echappeebelle

General

At the NE end of Isla Navarino and between Punta Eugenia and Islote Barlovento, Puerto Eugenia is only ten miles from Puerto Williams and is a good jumping off place for a trip to Cape Horn. It also provides shelter if there is a strong contrary wind in the Beagle when returning from Cape Horn. The entrance is clean and the holding is good in 6–12m.

10·12 Islas Holger– Caleta Echappeebelle

54°56'·74S 67°14'·81W (GPS)

Charts BA *1373*; US *22430*; Chile *13200, 13330* (Best shown on BA *3424* which is no longer published)

General

This is one of the prettiest and most sheltered anchorages in the area (except from the E) as is evidenced by the dense and luxuriant bush. In a strong W this anchorage was peaceful when Puerto Eugenia was subjected to hurricane force *rachas*.

Approach

Approach is straightforward along the Navarino shore from the E but can also be made between the islands from N or W by keeping a close watch on the kelp and water colour.

Anchorage

Shallow draught vessels can gain the best shelter in the shallow water at the head of the bay. Most will anchor in thick mud on the 2m shelf or a little further out in 5m.

10·13 Puerto Toro

55°04'S 67°04'W

Charts BA *1373*; US *22430*; Chile *13200, 13300*

General

This was one of the original settlements in Tierra del Fuego and has a small friendly community. The entrance is marked by Puerto Toro light (Fl.5s.7m6M white GRP tower, red band 4m. 150°-vis-301°) and has two drying rocks about 300m NE of the light. The hills round the bay are high. There is protection from all except NE and E winds.

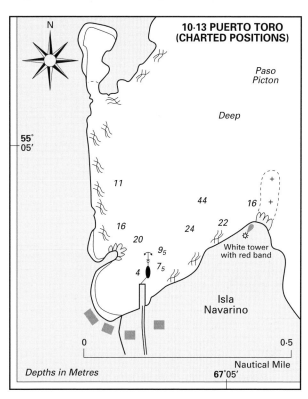

10·13 PUERTO TORO (CHARTED POSITIONS)

185

Anchorage

The *caleta* is very deep. It is possible to anchor in about 15m, but the shallow area is quite close to the shore. The other alternatives are to tie to the pier, which by local standards is in reasonable condition or to anchor off the pier with a line to it.

Cigarettes, meat, fruit and vegetables can be bartered for *centollas* (king crabs) and local craftwork.

10·14 Isla Picton – Caleta Banner

55°01'S 66°56'W
Charts BA *1373*; US *22430*; Chile *13200, 13300, 13322*

General

The *caleta* lies behind Isla Gardiner.

Anchorage

The best anchorage is in the deep bay on the S side of Isla Gardiner, the approach is between kelp beds but is straightforward. Holding is excellent in 4m sand; protection is total, though there is a long fetch to the SE.

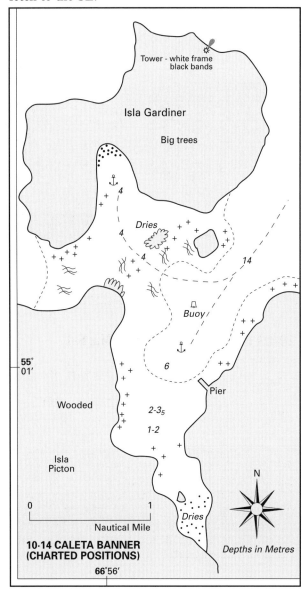

The main anchorage, near the buoy is more exposed, especially to the NE, and boats have dragged here in strong NW winds. Vessels may use the *armada* buoy in the centre of the bay. There is a boat pier on the E shore and a disused *armada* base. This is a tranquil and beautiful spot with many geese nesting along the shores.

10·15 Punta Yawl

55°12'·8S 67°05'·5W
Charts BA *1373*; US *22430*; Chile *13200, 13300*

General

This is an emergency anchorage, which is not normally included on a *zarpe*. The entrance can be identified by first spotting Islote Dingy. Anchor in between Islote Mariotti and Punta Yawl in 7m. Reasonable shelter and good holding though open to the E and best when wind is predominantly N or S. Puerto Toro would be better than Yawl in a westerly.

10·16 Isla Lennox – Caleta Lennox

55°17'S 66°50'W
Charts BA *1373*; US *22430*; Chile *13200, 13300, 13322*

General

Caleta Lennox provides excellent shelter from winds from the NW through to S and is a pleasant stop *en route* to the Horn, particularly if there are strong SW winds in Bahía Nassau. It is also a useful anchorage on the way N from the Horn if it is difficult to reach Toro because of fading daylight or strong NW winds. There is excellent holding in 3–4m over sand.

Formalities

The *armada* maintains a presence here.

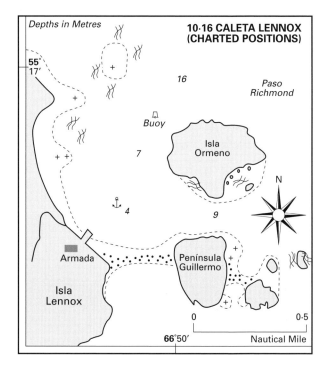

The S Islands

General

Bahía Nassau has variable and quickly changing weather. The prevailing winds are W but E is not uncommon and can be strong, kicking up a nasty sea. It is unwise to cross the bay in any condition of strong wind. There are some *caletas* on Islas Wollaston and Islas Hermite, which offer some shelter, none much good in an E wind.

10·17 Isla Wollaston – Caleta Lientur

55°44'S 67°18'W

Charts BA *1373*; US *22430*; Chile *13200, 13600, 13620, 13700*

The scale on *13200* and *13700* is the same and *13200* is easier to read.

General

Caleta Lientur is on the SE side of Isla Wollaston at the head of Bahía Scourfield. It has shelter to the NE and SW but SE and NW winds are directed into the *caleta* by the hills.

Approach and Anchorage

The entrance has a line of kelp across it in more than 15m. Anchor close in with lines ashore. Depths from 17m down to zero, sand and mud, good holding. Alternatively, use the *armada* buoy. If the weather is not too windy, a hike up to the nearby lake is worthwhile and gives great views of the Wollaston Islands.

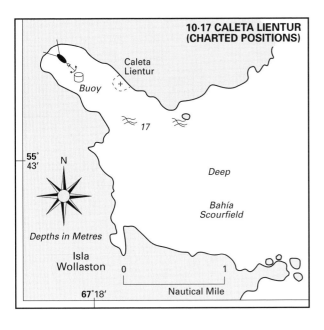

10·18 Isla Hermite – Puerto Maxwell

55°49'·4S 67°30'·7W (GPS)

Charts BA *1373*; US *22430*; Chile *13200, 13600, 13620, 13700*

The scale on *13200* and *13700* is the same and *13200* is easier to read.

General

Located inside Isla Jerdán at the NE end of Isla Hermite this anchorage is reached via Canal Bravo, Canal Franklin and Paso Oriental (not an approved route). Approaching by this route minimises exposure to the W wind and swell. Leaving Puerto Maxwell by the S opening gives access to the Horn from the NW and should provide fair winds for rounding the Horn.

Anchorage

The anchorage is the most secure in the area and is well sheltered from all directions, though there is a moderate fetch to the NE. The water here is tranquil when the W wind howls outside with only an occasional *racha*. Lines should be taken to the W shore of the anchorage shown. There is room for several boats. Walking here is excellent.

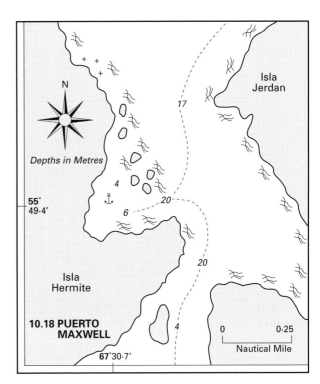

10·19 Isla Herschel – Caleta Martial

55°49'S 67°18'W

Charts BA *1373*; US *22430*; Chile *13200, 13600, 13620, 13700*

The scale on *13200* and *13700* is the same and *13200* is easier to read.

General

On the NE coast of Isla Herschel, Caleta Martial is the only anchorage in the Wollaston-Hermite group that the *armada* will authorise for use on a visit to Cape Horn. It is sheltered from all except E winds, in the event of which you should call Cape Horn or Wollaston Radio and request permission to move to Puerto Maxwell on Isla Hermite (preferred by yachts) or Caleta Lientur.

CHILE

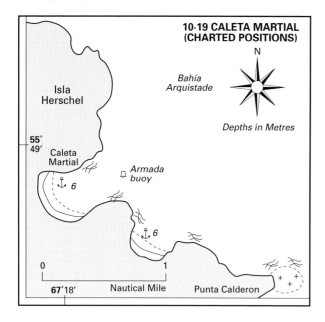

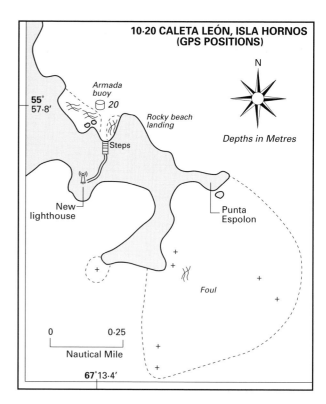

Approach and Anchorage

The yellow sand beach at the head of the *caleta* gives easy recognition. The entrance is clean and direct, and the holding is excellent in sand. The N anchorage is best for N to W winds and the S anchorage is better in SW winds.

Be prepared for hurricane force winds after a change to the SW. Heading S through Paso Mar del Sur on the way to Cape Horn, there is a clear safe passage through the islands if you stay close to the SE corner of Isla Herschel.

10·20 Isla Hornos – Caleta León

55°57'·8S, 67°13'·6W (GPS)

Charts BA *1373*; US *22430*; Chile *13200, 13600, 13620, 13700*

The scale on *13200* and *13700* is the same and *13200* is easier to read.

General

The anchorage 1·5M NW of Punta Espolon is a fair-weather one only (20–25m and rock) however if the yacht wishes to heave-to in the lee of Isla Hornos a safe dinghy landing can be made at the *armada* boat landing in all but the heaviest of weather. The *armada* has cut a narrow path through the kelp, which obstructs the approach. Wooden steps leading up the steep beach to the lighthouse mark the landing.

A young *armada* family will welcome visitors to the 'trophy room' (a club burgee etc. may be added to the collection of flags there), the small chapel, and of course the sculpture of a Wandering Albatross across the moor on a boardwalk. A beautiful and evocative spot to speculate on Patagonian travels to come, or reflect on a recent journey through the Chilean *canales*. Passports, logbooks etc. can be stamped by the *armada* creating a unique souvenir.

It has now been accepted that Drake landed at Cape Horn in 1578, well before Schouten's visit in 1616.

There is evidence to show that the Elizabethan Government suppressed Drake's discovery for reasons which, in today's terms, might be described as national security.

10·21 Islas Diego Ramirez

56°29'S 68°45'W

Charts BA *1373*; US *29002*; Chile *13700, 13711*

General

There are two anchorages, both in the S group: Fondeadero Oreste (25m, sand) on the E side of Isla Bartolome and Fondeadero Aguila on the NE side of Isla Gonzalo. They are only tenable after a prolonged period of calm weather. There is a manned *armada* base on Gonzalo, which will give permission to land if requested. The islands, which are bird sanctuaries, were named after the Brothers Nodal who first surveyed Tierra del Fuego in 1618–1619. It was one of the finest of the Spanish expeditions, particularly so as all the crew returned home alive.

Argentina – SE part of Tierra del Fuego

Warnings

Yachts should not call at Ushuaia from Chile unless the *zarpe* authorises the visit and all passports have Chilean exit stamps; to do so would be to leave Chile without clearance.

The Falkland Islands are considered to be Argentinian territory by Argentina though not by Chile. Any passage to or from Argentina, which includes the Falkland Islands should take that into account. For instance, a yacht moving from Ushuaia

188

to Buenos Aires via the Falklands will be deemed not to have left Argentina; this is permitted, but the vessel will be considered to be within the Republic of Argentina for all official and immigration purposes. It is better to leave from Chile.

When leaving Argentina, official permission will not be given to anchor anywhere in Argentine waters although it may be agreed verbally that anchoring is permitted for safety reasons (this means that the Argentine anchorages mentioned below and Staten Island may not be visited en route to another country). A yacht coming from the Atlantic bound for the *canales* but wishing to stock up in Ushuaia should consider visiting Ushuaia first and then returning to Puerto William for a *zarpe*. In this case, enter along the Argentine shore of Canal Beagle and fly the Argentine courtesy flag. The Chilean *armada* may call to check your destination.

10·22 Bahía Lapataia

54°51'·6S 68°34'·7W

Charts BA *554, 1373*; US *22430*; Chile *13100, 13200*

General

This bay, lying 10M W of Ushuaia, almost on the border with Chile, is a very nice place to visit, especially in springtime. The choice of two anchorages ought to provide shelter in most conditions. Note that entry to the small *caleta* near the head of the bay requires passing close to the north of the small islands shown in order to avoid a dangerous rock.

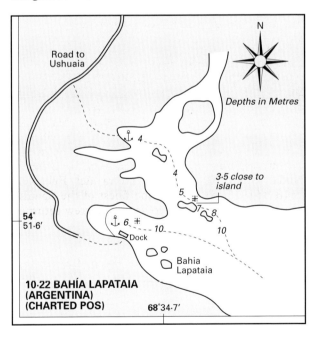

10·22 BAHÍA LAPATAIA
(ARGENTINA)
(CHARTED POS)

10·23 Ushuaia

54°49'S 68°19'W

Charts BA *554, 1373*; US *22430*; Chile *13100, 13200*

Port communications

Call on VHF Ch 16 c/s *L3P* (and enunciate LIMA TRES PAPA or they won't answer).

Lights

1323 **Paso Chico Ldg Lts 019·22°** *Front* 54°50'·4S 68°15'·7W Fl.6s10m7·5M White metal framework tower, red band 8m

1323·1 **Isla Casco** *Rear* 465m from front Fl.R.3s15·6m5·6M White metal framework tower black bands

General

Ushuaia, population 50,000, is much the best place to stock up before heading through the canals or going to Antarctica. The big charter yachts based here are good sources of information on Antarctica and the Cordillera Darwin area.

The Naval Museum located in the old jail is excellent and well worth the $5 entrance fee.

Approach

Coming from the W, the entrance to Bahía Ushuaia is through Paso Chico (1323 leading marks above). The bay is very shallow and the wind frequently blows very strongly from the W in the afternoon.

Formalities

Ushuaia is a port of entry. Call *Lima Tres Papa* on Ch 16 in advance and obtain instructions; immigration formalities may be carried out aboard. Customs should be cleared at the Customs Office on the main pier as soon as possible during working hours. There are charges for movements out of hours and at weekends. Details of these procedures change from time to time.

Anchorage

The bay is very shallow and the wind frequently blows very strongly from the W in the afternoon. The holding is not good. The most convenient anchorage is just off the Club Náutico (in 2001 this was no longer a yacht club, just a restaurant, though there were plans to reactivate it). Most boats raft to a grounded dry dock connected to the Club Náutico by a wooden walkway. It is best to tie on the E side due to the strong W winds. It is very shallow and keel boats can only tie at the extreme S end; shallower draught yachts can tie further along the wharf leading to the land. In summer this spot tends to be overcrowded.

An alternative anchorage is at AFACYN, the sailing and diving club, a $3 taxi run to the W and S of town. There is a jetty, with a water hose, charges in 2001 were $6 per day. There may be moorings available if resident yachts are away.

Facilities

Diesel and kerosene in cans by dinghy from a YPF gas station about half a mile E of the Club Náutico. Arrangements can be made to take fuel by hose and at a cheaper price from the YPF fuel dock 'Terminal Orion', located to the E of the main pier, after booking by ☎ 421 397 or VHF.

Water from hoses on the jetties.

There are several good supermarkets. The usual practice is for the supermarket to provide a complimentary taxi if the purchase is substantial.

Butcher on Belgrano and San Martin. Some yachts

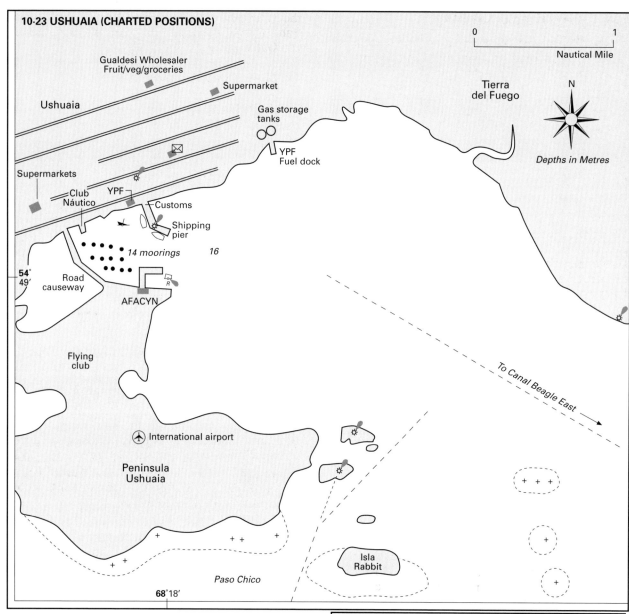

10·23 USHUAIA (CHARTED POSITIONS)

Gualdesi Wholesaler
Fruit/veg/groceries

Supermarket

Ushuaia

Gas storage
tanks

Tierra
del Fuego

N

Depths in Metres

0   1
Nautical Mile

YPF
Fuel dock

Supermarkets

Club
Náutico

YPF

Customs

Shipping
pier

14 moorings   16

54°
49′

Road
causeway

AFACYN

R

To Canal Beagle East

Flying
club

International airport

Peninsula
Ushuaia

Isla
Rabbit

Paso Chico

68°18′

purchase a whole or half sheep; they say it keeps, if hung in the rigging. Supermarkets sell high quality vacuum packed meat that will keep in a cool place for up to a month, longer with refrigeration.

Almost all food supplies, including vegetables and fruit can be obtained from a wholesaler in case or half-case lots (Gualdesi, 771 Gov. Campo or Allatuni, Godor Godoy 261 and Paz).

Self-service launderette Los Angeles on J M Rosas – expensive.

Club Náutico has a pricey bar and restaurant and AFACYN has showers.

Communications

There are many internet cafés.
Daily flights available to Buenos Aires.
Car hire.
Taxis.
Mail from Europe takes about a week.
Telephone: Area Code 901.

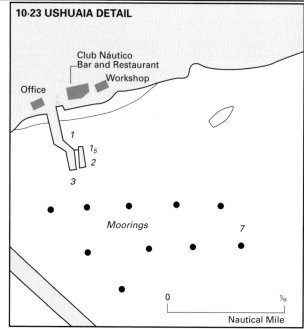

10·23 USHUAIA DETAIL

Club Náutico
Bar and Restaurant

Workshop

Office

1

1₅

2

3

Moorings   7

0   ¹⁄₁₆
Nautical Mile

Isla Gable/Harberton Area

To the NE of Puerto Williams there are a number of delightful anchorages and winding waterways on the N side of the Canal Beagle. These are mentioned because they are on the Canal Beagle but they can only be visited after entering Argentina and may not be visited after leaving Argentina *en route* to another country.

10·24 Bahía Almirante Brown

54°53'S 67°24'W

Charts BA *1373*; US *22430*; Chile *13300*

General

The entrance to Bahía Almirante Brown is Paso Remolcador Guaraní around the N side of Isla Gable, negotiable in daylight only, giving access to numerous sheltered anchorages amongst the low-lying rural islands. There are range markers to lead one through the narrow canal. The charts show a drying bar across the boat passage N of Isla Gable, but there is in fact at least 2·5m of water at LW all the way, and it is well marked with numerous transits. There is a nice anchorage about half way, just off the abandoned farmhouse. Fishing boats and gun boats from Ushuaia use this passage every day. The best chart for this area is the Argentinian strip chart for Canal Beagle *De Isla Becasses A Bahía Lapataia*.

10·25 Puerto Gable

54°53'·4S 67°25'·7W (GPS)

Charts BA *1373*; US *22430*; Chile *13300*

General

Of the various Argentine anchorages near Isla Gable, Puerto Gable is by far the best. The depth is 3m in heavy mud with no kelp, protected from all winds. There are a number of very nice walks ashore with easy dinghy landing on the beach.

Outside the canal there are well protected (ship size) mooring buoys in the bay on Isla Gable just to the W of Isla Martillo (54°54'·1S 67°25'·1W) and Bahía Relegada (54°52'·2S 67°20'·5W) to the east of Isla Gable.

10·26 Puerto Harberton

54°53'S 67°20'W

Charts BA *1373*; US *22430*; Chile *13300*

General

Puerto Harberton is choked with kelp, as is Bahía Cambaceres. On the N side of Cambaceres there are ruins of an old Yagan Indian house and wild foxes inhabit the area. Harberton is the site of the original settlement in this area by the Bridges family. It is now a large sheep *estancia* and a popular tourist attraction. Catamarans bring visitors each day from Ushuaia. The *estancia* welcomes visiting yachts and the guided tour is well worth the $6. It may be possible to use the pilot boat's mooring; check with the *estancia*. Holding for an anchor is good if a patch clear of kelp can be found. Two vessels with good gear reported dragging in a strong NW due to kelp on the anchor.

10·27 Bahía Aguirre

54°55'·7S 65°58'·3W

Charts BA *1373*; US *22430*; Chile *13400*

General

Travelling from W to E, Bahía Aguirre, on the S side of Península Mitre, is the last shelter available before entering the Estrecho de Le Maire. Punta Pique 54°56'S 65°57'·8W Fl.6s9m6·6M white conical tower 3m marks the bay.

Anchorage

The first anchorage is in the bay NW of Punta Pique and provides excellent protection from W winds but it is subject to swell particularly during strong SW winds. In the past there has been an *armada* buoy in this bay.

The second anchorage is further to the N in Puerto Español; holding is good in sand. There is a

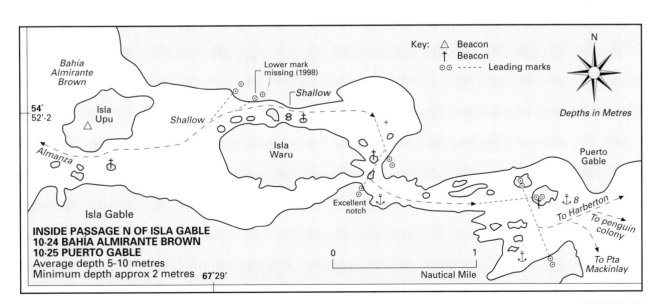

191

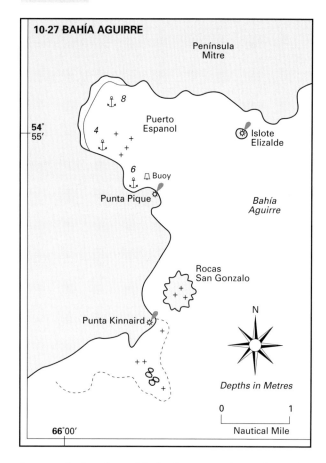

10·27 BAHÍA AGUIRRE

long reef of rocks and kelp that extends out from the W entrance to Puerto Español which cuts down on the swell. This anchorage would probably be better than behind Punta Pique in strong NW winds.

The first anchorage appears to be the most sheltered from SW winds which can be very fierce in Puerto Español. Neither bay provides shelter from the E or SE.

10·28 Bahía Buen Suceso

54°48'S 65°15'W
Charts BA *1373*; US *22430*; Chile *13400*

General

This wide-open bay on the E coast of Península Mitre, just S of the narrow part of the Estrecho de Le Maire, provides shelter from N through SW winds. It is a rolly anchorage but the holding is excellent at the head of the bay, in sand. The large *armada* buoy in the middle of the bay might be available. There is an Argentinian Naval Station at the head of the bay, and yachts transiting the straits should report their position on Ch 16.

Passage

Estrecho de Le Maire

54°40'S 65°00'W
Charts BA *1373*; US *22430*; Chile *13400*

General

The overfalls in Estrecho de Le Maire are notorious. A transit of the straits must be made with great respect for the risks involved, particularly going from S to N where a NW wind against a flood tide can create standing waves of 10–12m off Cabo San Diego. Yachts should keep to the centre of the straits where the current is usually about three knots. Care should be taken to stay at least 8M off Cabo San Diego and 4–5M off the W end of Isla de los Estados. The current floods N and slack tide in the straits is at low and high water at the tidal station in Bahía Buen Suceso.

Local charter boats and fishermen have another approach to transiting the straits which was used with ease and success by at least one yacht in 2001. Sail along the SE side of Tierra del Fuego, right next to the kelp in about 20m. Alongside the kelp, even in wind against tide situations, a path of smooth water will be found, although tide rips can be seen a couple of hundred metres to the S. One yacht used this route entering the straits eastbound against the full ebb, but inshore found the ebb current never exceeded 1kt. Counter currents of up to ¾ of a knot were common. The result was that the transit was easily made with the yacht arriving at Cabo San Diego at slack tide.

10·29 Isla de los Estados – Puerto Hoppner

54°46'·9S 64°24'·5W (All positions GPS)
Charts BA *1373*; US *22430*; Chile *13400*

General

Yachts approaching the area of Canal Beagle from the north often use this anchorage. It provides a suitable place to recover from a rough trip heading S and wait for favourable weather conditions in which to sail to the W.

Approach

Puerto Hoppner's outer bay (entrance 54°45'·2S 64°25'·8W) is too deep for anchoring, but there is a narrow gorge (least depth about 4m) at the back of this bay into a completely protected inner lagoon (Entrance 54°46'·4S 64°24'·8W). There is a visible rock exactly in the middle of this narrow channel that should be left to port. A five-knot current runs through the channel so it should be traversed at low or high tide (tides are approximately Bahía Crossley −0030hrs).

Anchorage

There are three good spots to tie up, but the best is at 54°46'·8S 64° 24'·3W between the small island and shore. It's possible to pass around the N end of the island with least depths of 3m but it is narrow

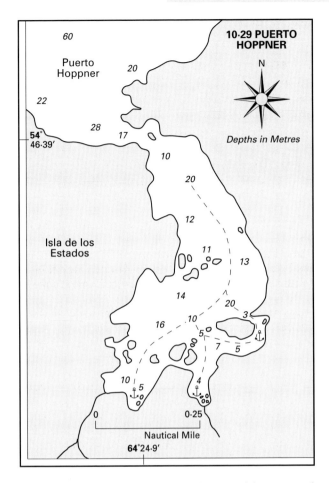

with little room to manoeuvre. Approaching around the S end there is more room with least depths of 5m, but care must be taken of the rocks that extend SW from the island.

To the E of Hoppner is Puerto Perry, which could be entered in all weather. The *armada* have laid a large (ship size) and surprisingly well-protected mooring buoy at 54°46'·8S 64°23'·7W.

11. Isla de Pascua and Islas Juan Fernandez

Isla de Pascua
(Rapa Nui, Easter Island)

27°09'S 109°27'W

Approximate Distances
Galápagos–1950–Isla de Pascua–1945-Valdivia
Pitcairn–1100–Isla de Pascua–1620–Juan Fernandez

Charts BA *1389*; Chile *2500, 2510, 2511, 2512, 2513*
Note that in the *Atlas Hidrográfico de Chile* these charts come at the end.

Tides
Standard Port – Pago Pago
Spring Range 0·5m
Neap Range 0·m

Port communications
VHF Ch 16 c/s *CBY*

General

Known as Easter Island in English and Rapa Nui by the Polynesians, the island is administered as part of the *región* of Valparaíso. It is largely dependent upon tourism and not much of the original culture remains – what does, is highly visible. The island's hundreds of huge and very famous stone statues, *moais*, are extraordinary, unexplained and well worth visiting.

The island is not a good stop-over for fuel and stores. Facilities are limited. The anchorages are open. Moreover landing can be difficult; it may be necessary to wait days for conditions to ease before it becomes possible. If landing is possible, always leave enough crew on board to handle the boat when the wind shifts, as it can do suddenly and dramatically. The *armada* requires that one person remain on board at all times.

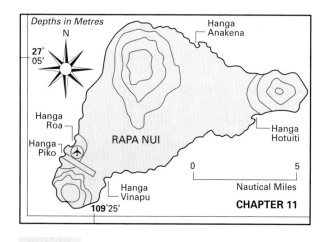

Approach

Contact the *armada* on Ch 16 for advice and negotiate for clearance. Although there is no clearance charge as such, if officials use a boat to come out there may be a charge by the local boatman (about US$20).

Facilities on Isla Pascua

Fuel Sunoco (Juan Edmunds), Airport Road.
Water Hose at Hanga Piko.
Bank and Change Banco del Estado at Tuumaheke accepts Visa cards only (2001). Sunoco fuel station accepts American Express and possibly other cards. US dollars widely accepted.
Fruit and vegetables market (pick-up truck sales) early in the morning at Atamu Tekena crossing Tuumaheke.
Car hire Most of the hotels have cars for rent but a better deal can be made with one of the many souvenir shops. Many of these shops have one or two 4WD's for rent. (Use a 4WD if possible; rain quickly turns tracks to mud),
Motorcycle hire Juan Edmunds, Sunoco; Hertz at airport.
Provisions reasonable shops. LanChile fly in supplies twice a week.
Laundry available on request.
General facilities Ask Juan Edmunds who can arrange everything from finding a pilot to hiring a horse.

Communications

Air: LanChile twice a week en route between Santiago and Tahiti & vice versa, more frequently in summer when it is heavily booked.
Telephone: Area Code 39. Entel office for phone and fax.
Coast Radio accepts public correspondence on Ch 16, 09, 10, 14, & 26 24hrs.
Internet café in the main shopping street Atamu Tekena.

Tourism

Apart from paying respects to *moais*, there is a delightful beach at Anakena as well as Thor Heyerdahl's restored *moai*; anchor off or drive there.

Anchorages

11·1 Hanga Roa

500m NE of Punta Roa, 27°08'·6S 109°26'·6W approx
Chart Chile *2512*

General

This is the chief anchorage for visitors. Approach the main anchorage, on the direction line 1993 Hanga Roa (Fl.8s12m13M Dir 134°-154° White steel tower with horizontal red stripes). Anchor in 12m, sand and rock, variable holding; inshore are rocks and foul ground.

11·2 Hanga Piko

Half a mile away to the S of Punta Roa 27°08'·6S 109°26'·6W approx
Chart Chile *2512*

General

Now open to yachts up to about 15m LOA and 2m draught. Permission should be sought from the *armada* who will require the vessel to use a local pilot when you enter and leave this small harbour.

The *armada* can arrange a local fisherman to do the pilotage, very expensive (US$100 in 2001) however prices are negotiable and it is possible to make more economical arrangements directly with a fisherman.

Have long lines and two stern anchors ready before entering the harbour, as there is hardly room to manoeuvre.

In unsettled weather Hanga Piko is not a safe place: the surge inside can be tremendous and with a bit more than a breeze it is impossible to leave because the sea breaks right over the entrance.

Remove loose items, especially lines from the deck when leaving the boat unattended in Hanga Piko.

11·3 Hanga Anakena

27°04'·8S 109°19'·5W
Chart Chile *2511*

General

This is a beautiful anchorage on the N coast, subject to suitable winds. Be careful not to go too far into the bay since there is a safety line for swimmers tied across. Don't pass the stone jetty on the E side.

11·4 Hanga Vinapu

27°10'·8S 109°24'W
Chart Chile *2513*

General

On the S coast Hanga Vinapu provides shelter from the SW as well as W winds though it is subject to swell. Landing, via an oil structure, is difficult and there is nowhere to leave a dinghy. This may be no bad thing, as someone will have to stay aboard as taxi-driver as well as ship-minder.

11·5 Hanga Hotuiti

27°07'·5S 109°16'·5W
Chart Chile *2513*

General

On the S coast, E end, Hanga Hotuiti is dramatic but not such a good anchorage as the others.

11·6 Islas Juan Fernandez

33°38'S 78°51'W
Approximate Distances
Pascua–1620–Fernandez-368–Viña del Mar
Arica–900–Fernandez–454–Valdivia
Charts BA *1389*; US *22492*; Chile *5410, 5411, 5412, 5413*
Tides
Standard Port – Valparaíso
   Spring Range 0·9m
b. Neap Range 0·9
c. HW +0015hrs LW +0026hrs
Port communications
Ch 16 c/s *CBF*

General

The two inhabited islands are Alejandro Selkirk and, 84M to the E, Isla Robinson Crusoe (ex *San Juan Bautista*). The two are also called Isla Más Afuera ('further away') and Más a Tierra ('closer to land') for obvious reasons. Both are National Parks. Alejandro Selkirk is wooded, steep-to and rises to 1645m. About 20 fishing families live on it during the season (September to April) and are visited by boat about once a month for their catch of *langosta* (crayfish, which are not found on the continental coast of Chile). Be prepared to carry mail to Robinson Crusoe, if going there.

Robinson Crusoe has a population of about 600, living mainly in the village of Juan Bautista and occupied with fishing, tourism and some local government. A mainland boat calls every three weeks or so bringing a few visitors. Few yachts call though there is an annual race to the island organised by the Club Náutico Oceánico de Chile. The climate is warm and humid and the island, like the Galápagos, has several unique species of flora and fauna.

The office of the Chilean Forestry Organisation, CONAF, is worth visiting.

Approach

Straightforward in both cases.

Anchorage

Alejandro Selkirk A visitor will be offered a mooring opposite the former penal colony, midway down the E side.

Robinson Crusoe Anchor in Bahía Cumberland, a beautiful wide bay but subject to strong gusts off the mountains. In strong southerlies yachts have dragged out to sea and conditions are rolly.

Formalities

Contact the *armada* on Ch 16.

Facilities

On Alejandro Selkirk there is spring water, otherwise nothing except the possibility of trading cigarettes or liquor for *langostas*.

On Robinson Crusoe supplies are very restricted in the few shops. Fish is available and red snapper may be caught on a line over the side. Water is available.

Communications

Robinson Crusoe: an airstrip for light aircraft.
There is a post office with telephone.

Appendix

APPENDIX A
Direction Finding stations
Note Ranges for aero beacons are indicated in terms of the power of the transmitter and for marine beacons in nautical miles. (Details are corrected from *Chilean List of Radiosignals* to Nov. 2001. Numbering shown is that of *ALRS*, where known.)

3776 Arica, Chacalluta Airport 18°21'S 70°21'W c/s *ARI* 340kHz 1·0kW 24hr

3778 Iquique, Chucumata Airport 20°34'S 70°11'W c/s *UCU* 368kHz 0·4kW 24hr

3780 Mejillones, Aero 23°07'S 70°27'W c/s *MJL* 240kHz 1·0kW 24hr

3782 Caldera 27°04'S 70°50'W c/s *CLD* 227kHz 1·0kW 24hr

3784 Punta Tortuga 29°56'S 71°21'W c/s *TUGA* 322·5kHz 160M When required (call *Coquimbo Radio* on Ch 16 or 2182kHz)

3786 Tongoy 30°16'S 71°29'W c/s *TOY* 260kHz 3·0kW 24hr

3788 Quintero 32°44'S 71°29'W c/s *ERO* 384kHz 1kW 24hr

3790 Punta Angeles 33°01'S 71°39'W c/s *VASO* 300kHz 110M When required (call *Valparaíso Radio* on Ch 16 or 2182kHz)

3792 Santo Domingo 33°38'S 71°36'W c/s *SNO* 355kHz 1kW 24hr

3794 Constitución 35°18'S 72°23'W c/s *CTN* 340kHz 1kW 24hr

3798 Concepción 36°51'S 73°07'W c/s *CE* 254kHz 1kW 24hr

Valdivia, Pichoy 39°43'S 73°05'W c/s *VLD* 208kHz 1kW 24hr

3802 Punta Corona, Isla Chiloé 41°47'S 73°53'W c/s *CONA* 290kHz 110M When required (call *Faro Corona* or *Puerto Montt Radio* on Ch 16 or 2182kHz)
Puerto Montt, El Tepual 41°26'S 73°05'W c/s *TEP* 400kHz 1kW 24hr
Castro 42°28'S 73°46'W c/s *STR* 285kHz 1kW 24hr

3804 Chaitén 42°55'S 72°43'W c/s *TEN* 234kHz 0·4kW 24hr
Puerto Aguirre 45°09'S 73°32'W c/s *PAR* 350kHz 1kW 24hr

3806 Isla San Pedro 47°43'S 74°55'W c/s *ISP* 295kHz 1·0kW 24hr

3808 Isla Guarello 50°22'S 75°20'W c/s *IGU* 315kHz 0·5kW 24hr

3810 Punta Arenas 53°06'S 70°54'W c/s *NAS* 270kHz 3·0kW 24hr

3812 Punta Dungeness 52°24'S 68°26'W c/s *GENE* 322·5kHz 110M When required (call Punta *Dungeness* or *Magallanes Radio* on Ch 16 or 2182kHz)
Faro Cabo Vírgenes 52°20'S 68°22'W c/s *CV* 300kHz 0·2kW 24hr
Puerto Williams 54°55'S 67°34'W c/s *PWL* 288kHz 24hr

APPENDIX B
Short wave broadcasting
Good reception can be obtained for broadcasts by the BBC, VOA, Dutch, French and German services. Up-to-date information can be obtained at the relevant station's website. In practice, especially in the S, transmissions intended for other areas may be received better than those intended for S America. Listening varies with propagation conditions, which also change with the time of year. In general, listening is good early in the morning and in the evening with strong signals intended for African listeners being heard in the afternoons. The following are frequencies (in kHz) that have been used for reception of BBC World service:

5970, 6110, 6195, 7325, 9560, 9825, 9915, 11750, 11765, 12095, 15190,15175, 15220, 15390, 15400, 15565, 17790, 17830, 17840, 17790.

APPENDIX C
Bibliography (Compiled by Pedro Vergara)
It is difficult for a bibliographer to find a happy compromise between listing every book ever published on a subject and being so superficial as not to provide some fascinating gems. The majority of the books mentioned are out of print today but copies can usually be found through book search companies. To limit the bibliography to English titles would be very restrictive so some classic reference books in Spanish have been included. The books often have their own bibliographies and are excellent sources for further research.

Historical and Exploration
The Exploration of the Pacific J C Beaglehole (Black) 3rd ed. 1966. This is a classic, first published in 1934. The book covers, very comprehensively, the early exploration of the route from the Atlantic to the Pacific by Magellan and others.

The Circumnavigators Derek Wilson (M Evans & Co, New York and Constable & Co. Ltd, UK 1989).

The Wager Mutiny S W C Pack (Alvin Redman, London 1964).

Byron of the Wager Peter Shankland (Collins 1975). These books cover the shipwreck of the *Wager* just S of the Golfo de Penas in 1740. The *Wager* was part of Anson's fleet sent to attack Valdivia. The books describe the mutiny and how the majority of the crew sailed by open boat back via the canals to Brazil.

In Darwin's Wake John Campbell (Waterline). ISBN 1 85310 755 7.

The Voyage of Charles Darwin. A book linked to the BBC film about the voyage of a replica of the *Beagle*. Christopher Ralling has selected Darwin's autobiographical writings to form the text of the book.

Three Men of the Beagle R Lee Marks (Alfred A. Knopf, New York 1991). The tale of Fitzroy, Darwin and Jeremy Button.

Cruise of the Alert – in Patagonian and Polynesian Waters
Dr R W Coppinger (Swan Sonnenschein & Co,
London 1885). The book describes the cruise of the
British ship, the *Alert*, between 1878 and 1882, on a
comprehensive survey trip that included key
anchorages in Patagonian waters.

Cap Horn 1882-1883. Rencontre avec les Indiens Yahgan
A Chapman, C Barthe, P Revol and J Dubois
(Editions de la Martinière, Paris, 1995).

*The Wilds of Patagonia – A narrative of the Swedish
Expedition to Patagonia* Carl Skottesberg (Edward
Arnold, London, 1911).

Mis Viajes a la Tierra del Fuego published in Milan, 1946;

*Andes Patagonicos Viajes de Exploracion a la Cordillera
Patagonica Austral* published in Buenos Aires, 1945;

Trenta Amos en Tierra del Fuego published in Buenos
Aires in 1956.

These three books were written and published by
Alberto M de Agostini. They relate the extraordinary
explorations by yacht of this priest who was the first to
describe many of the mountains of Patagonia.

Sailing Sward from the Straight of Magellan Rockwell Kent
(G P Putnam's Sons, 1924). A classic sailing
adventure in the canals, without engine. A book that
contains many wonderful woodcuts.

The Eight Sailing Mountain Exploration Books – including
Mischief in Patagonia H W Tilman (Diadem Books,
London, 1987).

Anuario Hidrográfico de la Marina de Chile. A series
published in 14 volumes by the Servicio Hidrográfico
y Oceanográfico de Chile. The series covers very
comprehensively the exploration and charting of the
Canals and has extracts from many authors. It is
probably the most comprehensive source of historical
information on the canals.

Land of Tempests Eric Shipton (The Travel Book Club,
1963). The travels and climbs of Eric Shipton over
the period 1958–62.

The Springs of Enchantment John Earle (Hodder and
Stoughton, London, 1981). An account of two trips
to Patagonia, the first with Eric Shipton.

Two against the Horn Hal Roth (Stanford Maritime,
London, 1979).

The Totorore Voyage – an Antarctic Adventure Gerry Clark
(Century Hutchinson, New Zealand, 1988).

By way of Cape Horn and *The War with Cape Horn* A J
Villiers (Henry Holt and Co, New York, 1930 and
Hodder and Stoughton, 1971 respectively).

Cape Horn: The Logical Route (William Morrow and Co,
New York, 1973) and *Cap Horn à la Voile* (Arthaud,
Paris, 1995). Two books by Bernard Moitessier.

The Great Days of Cape Horners Yves Le Scal (Souvenir
Press, UK, 1966).

Because the Horn is There and *Once is enough* Miles
Smeeton (Grafton Books, London, 1987 and 1991
respectively).

Sailing Cape Horn – A Maritime History Robin Knox-
Johnston (Hodder and Stoughton, 1971).

Then we sailed away – A family adventure by John, Marie,
Christine and Rebecca Ridgeway. ISBN 1-85130-
775-7.

Patagonia Paul van Gaalen (El Mercurio (Santiago),
1997). Good photographs, interesting text. ISBN
9567 4020 51.

Diccionario de la Toponimia Austral de Chile Carlos
Alberto Mantellero Ognio. Published by the Author,
Valparaíso. Etymology of names along the Chilean
waterways. In easy Spanish, a fascinating companion
for a voyage in this region. Two volumes: ISBN 9562

3501 17 (1984), 9562 3501 33 (1991).

Savage The Life and Times of Jeremy Button Nick
Hazelwood. (Hodder & Stoughton). ISBN 0340 7391
18.

Chile – General Travel

Full Circle – A S American Journey Luis Sepulveda. ISBN
0 86442 465 5 (Lonely Planet Journeys).

Travels in a Thin Country Sara Wheeler. ISBN 0 349
10584 7 (Abacus Travel).

In Patagonia. Bruce Chatwin (Vintage reprint 1998).
Classic, idiosyncratic, a good read but not entirely
reliable. ISBN 0099 7695 14.

Chile and Easter Island. A Lonely Planet Travel Survival
Kit. ISBN 0-86442-181-8.

Chile and Easter Island. Lonely Planet Atlas. ISBN 0
86442 517 1.

Travel Companion: Chile and Easter Island Gerry Leitner.
ISBN 0 646 06042 2 (Companion Travel Guide
Books, Australia).

S American Handbook Ben Box. ISBN 0 900751 74 6.
(Footprint Handbooks, UK).

The general travel books listed above can be obtained
through bookshops in the UK such as Stanford's
International Map Centre, 12-14 Long Acre, London
WC2E 9LP ☎ 020 7836 1321 *Fax* 020 7836 7960.

Chile – A Remote Corner on Earth (Turismo
Comunicaciones SA). This book is the English
version of a guide normally printed in Spanish is
probably the best guide to the country.

Turistel: Guia Turistica de Chile (Compania de
Telecomunicaciones de Chile SA, Santiago). The
nearest thing to a combined Green and Red Michelin
of Chile. In Spanish.

Both the above books are available in bookshops or
magazine stalls in Chile.

Chile – Natural History

The Flight of the Condor Michael Andrew (William
Collins & Sons Ltd, 1983). The story of an excellent
BBC natural history series.

*Flora Silvestre de Chile – zona Central. Flora Silvestre de
Chile – zona Araucana. Flora Silvestre de Chile – zona
Austral* Adriana Hoffman J (Fundacion Claudio Gay,
1979,1984 and 1982 respectively).

Flora of Tierra del Fuego David Moore (Anthony Nelson,
London, 1983).

Guia de Campo de Las Aves de Chile Braulio Araya M and
Guillermo Millie H (Editorial Universitaria, Chile,
1996).

APPENDIX D
Chart lists
The charts mentioned in this volume are listed below.
All three Hydrographic Offices produce charts, which are
not mentioned in the text.

Chilean charts have the most detailed information but
BA charts are sometimes easier to handle, especially
when trying to locate places.

UK Hydrographic Office
Note All the charts at 1:500,000 have plans of selected
ports.

554	Estrecho de Magallanes	550,000
631	Estrecho Magallanes Paso del Mar and Canal Smythe – S part	100,000
887	Paso Inglés, Tortuoso, Largo and del Mar	100,000
1281	Segunda Angostura to Paso del Mar	300,000
1282	Estrecho de Magallanes to Canal Concepción	300,000

1282	Estrecho de Magallanes to Canal Concepción	300,000
1286	Canal Concepción to Canal del Castillo	300,000
1287	Canal del Castillo to Estero San Esteban	300,000
1288	Seno Cornish to Boca del Guafo	300,000
1289	Islas Guaitecas to Bahía San Pedro	440,000
1313	Channels between Maullin and Montt	152,300
1332	Isla de Los Estados to Estrecho de le Maire	
1373	S-E part of Tierra del Fuego	550,000
	Cabo Virgines to Primera Angostura	
	Primera Angostura to Segunda Angostura	
1694	Segunda Angostura to Punta Arenas	100,000
3070	Bahía Algodonales to Rada de Arica	500,000
3071	Puerto Pan de Azúcar to Bahía Algodonales	500,000
3072	Caleta Totoralillo to Puerto Pan de Azúcar	500,000
3073	Bahía Valparaíso to Caleta Totoralillo	500,000
3074	Golfo Arauco to Bahía Valparaíso	500,000
3075	Bahía San Pedro to Golfo Arauco	500,000
3076	Ports on the coast of Chile	Various
3077	Ports on the coast of Chile	Various
3078	Ports on the coast of Chile	Various
3079	Plans on the coast of Chile	Various
3080	Plans on the coast of Chile	Various
3081	Plans on the coast of Chile	Various
3749	Golfos Corvocado and Ancud	152,300

**Defense Mapping Agency,
US Department of Commerce**

Note although not all are mentioned in the text, this agency produces Charts of the whole coast at 1:500,000.

22205	Arica to Mejillones	500,000
22221	Plans on the coast of Chile	Various
22225	Mejillones to Puerto de Caldera	500,000
22250	Puerto de Caldera to Coquimbo	500,000
22259	Bahía de Valparaíso and Puerto Valparaíso	10,000
22261	Plans on the coast of Chile	Various
22262	Puerto Huasco	12,000
22263	Bahía Quintero	15,000
22264	Approaches to Bahías Quintero and Valparaíso	50,000
22275	Bahía de Coquimbo to Bahía de Valparaíso 500,000	
22281	Punta Porotos to Punta Lengua de Vaca	100,000
22282	Bahías de Coquimbo and Guayacán	36,500
22290	Bahía de Valparaíso to Golfo de Arauco	500,000
22295	Plans on the coast of Chile	Various
22305	Port Talcahuano to Bahía Corral	500,000
22312	Golfo de Arauco	80,000
22335	Bahía Corral to Isla Guafo	500,000
22341	Golfo de Ancud – N Part	140,000
22342	Canal de Chacao	60,000
22345	Puerto Montt	20,000
22352	Golfo Corcovado and S Golfo de Ancud	150,000
22360	Boca del Guafo to Canal Moraleda	200,000
22370	Isla Guafo to Golfo de Penas	500,000
22371	Bahía Darwin to Seno Aisén	200,000
22404	Isla Richards to Islotes Fairway	30,000
22405	Isla Cutter to Isla Richards	30,000

22410	Cabo Deseado to Isla Noir inc. W of the Estrecho de Magallanes	276,600
22412	Islote Fairway to Cabo Cooper Key	100,000
22415	Paso Largo, Canal Jerónimo and Paso Tortuoso Various	
22418	Bahía Desolada to Punta Yamana	200,000
22420	Canal Trinidad to Estrecho Magallanes	500,000
22425	Canal Magdalena, Canal Cockburn and Adjacent Channels 165,000	
22430	Canal Beagle to Cabo de Hornos	200,000
22471	Primera Angostura to Punta Dungeness	100,000
22481	Bahía Gente Grade to Primera Angostura	100,000
22482	Rada Punta Arenas	20,000
22492	Islands off the coast of Chile Robinson Crusoe Islands 40,000	
29002	Antarctic Península	1,500,000

Servicio Hidrográfico y Oceanográfico de la Armada de Chile (SHOA) Casilla 324 Valparaíso Chile

The Chilean *Armada* produce about 280 coastal charts plus various instructional charts. Please refer to the SHOA catalogue or Atlas Hidrográfico. It is strongly recommended that the catalogue be on board in addition to the atlas. Chilean charts have recently been renumbered so beware of confusion. The complete catalogue which includes notes on renumbering, electronic charts and corrections for varying datums in use with Satellite Navigation is available free on the internet at: www.shoa.cl. It would be wise to have a copy on board.

Appendix H gives conversions between numbers in the 2001 edition of the atlas and the numbering from the 2003 edition used in this book.

APPENDIX E
Glossary

The following limited glossary relates to the weather, the abbreviations to be found on charts and some words likely to be useful entering port. For a list containing many words commonly used in connection with sailing, see *Webb & Manton, Yachtsman's Ten Language Dictionary* (Adlard Coles Nautical).

General

aduana, customs
armada, navy
bahía, bay
caleta, inlet, bay
canal, strait, canal, channel
estero, sound
morro, headland
puerto, port, bay
seno, sound
surgidero, anchorage, roadstead

Weather

On the radio, if there is a storm warning, the forecast starts *aviso temporal*. If there is no storm warning, the forecast starts *no hay temporal*. Many words are similar to the English and their meanings may be guessed. The following may be less familiar:

viento, wind
calma, calm
ventolina, light air
flojito, light breeze
flojo, gentle breeze
bonancible, moderate breeze

fresquito, fresh breeze
fresco, strong breeze
frescachón, near gale
duro, gale
muy duro, strong gale
temporal, storm
borrasca, violent storm
huracán, hurricane
tempestad, *borrasca*, thunderstorm
chubasco, squall
racha, squall
ráfaga, squall
remolino, whirlwind

Note We have not found a qualitative difference between *chubasco*, *ráfaga* and *racha*. *Chubasco* is a Chilean word; *El Diccionario Enciclopédico 'La Fuente'* defines *racha* as *ráfaga*. All three are commonly translated into English as *williwaw*, a word which used to be heard only in connection with the Magallanes.

visibilidad, visibility
buena, good
regular, moderate
mala, poor
calima, haze
fosca, haze
neblina, mist
niebla, fog
precipitación, precipitation
aguacero, shower
llovizna, drizzle
lluvia, rain
aguanieve, sleet
nieve, snow
granizada, hail
el cielo, the sky
nube, cloud
nubes altas/bajas, high/low clouds
nuboso, cloudy
cubierto, covered, overcast
claro, *despejado*, clear

Names of cloud types in Spanish are based on the same Latin words as the names used in English.

sistemas del tiempo, Weather systems
anticiclón, anticyclone
depresión, depression
vaguada, trough
cresta, ridge
cuna, wedge
frente, front
frio, cold
cálido, warm
ocluido, occluded
bajando, falling
subiendo, rising

Lights and charts – major terms and abbreviations

Abbr	Spanish	English
A	*amarilla*	yellow
Alt	*alternativa*	alternative
Ag Nv	*aguas navegables*	navigable waters
Ang	*angulo*	angle
Ant	*anterior*	anterior, earlier, forward
Apag	*apagado*	extinguished
Arrc	*arrecife*	reef
At	*atenuada*	attenuated
B	*blanca*	white
Ba	*bahía*	bay
	bajamar escorada	chart datum
Bal. E	*baliza elástica*	'elastic' (plastic) buoy
Bco	*banco*	bank
Bo	*bajo*	shoal, under, below, low
Boc	*bocina*	horn, trumpet
Br	*babor*	port (left, not harbour)
C	*campana*	bell
Card	*cardinal*	cardinal
Cañ	*cañon*	canyon
cil	*cilíndrico*	cylindrical
C	*cabo*	cape
Cha	*chimenea*	chimney
Cno	*castillo*	castle
cón	*cónico*	conical
Ct	*centellante*	quick flashing (50-80/min)
Ctl	*centellante interrumpida*	interrupted quick flashing
cuad	*cuadrangular*	quadrangular
D	*destello*	flash
Desap	*desaparecida*	disappeared
Dest	*destruida*	destroyed
dique		jetty, quay
Dir	*direccional*	directional
DL	*destello largo*	long flash
E	*este*	East
edif	*edificio*	building
Er	*estribor*	starboard
Est	*esférico*	spherical
Esp	*especial*	special
Est sñ	*estación de señales*	signal station
ext	*exterior*	exterior
Extr	*extremo*	end, head of pier etc
F	*fija*	fixed
Fca	*fabrica*	factory
FD	*fija y destello*	fixed and flashing
FGpD	*fija y grupo de destellos*	fixed and group flashing
Flot	*flotdora*	float
Fondn	*fondeadero*	anchorage
GpCt	*grupo de centellos*	group quick flashing
GpD	*grupo de destellos*	group flashing
GpOc	*grupo de ocultaciones*	group occulting
GpRp	*grupo de centellos rápidos*	group very quick flashing
hel	*helicoidales*	helicoidal
hor	*horizontal*	horizontal
Hund	*hundida*	submerged
I	*interrumpida*	interrupted
Igla	*iglesia*	church
Inf	*inferior*	lower
Intens	*intensificado*	intensified
Irreg	*irregular*	irregular
Iso	*isofase*	isophase
L	*luz*	light
La	*lateral*	lateral
	levante	East
M	*millas*	Nautical miles
Mte	*monte*	mountain
Mto	*monumento*	monument
N	*norte*	North
Naut	*nautófono*	foghorn
NE	*nordeste*	NE
No	*número*	number
NW	*noroeste*	NW
Obst	*obstruction*	obstruction
ocas	*ocasional*	occasional
oct	*octagonal*	octagonal
Pe A	*peligro aislado*	isolated danger
	poniente	West
Post	*posterior*	posterior, later
Ppal	*principal*	principal
	prohibido	prohibited
Obston	*obstrucción*	obstruction
Prov	*provisional*	provisional
prom	*prominente*	prominent, conspicuous
Pta	*punta*	point
Pto	*puerto*	port
PTO	*puerto*	port

Note 'puerto' covers any landing place from a beach to container port.

| R | *roja* | red |
| Ra | *estación radar* | radar station |

Ra+	radar + suffix	radar+suffix (Ra Ref etc)
RC	radiofaro	circular (all-round) radiobeacon
RD	radiofaro dirigido	directional radiobeacon
rect	rectangular	rectangular
Ra	rocas	rocks
Rp	centeneallante rápida	very quick flashing (80-160/min)
Rpl	cent. rápida interrumpida	interrupted very quick flashing
RW	radiofaro giratorio	rotating radiobeacon
S	segundos	seconds
S	sur	South
SE	sudeste	SE
sil	silencio	silence
Silb	silbato or silbido	whistle
Sincro	sincronizda con	synchronised with
Sir	sirena	siren
son	sonido	sound, noise, report
Sto/a	Santo, Santa	Saint
SW	sudoetse	SW
T	temporal	temporarily
Te	torre	tower
trans	transversal	transverse
triang	triangular	triangular
troncoc	troncocónico	truncated cone
troncop	troncopiramidal	truncated pyramid
TSH	antena de radio	radio mast
TV	antena de TV	TV mast
U	centellante ultra- rápida	ultra quick flashing (+160/min)
UI	cent. ultra-rápida interrumpido	interrupted ultra quick flashing
	Ventisquero	Glacier
V	verde	green
	vivero	shellfish raft or bed
	visible	visible
W	oeste	West

Ports and Harbours

a popa	stern-to
a proa	bows-to
abrigo	shelter
al costado	alongside
amarrar	to moor
amarradero	mooring
ancho	breadth (see manga)
cabo	warp, line (cape)
calado	draught
compuerta	lock, basin
dársena	harbour
dique	dock, jetty
esclusa	lock
escollera	jetty
eslora total	length overall
espigon	spur, spike
fondear	to anchor
fondeadero	anchorage
knudos	knots
fondo	depth (bottom, base)
longitud	length (see eslora)
lonja	fish market (wholesale)
manga	beam
muelle	mole
nudo	knot
noray	bollard, mooring
pantalán	jetty
parar	to stop
pila	pile
práctico	pilot
profundidad	depth
rompeolas	breakwater
varadero	slipway
vertedero (verto)	spoil ground

Direction

babor	port
estribor	starboard
norte	N
este	E
sur	S
oeste	W

Administration

aduana	customs
astillero	shipyard
capitán de puerto	harbourmaster (an armada officer)
carabineros	police
combustible	fuel, in the general sense
derechos	dues, rights
dueño	owner
fabrica	factory
ferrocarril	railway
gasoleo	diesel
gasolina or bençina	petrol (UK) gasoline (US),
Investigaciones	CID and international Police
kerosina	paraffin
manguera	hose-pipe or flexible tubing
parafina	paraffin
patrón	skipper (not owner)
prorroga	extension to a document, customs permit, for instance
petróleo	diesel
señalizacion	
maritima annual	light dues
título	certificate

APPENDIX F
Names of contributors

The editor and RCC Pilotage Foundation are very grateful for all the assistance they have received. This guide represents an enormous amount of work on the part of many people over a number of years. More contributions are being received all the time. Every effort has been made to include all contributors known to the editor; please excuse and correct any omissions.

Arthur and Germaine Beiser
Beatrice Roters and Heinz-Juergen Scheld – *Spirit of Assy*
Bill Tilman
Bjorn Bratlie and Marit Aasdal Svendsen – *Kuven*
Burkhard and Sabine Strauch – *Penelope*
Chris West and his father, Mr West snr.
Corine and Gerard Saint-Jalmes – *Millennium Falcon*
Corri and Willem Stein – *Terra Nova*.
David Lewis
Eric B. Forsyth – *Fiona*
Evans Starzinger and Beth Leonard – *Hawk*
Francis Hawkings – *Plainsong*
Greg Landrein and Keri Pahuk – *Nanger*
Greger and Eva Dahlberg – *Noomi*
Hal Roth
Hans-Petter Lien – *Felice*
Harry Ross-Skinner
Hugh Clay
Ian and Maggy Staples – *Teokita*
Jay Davison and Austin Brookes – *Stokes*
Jean Francois and Michele Delouye – *Echapppeebelle*
Jeremy Burnett
Jim Gallup and Lena Anastacio-Gallup – *Mist*
John and Fay Garey
Juan Carlos Schidlowski
Keith and Liz Post – *Najat*
Ken Murray – *Pelagic*
Knick and Lynn Pyle
Laurence Ormerod
Marie Christine Duputel and Guy Aubonnet – *Flanneur*

Mariolina and Giorgio Ardrizzi
Members of the Valdivia Yacht Club, especially:
Miles Horden – *Gordian*
Oscar Prochelle – *Clipper*
Rémi, Hélène and Felix Barnaud – *Caouane*
Roger Wallis – *Parmelia and Toluka*
Skip Novak and Hamish Laird – *Pelagic*
Tim and Sophie Trafford – *Ardevora*
Tina and Gustaf – *Caminante*
Tony and Coryn Gooch – *Taonui*
Willy Ker
Yves and Florance Monier – *Morgane*
Yves Beauvillen and Marie Gauvrit – *Toupa*

APPENDIX G
Lights on the northern coastline
Navigation at night off this shore should only be conducted with an up-to-date light list. In case of emergency for passage making vessels forced inshore a selection of lights that may be of use to a vessel making a passage (correct to the Chilean Light List of December 2001) is included.

1987 La Concordia 18°20'·8S 70°21'·5W
Fl.G.5s41m14M White tower, red bands 21m Ra refl
1978 Punta Pichalo 19°35'·9S 70°14'·2W
Fl.12s55m13M White GRP tower, red band 4m 309°-vis-221°
1964 Punta Gruesa 20°21'·7S 70°10'·8W Fl.10s27m 14M White truncated conical tower with blue base 10m 004°-vis-205° 4 masts F.R
1963 Punta Patillos 20°45'·2S 70°11'·9W
Fl.5s41m13M White round GRP tower red band 4m. 073°-vis-186°, 348°-vis-063°
1956 Punta Algodonales (Islote Blanco) 22°05'·5S 70°13'·0W Fl.12s23m16M White round GRP tower, red band 8m 048°-vis-041°
1952 Punta Angamos 23°01'·4S 70°30'·9W
Fl.10s108m14M White GRP tower, red band 8m 036°-vis-267°
1948 Punta Tetas 23°31'·0S 70°37'·2W Fl.18s33m15M White GRP tower, red band 8m 287°-vis-166°
1938 Punta Ballenita 25°46'·6S 70°43'·5W
Fl.10s48m9M White GRP tower, red band 4m 003°-vis-241° Obscured 009°-010°
1936 Punta Achurra 26°17'·9S 70°40'·5W
Fl.15s32m15M White GRP tower, red band 8m 330°-vis-150°
1924 Punta Caldera 27°03'·0S 70°51'·1W
Fl.12s38m15M White truncated wooden tower, red bands 18m 020°-vis-278°
1922 Puerto Viejo (Bahía Copiápo) 27°20'·5S 70°57'W Fl.10s15m5M White GRP Tower, red band 3m 045°-vis-270°
1918 Península Guacolda 28°27'·6S 71°15'·3W
Fl.15s39m20M White GRP tower, red band 8m 090°-vis-320°
1916 Isla Chañaral 29°01'·8S 71°35'·0W
Fl.12s58m13M White round tower, GRP top, red bands 10m 010°-vis-214°
1904 Islotes Pájaros 29°35'·0S 71°31'·5W
Fl(2)10s39m11M Black tower, red band 162°-vis-158°
1900 Punta Tortuga 29°56'·0S 71°21'·4W
Fl.13s23m27M White round metal tower, red band 4m 042°-vis-255°
1896 Punta Laguna de Vaca 30°14'·8S 71°37'·8W
Fl.15s40m16M White GRP tower, red band 4m 039°-vis-265°
1896 Cabo Tablas 31°52'·5S 71°34'·1W Fl.10s72m10M

White GRP tower, red band 5m 284°-vis-170°
1874 Punta Angeles 33°01'·2S 71°38'·7W
Fl.10s59m32M White round metal tower, orange bands 18m 048-5°-250°
1870 Punta Curaumilla 33°06'·0S 71°45'·0W
Fl.15s83m16M Siren(3)30s White metal tower, red band, white house 3m 344°-vis-224°
1850 Punta Topocalma 34°08'·5S 72°00'·0W
Fl.10s118m16M White GRP tower, red band 4m 347°-vis-210°
1846 Cabo Carranzana 35°33'·1S 72°36'·6W
Fl.10s52m21M White steel tower, red band 18·8m 038°-vis-211° Manned
1796 Punta Tumbes 36°36'·7S 73°06'·9W
Fl.5s39m18M Siren (3)30s White round metal tower, red bands 6m 028°-vis-273°
1798 Isla Quiriquina 36°36'·3S 73°02'·9W
Fl.10s90m32M Siren(2)30s White metal tower, red bands 7m−048°-vis-015°
1764 Isla Santa Maria 36°59'·1S 73°32'·1W
Fl.15s73m17M White GRP tower, red band 8m 006°-vis-344°
1750 Isla Mocha (S) 38°24'·7S 73°53'·5W
Fl.12s33m15M White GRP tower, red band 8m 205°-vis-063°
1744 Morro Bonifacio 39°41'·3S 73°24'·0W
Fl.10s44m14M White concrete tower, red band 4m 014°-vis-218°
1724 Punta Galera 40°00'·0S 73°42'·0W
Fl.12s43m15M White GRP tower, red band 4m 326°-vis-208°

APPENDIX H
Conversion list for Chilean chart numbers in the 2003 and 2001 editions of the *Atlas Hidrográfico*.

2003	2001	2003	2001
9510	9470	11114	11141
9511	9472	11120	11131
9520	9510	11212	1115
9530	917	11311	1117
9531	905	11312	1118
10212	920	11411	11410
10310	10350	12310	12350
10325	915	12400	1201
10341	916	12421	1202
10350	10370	12700	1206
10511	1002	12711	1221
10611	10620	12711	1207
10631	10641	12713	1205
10640	10650	12720	1251
10641	10651	12800	1203
10643	1104	13100	1307
10700	1007	13142	13150
10712	1003	1320	1301
11111	10570	13300	1318
11112	11110	13400	1340
		13711	1315

Index